Challenges, Opportunities, and Dimensions of Cyber-Physical Systems

P. Venkata Krishna
VIT University, India

V. Saritha
VIT University, India

H. P. Sultana
VIT University, India

A volume in the Advances in Systems Analysis, Software Engineering, and High Performance Computing (ASASEHPC) Book Series

Managing Director: Lindsay Johnston
Managing Editor: Austin DeMarco
Director of Intellectual Property & Contracts: Jan Travers
Acquisitions Editor: Kayla Wolfe
Production Editor: Christina Henning
Development Editor: Hayley Kang
Typesetter: Amanda Smith
Cover Design: Jason Mull

Published in the United States of America by
Information Science Reference (an imprint of IGI Global)
701 E. Chocolate Avenue
Hershey PA, USA 17033
Tel: 717-533-8845
Fax: 717-533-8661
E-mail: cust@igi-global.com
Web site: http://www.igi-global.com

Library of Congress Cataloging-in-Publication Data

Krishna, P. Venkata, 1977-
Challenges, opportunities, and dimensions of cyber-physical systems / by P. Venkata Krishna, V. Saritha, and H.P. Sultana.
pages cm
Includes bibliographical references and index.
ISBN 978-1-4666-7312-0 (hardcover) -- ISBN 978-1-4666-7313-7 (ebook) -- ISBN 978-1-4666-7315-1 (print & perpetual access) 1. Embedded computer systems. 2. Embedded Internet devices. 3. Internet of things. 4. Ad hoc networks (Computer networks) I. Saritha, V., 1977- II. Sultana, H. P., 1973- III. Title.
TK7895.E43K75 2015
006.2'2--dc23

2014036866

This book is published in the IGI Global book series Advances in Systems Analysis, Software Engineering, and High Performance Computing (ASASEHPC) (ISSN: 2327-3453; eISSN: 2327-3461)

British Cataloguing in Publication Data
A Cataloguing in Publication record for this book is available from the British Library.

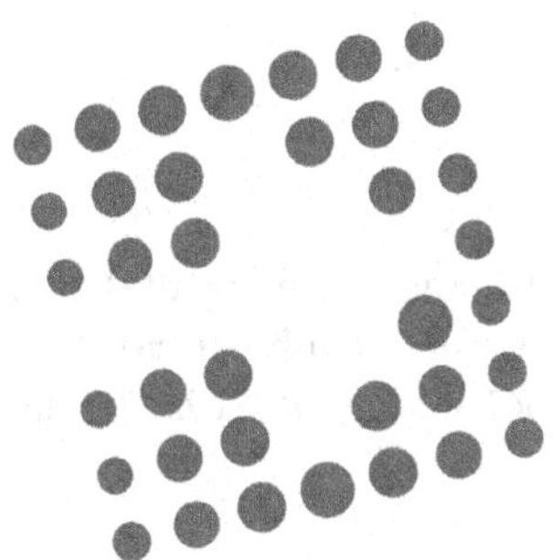

Advances in Systems Analysis, Software Engineering, and High Performance Computing (ASASEHPC) Book Series

Vijayan Sugumaran
Oakland University, USA

ISSN: 2327-3453
EISSN: 2327-3461

Mission

The theory and practice of computing applications and distributed systems has emerged as one of the key areas of research driving innovations in business, engineering, and science. The fields of software engineering, systems analysis, and high performance computing offer a wide range of applications and solutions in solving computational problems for any modern organization.

The **Advances in Systems Analysis, Software Engineering, and High Performance Computing (ASASEHPC) Book Series** brings together research in the areas of distributed computing, systems and software engineering, high performance computing, and service science. This collection of publications is useful for academics, researchers, and practitioners seeking the latest practices and knowledge in this field.

Coverage

- Distributed Cloud Computing
- Enterprise Information Systems
- Performance Modelling
- Computer Graphics
- Network Management
- Human-Computer Interaction
- Metadata and Semantic Web
- Storage Systems
- Engineering Environments
- Computer Networking

IGI Global is currently accepting manuscripts for publication within this series. To submit a proposal for a volume in this series, please contact our Acquisition Editors at Acquisitions@igi-global.com or visit: http://www.igi-global.com/publish/.

The Advances in Systems Analysis, Software Engineering, and High Performance Computing (ASASEHPC) Book Series (ISSN 2327-3453) is published by IGI Global, 701 E. Chocolate Avenue, Hershey, PA 17033-1240, USA, www.igi-global.com. This series is composed of titles available for purchase individually; each title is edited to be contextually exclusive from any other title within the series. For pricing and ordering information please visit http://www.igi-global.com/book-series/advances-systems-analysis-software-engineering/73689. Postmaster: Send all address changes to above address.

Titles in this Series

For a list of additional titles in this series, please visit: www.igi-global.com

Human Factors in Software Development and Design
Saqib Saeed (University of Dammam, Saudi Arabia) Imran Sarwar Bajwa (The Islamia University of Bahawalpur, Pakistan) and Zaigham Mahmood (University of Derby, UK & North West University, South Africa)
Information Science Reference • copyright 2015 • 354pp • H/C (ISBN: 9781466664852) • US $195.00 (our price)

Handbook of Research on Innovations in Systems and Software Engineering
Vicente García Díaz (University of Oviedo, Spain) Juan Manuel Cueva Lovelle (University of Oviedo, Spain) and B. Cristina Pelayo García-Bustelo (University of Oviedo, Spain)
Information Science Reference • copyright 2015 • 745pp • H/C (ISBN: 9781466663596) • US $515.00 (our price)

Handbook of Research on Architectural Trends in Service-Driven Computing
Raja Ramanathan (Independent Researcher, USA) and Kirtana Raja (IBM, USA)
Information Science Reference • copyright 2014 • 759pp • H/C (ISBN: 9781466661783) • US $515.00 (our price)

Handbook of Research on Embedded Systems Design
Alessandra Bagnato (Softeam R&D, France) Leandro Soares Indrusiak (University of York, UK) Imran Rafiq Quadri (Softeam R&D, France) and Matteo Rossi (Politecnico di Milano, Italy)
Information Science Reference • copyright 2014 • 520pp • H/C (ISBN: 9781466661943) • US $345.00 (our price)

Contemporary Advancements in Information Technology Development in Dynamic Environments
Mehdi Khosrow-Pour (Information Resources Management Association, USA)
Information Science Reference • copyright 2014 • 410pp • H/C (ISBN: 9781466662520) • US $205.00 (our price)

Systems and Software Development, Modeling, and Analysis New Perspectives and Methodologies
Mehdi Khosrow-Pour (Information Resources Management Association, USA)
Information Science Reference • copyright 2014 • 365pp • H/C (ISBN: 9781466660984) • US $215.00 (our price)

Handbook of Research on Emerging Advancements and Technologies in Software Engineering
Imran Ghani (Universiti Teknologi Malaysia, Malaysia) Wan Mohd Nasir Wan Kadir (Universiti Teknologi Malaysia, Malaysia) and Mohammad Nazir Ahmad (Universiti Teknologi Malaysia, Malaysia)
Engineering Science Reference • copyright 2014 • 686pp • H/C (ISBN: 9781466660267) • US $395.00 (our price)

Advancing Embedded Systems and Real-Time Communications with Emerging Technologies
Seppo Virtanen (University of Turku, Finland)
Information Science Reference • copyright 2014 • 502pp • H/C (ISBN: 9781466660342) • US $235.00 (our price)

www.igi-global.com

701 E. Chocolate Ave., Hershey, PA 17033
Order online at www.igi-global.com or call 717-533-8845 x100
To place a standing order for titles released in this series, contact: cust@igi-global.com
Mon-Fri 8:00 am - 5:00 pm (est) or fax 24 hours a day 717-533-8661

Table of Contents

Chapter 9

Chapter 10

Chapter 11

Chapter 12

Chapter 13

Foreword

I am happy that the faculty members of VIT University are quite active in preparing learning materials for use by students of engineering and other disciplines. This book, *Challenges, Opportunities, and Dimensions of Cyber Physical Systems,* authored by the faculty team comprised of Dr. P. Venkata Krishna, Dr. V. Saritha, and Ms. H. P. Sultana of the School of Computer Science and Engineering is the latest addition to the list of books published by VIT faculty members. I hope that the book will be of immense use to students, teachers, and professionals.

I understand that Cyber Physical Systems (CPS) is an emerging area that integrates every branch of the cyber world, including networking, data mining, programming, etc., and that it involves almost every aspect the physical world as well. Every stakeholder from the physical world, such as humans, organizations, utilities, other physical entities, etc., stands to benefit from this technology. The prime objective of CPS is to enrich this world and make it a better place to live. Hence, this domain needs to be explored meticulously to bring out its potential advantages.

I congratulate the authors on their remarkable efforts in bringing out a detailed and well-organized book about cyber physical systems, which I hope would fulfill the requirement for scholarly material on the topic. I am confident that the wide and detailed discussions on various topics will augment further research in this evolving field. This book should meet the intellectual demand of researchers, students, and curriculum developers. Being one of the earliest books in this emerging field, it is a pioneer in the domain of the convergence of cyber and physical worlds.

I wish the authors all the best.

G. Viswanathan
VIT University, India

G. Viswanathan, *the Founder-Chancellor of VIT University, was born on December 8, 1938, in a remote village near Vellore in Tamil Nadu. Dr. GV's life is a source of inspiration to the modern-day youth. Dr. GV completed the Advanced Management Program at Harvard Business School in 2003, nearly four decades after his university education, reaffirming his urge to be an eternal student. He excelled in academics from the beginning. His pre-university education at Voorhees College, Vellore, initiated him to the world outside. From there, he went on to obtain his bachelors and Master's degrees in Economics from the prestigious Loyola College, Chennai. Following this, he graduated in Law from the Madras Law College. Dr. GV founded Vellore Engineering College in 1984 at Vellore. He envisioned that this institution would offer world-class education to students who would in turn create an indelible impact on society. The engineering college that started with an intake of 180 students in 1984 has evolved as a VIT university with two campuses. Dr. GV's passion for societal development and compassion for the underprivileged have resulted in the introduction of several schemes for uplifting the women and unemployed youth in the region to help them become self-reliant. Dr. GV offers scholarships to students from disadvantaged sections of society to enable them to pursue higher studies. Dr. GV has established the Universal Higher Education Trust to create opportunities for higher education to every deserving student in the region. He has adopted several villages in an effort to improve the quality of lives of the rural people. His vision of transforming Vellore into a greener and cooler town by planting one million saplings has begun to yield fruit. Dr. GV's farsightedness extends beyond horizons.*

Preface

In 2007, the US National Science Foundation (NSF) recognized Cyber Physical Systems as a key area of research. A Cyber Physical System (CPS) is a system that combines and coordinates the Internet and physical elements. These systems are distributed networks executing in unpredictable environments and built from control systems and embedded systems to monitor and regulate the physical world in real time. Cyber Physical Systems can be found in aerospace, automotive, chemical processes, civil infrastructure, energy, healthcare, manufacturing, consumer appliances, and transportation. Unlike embedded systems, Cyber Physical Systems are designed as a structure of interacting elements with physical input and output. In embedded systems, the importance is more on the computational elements and less on the connection between the computational and physical elements. Enhancements in science and engineering will significantly increase the flexibility, independence, competency, functionality, consistency, and security of Cyber Physical Systems. They also widen the prospective of Cyber Physical Systems in several dimensions like collision avoidance, nano-level manufacturing, search and rescue in inaccessible environments, air traffic control, and healthcare monitoring.

This is not about adding computing and communication techniques to conservative inventions where both sides maintain distinct individualities. This is about the integration of computing and networking with physical systems to generate novel innovations in science, technical skills, and creations. CPS will have an amazing impact on the future of industry. Lagging behind in the fundamentals of CPS may render our scientific and technological arrangement antiquated. Whether we recognize it or not, we are in the center of a pervasive, thoughtful change in the way humans arrange physical systems and design their physical environment.

The main objectives of this book are to shed light on the significance of CPS for the future and to explain the fundamental wireless communication architectures with the computing systems to understand the design methodologies of CPS, which addresses the design and security challenges while communicating between systems in CPS. The book also includes open research issues in CPS. It consists of the following 15 chapters, each of which contains multiple sections focusing on various aspects in that section. Each chapter ends with a conclusion specifying future research challenges related to it. In the following paragraphs, we present a brief overview for each of the chapters and the sections therein.

Chapter 1 defines Cyber Physical Systems with its features. *Cyber* is an integration of computation, communication, and control systems. *Physical* means natural and human-made systems that are managed and governed by the physics regulations and functioning in constant time. In Cyber Physical Systems, the cyber and physical systems are those firmly incorporated at all stages and dimensions. Starting in late 2006, the US National Science Foundation (NSF) and other United State federal agencies sponsored several workshops on CPSs. In 2007, the NSF identified CPSs as a key area of research. CPS uses embedded computers and networks to compute, communicate, and organize physical actions. Simultaneously, a CPS receives feedback on how physical events impact computations and vice versa. Just as the Internet transforms how humans interact with one another, CPSs will transform how we interact with the physical world around us. In the latter part of this chapter, the challenges and opportunities in CPS are discussed. It also focuses on research trends in CPS. A summary of Wireless Cyber Physical Systems is explicated at the end of this chapter.

Chapter 2 focuses on prototype architecture for CPS and explains the approach to design open data service architecture for CPS. This chapter deals with the CPS architectural style, which can be used to provide support to the plan and assessment of other structural designs for cyber physical systems. It also shows the interconnections between physical and cyber components. In this prototype architecture, the important attributes of this architecture for CPS, which helps to identify many research challenges, are described and explained. We also discuss the open information service structural design to deal with the issues related to management of data in CPS. Along with the single-layer and multi-layer survivability of architecture, a portable CPS structure, which is known as multi-layer widespread structure, is discussed. This system uses unlicensed and licensed networks with various spectrums to connect CPS through different gateways. A research-related wireless access network project is described. In multilayer wireless networking, it describes the functionality of heterogeneous CPS networking. The last section focuses on mobile networking between various reachable networks and mobile devices.

Chapter 3 provides an overview on CPS design and discusses various CPS design components to create a network control for CPS. A large set of CPS physical processes are referred to as Cyber Physical System community. This CPS community deals with the modelling and design optimization of CPS. The network elements that are model-based emphasize control over system with various temporal semantics. Model-based design is a great technique for CPSs and are mainly used for developing mathematical modelling to plan, examine, prove, and certify dynamic systems. This is described in ten fundamental steps. This design methodology helps in assessing the development of CPS. Due to difficulty and nonexistence of accurate and technical tools, the three necessary elements in the strategy and study of existing and forthcoming cyber-physical systems are also explained in the chapter. The latter section of this chapter deals with the network latency in CPSs. At the end of this chapter, CPS design challenges are addressed.

Chapter 4 lists a variety of issues and challenges in connecting wireless and ad hoc networks. This chapter shows the interconnection issues in different wireless networks such as ad hoc networks and sensor networks. It also specifies the need for multicast routing protocols in mobile networks, because these wireless networks are suitable for multicast communication due to its inherent transmission ability. Based on the area to be covered, mechanism used for sensor deployment, and various properties of sensor network properties, different coverage formulations have been suggested. In addition, several constructions reachable areas and their expectations along with an outline of the explanations are described. Though IEEE 802.11 planned for organization-based systems, the Distributed Coordination Function (DCF) offered in IEEE 802.11 permits mobile networks to communicate with the channel exclusive of the base location. Several performance issues related to IEEE 802.11 are revealed. This chapter identifies the main reasons for performance losses and provides solutions for the scenarios in which issues were raised. The chapter discusses the issues arising during transmission in different wireless networks, such as Wi-Fi, 802.11-based wireless networks, etc. It also addresses the issues related to mobile IP and location tracking.

Chapter 5 describes the Cyber Physical Internet (CPI). The first section provides an overview of Large-Scale CPSs components, which describes protocol architecture of CPI. This chapter also focuses on CPS Interconnection Protocol (CPS-IP) and specifies a detailed design of CPS-IP. This chapter explores the concept of the Cyber Physical Internet (CPI) and discusses the design necessities of it. In addition, it provides the restrictions of the present networking concepts to satisfy these necessities. The structural design of protocol stack for CPI has an extra layer Cyber-Physical Layer (CY-PHY Layer) to offer a conceptual description of the properties and type of cyber physical information. To enable standard communication between heterogeneous systems, Cyber Physical System-Interconnection Protocol is used. This protocol is mainly designed for special CPSs, which require overall instruction and performance guarantee for cyber physical interaction. The main objective of this protocol is to offer CPSs heterogeneity at three different levels: function interoperability, policy regulation, and performance assurance. Later, the transport protocol services used in the design of CPS-IP are explained.

Chapter 6 deals with the network QoS management and discusses the network characteristics and QoS requirements for CPS. An overview of aspect-oriented QoS modeling is dealt along with its specification for CPS. Wireless Sensor Actuator Networks (WSANs) perform a vital role in CPS. This chapter describes the key features of WSANs and the necessities of QoS provisioning in the perception of cyber physical computing. Network Quality of Service (QoS) is one of the research issues that is focused on in wide way. To address the challenges identified, a feedback scheduling framework is explained in the latter part of this chapter. It is a difficult task to satisfy end-to-end QoS requirements in CPSs. To overcome this, a model-driven middleware called NetQoPE is used to protect the application designers from the complications of programming at lower level CPU and by streamlining network QoS mechanisms. The chapter shows how NetQoPE provides QoS assurance for CPS applications. The chapter concludes with the possible challenges in Internet QoS.

Chapter 7 elucidates the security issues and challenges for CPS. This chapter gives a brief view on security control for CPS, which analyzes threats and uncertainties in cyber physical networks. It also describes a robust context-aware security framework for CPS. IT and CPS have a well-built organization of information and a set of skilled professionals for providing information security, but providing security to CPS is a new challenge as systems are interconnected. This chapter gives a brief study of CPS security by identifying and defining the problem of secure control systems and also observes the protections that information security and control theory provide to the system. Later, a set of challenges are described, which are required to enhance the security of CPSs. As today's cyber physical systems are part of critical structure, an open and interconnected situation strengthens the effect of malicious actions. Even though in distributed systems delay is bearable, CPSs should follow certain timing requirements to perform regular process.

Chapter 8 addresses the security issues with respect to cyber physical systems. As cyber physical system security is not satisfactory, the security of a particular infrastructure depends on both internal and other related vulnerabilities. Communications between components in the cyber and physical realms lead to unintentional information flow. This chapter describes the difficult communications that occurs between the cyber and physical domains and their impact on security. Assailants may be competent to initiate exclusive attacks to cyber physical systems. There are several types of attacks that affect the interactions between the cyber and physical devices, which might be in a passive way or in an active method. Even though the communication provides authenticity and confidentiality, a few attacks form some threats against ad hoc routing protocols as well as location-based security systems. It has been said that many attacks modify the activities of the targeted control system. At the end of the chapter, we describe how control systems are affected by malicious attacks and also how to resolve these issues.

Chapter 9 describes the interoperability and communication issues in cyber physical systems. Cyber physical systems involve multi-domain models during the development process of the design. This chapter focuses on integrated design methodology that provides reliable relationships between various system models of heterogeneous types. Each model is linked with the base architecture over the abstraction of an architectural view framework. From quadrotor perspective, this framework compares system models from different domains. Present methods lack in modeling, analysis, and design of CPSs due to nonexistence of an integrated framework. To overcome these difficulties, an architectural level system model is defined to capture the structural interdependencies. A base architecture for the complete system is described in this chapter to confirm the structural reliability the model elements and components present in it. The usefulness of this process is exemplified in the quadrotor air vehicle.

Chapter 10 discusses different networking issues in heterogeneous networking. To make a network survivable it must be heterogeneous. The functionality of this network is defined by a set of protocols and its operations. In heterogeneous networks, if a protocol is weakened by any attack, it will not affect the entire network. Applying this heterogeneity concept, a new survivability paradigm is described in this chapter. This network architecture improves the network's heterogeneity without losing its interoperability. Several issues discovered in security and survivability applications can be converted into scheduling problems. To overcome this, a new model is described to support design and analysis with security and survivability concerns. A five-step model is introduced to transmute applications into model abstraction and representations with solutions resulting from scheduling algorithms. A reverse transformation converts the solutions back to the application domain.

Chapter 11 focuses on mobile computing issues in the heterogeneous environment. The fast development of mobile computing has produced a wide variety of technologies that affect systems in the mobile computing realm. Even though mobile computing focuses the importance of interrelated systems, the qualifying of interoperability remains an important constraint. In this chapter, several techniques are explained to manage various heterogeneity characteristics along with the key concepts related to these systems. A general approach is described to manage the heterogeneity. It has been seen that to have a better performance in overlapping networks, it is necessary to switch between the networks due to mobility and congestion. This problem is overcome by overlay networks that identify the existing network and then select the best network and allow transmission from one node to another node in the same network or create a novel network. In this way, this architecture provides a way to transmit packets to the mobile host using the available network.

Chapter 12 describes the cluster-based architecture for the heterogeneous environment. Along with the heterogeneous devices, Web-based content increases the necessity for computational services. However, recent trends make it difficult to execute such computations at the terminal side, whereas service providers often allow computations during different load operations. Many computational services are using conventional distributed systems, which provide successful packet transmission in IP networks. In this chapter, proxy architecture and its related tasks are discussed. Some of the necessary requirements, such as incremental scalability, 24x7 availability, and cost-effectiveness, are recognized for scalable network services. To administrate a large cluster and to construct a cluster-based scalable network services, a layered architecture is recommended. This architecture captures the scalable network service requirements and utilizes service-programming models to perform Transformation, Aggregation, Caching, and Customization (TACC) of Internet substance. For better performance, the architecture with the TACC programming model uses data semantics to create novel network services.

Chapter 13 discusses different network services required for cyber physical systems. A novel framework formed from a collection of independent agents that interact with each other is determined to provide a network service. Agents in this structure have the capability to perform independent activities such as duplication, migration, etc. A new method is developed in this chapter by means of genetic algorithms to change the behavior of agents over peers and also to improve the network service performance in a distributed and well planned way. Architecture with a remote control device, Personal Universal Controller (PUC), is described. The PUC provides two-way communication with the applications for copying specification for its functionality and constructing an interface for monitoring that electrical device. The requirements of every application hold the information about its dependency information and availability of appliance conditions. The network protocols, such as Service Discovery Protocols, are explained with their types and functionality.

Chapter 14 shows the different cyber physical control systems with respect to intelligent and real time systems. The focus of algorithmic design is to solve composite problems. Intelligent systems use intellectual concepts like evolutionary computation, artificial neural networks, fuzzy systems, and swarm intelligence to process natural intelligence models. Artificial intelligence is used as a part of intelligent systems to perform logic- and case-based reasoning. Systems like mechanical and electrical support systems are operated by utilizing Supervisory Control and Data Acquisition (SCADA) systems. These systems cannot accomplish their purpose, provided the control system deals with the reliability of it. In CPSs, dimensions of physical processes are taken by sensors and are processed in cyber subsystems to drive the actuators that affect the physical processors. CPSs are closed-loop systems. The adaptation and the prediction are the properties to be followed by the control strategies that are implemented in cyber subsystems.

Finally, Chapter 15 discusses various cyber physical systems management techniques. Most of the systems are unsuccessful during integration due to insignificant consequences occurring in them. This is due to lack of system scalability that fails to provide an improved workload of the system. This chapter describes the parameters to be measured while evaluating the scalability of the structure. The parameters to be measured are described in a scalability review that represents the problems in it. The primary requirement of CPSs is system reliability because an unreliable system yields service interruption and financial cost. A CPS cannot be set up in critical applications in which system reliability and predictability are inefficient. To provide safety critical systems, a high volume of data is dealt, containing operator-in-loop and operating online constantly. The combined characteristics of physical and computational components allow CPSs to use hybrid dynamical models to integrate discrete and continuous state variables that use computational tools to resolve composite problems.

As an intellectual challenge, CPS is about the intersection, not the union, of the physical and the cyber. It is not adequate to individually understand the physical components and the computational components. We must instead understand their interaction. The design of such systems, therefore, requires understanding the joint dynamics of computers, software, networks, and physical processes. It is this study of changing aspects that sets this discipline apart. This book will be of considerable interest to researchers, professionals, and students with the backgrounds of computer science and electrical and electronics communication.

P. Venkata Krishna
VIT University, India

V. Saritha
VIT University, India

H. P. Sultana
VIT University, India

Chapter 1
Cyber Physical Systems (CPSs)

ABSTRACT

Cyber is an integration of computation, communication, and control systems. Physical means natural and human-made systems that are managed and governed by the physics regulations and functioning in constant time. In Cyber Physical Systems, the cyber and physical systems are those firmly incorporated at all stages and dimensions. Starting in late 2006, the US National Science Foundation (NSF) and other United State federal agencies sponsored several workshops on CPSs. In 2007, the NSF identified CPSs as a key area of research. CPS uses embedded computers and networks to compute, communicate, and organize physical actions. Simultaneously, a CPS receives feedback on how physical events impact computations and vice versa. Through the Internet and how people communicate with each other, CPSs will change the way people interrelate with the world around them. This chapter explores CPSs.

INTRODUCTION

Cyber Physical Systems gives a new dimension of correlating present systems with the humans. And also shows how these systems combine computations and physical actions. These processes communicate with the physical world with the latest approaches. As in Figure 1 CPS has the facility to interrelate physical resources with the help of organization, estimation, and transmission. It is a main factor for improving future technologies (Baheti & Gill, 2011).

Basically CPS means observing the physical behaviour actions and performing some processes to alter its behavior. This is to construct a physical system which should function appropriately in an enhanced way. In other words the physical action is observed by the cyber system. In turn this system is associated with various small devices having wireless communication recourses, sensing capability and computing ability. In the physical environment the actions are managed by natural happening, a human-made physical system or a more complex combination of the two which is depicted in the Figure 2 as in (Shi, Wan, Yan, & Suo,2011).

More than years, researchers in the fields of systems and control, have established a way to the progress of authoritative system with science and engineering processes and equipments such as (Baheti & Gill, 2011):

- Methods in frequency and time domains,
- State space analysis,

DOI: 10.4018/978-1-4666-7312-0.ch001

Figure 1. CPS communication

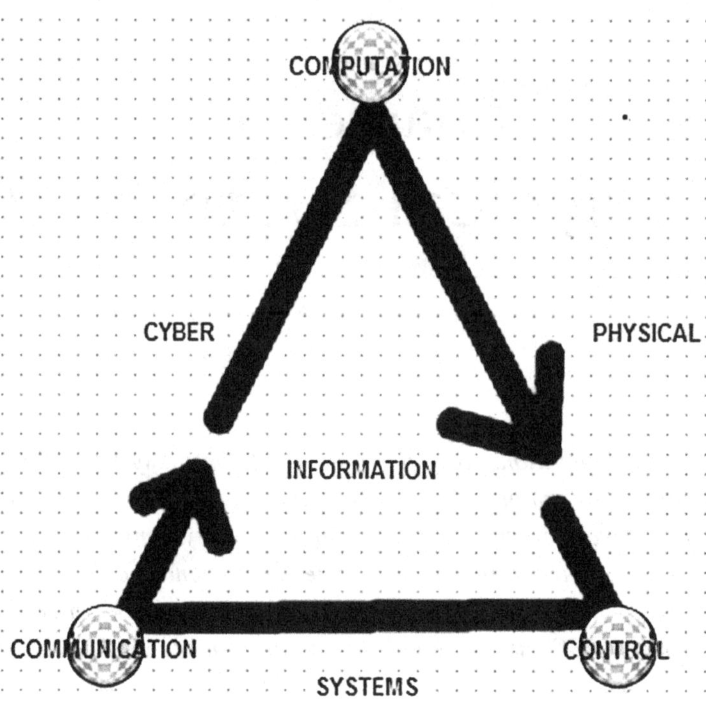

Figure 2. CPS architecture

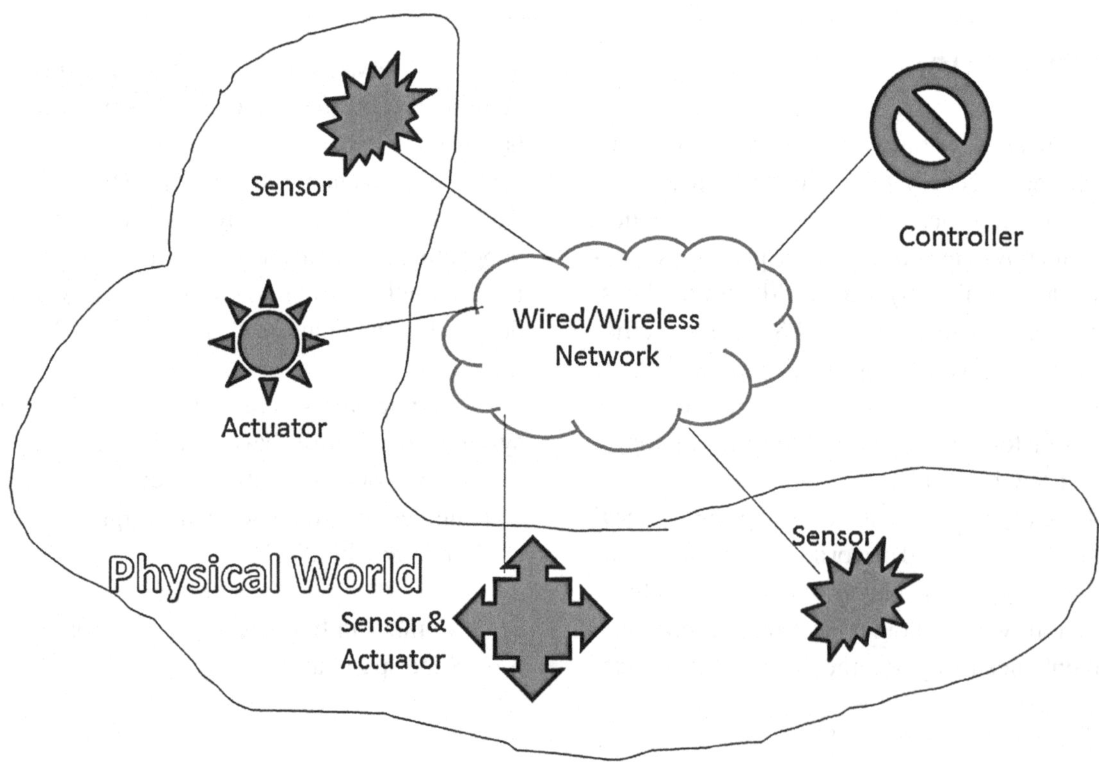

- Classification of a system,
- Optimization,
- Estimation,
- Filtering, and
- Management of Robust and Stochastic.

At the same time, computer science researchers have made breakthrough in new programming languages, real-time computing techniques, visualization methods, compiler designs, embedded systems architectures and systems software by new methods to have secured reliable computer system, cyber security and fault tolerance.

CPSs incorporate physical action dynamics with the transmission and software. This incorporated system provides concepts and modeling along with the proposed and exploration techniques. CPSs research aims to integrate information and developed regulations with the engineering and estimated regulations such as supervise, code, individual communication, theory of learning, networks as well as electrical, biomedical, mechanical (Baheti & Gill, 2011) and other developed regulations to create novel CPS science with the supporting approaches. In many industries, various engineering systems have been designed by decoupling the control system design from the specified hardware or software details. To do so, it necessitates extensive simulation to verify and require ad hoc tuning methods to address modeling uncertainty and random disturbances. While keeping the system functional and operational, the combination of various subsystems has been time consuming and more cost effective.

BACKGROUND

Workflow of CPS

Cyber Physical Systems (CPSs) are executable physical systems that are implemented to be monitored and manipulated by centralized computing resources. CPSs are just running everywhere that we could possibly identify. CPS plays a very important role in ensuring the stateful services with communication process. The condition of CPS looks up to new propagation of solutions with embedded and integrated systemized physical features that move together and extend features of, real world via systemization. Communication holds a path of enabling the technologies with successful improvements. Likelihoods and exploring complexities of includes solutions for future-generation everything that exists with the current world which keeps human life at the limit of customization.

The global communication system which in other words known as Internet, made our human life much less complex than we could always visualize. CPSs are really takes the idea of global communication into new direction and realize the unimaginable aspects in to real time solutions. Throughout the times of digital life innovators are initiated the process of developing more hefty systems and solutions to work with many aspects of its core components. CPS holds numerous and singular differences. Edges between cyber and physical world can never be predicted and the extending boundaries are always challenging, to be exact, CPS has come out of distributed computing systems.

CPS integrated workflow and communication and along with physical address. Information Technology uses embedded computers and multi networks to reckon and pass along and manipulates the physical process and obtains the result on how physical process affects the computation the other way around. To transit fundamental interaction with physical world, CPS system today are so anticipated in new category of systems that profoundly implant cyber possibilities in the physical world, either on domestic or base program.

The general workflow of CPS (Wang et al., 2010) can be classified into four major steps, namely monitoring, networking, computation, and actuation.

- **Monitoring:** The essential function of CPS is to examine the methods in the physical environment, where the aim of physical event is to attain a novel physical objective. This process is helpful in giving feedback on the previous actions obtained by CPS. This is to perform precise actions in the future.
- **Networking:** Data collection and dissemination done by this process. There are many sensors in the CPS, which can produce information in instantaneous. Similarly different sensors can be used to produce large voluminous data that should be collected or disseminated to execute .The produced data can be used for analyzers. At the same time various technologies have to be associated with the interlinked communication.
- **Computing:** This process investigate and calculate the obtained data from the monitoring phase. This is to verify whether the physical event occurred according to the well-defined conditions. The remedial actions have to be carried out, if the required actions have not been met. For example, a datacenter CPS can use dissimilar scheduling algorithms to estimate the boost in temperature. This is used to establish upcoming processes.
- **Actuation:** This phase carry out the events obtained from the previous phase. Actuation can activate variety of events such as rectification of CPS virtual performance and change the CPS physical events. For example, in the healthcare field, medical CPS is used to deliver the medicine required. As in (Wang et al., 2010) the figure. 3 shows the workflow of CPS. In this data_ac correspond to collection of data from sensors, data_ag means obtaining physical data from the network, valid_cmd represent valid commands selected by the controller and cntrl_cmd means the managing instructions transmitted to the actuators.

Due to advancement in the complexity of components and the utilization of highly developed technologies for sensors and actuators, wireless communication and multicore processors cause an important challenge for building next-generation vehicle control systems. Both the supplier and integrator necessitate new system science that enables reliable and cost-effective integration of independently developed system components (Baheti & Gill, 2011) . The tools required for developing cost-effective methods are used to

- Design, analyze and verify components at different levels of abstraction which include system and architecture levels.
- Analyze and understand interactions between the main system (vehicle control system) and its subsystems.
- Ensure safety, stability, and performance while minimizing the system cost to consumer.

It is expected that in future the enduring enhancements in science and construction will create a progress between physical and computational elements. It also gradually improves Cyber Physical Systems flexibility, self-government, competence, functionality, consistency, security and usability. The progress will expand the prospective of CPSs in various levels such as intervention like preventing collision, correctness like surgery using robots, operation in unreachable location like search and rescue, coordination like fighting in battle, competence like Zero Net Energy (ZNE) (Baheti & Gill, 2011) buildings and strengthening of human abilities like supervising health related problems.

Figure 3. CPS workflow

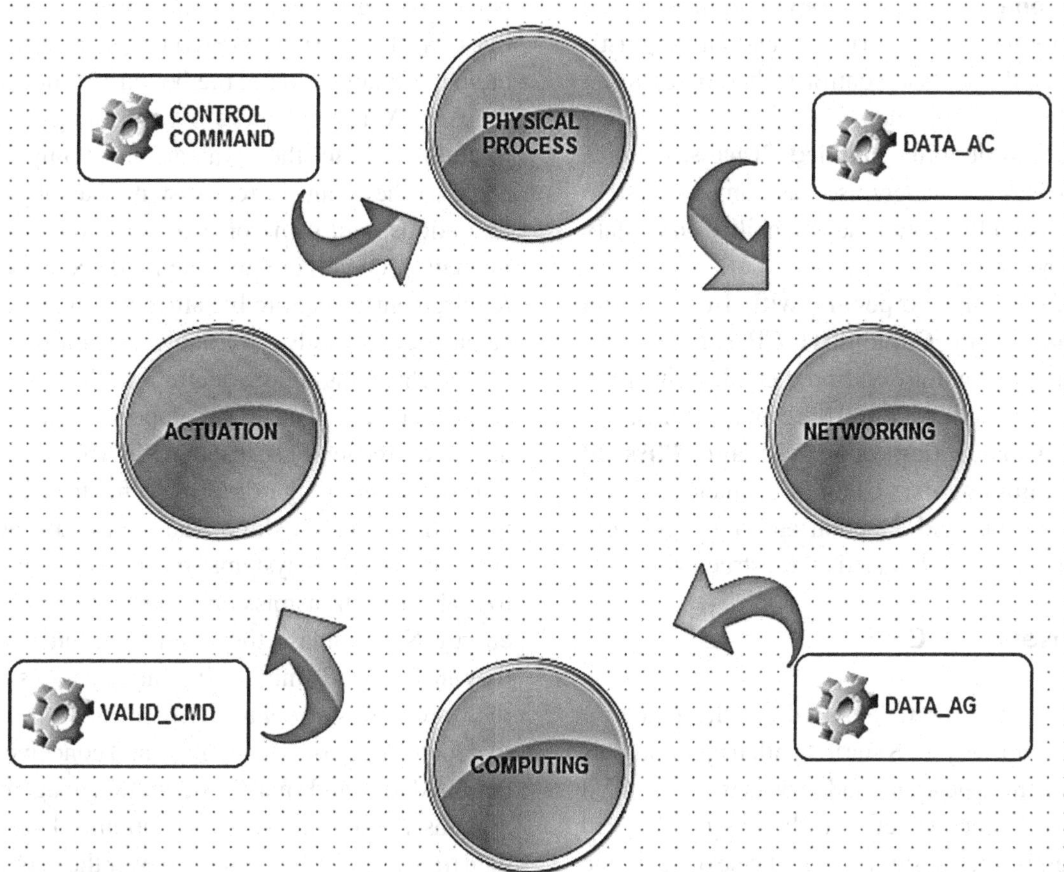

Features of CPSs

The objective of the program study of the CPSs is to incorporate physical and cyber design. CPSs are dissimilar compared to traditional computing, predictable embedded real-time systems and Wireless Sensor Network (WSN). The following are some of the characteristics of CPSs (Wang et al., 2010).

- **Tightly Coupled:** In CPSs physical and computation tasks are linked together.
- **Intervention of Cyber Capability in Physical Component with Limited Resource:** Instructions related to real-time systems are available in the system itself. And also it has restricted system resources like operations, bandwidth of network, etc.
- **Association of Various and Excessive Levels**: CPSs are a combination of infrastructure based or infrastructure less networks which has WLAN, Bluetooth, GSM, etc. In these distributed systems the types of devices and levels of system are different.
- **Complexity of Various Sequential and Spatial Levels:** The various resources of have probably in equably constrained by spatiality and real time.
- **Dynamic Restructuring/Rearrangement:** Though CPSs are highly complicated but it should have adjustable competencies.

- **High Measures of Tightly Coupled Computerization Control Loops:** CPSs are mostly user friendly and has sophisticated response control technologies in an extensive manner.
- **Reliable and Qualified Processes:** Since CPSs are widely used as complex system it should contain dependability and safety measures.
- **Physical Component with Intervention of Cyber Capability:** CPSs have sensing technology and predictable behaviour, high confidence software and systems.
- **Incorporation of Cyber and Physical Components:** CPSs are integrated for learning and adaption and are highly executable, automated and restructuring.

The Need for CPS

Exploration over CPS is still in the phase of scratch. Initially CPS started with major computing system as desktops and servers which bonded them as client and server technology and ended with embedded systems. Then the next discipline holds mainframe computing (Baheti & Gill, 2011) which had the ability to handle hefty processed and worked with client and server in large amount. Personal systems and the internet enabled both commercial and enterprise communication possible and helping the industries grows much larger than they could anticipate. Embedded computing which is always would untraceable to the normal computing world. Embedded computing which also shifted industries into both commercial and technical aspects. There are certain types of characteristics (Baheti & Gill, 2011) associated with CPS such as Network boding, Detection technology, Primitive certainty, Period procedure, Reliable systems and technology. CPS modules are integrated for adaptability, mixed performance, automated system and systemized fabrication.

Cyber physical systems convey a various disputes, halting of its range and content. Since it must travel where the process occurs, it must trust radio communication at the bound if connective property. Various devices act according to it is forcible attributes they evaluate and manipulate. More to the point, in real systems has physical limitations, and some of it is attributes will be main players with unlike, potentially contending requirements. The forcible attributes in any CPS cannot be absolutely governable. Sensing devices and mechanisms endure qualities for it is forcible world boundaries and those components can fail at any time. Frequently, such failures will be overtone. The scope and range of CPS seems to increase more challenges of its kind. Radio communication systems (Wireless systems) must show response to usable data transmission rate and the available energy. Nevertheless, they seem to be unordered, they are frequently implicit in generalizations with their properties of connectivity. It might be able to good to forecast connectivity and conceive accommodative and smart bandwidth management systems. Possibilities of manipulation are based on data transmission rate available over the network. The measure and the range of CPS propose that a standalone and well-designed preparation is merely unimaginable and the devices are overly legion. Further, it is unbelievably the selfless could be mattered on system's precise conduct.

CPS research is still in its early stage. Expert and organizational survey have found division specific study and learning position in the university circles for the knowledge and production based disciplines. Investigation study is separated into further subdivisions like sensors, interaction through connections, computer science, and numerical theory of control, arithmetic operations and software engineering. For example, systems are evaluated and constructed using various representations of methodologies and mechanisms. Every methodology enlightens particular characteristics and creates way for others to investigate in an efficient way. Usually, a specific methodology signifies the process related to virtual or physical, but not together. Different mathematical notations are used for representing the physical processes, whereas to characterize the individual behaviour and process flow, mathematical approaches such as automata are used. Though the methodology and mathematical approaches are sufficient to sustain a element-based divide and conquer method to CPS growth, but it is a difficult task to verify the security and general accuracy at the system level and physical and behavioral communications between components. The following topics describe the investigation study for CPS (Baheti & Gill, 2011) .

- **Abstraction and Architectures:** Advanced approaches to abstraction and architectures (Baheti & Gill, 2011) that allow faultless combination of organization, interaction and calculation should be established for fast proposed and process of CPSs. For instance, in network communication the links have been generated by involving various levels and the segmentation permits certain improvements in each level. The whole structure allows establishing a mixed variety of systems in an easy manner. This has created possibilities for advance and substantial growth of technology and the improvement of the connection of network.
- **Distributed Computations and Networked Control:** Several challenges with respect to discrete and event-driven processing, instruction, time delay variation, breakdown, reconstruction and distributed decision support systems (Baheti & Gill, 2011) have been created for the accomplishment of networked control system. There are certain CPS research challenges such as protocol design for providing real-time QoS assurance over wireless networks, transactions connecting design of control and accomplishment of real-time complexity, eliminating the detachment of constant and variable time systems and huge systems robustness. To fulfill the heterogeneous components (Baheti & Gill, 2011) dependability and security necessities certain frameworks, algorithms, methods and tools are required. These methods and tools are used in a compound, tightened physical situation to communicate over several spatial and sequential measures.
- **Verification and Validation:** Components of type hardware and software, systems of type operating and middleware require to be recognized so that it can be ahead of the current method. The elements of type hardware and software should be extremely reliable, reconstruct and confirmable (Baheti & Gill, 2011) from components to assimilated systems. In a present cyber systems reliability of complex systems is missing that should be maintained. For instance certification is required to consume more resources to develop new, safety-critical systems in the aviation industry. Efforts have been taken to maintain in the application domains such as biomedical, automotive and energy systems (Baheti & Gill, 2011). Till today this method is challenging for complex designs and moreover interoperability is necessary for the systems. To combine verification and validation of software systems (Baheti & Gill, 2011), essential models, algorithms, methods and tools are needed.

Applications of CPSs

Uses of CPSs consist of medicinal devices and structures, transportation control and protection, self-propelled systems, energy conservation, development control, eco-friendly mechanism (aviation software), arrangement, precarious set-up, distributed robotics, financial networks, biosystems, disseminated detecting facility and control, shrewd systems, military systems, etc. Common uses of CPSs naturally cascade under sensor built structures and self-driven systems. For instance, several WSNs observe particular phase of the location and transmit the managed information to a dominant node. Some of the applications of sensor-based are given below:

- A group of robots have been used in a scattered robot garden at MIT, Cambridge to supervise tomato plants. This structure uses detecting devices which are dispersed in it. Each plant is furnished with a detecting device that observes its condition, routing, operation (objects to pick up, modify, and destroy) and wireless interacting.
- An attention on the control structure phases of CPSs that pass through precarious structure (electricity generation, water supply and telecommunication) can be discovered in the efforts of the Idaho National Laboratory at Eastern Idaho and traitors investigating robust mechanism systems (tolerate fluctuations via their structure and control parameters).
- MIT's CarTel assignment in which a group of taxis gather instantaneous movement information in the Boston area. Together with past data, the current data is then used for computing clear ways for a given period of the day.
- Fitness maintenance and medication domain contains National health information set-up, Automatic patient documentation resource, Home-based maintenance, Operational area, etc. Some of these are measured by workstation structures with hardware and instructional mechanisms and instantaneous structures with safety and scheduling necessities.
- Many sensor nodes create wireless systems with characteristics of self-motivated restructuring and reforming. Integrate intelligent road with unmanned vehicle with detecting devices fetch data from wireless sensor networks and manage information to regulate the behaviour of automobiles. This includes visualization system, Global Positioning System (GPS), central board, etc. The GPS and visualization system assist as a supporting place, while the unmanned automobiles mostly understand routing dependent on WSNs.
- The disseminated micro control production is combined with the power network, where scheduling accuracy and safety disputes appear huge. The Electric Power Grid CPS is constituted with the combination of power electronics, power grid and embedded control software. This electric power grid CPS design is inclined by error reception, safety and dispersed mechanism.
- Transport systems could be benefit substantially from automobiles with implanted intellect, which could increase security and competence.
- Self-governing interconnected vehicles could intensely increase the effectiveness of army and could propose significantly further operative calamity rescue methods.
- Interconnected structure control methods such as Heating, Ventilation, and Air-Conditioning (HVAC) system and lighting could considerably upsurge dynamic effectiveness and request inconsistency, decreasing reliance on hydrocarbon fuels.
- In transportations, intellectual radio could be profit a lot from disseminated agreement about obtainable bandwidth and from dispersed control tools.
- Huge measure amenities systems leveraging RFID and other tools for chasing of

things and facilities could obtain the setting of circulated concurrent control structures.

- Current dispersed present games that incorporate measuring devices and actuators could alter the environment of online group communications.

Challenges and Opportunities

Precariousness in the surrounding and protection blast, and fault in the physical components and in wireless transmission laid a vital dispute to guarantee whole system hardness, security and protection. Regrettably, it is too one of the minimum realized challenges in cyber-physical systems. However, there is a clean rational chance in applying the technological basis for hardness, surety and security of relating to CPS in common and any systems in specific. Security and the privacy implication can be more complex than it is anticipation.

The U.S. National academy of Engineering has listed some grand challenges related to environment, health, and social issues. These issues will be hugely benefited from progress achieved in cyber-physical systems. The control engineering research community can show a leading task in the growth of cyber-physical systems. Some of the opportunities (Baheti & Gill, 2011) are described below.

- CPS study is providing various prospects and tasks in medicinal and biomedical manufacturing. These engineering fields contain intellectual functioning rooms and clinics, surgery using images and treatment, liquefied flow controller for medication and scientific experiments. Healthcare depends on therapeutic devices and structures that are networked and need to satisfy the requirements of patients with special circumstances. Thus, therapeutic devices and structures will be required that are vigorously reconstructed, distributed and interrelate with patients and caretakers in complicated locations.
- Another challenging area for CPS research is neuroscience for understanding the fundamental principles of human motor functions and exploiting this understanding in engineered systems. Instances of these functions are brain-machine interfaces, restorative and entertainment robotics and orthopedic devices (alter or modify foot function).
- In-home healthcare delivery, more capable biomedical devices are used for measuring health, within and outside the body. Networked biomedical systems that increase automation and extend the biomedical device beyond the body.
- CPSs research is likely to have an impact on the design of future aircraft and air traffic management systems as well as on aviation safety.
- In confirmation and authentication of aviation, flight-critical structures contain approaches for careful and high level of logical authentication of structure safety properties and requirements. These have been provided from primary strategy through execution, preservation and alteration, as well as thoughtful transactions among difficulty and confirmation procedures for assisting vigorous and fault acceptance.
- Smart grid and renewable energy research and development are to improve energy efficiency by investing in modernization of the energy infrastructure. Advances in optimization of multiscale non-deterministic dynamic systems as well as in distributed

control are necessary to improve smart grid performance with respect to security, efficiency, reliability and economics.

- More capable defence systems that make better use of networked cluster of autonomous vehicles.
- New and renewable energy sources used in energy and industrial automation. Homes, offices, buildings and vehicles are more energy efficient and cheaper to operate.
- Energy efficient technologies used in agriculture are aimed to increase automation and closed-loop bioengineering processes. It is for resource and environmental impact optimization and improved safety of food products.
- Highway systems that allow traffic to become denser while also operating more safely. A critical infrastructure CPS used is a national power grid that is more reliable and efficient.
- Computational abstractions need to include physical concepts such as energy and time, to realign abstraction layers in design flows. Concepts developed for describing physical dynamics should be widespread to capture uncertainties such as network delays, finite word length and round-off errors.
- To describe different physics and logics, there is need to improve semantic bases for generating dissimilar representations and patterning languages. Mathematical frameworks should be developed in such a way that it can be understood by system as well as tool developers.
- The compositionality in dissimilar structures permits for creating huge interrelated systems, which satisfy required physical resources and execute the necessary functionality in a consistent method. Progress of technology for attaining expectedness in moderately compositional approach is a difficult task that must be addressed.
- It is a big challenge to convert structure combination from a great risk manufacturing exercise into learning based engineering regulation, which requires secure association between engineering and academy.
- Compositional authorization of CPSs requires novel approaches as this certification can be used as verification in confirming the superior system rather than on analysis.
- The existing tool base in the current system must be able to adapt to a new application domains of cyber-enhanced physical systems. Hence there is need to create a new approachable design automation of CPSs.
- Need to design new open architectures for CPSs, which allows building national as well as global scale facilities. These architectures can be easily customized to different operational conditions.
- Require strategies and tools which provide dependable CPSs from changeable modules and build vigorous CPSs that endure malicious outbreaks from either virtual or physical areas.

The destinations of cyber physical systems are new and the effects of results are would sound louder. Analytical methods need to grow at the pace of quickened. More available tools are contrived to let us determine on multi proportion. Future's cyber physical systems have to be capable enough to follow the natural world and its organic evolution. Realizing and formulating novel systems that are visceral and incorporate with mankind's needs. Loads of cyber physical systems' intentions are null in human death and it can be only achieved by formulating systems that are nature and human friendly with comprehensive conventional realizing of man's behavior under varying situation includes casualty and trying scenes. Since those systems alter into composite CPS with vital physics and the manipulation of physical attributes, the chance of unsought emerging conducts on runtime interactions would only gain up.

Existing hardware design and programming outlines are hugely built on the assumption that the principal task of system is primarily a communication and transformation of various types of data. This demands a decisive test on subsisting hardware and software architecture built decades ago. Foundational opportunities got potentials of determining the view of computation and in the world of CPS. While computation moves with physical world, it needs us expressively work with cases distributed with both universe and phase. Sequential and spatial data's expressively to be caught into programming models. Rest of the parameters and properties such as logical and forcible rules, protection, energy restraints, hardness and characteristics of protective parameters must be caught in writable fashion in programming generalizations.

These programming generalizations may demand a strike conceiving of the standard gap between software design languages and operational systems. Similar updates remain expected by the software and hardware degree of afforded performance. It also expects a robust real time parallel software design concepts. Application engineers must be able to show the strong disapproval of functionality of software element while it carries out on a device with fixed resource. Programming generalizations that pictured would need to defense at the middleware and operating systems levels for:

- Sequential effect activator.
- Ordered opinion of shared states in period of time over the circle of shape. This dispute is heavy in mobile computing.
- Port to approach the similar type of control anyway of implicit in network science.

The omnipresence of CPS gives possible to expose to various information of our experiences that people consider a common secret. What is more, their possibility to manipulate physical views of the world triggers potentially a huge advantage to vicious striker. Thus, the systems must be built to ensure complexity of breaking the security and realizes the value of privations and it is users without flex bling the practical functions with the second thought of protection and authentication and authorization.

CPS systems precisely and hardly confirm in energy consumption and it's one of and always will be part of strong challenges with CPS. Couple of biggest challenges of our life time is paired with energy insufficiency and the rapid improvements in requiring energy sources. Construction and deportation are spheres with hard energy intake. We should strongly incorporate computers on the internet with physical world. Hybrid systems technology expected to be developed that is forcible and computational at the same time, enables the merged model for handling the feed of batch, energy and details in ordered manner.

Developing technological and advanced systems in CPS will surely take place due to permeate utility and it leads in social and frugal benefits:

- Utmost-concede farming,
- Protective and speedy excretion in reaction to life-like or synthetic disasters,
- Constant life supporter for meddling and elderly and incapacitated souls,
- Position independent approach to foremost medication,
- Energy-cognizant establishments and urban centers, and
- Uninterrupted energy production and dispersion.
- Auto-adjusting cyber physical systems for natural event applications.

Cyber physical systems elevated challenges are vocalized in various industry sectors. Exploration with CPS brings out hefty number of opportunities and challenges in the following areas such as clinical medicine, automotive and more as it can diversify into.

Research towards CPS in clinical medicine industry opens up loads of opportunities in both engineering and as well as analysis. Smart functioning suits, imaging aided surgical and medical cares. Clinical medicine systems utmost depend on remedial systems that are intercommunicated and needed to match the requirements of affected roles through peculiar conditions. Therefore, clinical medical systems are actively to be arranged and setup in a new way. Frequently, these gimmicks need to be set up into a modern system to cope up with particular people or process. A raw system that is intended to develop with CPS for clinical medicine science must follow and abide to those goals mentioned such as Practical and more exposed systems, disseminated supervising, disseminated manipulation, and period of time network for medical cares, Credential methods for applications and systems and patient supervising and help. Serious analysis over CPS in automotive industry can be divided into current status and for the improved future.

A Cyber physical system in automotive industry primarily focuses on largely single vehicle and it works toward integrating the science of undercrossed fuel economy. But, in future the technology must diversify into multi vehicle more equipped with more accommodative routes for highway transport solutions. Social needs as well as competitive pressure from other countries have radically increased their investment in CPS related research, to go ahead with our national R&D investment strategy. Investment in CPS strongly supports all design and manufacturing industries as well as health care, agriculture and infrastructure. We make industries more competitive across the country, by investing in the fundamental technology of CPSs.

INTRODUCTION TO WIRELESS CPS's

In a wireless system one cannot avoid nodes from wandering to the point of connectivity. Environment concerns like stream and territory types cause major deviations in the wireless bandwidth. Furthermore, one cannot stop malicious nodes from occupying the wireless range. At some point the connection dispute recommends that a particular, widespread, high rapidity network is impossible. Instead, it will provide a way to develop a range of insignificant wireless provisioning sockets, creating movements of nodes with power in it.

Correspondingly, the physical objects in our structure will not be faultlessly manageable. Detecting devices and actuators undergo flaws due to environmental boundaries and these tangible components can be unsuccessful. Regularly, such breakdowns will be unfinished and create errors in semantics that are more problematic than the familiar malfunction hardware machines which are independent like the system used by people. For illustration, an intellectual self-propelled structure is still issue to the determination of its social driver. These operators will often have incompatible, challenging desires and requirements to reduce the opportunity of integrated foundation.

In addition to the management tasks, the possibility and measure of CPS give escalation to additional noteworthy task such as maintaining the secrecy of the people who utilize them. Still now many important revelations of behaviour are considered to be secretive. Furthermore the design of safety, verification and approval are not likely to deliver much hold in the cyber-physical world.

Wireless systems in CPSs are said to be adaptive and proactive systems, because the wireless structures respond to deviations in existing bandwidth, power of battery, etc. But they seem to be disordered; there are frequently essential reliabilities in their connectivity and flexibility. These consistencies can be used in a different ways by refining connectivity, proactively planning adaptable interaction information and providing a way for fetching geographical data, duplication and decreasing risk in the systems.

It can also be useful to calculate and make appropriate alterations for product behavior. For instance consider a supportive, smart transportation supervision systems, consuming inter automobile transmission. Mechanism is determined by bandwidth and rapidity needs constricted limits on round trip control communications. When connectivity environments are likely to worsen, the automobiles can sluggish down in hope by conserving the protection of the transport organism.

Mobile CPSs, in which the physical structure has essential flexibility, are a well-known subgroup of CPSs. Mobile CPS is used in portable robotics and integrated circuit equipment carried by individuals or creatures. The attractiveness of smart mobiles has improved curiosity in the region of portable CPSs. Smartphone programs make perfect portable CPSs for the following motives:

- Substantial executable tools used such as local storage, ability to develop.
- Various sensing machines such as android devices, cameras, microphone, light sensors, etc.
- Different transmission techniques such as Wi-Fi, Bluetooth, EDGE and 3G.
- Software required for Mobile CPSs is developed using high level programming languages such as Java, C#.
- The approaches of dispersal functionalities are android marketplace and apple application store.
- Providing customer support such as recurrent renewal of battery.

However, a fast growth of smart phone based mobile CPS devices, make use of interconnected structure to add the portable structure either with a main network or a distributed system. It facilitates composite executable processes that are unfeasible under limited source restriction. Some of the applications of mobile CPSs are tracking and analyzing CO_2 emissions, monitoring cardiac patients, detecting traffic accidents and providing services to first responders.

In this methodology, anyone can construct a system in which a sensible node locates it advantage to create results that also assist the overall system. For instance supportive systems can be planned to determine or construct interactions pair wise, presenting equality without expecting well-built characteristics or centralized management. Related planning methods can supply secured building management and dependable systems. In addition to reconfiguring, anyone can relate procedures to particular devices to enhance the functioning, consistency and effectiveness of processing systems. For instance, one can use such affirmations of objective to choose system services by permitting functions to depict their objective.

The presence of CPSs gives the prospective to depict about various confidential information of our existence. In addition, the capacity to manage features of the tangible world offer more authority to an immoral invader. It is recommended to construct systems that value the confidentiality of their members without negotiating functionality and reorganize our safety, certification, and approval concepts.

RESEARCH TRENDS

It is difficult to point out the CPSs research areas, because of following reasons:

- No clear frontiers between cyber and physical worlds
- Restrictions are always changing
- No perfect digitization of the continuous world
- Unpredictable compound systems

- Basically multi-disciplinary

The invention and engineering and substantiation of cyber physical systems places disputes in large number in terms technology and discipline to its researchers and instructors. Computation and communication process will soon be implanted into every type forcible type in natural world. The merging of fundamental CPS science proved new chances and presents novel research challenges. CPS would get compiled of internetworked clumps of working attributes and big medium networks of both wire and wireless networks that link to numerous kinds of sensing elements and mechanisms.

Some of the experts from across the world researchers from various countries conversed about the correlated views, methods, approaches and disputes in the CPS workshops and the International conferences organized on topics related to CPS. As a result of this, it mainly concentrates in the following domains (Baheti & Gill, 2011; Lee, 2006).

- **Energy Control:** In CPSs most of the devices require less energy, but still power supply is a huge dispute. This is due to inconsistent demand and supply of energy. A good approach has to be planned for recognizing greatest way to exchange data in data centre for consuming energy.
- **Secure Control:** In the investigation studies, safety methods and grand challenges are reviewed and planned. In addition, many researchers have explored the concept of consistency in CPSs, demonstrated the concept of how data is transmitted to CPSs in a secured approach, presented a friendly healthcare management and observation system that describe the metrics for diagnosis error and also provide the necessity condition for diagnosis. And also provide solutions through message transfer to enhance the quality of security in wireless networks for cyber-physical function like mission critical.
- **Communication and Managing:** CPSs have to perform the communication and administration of multi-model information produced by diverse sensor devices. Usually real-time secured data services are proposed in CPSs using data-centric method. In order to attain the critical data for finest environment notion, a study is done on the spatio-temporal distribution of CPS nodes in WSNs. Though research is done on CPS applications which require expected real-time data services through the evaluation of systems and methods, still there are various issues to be considered.
- **Model Based Software Design:** On the basis of embedded system design, most of the learners perform model-based software design such as event and physical model, consistency for CPSs. However the model-based software design emerged earlier, the researchers of CPSs are very keen in developing challenges to improve themselves in it.
- **Control Technique:** The organization methods of CPSs are basic compared to other control applications. A plan and accomplishment of CPSs for impartially controlled virtual legs is proposed by some researchers. This approach had a problem of verifying a digital controller execution from a viewpoint of input-output and robust control.
- **Allocation of System Resources:** Allocation of system resource is a comparative study till now and primarily has been focusing on systems that are implanted, network controlled, interrelated with wireless sensors, etc. Resource allocation in CPSs is at the earlier stage and a new

study is on bandwidth allocation in CPSs. According to resource allocation, an investigation is proposed to recognize the difficulty of planning a disseminated procedure for combined ideal congestion control and allocation of channel in the multi receiver and transmitter networks for CPSs.

Since every developing country has treated the science of CPS as new growing scheme and researchers around the world tend to focus on certain aspects as follows:

- **Power Management and Manipulation:** Shared or distributed system is one of the features of cyber physical systems. Despite, various gimmicks used in CPS requires very smaller amount of energy to operate, it sill raises a question and demands in terms of power consumption and availability to perform the whole process of communication and computation without any issues. Operative scheme is being suggested from various forms to understand requirement and the intake of energy in the information warehouses. The authors Zhang & Shi (2009) proposed an ideal adaptive expulsion strategy to obtain full battery energy for a square wave imprudent current. Some researchers have developed an idle scheduler to accomplish facilities with least power outflow but not disturbing the constraints that are time-sensitive. In a top stream, the task of decreasing temperature is devised to increase the power competence. In many research papers it has been shown that a grouping construction is used to attain better achievement in power efficacy protection management.
- **Safe and Security Manipulation:** Systems will transmute the way we move with physical world with similar way how it acts with some other. Cyber security refers to combined cyber physical systems since the development of CPS exposure may have prompt and frightening effects in a new range. Instinctively, CPS may also be qualified as contains these characteristics. Uncertainness in the environment and safety hazard and faults in physical elements ensures the whole system's hardness, safety, at a vital dispute. Protective solutions may overwork the physical quality of cyber physical systems by purchasing position and mark based mechanisms. The quality of human life compared to decades ago and the world today for them and what it has to offer for better life.

CPS IN THE REAL WORLD

Cyber-physical systems – the new mantra for future Information and Communication Technology (ICT).It could be abstractly defined as the fusion of cyber (or) virtual worlds. In Pure technical terms, CPS comprises off four prime elements such as computing entity, a communicating entity, sensing (or) monitoring entity and an actuating entity. In simple terms, CPS means providing intelligence to the physical processes (or) phenomenon (or) physical entities such as an automobile, a motor, a refrigerator, an air-conditioner, a boiler, a traffic-controller (or) processes such as a heating process, a packaging, process (or) phenomenon such as pressure, temperature, moisture, force, etc. Cyber-physical systems will have innumerous opportunities across different sectors such as transportation, navigation, surveillance, manufacturing, logistics, etc. Hence, CPS should be explored and simplified and make it viable as well as affordable technology in near future. Even though cyber-physical systems could used in different sectors such as medical, industrial, military, etc., it could be used to solve two critical issues namely artificial disaster management such as structural collapse and natural pre disaster as well as post disaster management that could save human lives.

Disaster Management for Structural Collapse

In recent times building collapses are happening around the world during construction as well as after construction. In some places structural collapses (bridges, dams, etc.) also occurs during infrastructure development as well as existing infrastructure management. Smart miniaturized sensor nodes could be designed using cost effective microcontrollers and integrated with different sensors to sense or monitor individual physical phenomenon such as vibration, pressure, temperature, moisture, force, etc. These sensor nodes could be packaged with water proof container and provided with wirelessly charging capability at select points. These miniaturized smart nodes are then planted inside concrete roof, concrete pillars, concrete belt-beams, concrete wall and planted at the corners in every building structure. These smart nodes could be charged electrically through micro probes at the select places. Every smart node work cooperatively and convey the information related to the pressure, moisture, load, mild cracks, etc., to the centralized smart gateway. The centralized gateway mines all the data and prepares the structural health report. Hence, the CPS would create a real-timed based ad hoc connected structural health monitoring system to monitor, pre-warn as well as suggesting solution for the above mentioned issue.

Natural Disaster Management using Cyber-Physical System

The natural disasters such as Tsunami, Floods, Cyclones and earthquakes take hundreds of lives at few places every year across the globe. The cyber-physical systems could provide a great relief in pre as well as post natural disaster management. Smart miniaturized nodes could be designed using low-cost hardwares and could be integrated with specific sensors such as acoustic, vibration, ultrasonic or infrasonic based sensors. These smart nodes could be deployed at select places where natural disasters are expected frequently (based on historical data) to form an intelligent cyber-physical system based networks. These networks could be used to fore warn the people regarding the potential occurrence of natural disaster.

CONCLUSION

For the past few years this field is an interesting and likeable topic for researchers. Cyber Physical Systems will change the way of communication by connecting human with the world through internet depicts how information is transformed. CPSs must accomplish reliably, safely, securely and efficiently in real time. This domain includes energy and secure control, model-based software design. CPSs represent a convergence of technologies in embedded systems, distributed systems and dependable systems. CPSs advances in energy-efficient networking, sensors and actuators. CPSs technologies must be scalable with time and space. CPSs deal with uncertainty, privacy concerns and security issues. CPSs require new mathematical foundations to specify, analyze, verify and validate systems to monitor and control physical entities. Advances in CPSs research can be progressed by effective collaborations between engineering and computer science disciplines.

REFERENCES

Baheti, R., & Gill, H. (2011). Cyber-physical systems. In *The impact of control technology*, (pp. 161-166). Academic Press.

Lee, E. A. (2006, October). Cyber-physical systems-are computing foundations adequate. In *Proceedings of NSF Workshop on Cyber-Physical Systems: Research Motivation, Techniques and Roadmap* (vol. 2). NSF.

Shi, J., Wan, J., Yan, H., & Suo, H. (2011, November). A survey of cyber-physical systems. In *Proceedings of Wireless Communications and Signal Processing (WCSP),* (pp. 1-6). IEEE.

Wang, E. K., Ye, Y., Xu, X., Yiu, S. M., Hui, L. C. K., & Chow, K. P. (2010, December). Security issues and challenges for cyber physical system. In *Proceedings of the 2010 IEEE/ACM Int'l Conference on Green Computing and Communications & Int'l Conference on Cyber, Physical and Social Computing* (pp. 733-738). IEEE Computer Society. doi:10.1109/GreenCom-CPSCom.2010.36

Zhang, F., & Shi, Z. (2009, December). Optimal and adaptive battery discharge strategies for cyber-physical systems. In *Proceedings of Decision and Control, 2009 Held Jointly with the 2009 28th Chinese Control Conference* (pp. 6232-6237). IEEE. doi:10.1109/CDC.2009.5400561

ADDITIONAL READING

Broy, M. (2013, April). Challenges in modeling cyber-physical systems. In *Proceedings of the 12th international conference on Information processing in sensor networks* (pp. 5-6). ACM.

Conti, M., Das, S. K., Bisdikian, C., Kumar, M., Ni, L. M., & Passarella, A. et al. (2012). Looking ahead in pervasive computing: Challenges and opportunities in the era of cyber–physical convergence. *Pervasive and Mobile Computing, 8*(1), 2–21. doi:10.1016/j.pmcj.2011.10.001

Gupta, S. K., Mukherjee, T., Varsamopoulos, G., & Banerjee, A. (2011). Research directions in energy-sustainable cyber–physical systems. *Sustainable Computing: Informatics and Systems, 1*(1), 57–74.

Huang, B. X. (2008). Cyber physical systems: a survey. *Presentation Report, June.*

Lee, E. A. (2007). Computing foundations and practice for cyber-physical systems: A preliminary report. *University of California, Berkeley, Tech. Rep. UCB/EECS-2007-72.*

Lee, E. A. (2008, May). Cyber physical systems: Design challenges. In *Object Oriented Real-Time Distributed Computing (ISORC), 2008 11th IEEE International Symposium on* (pp. 363-369). IEEE.

Rajkumar, R. R., Lee, I., Sha, L., & Stankovic, J. (2010, June). Cyber-physical systems: the next computing revolution. In *Proceedings of the 47th Design Automation Conference* (pp. 731-736). ACM. doi:10.1145/1837274.1837461

Sha, L., Gopalakrishnan, S., Liu, X., & Wang, Q. (2009). Cyber-physical systems: A new frontier. In Machine Learning in Cyber Trust (pp. 3-13). Springer US.

Wu, F. J., Kao, Y. F., & Tseng, Y. C. (2011). From wireless sensor networks towards cyber physical systems. *Pervasive and Mobile Computing, 7*(4), 397–413. doi:10.1016/j.pmcj.2011.03.003

KEY TERMS AND DEFINITIONS

Actuators: Analyses the behavior of physical processes.

Computation: Reasoning and analyzing the data collected.

Cyber Physical Systems: A new generation of systems with integrated computational and physical abilities that can interact with humans through many new approaches.

Cyber: Integration of computation, communication and control systems.

Monitoring: Observing physical processes.

NSF: National Science Foundation.

Physical: Natural and human-made systems governed by the laws of physics.

Sensors: Perform the task by sensing the data.

WSN: Wireless Sensor Network.

Chapter 2
CPS Architecture

ABSTRACT

This chapter deals with the CPS architectural style, which can be used to provide support to the plan and assessment of other structural designs for cyber physical systems. It also shows the interconnections between physical and cyber components. In this prototype architecture, the important attributes of this architecture for CPS, which helps to identify many research challenges, are described and explained. The authors also discuss the open information service structural design to deal with the issues related to management of data in CPS. Along with the single-layer and multi-layer survivability of architecture, a portable CPS structure, which is known as multi-layer widespread structure, is discussed. This system uses unlicensed and licensed networks with various spectrums to connect CPS through different gateways. A research-related wireless access network project is described.

INTRODUCTION

Present models and methods for cyber-physical systems (CPS) analysis and design are disoriented with an impact of different mathematical formalisms and principles in engineering and computer science. Dissimilar analytical approaches for achieving flexibility often results in preliminary partition among virtual and physical requirements of the procedural structure. This separation is creating a complexity to estimate the effects and tradeoffs that flatten the boundaries between these domains. It extends to software architectural descriptions to include the complete elements of cyber-physical organization.

The aim is to generate an extendable structure that can create a wide-ranging set of pattern devices. A new CPS architectural style as a new direction along with operational observations and connected appliances are used for confirmation. A decade before, the instruction structural design has become one of the ultimate primary techniques in the discipline of significant instruction systems engineering. Typically instruction structural design develops a system as a chart of elements and connecting objects. These components signify the major executable elements of a system's executable structure (Rajhans et al.,2009) and the connecting objects denote the pathways of interaction between elements (Rajhans et al.,2009).

These elements are remarked with resources that distinguish their conceptual performance and allow the analysis of system-level design tradeoffs. There is a continuous extensive investigation and

DOI: 10.4018/978-1-4666-7312-0.ch002

growth in Architecture Description Languages (ADLs) (Rajhans et al.,2009) and devices to support their study and understanding as code.

Standard representations such as Unified Modeling Language (UML 2.0) (Rajhans et al.,2009), Systems Modeling Language (SysML) (Rajhans et al.,2009) and Architecture Analysis Design Language (AADL) (Rajhans et al.,2009) offer modeling vocabularies (Rajhans et al.,2009) of elements, connecting objects and properties. Many investigators has explored techniques to model structural design performance such as protocols described by process algebras or state machines (Rajhans et al.,2009) .

Tools render support to the above mention standard notations in the following ways:

- Visual editing and screening,
- Expansion of hierarchy, and
- Inspecting for element consistency or replacement and consideration of superior characteristics such as presentation, dependability, and protection.

Instructional structure design also supports reprocess of draft capability and system communications. Typically, system architecture suits inside a widespread family and referred as an architectural style (Rajhans et al., 2009). An architecture style comprises a set of element and object connector types collectively restraints that describe modes of factor composition. Few ADLs allow defining architecture styles, develop systems in it, and supply support tools for checking the compliance of system with that style. Software architecture is effectively used on many implanted and organized systems. For example, structural design narrative languages such as Meta-H and AADL are used to build air and spacecraft systems (Rajhans et al., 2009) and automotive control systems. CPS architectural style usually indicates structures at a superior level than replication models which denotes the system implementation particulars.

BACKGROUND

CPS Architecture Style

Despite the fact that structural design process is used in precise discipline to integrate certain tangible elements as components, currently there is rejection way of considering virtual and material elements as similar. The reason behind this is, the elements and connecting objects in instructional structure design approaches are incompetent for supporting the kinds of physical elements found in CPS and their connections with virtual entities. It extends to permit both material and virtual elements to be represented collectively in a CPS structural design approach. Acme ADL (Rajhans et al.,2009) is used which is a strong platform for defining flexible architectural approaches. In Acme, a structural design approach is denoted as a collection of component types that pursue certain configuration and regulations. This representation is in the form of physical elements and connecting object types that exist in the system and the pattern of their connection with all. A wide-ranging unit can be composed into a particular functional group (Rajhans et al., 2009) by accumulating extra elements and regulations.

The dispute in creating a structure design approach is to establish stability by linking specification and generalization. The CPS field focuses on implanted observation and management systems. The purpose is to generate a group of wide-ranging equipment's and connecting objects that can assist in this extensive domain as foundation for application-specific styles.

Cyber Family

It has been known that fundamental face of CPS is based on the established field for ADLs. The following elements and connecting devices offer a better aid for regular instantaneous supervising and manageable applications (Rajhans et al.,2009) . The component types are

- **Data Stores:** It is type of components that store data to create a line between executable elements in the structure. In uncomplicated organization, it could be submissive storage units, where as in composite systems details are provided to know that which elements can fetch and send to the data store elements.
- **Computation:** The approach of executable elements is to provide better components which aim in maintaining up to date data posted in data store components and operate things such as filtering, state estimation and control.
- **IO Interfaces:** In this implementation and discrete operations are executed to detect and manage the real world and these components enhance their performance like raw sensor data processed by smart sensor software.

The computational aspect of software plays a vital role to represent communication elements in the system. For this reason, it is important to closely observe the instructional elements and this change the physical performance of a whole organization. There are types of cyber connectors such as call-return connector and publish-subscribe connector represent one-to-one and one-to-many communication respectively. Further these connectors can be used to signify a balance between communication protocols (Rajhans et al.,2009) and network characteristics.

Physical Family

The architecture level is ready to face upcoming issues in designing an appropriate depiction of the cyber physical systems. Architectural models need not to maintain the essential details of physical dynamics simulation. The architectural components and connectors are used to represent the some of the concepts of physical dynamics. Similarly cyber elements and connecting devices connect the essentials of executable systems. To maintain the stability between physical elements and connecting objects with respect to force the interactions between various physical domain and its properties are represented.

Types of physical component are (Rajhans et al., 2009):

- **Sources:** These are the components that provide power to other components. Since this component has output port which is used to provide flow to the system.
- **Energy Storage:** A dynamic element or subsystems of an energy storage component models should have capacitive and inductive properties (Rajhans et al., 2009) in electrical systems. These component ports permit assignment of energy to further subsystems.
- **Physical Transducers:** Transducers balance energy conversation among dissimilar types of physical regions. Mainly these elements are used for demonstrating multidomain systems such as electromechanical devices. The electromechanical devices exchange force between electrical and machine-driven areas.

The following are the physical connector types (Rajhans et al., 2009):

- **Power Flow:** Connectors with energy stream provide dynamic coupling between physical elements by offering bidirectional exchanges to it.
- **Shared Variable:** It is a variable in two components that has adopted the same strategy and there is no directionality process of acquiring its connector.
- **Measurement:** It is a collection of connectors that uses any physical element as a key in another component. Such type of connectors has one way communication that corresponds.

Cyber-Physical Interface Family

It is known fact that the basic approach of cyber-physical connection family holds all fundamentals of cyber physical families. It would further add up better elements and acts as a link between various computational and physical approaches. To model and create enhanced interactions and to enact with cyber-physical world constraints, two connector types are used. They are physical-to-cyber (P2C) and cyber-to-physical (C2P) (Rajhans et al., 2009). Simple sensors which are designed based upon P2C connectors and actuators are modeled as C2P connectors. There are far more complex use of interface like cyber and key physical elements like defining P2C and C2P transducer components. These components have ports to either side of cyber and physical elements which would maintain better cyber-physical approach. These devices can be modeled and act as a better transformation between cyber and physical domains.

PROTOTYPE ARCHITECTURE

Cyber Physical system can make up a better network interconnector which acts as a collection of loosely coupled cyber systems. There are other issues of physical systems which help in monitoring and controlling user define laws. There are further approach of controlled logic and units having better actuator units. There are certain amenities that include various global reference time and subsequent group network. There is a clear need to derive better system components containing the individuals, devices and other cyber logic design. There is varied architecture of CPS, which highlight better architecture shown in Figure 1 as in (Ying et al,2008):

- A global reference time is a process that makes all system components function and interconnect properly. Though the system components are interrelated with the real world in parallel and non-parallel ways but components of communicating system can still accomplish a precise arrangement of activities and actions.
- Human society is nothing but events or information system (Ying et al,2008). These events are concepts of the tangible world created by system modules. These constructs have live events or information that determines the current position of the corporal world, whereas previous status of physical world is determined by out-of date events or information (Ying et al,2008). Events are of type raw facts or actuations generated by sensors or humans. The information is a physical world representation determined by CPS control units.
- Any event or information of this architecture hold the build-in properties such as global reference time, life-span, confidence fading equation, digital signature, trustworthiness, dependability and criticalness.
- According to previous experience and knowledge, various system components are used to represent dissimilar dependability and reliable values to different input sources. For similar abstractions as input, various system components yield different results.
- Publish and Subscribe are two simple transmission sources that are used in social humanity. With the aid of global reference time (indirectly or directly), anybody can publish their overview of the real world, which may be contributed and understood appropriately by other interested personalities.
- Semantic Control Laws are used to create an essential CPS mechanism which is represented in an event-condition-action (Ying et al,2008) form. Based on user defined scenarios, the system behaviors are

Figure 1. Prototype architecture of CPS

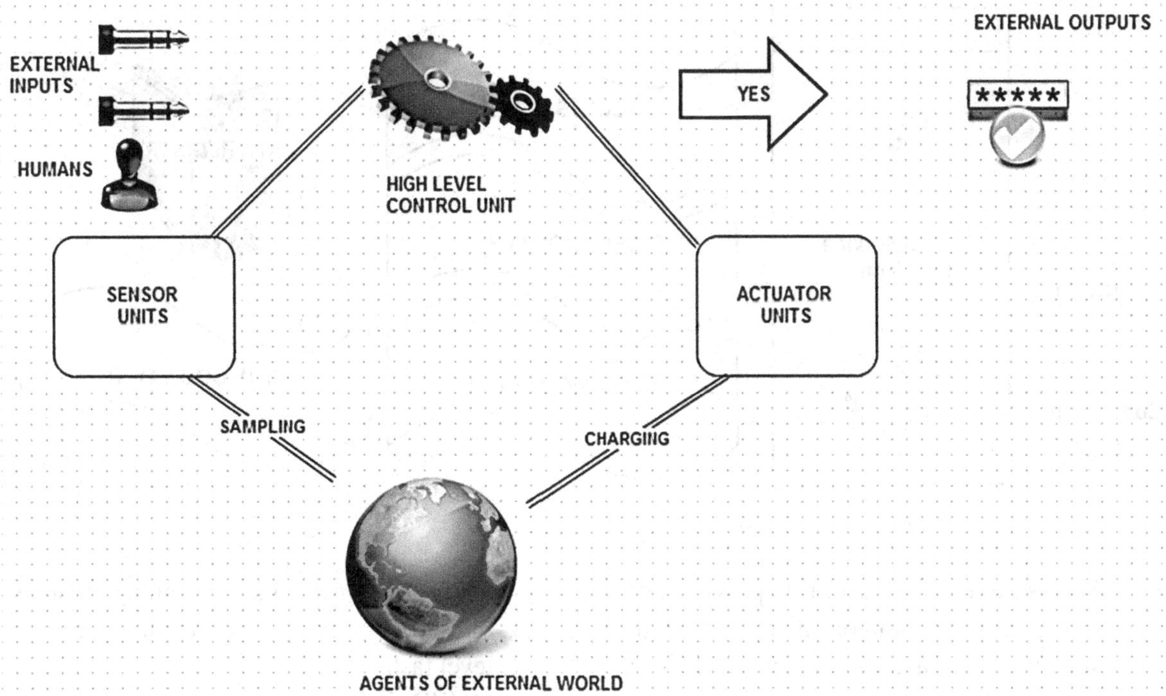

controlled with respect to the environment context.

- In extent to the availability of global reference time, the subsequent group network needs to offer new event or information channeling and structures of data management (Ying et al,2008). According to current conviction each node in a interrelated system should use a broadcast scheme for transmitting information or task to its neighbor nodes. As the assurance of the information or task falls to nil, the significance of this information or task remains live in the system.

OPEN DATA SERVICE ARCHITECTURE DESIGN FOR CPS

There are various services of data which helps in collating better storage and process of exports of data. By recommending, a better data service architecture having various layers of programming abstracts. The architecture layer majorly permits various divisions of data to measure a better abstraction on data services. The architecture is designed in such a way that suppose any developer wants to control data services can avail only low level interfaces rather than the interface of higher level. Since the design is mainly aimed for general applications. Moreover the routes of the layers are reachable and outlined by web service structure which is considered as communication protocol. This protocol is supported by various vertical and horizontal platforms to perform operations between them. In WSN back-end servers are treated as alternative data server to provide powerful web based data services as sensor nodes cannot perform this.

The open data service structural design has three layers which is shown in Figure 2 as in (Kang & Son,2008) and the role of each layer (Kang & Son,2008) in it is described below.

Figure 2. Open data service architecture

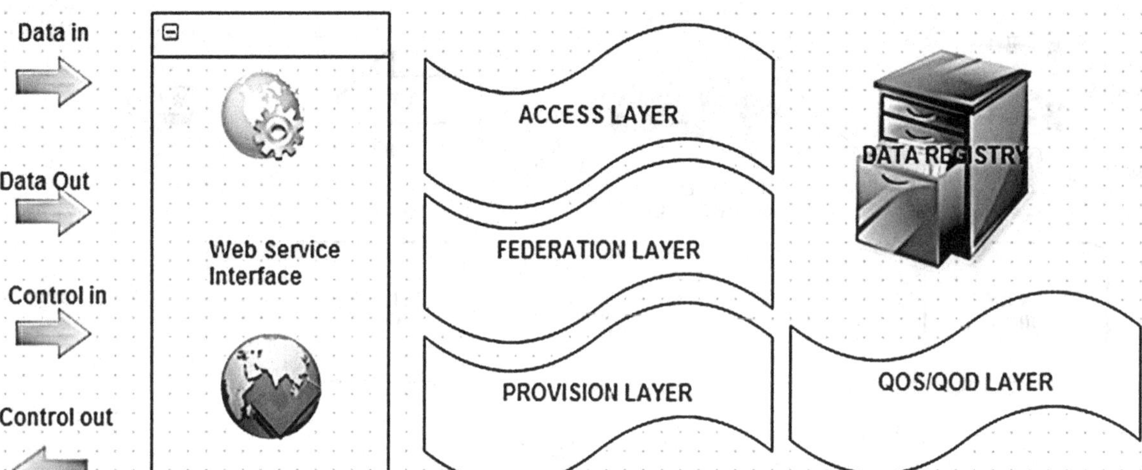

- **Access Layer:** This layer is to provide data access through common interface such as SQL which is a query language. This is to support continued operations against data flow as most of the information from sensing devices are in constant flows. The characteristics and level of the provision are Quality of Service (QoS) and Quality of Data (QoD). QoS is to acquire the target deadline miss ratio and QoD is to update and correct data which can be achieved through this layer. Through interface the performance of a data service is controlled by applications in it.
- **Federation Layer:** This layer permits well organized data to be applied in various locations. A Web Service Definition Language (WSDL) describes interfaces for data service accessibility. By providing distributed data services, the organization and allocation of data between data services can be accomplished.
- **Provision Layer:** Through this layer there are various functions which would help us in deriving better requirements among advanced layers. The services delivered contain both assignment of data among various locations and data reproduction and consistency, data streaming, managing storage capacity and maintaining lower level tasks.
- **QoS/QoD Enforcement Layer:** The main objective of this layer is to enforce access layer requirements that can communicate with the above two mentioned provision and federation layer of this architecture. Based on federation and provision layer abilities, QoS/QoD is forced by monitoring local resources. In this layer data service wide-spread data sources and to meet the performance objectives it involve dynamic storing and streaming of data. The assurance of QoS/QoD requirement from access layer is achieved only if federation and provision layer provide sufficient resources which is enabled through the enforcement layer.

In the above mentioned Figure 2, data service is provided by data registry service such as s defining, processing, reproducing and modifying data. A data service is categorized by data objects to achieve assurances of QoS/QoD. For a vast usage relational data model is represented in this data service architecture. Moreover data flows are transformed to associations as in persistent query language and every data object is recognized by End Point Reference (EPR) which is a unique identifier.

MULTILAYER WIRELESS NETWORKING

Present communication networks are established using layered approach. This type of networks basically built upon a fiber network. There are various works related to particular view and has a different approach in multilayer and has better survivability. There are other earlier works which would set stage for better rising of end to end and has better broadband networks. Various research projects establishing a better framework and having survivability strategies. There are various research views and better link up emphasis on Internet Protocol (IP) over Wavelength Division Multiplexing (WDM) (Lee & Modiano, 2009) based networks. There are other relative perceptions that make up a better multilayer and survivability. There is various issue of layer which acts as a defined point and come across various network. There are various sections of network which would help us in defining a better network and has better different services with different types of traffic.

In this topological layering there are various layers defined based on the physical and logical network topology. Further, there is an issue which would act as better identifier of topology which consists of one tier and internet providers. There is another approach with two layers which largely based upon the regional Internet Service Providers (ISP's). By considering a key use of the ISP's and presenting them in a better way, it performs better management and structured communication path among various domains. There are various links which act as a better regional ISP and further ISP fails to coordinate efforts to establish communication over a links.

In WDM based network the light paths are specifying the logical connection of nodes whereas fibers specify the physical connection of nodes. Networks frequently depend on logical layer for providing security and recovery of services. Though logical link is capable of handling single logical connection failures, when it is combined with the physical topology, it will not be available to single physical link failures. The multiple light paths in every physical link lead to several link failures in logical connection due to one link failure. And this in turn disconnects the logical connection. There are far more many layers which would provide better mechanisms in the network stack. In real life, networks are very complicated and layered. Due to many problems in cross-layer survivability, the protection and recovery approaches are associated only to single-layer network situations.

Consider a scenario of light paths which help in carrying a various different Label Switched Paths (LSP) (Lee & Modiano,2009) . There are various IP routers, which would help in coordinating failures and fiber span act as a light path. However, maintaining a better Multi-Protocol Label Switching (MPLS) (Lee & Modiano,2009) layer which would establish a new set of LSP's. There are various processes which would help in updating network wide routing tables and take up various orders through a light path. Taking a wide matter and restoring LSPs used through IP for a better routing of bypass and LSP affected. Taking a far better assumption of cost of activity and providing necessary steps to develop a better losing capacity in a single fiber span. The coordinated reconfigurations can result in developing better light paths and has multiple paths. The recovery of these would further help us in discovering traffic and no longer balance various paths and least can make up a better on round of re-routing.

Single-Layer Survivability

Basically, there are two approaches are presented to make recover process in single-layer survivability, such as retrieval at the lowermost layer and recovery at the uppermost layer. In this multilayer stack of network each layer maintains client/server relationship between adjacent layers. Each lower layer of network provides accessibility to higher layer of network. A single-layer recovery scheme is applied to each layer of network. These recovery approaches are developed during many failures such as fiber cuts and recovery of these failures are enabled in the lower layer of network. On the other hand, higher layer of network recovery demand more flexibility. The highest-layer recovery is the best option in some situations because it efforts are very near to the traffic/service provider sources. It gives superior efforts on the situation and works effectively to optimize the network globally and eliminates the in-appropriate local decisions.

Multilayer Survivability

Generally, escalation (Demeester et al.,1999) is a procedure that can determines about the activities like when to start/stop and how to organize various recovery methods. The survivability method is very difficult in multi-layer networks. There are three aspects in the escalation process (Demeester et al.,1999) as key roles are Activation method, Escalation direction method and Inter-layer coordination method. The Activation method works for a recovery of particular layer and it could be either parallel (all layers starts at the same time) or sequential (one layer at a time). Parallel activation is the first choice to perform this process because of its faster and no need of interactions among the layers which is required in sequential activations.

There are two basic escalation types are available for recovery process such as bottom-up and top-down. As we studied prior in single-layer strategies, the recovery process in bottom-up case is having many failures which is not happening in highest-layer in top-down. But, the escalation process of single layer strategy might be a bottom-up or top-down which is based on pre-defined instructions.

HETEROGENEOUS CPS NETWORK ARCHITECTURE

Cyber Physical Systems network is mainly for communicating various CPS terminals such as smart phones, sensors, automatic machines and wearable computers. Mobile CPS study has shown that how CPS can facilitate ubiquitous wireless networking (Shen, Xu, Lu, & Li,2010) with the help of Wireless Local Area Network(WLAN) (Shen et al.,2010) and Wireless Wide Area Network(WWAN) (Shen et al.,2010) . WLAN coverage range is short compared to WWAN, but it can be widespread using multi-hop mesh network. A portable CPS system is known as multi-layer heterogeneous system because it uses WLAN (unlicensed) and WWAN (licensed) with various spectrums. As WLAN provides specific coverage and WWAN provides complete coverage, heterogeneous CPS system can access several techniques with various coverage spectrums. Moreover CPS network is connected with WLAN and WLAN through gateways.

In WLAN few CPS terminals can be linked with CPS through wired connection whereas other CPS devices can be connected through multi-hop nodes. Because of this difficulty, CPS cannot use WLAN topology. To overcome this issue real CPS network uses WLAN with high frequency (2.4GHz) band and WWAN with low frequency (800-900MHz) band. In this multi-layer heterogeneous CPS network, devices deployed in WLAN region can access coverage area of WWAN or WLAN. As the WWAN uses licensed spectrum which is costly, the resources accessed in this range have higher value. Now a question rises that how to choose an appropriate access scheme with a required band for a desired CPS station by matching the resource cost and value (Shen et al.,2010). The following steps are helpful in selecting the coverage regions such as WLAN or WWAN.

- If a workstation is situated in WLAN region, then it can avail WLAN resources with low-cost and low-value.
- If a workstation is situated beyond the WLAN region, then it can avail WWAN resources with high-cost and high-value.
- If a workstation is situated in WLAN area and has high flexibility then it can avail WLAN resources rarely, since WLAN do not allow high mobility.

The heterogeneous multi-layer architecture can be simplified to dual-layer heterogeneous architecture network (Shen et al.,2010) . The dual-layer heterogeneous consists of WLAN layer WWAN layer. In this WLAN access points and base locations of WWAN are situated, as WLAN coverage is less compared to WWAN. If a low mobility device is situated in the WLAN zone then the supply is accessed from WLAN layer. Suppose a device has high mobility or situated outside the WLAN coverage area then it can avail the resource from the WWAN layer.

Multilayer Resource Management for CPS

The multi-layer resource management operation is performed in a combined way by utilizing both the layers (WLAN and WWAN). The WWAN use its frequency for resource on cell-edge region with high mobility device to attain a superior throughput of the system. But WLAN covers the center region for low mobility devices. The access the resources in an efficient way a joint scheduling process (Shen et al.,2010) is shown in figure 3.

The process of joint scheduling is given below.

- Signal behaviors of WLAN access points and base locations of WWAN are measured by the workstations.
- Based on the measurements of two layers the Channel Quality Indicator (CQI) is estimated by the workstation.
- Now network scheduler of CPS retrieves the reports of two CQIs from the workstation.

- WLAN's CQI is enhanced with an additional load to set a low cost to it and CQIs of both the layers are related by the CPS network scheduler.
- Once the decision is made by the CPS network scheduler, it informs to the workstation.
- Based on the result the workstation selects the layer for accessing the resources.

The joint scheduling process is mainly applicable to WWAN layer because the workstation need not be situated in WLAN region always.

Following are the various dimensions of network heterogeneity (Lehman et al.,2011) which can be determined in the heterogeneous infrastructures.

- **Multiservice:** These are the services provided by underlying network, when any user connected to the boundary of a network. The multiple services provided are based on certain combinational characteristics such as physical port type like Fiber channel, Ethernet (Lehman et al.,2011) and type of network transfer like routing via IP, Ethernet Virtual LAN (VLAN) (Lehman et al.,2011), etc.
- **Multi-Technology:** To accomplish essential network services, multiple technologies are need to be installed. The multiple technologies can be used are IP, Ethernet, MPLS, WDM, etc.

Figure 3. Multi-layer resource management for CPS

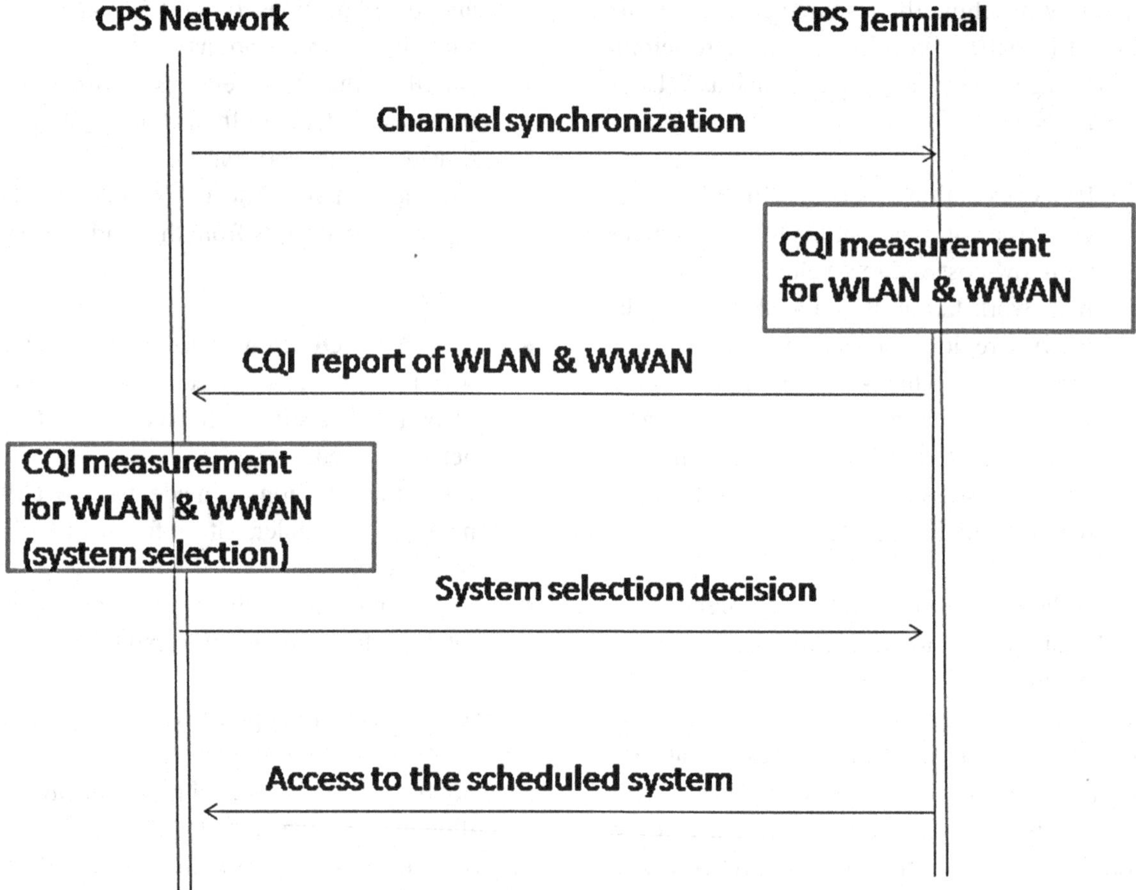

- **Multilevel:** It provides various routing regions that allow many domains to access its networks across the boundaries of related network regions.
- **Multilayer:** It describes the combination of Multilevel and Multi-technology notions which are to be covered.

ARCHITECTURE FOR HETEROGENEOUS MOBILE COMPUTING

Initially in the year 1994, there was lot of discussion contrary to the existing tendency towards moveable devices that were fundamentally keys of calculation (Brewer et al.,1998). The major focus is on almost all facets of the problem, containing link and transport layer protocols, mobile channeling, controlling power, provision of application, hypermedia streaming and native and widespread network services. In other words the portable computers were watching for a powerful app related to a personal controller. However, the idiom 'Access is the Killer App' (Brewer et al.,1998) is actually a dispute that matter of concern is not much about the capabilities of the device, but relatively about the information and processing power to which it has the access. It is feasible to control terabytes of facts and the supercomputers power until they are accessed over a universal network. The consequential structural design determines (Brewer et al.,1998):

- The way to build this network from the superimposed collection of networks,
- How to ramble in this network flawlessly and efficiently, and
- For mobile devices how to influence processing in the communications to facilitate innovative skills and facilities.

The focal point is to set up a universal networking that is confined to smaller areas which features the network as a whole having extensive coverage. But the quality of the connection and features might differ by locality to a greater extent. The network connections might differ from reinforced or ultraviolet in-room systems with remarkable execution, to urbanite cellular networks, to satellite networks with high invisibilities but vast exposure. Services might differ on a large scale such as from home access to restricted driving instructions, to universal services such as search mechanisms and web approach (Brewer et al.,1998).

This is unconventional to the initiative of universal computing in which the major focus is on the connectivity than on computing. Also there is a need to have a significant infrastructure that is easily accessible, less cost and adequately scalable to support many users. By and large, instead of the mobile devices, the main properties such as calculation, space and difficulty should be relocated into the infrastructure to enable new services, cost effective and less power tiny low-priced portable devices with incredible functionality. However, such an substructure is readily built and its new abilities are used as a simple mobile client such as Palm Pilot PDA (Brewer et al.,1998). The structural design discussed is designed by keeping some of the challenges in view by offering solutions to it such as:

- Flawless mobility is provided within a system and through diverse networks. The discovery and arrangement of network links is noticeable and programmed similar to the group of the finest network in series. For many systems, very little latency handoffs are also provided to facilitate audio and video while moving around the network.
- A TCP based dependable transport layer is provided to work with the servers. And concealing the properties of wireless thrashings and irregularity that usually damages the TCP functioning.
- To provide instinctive detection and arrangement of native network facilities.
- To support clients with the changing and regulating the content according to device.

Nevertheless, the prime notion is overlay networking (Brewer et al.,1998) that is comprised of various networks that differ from each other in terms of coverage and performance. This is further merged into a particular understandable network providing coverage which is the amalgamation of the networks' exposure with implementation. Besides the established cell-based traveling referred as parallel wandering, logical roving is provided that ranges across the basic networks known as vertical roaming as it changes its IP address or network boundary.

In the specified overlay network, the subsequent issue is all about the poor presentation of characteristic TCP in the wireless and dissimilar networks that allow mobility. TCP believes that the losses in the network are due to blocking and regular association, which is not true.

Key Themes

In this architecture there are four broad-spectrum themes such as dynamic adaptation, cross-layer optimization, agent-based capabilities and exploit soft state (Brewer et al.,1998). But our concentration is only on the first two themes for discussion. Self-motivated adjustment is the usual method to deal with diverse network environment and with customer heterogeneity. This incorporate innovative adaptive procedures for TCP, on demand conversion of layout, instantaneous visual transcoding, vigorous quality or performance trade-offs, and personalization of user linkage for smaller devices (Brewer et al.,1998). The second theme is the cross-layer optimization. There are certain situations where we unambiguously crack the OSI model of model for enabling improved accomplishment or smarter variation. While doing so, it usually includes the use of information in physical level to activate handoffs and develop information in transport level to direct retransmission of link layer and vibrant adaptation of application layer (Brewer et al.,1998).

The primary goal of the agents in network architecture is to improve the performance by increasing the opportunities to perform with client systems, TCP stacks and servers (Brewer et al.,1998). The main role is to conceal to whims of wireless networking, portability and outermost diversification from all of the clients and organization (Brewer et al.,1998). The agents work at their best to depict the way it is believed to be. Another way is to obtain an end-to-end methodology in which the user is permissible to transform all components comprising clients and servers. This method is considered as a better solution on the whole, but it is almost impossible to install it, since clients and servers require enhancement often. However, it is also shown that the agent-based solutions can perform better in many cases and have a better deployment path. In few cases it is only option as it manage information of the particular end-to-end connection. To improve the TCP performance in the networking, the agents are used to control mobility and vertical handoff. Exploit Soft State is type of soft state which assists in the presentation of a system. It is not necessary to recover the soft state after failures but it can be discarded at any time. It can usually be unpredictable without affecting accuracy. In general, most of the agents use soft state to make them unsophisticated and immaterially fault tolerant.

BARWAN

To enable the actual functional mobile networking across an enormously extensive range of real world networks and portable devices, the BARWAN (Bay Area Research Wireless Access Network) (Brewer et al.,1998) project was used. It was a three-year DARPA-funded project at the University of California at Berkeley, was done that had focused majorly on this issue and provided its best at it. The BARWAN architecture has elements such as heterogeneous clients, networks and servers. In addition to this, proxy is used for mobility and self-motivated variation (Brewer et al.,1998). In this architecture horizontal and vertical handoffs happen amongst the different nodes of the identical network and between various networks respectively. It also provides high performance to deliver consistent data transport. The architecture of BARWAN is shown in figure 4 as in (Brewer et al.,1998). The following are the four networks in the overlay BARWAN test bed.

- **IBM Infrared Wireless LAN:** This is an infrared network that forms the fundamental in-room network (Katz et al.,1996; Brewer et al.,1998). However, the reuse of spectrum is provided insignificantly by the Infrared that further high bandwidth is enabled per cubic meter in constructions. It's a very cost-effective network.
- **Lucent Wave LAN:** According to building-size network both the 900-MHz and 2.4-GHz forms are considered for this network. In this coverage is for all the floors having at least one or two base stations per floor.

Figure 4. BARWAN architecture

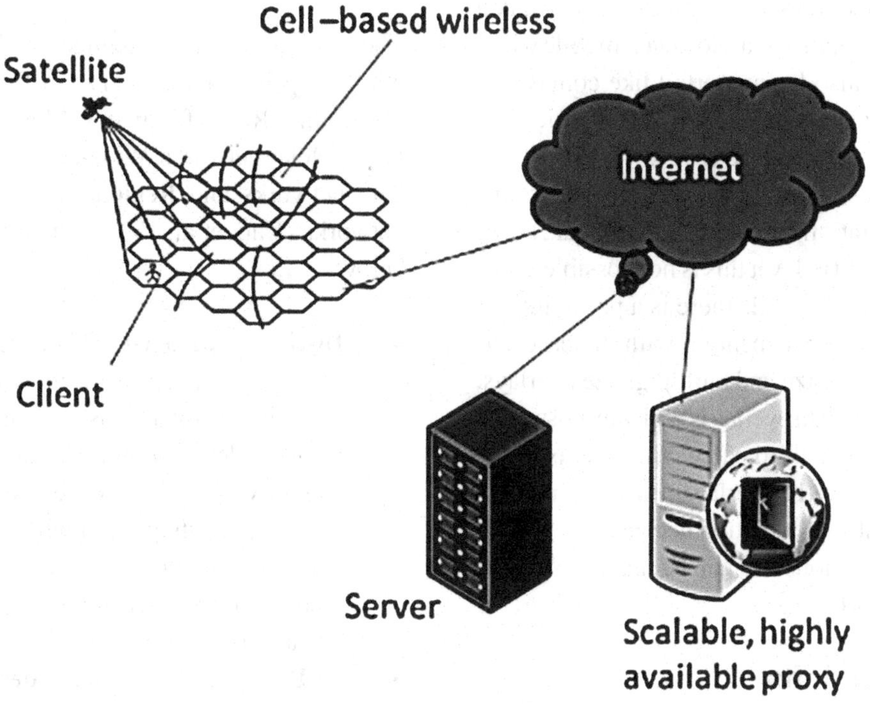

- **Metricom Ricochet:** It is a packet-based broadcasting network for urban areas including the Inlet region. In this test bed private network is also used for testing.
- **Hughes Direct-Broadcast Satellite (DBS):** There is only one dish on top of the building and also have a moveable dish at isolated regions.

The bandwidth, latency, cell size and registration times are specified in the above mentioned networks. The registration times that refers to the setting up of the initial connection, were calculated by sending set of UDP packets to a movable host, activating the network link and estimating the time between the transmission i.e., the time taken to activate the network interface and the time taken to deliver the initial data packet to the mobile. From the above facts it is known that there is an extensive discrepancy in all dimensions and it is further concluded that there is no single network that can be considered as finest.

Overlay Networking

In future most of the systems will be built based on heterogeneous wireless overlay networks which provide communication between wired as well as internetworking over a wide region. And also to provide cost-effective connectivity between In-Room infrared (IR) and Radio Frequency (RF) the wireless overlay networking architecture is used. In this network structure lower levels consist of high bandwidth wireless cells that usually cover a small area. However, in a wider geographic area the higher levels offer a lower bandwidth per unit area connection. In this network structure there are three overlay levels. The lowest level includes a collection of disjoint room-size with higher bandwidth networks that supply the highest bandwidth (one Mb per sec) per unit area. The subsequent level include higher bandwidth of building size networks that offer bandwidth according to the room-size networks, but cover huge area like any level of a building. The last level is a wide-area data network that provides comparatively lesser bandwidth link (tens of kilobits), over a much extended geographic area. However, mobile wired networks can also be supported like connecting local Ethernet subnet robustly via Dynamic Host Configuration Protocol (DHCP).

Nevertheless, some elements of these systems such as base station software (Brewer et al.,1998) are ideally modified, yet this is not possible every time. For instance, while there is a possibility of modifying and experimenting with the base stations for the area size and building-size overlays, the wide-spread data overlay is typically possessed and managed by a third party. This results in the indirect control on the overlay infrastructure. This is a significant consideration because it sets limit for the modifications that can be made to support vertical handoff.

Vertical Handoffs

The main purpose of a vertical handoff system is to diminish the handoff delay by keeping the bandwidth and power outlays as much low as possible for a particular user. There are some significant distinctions between the horizontal and vertical handoffs. As a first difference, there are two types of vertical handoffs such as upward and downward vertical handoff. An ascendant vertical handoff is a handoff to an overlay with a superior cell size and lesser bandwidth per area whereas a downward vertical handoff is a handoff to an overlay with a lesser cell size and superior bandwidth per area. As a device often linked to the upper overlay during handoff, downward vertical handoffs are less critical in terms of time. The second dissimilarity is that in a diversified network, selection of best network can be exigent. For instance, an in-building RF network with a poor sign may produce superior function than a wide-area data network with a well-built indicator. Sometimes there might be variation in the financial concerns that might not arise in a particular network.

Overlay Wireless Technologies

The overlay wireless architecture has different wireless technologies such as In-Room Infrared, In-building Radio frequency, Metropolitan Area Packet Relay networks, Wide-area packet switched data networks and Regional-area satellite data networks (Katz et al.,1996) which are described below.

- **In-Room Infrared:** This infrared technology is effectively used in physical places like discussion rooms and offices to provide wireless communication. It has latencies as wire line networks uses. This technology permits good quality of video and audio information in a compressed format. And it can be used for laptops and PDAs because of its less cost.
- **In-Building Radio Frequency:** Several wireless local area networking devices are accessible in the market with wide spectrum having unlicensed bandwidth. The bandwidth range might be up to 1 to 2 mbps. It has a provision to transmit compacted video and audio information and the coverage area is limited to certain part of a building like half the floor of the building. It follows the concept of Pico-cellular architecture (Katz et al.,1996) which is quite expensive.
- **Metropolitan Area Packet Relay Networks:** The packets are transmitted between the hosts, wired access points and infrastructure radios (Katz et al.,1996) by the packet radio systems. The network deployed in S.F. Bay area (Katz et al.,1996) uses this network architecture that has radio link range up to 100kbps which is to be spread between the users inside the cell. Based on the number of radio hops (2 to 3 hops) between the wired connection and the mobile host latency is calculated.

- **Wide-Area Packet Switched Data Networks:** It is a type of Cellular Digital Packet Data (CDPD) used as wide-area data overlay (Katz et al.,1996) to the analog cellular system. Based on the cellular voice data latency of the system varies. And the transmission range is up to 19.2 kbps which is difficult to maintain.
- **Regional-Area Satellite Data Networks:** To provide low data rate processes to the system various Low Earth Orbiting (LEO) satellites (Katz et al.,1996) are planned for future. The high data rate download links are determined by both Deployed Direct Broadcast Satellite (DBS) (Katz et al.,1996) and Very Small Aperture Terminal (VSAT) (Katz et al.,1996) services. As a result of this high latency rates will be obtained due to satellite orbits such as geosynchronous orbits (Katz et al.,1996).

To make the network system more efficient, wireless overlay network architecture must deal with the following

- **Seamless Integration of Overlay Networks:** Overlay IP referred as mobile IP should choose a better subnetwork for delivering a packet with the help of policy-driven (Katz et al.,1996) approaches.
- **Support Services for Mobile Applications:** A new API to be used to initiate handovers through application, to represent its connectivity feature and to change its connection according to infrastructure requirement.

The Gateway-Centric Architecture

In a homogeneous networking approach the portable host is placed at the hub connected with the access point to provide services to new networks. But access-centric method provides a way from one subnet to other in the middle of the structural design for communication. Different types of networks are connected through software that transmits the information between the host (portable) and the connections linked to it. Moreover mobile host ramble between various wireless networks. In wireless networks service providers controlling the subnets are called as black pipes (Katz et al., 1996). Because packets are transmitted from or to the mobile host through wired gateway or wireless connection based on routing, priority, quality service, etc. Another network called cooperative network that provide control over networks by gateway and balance the network traffic among associated networks using management software.

To offer services to wireless overlay internetworking (Katz et al.,1996) and mobile applications a conceptual architecture with the (bottom up) layers approach is used. The different layers (Katz et al.,1996) used in this architecture are given below.

- **Wireless Overlay Subnetwork Layer:** To combine wireless subnetworks it uses physical, data link and subnetwork layers. All these are connected through overlay IP. The information like the routing protocols used, type of media access and physical channels used are noticeable only below this layer. On the other hand to restrict handoff, the in-building subnetworks are represented by essential methods.
- **Overlay Network Management Layer:** To handle various overlays this level associate to the transport and network levels. This layer establishes internetworking over the wireless subnetworks. By selecting a suitable subnetwork for continuous connectivity, it transmits the packets to the heterogeneous subnets with the required QoS. To handle the handoff between heterogeneous subnets it require algorithms to be applied based on feature of the interconnected system that creates routes among the mobile host and the home agent. And

also to preserve the energy in the network at a time only one network interface is made active while other interfaces are used based on its requirement. The protocols available in this layer need to be enhanced to improve the performance of transmission over the connections.

- **Session Management Layer:** This level offers session methods such as connections using messages to be used over a particular TCP link.
- **Data Type Specific Transmission Layer:** Some unique functions are used in this layer to control the transfer of precise objects in multimedia applications. These applications access only auditory, video, picture and other semantically rich data (Katz et al.,1996).
- **Application Support Services Layer:** In this layer applications can exchange information between the mobile host's region and the wired environment. These distributed services and allocation of resource management are offered by this layer.
- **Mobile Multimedia Applications Layer:** The main aim of this layer is to provide fundamental services and network administration operations to mobile applications in it.

Cyber-Physical Handshake

CPSs enhance the communications by linking the cyber and the real worlds and sensor supported group interconnections are one of the applications of CPS. The inventive design of sensor supported group network system is called as cyber-physical handshake (Wu, Chu, & Tseng,2011b). This architecture design is to allow data transfer between two persons after sensing and verifying the handshaking configurations. In the physical world data transfer like exchange of business cards between two authenticated users is called as handshake performance. Conversely in the cyber world the handshake method is implemented between two nodes before they initiate the process of data exchange. The process continues as handshake to implement an authenticated procedure. Once they have performed the handshake the sensing methods support the automatic transfer of data between two people. This light-weight procedure is suitable for simple sensor devices that yield few computations and need not to produce and endorse common solutions.

The primary objective of handshake method in cyber-physical system is to permit data transfer between two users who have performed handshake previously. In the real world the handshake among two friends creates shaking waves (Wu et al.,2011b) which are observed from the user's sensor nodes. This information will have better similarity in terms of time and frequency regions. Later this related information is used to endorse the handshake performance. In this handshake system architecture every client is provided with a intelligent devices and wearable wristwatch like transceiver node attached with a measuring instrument on the user's wrist. This type of communication by sensor nodes between two users is done through IEEE 802.15.4 (Wu et al.,2011b) Every user's smart phone is connected with the sensor nodes via Bluetooth. The sensor nodes are capable of sensing and delivering handshaking data to user's smart phone. The similarity between the two user's data is assessed by the smart phone. During comparison if the predefined threshold value is less than the estimated similarity, then the users will exchange the data such as E-card information through Internet.

Comparison between MANET, WSN, and CPS

Following are some of features (Wu, Kao, & Tseng,2011a) which are compared between different wireless networks such as MANET, WSN and CPS with respect to networking.

- **Network Formation:** The configuration of MANET is always random with the node mobility. WSN is usually area-specific and allows less mobility. It also allows self-motivated participation. However, the networks of CPS are wide spread across various regions that are internet dependent while connecting.
- **Communication Pattern:** The routing abilities differ in each network. Though WSN engross interactions like query-and-response communications, but MANET allows random interaction patterns like unicast, multicast and broad cast. In CPS different domain interactions are possible in addition to intra-WSN interactions. For instance in the flood prevention applications, to manage the water gates of a dam a set of water-level tracking sensors are coordinated with the various sets of rain-meters.
- **Power Management:** Though both MANET and WSN highlight to save power, this is impossible for WSN as sensing devices are situated in remote regions. In MANET change of node state is based on the network requirement which is possible. According to the applications used in CPS sensor activity is determined. Consider the dam control system application which has the sensors to change the mode either in flood mode or non-flood mode.
- **Network Coverage:** Wireless Sensor Network involve in maintaining both coverage and connectivity where as in MANET concentration is only on node mobility. Sensors are supposed to be allocated with the ranges of fixed sensing and communication. CPS uses the same requirements of WSN, but various phases of reachability and linking device is used for dissimilar WSNs.
- **Node Mobility:** Compared to MANET portability is very less in WSN. In most of the mobile sensing applications there are two types of mobility such as controllable like vehicular sensing and uncontrollable mobility like opportunistic sensing. In many CPS applications the data sensed is retrieved from mobile and static sensor nodes which might be of mobility type manageable and unmanageable.
- **Knowledge Mining:** In MANET simply set of connections concerns are dealt. In WSN more concentration is on how to gather and supervise the sensed data. On the other hand CPS focuses on acquisition of information from various network regions to exploit the intelligence efficiently. For instance the energy distribution is done wisely in wind and solar energy metering (Lehman et al.,2011) sensors.
- **Quality of Services:** Quality of Services differs from one network to another network. In MANET more importance is given to transmission of data where as in WSN main focal point is sensing of data. However CPS concentrates more on network availability, sensed data and its security and the intellectual information.

CPS performs several computations by combining WSN from various domains to it. The networks and the embedded computers manage and observe physical processes as well as computations carried out in CPS. Existing new embedded technologies have an important role in communicating factual things in a concealed manner.

CONCLUSION

A CPS network should be intended to universally access various types of networks, including WLAN and WWAN. A joint resource administration design for a multi-layer widespread structure network for the CPS network is portrayed. The WWAN and WLAN layers are stable based on the cost of the cellular network layer when there is possibility to access required devices. On the other hand, our structural design data service facilitates particular implementation conclusion more logically than others. For example, the data service arrangement through federation layers permit data flow in an order from data sources to destinations and hierarchical feedback control to assure QoS and QoD becomes a normal selection.

Wireless overlays are represented as a way to merge the offering of wide-area coverage while accomplishing the top reachable bandwidth and latency for movable devices. Some of the support procedures are designed to facilitate applications and to adapt to the amendments in the excellence of their network connectivity. BARWAN is being planned, arranged and assessed with wireless procedures and network services from AT&T, IBM, Metricom and Pacific Telesis. It is possible to wander between various networks and the accomplishment of the networks is quite fine. The proxy is well accessible and supports thousands of customers, various quality services and a wide variety of portable devices.

The assistance for restricted network services permit mechanical configuration of portable devices so they can develop local sources, and the inaccessible power functionality makes it possible to manage your surroundings with your personal PDA, even if the user is unavailable in the room before. While the people of WSN concentrate more on the plans of sensing, managing data, retrieval of data, interaction and exposure issues. But the humanity of CPS concentrate more on the growth of cross-functionality intelligence from various WSNs and the communications between the cyber and physical world. A CPS application may link various inaccessible WSNs and perform corresponding actions. The achievement of CPS includes administration of cross-discipline sensing data, implanted and movable sensing approaches, expandable computing or storing techniques with confidentiality and safety patterns.

REFERENCES

Brewer, E. A., Katz, R. H., Chawathe, Y., Gribble, S. D., Hodes, T., & Nguyen, G. et al. (1998). A network architecture for heterogeneous mobile computing. *IEEE Personal Communications*, *5*(5), 8–24. doi:10.1109/98.729719

Demeester, P., Gryseels, M., Autenrieth, A., Brianza, C., Castagna, L., & Signorelli, G. et al. (1999). Resilience in multilayer networks. *IEEE Communications Magazine*, *37*(8), 70–76. doi:10.1109/35.783128

Kang, W., & Son, S. H. (2008). The design of an open data service architecture for cyber-physical systems. *ACM SIGBED Review*, *5*(1), 3. doi:10.1145/1366283.1366286

Katz, R. H., Brewer, E. A., Amir, E., Balakrishnan, H., Fox, A., Gribble, S., et al. (1996, February). The bay area research wireless access network (BARWAN). In Proceedings of Compcon'96: Technologies for the Information Superhighway (pp. 15-20). IEEE.

Lee, K., & Modiano, E. (2009). Cross-Layer Survivability in WDM-Based Networks. In *Proceedings of INFOCOM 2009. IEEE*. doi:10.1109/INFCOM.2009.5062013

Lehman, T., Yang, X., Ghani, N., Gu, F., Guok, C., Monga, I., & Tierney, B. (2011). Multilayer networks: An architecture framework. *IEEE Communications Magazine*, *49*(5), 122–130. doi:10.1109/MCOM.2011.5762808

Rajhans, A., Cheng, S. W., Schmerl, B., Garlan, D., Krogh, B. H., Agbi, C., & Bhave, A. (2009). An architectural approach to the design and analysis of cyber-physical systems. *Electronic Communications of the EASST, 21*.

Shen, J., Xu, F., Lu, X., & Li, H. (2010, October). Heterogeneous multi-layer wireless networking for mobile CPS. In *Proceedings of Ubiquitous Intelligence & Computing and 7th International Conference on Autonomic & Trusted Computing* (UIC/ATC), (pp. 223-227). IEEE. doi:10.1109/UIC-ATC.2010.30

Wu, F. J., Chu, F. I., & Tseng, Y. C. (2011, August). Cyber-physical handshake. *Computer Communication Review*, *41*(4), 472–473. doi:10.1145/2043164.2018527

Wu, F. J., Kao, Y. F., & Tseng, Y. C. (2011a). From wireless sensor networks towards cyber physical systems. *Pervasive and Mobile Computing*, *7*(4), 397–413. doi:10.1016/j.pmcj.2011.03.003

ADDITIONAL READING

Modiano, E. (2001). Traffic grooming in WDM networks. *IEEE Communications Magazine*, *39*(7), 124–129. doi:10.1109/35.933446

Tabuada, P., Caliskan, S. Y., Rungger, M., & Majumdar, R. (2014). Towards Robustness of Cyber-Physical Systems. *IEEE Transactions on Automatic Control*, 1. doi:10.1109/TAC.2014.2351632

KEY TERMS AND DEFINITIONS

ADL: Architecture Description Languages.

CQI: Channel Quality Indicator.

Cyber Family: Collection of components and connectors for real time monitoring.

ISP: Internet Service Providers.

Physical Family: Maintaining energy balance between physical components and physical connector types.

WDM: Wavelength Division Multiplexing.

WLAN: Wireless Local Area Network.

WWAN: Wireless Wide Area Network.

Chapter 3
Cyber Physical System Design

ABSTRACT

A large set of CPS physical processes are referred to as Cyber Physical System community. This CPS community deals with the modelling and design optimization of CPS. The network elements that are model-based emphasize control over system with various temporal semantics. Model-based design is a great technique for CPSs and are mainly used for developing mathematical modelling to plan, examine, prove, and certify dynamic systems. This is described in ten fundamental steps. This design methodology helps in assessing the development of CPS. Due to difficulty and nonexistence of accurate and technical tools, the three necessary elements in the strategy and study of existing and forthcoming cyber-physical systems are also explained in the chapter.

INTRODUCTION

Cyber-physical systems are an emerging trend around the world because of fundamental technological and economic forces. Cyber-physical systems are the primary area where disruptive technologies emerge that create new industries and rearrange the status quo in entire industrial sectors.

Cyber Physical System (CPS) is an engineered system (Bogdan & Marculescu,2011) which features the combination of computations, networking, and physical processes. Physical processes are controlled and supervised by computers using networks; feedbacks are given to the computers controlling the physical process and vice versa. With Cyber Physical System, interaction and estimation are intensely embedded in and physical procedures are interrelated to increase different characteristic and possibilities to physical structures. This means that the software and the system cannot be designed independent of each other. In those systems commercial and communal prospective is superior to what had been projected initially, and throughout the universe primary reservations are exist to enhance this technology. Applications of Cyber Physical Systems include smarter power grid, intellectual transportation, intellectual medical approaches and buildings, supervision of future air transportation, progressive engineering and many more.

The Cyber Physical System is about integration of physical systems processing and interactions to improve quality of product and construct different proficiencies. The Cyber Physical System will change the way people interrelate with planned systems, as like internet helps the people to ac-

DOI: 10.4018/978-1-4666-7312-0.ch003

Figure 1. CPS community

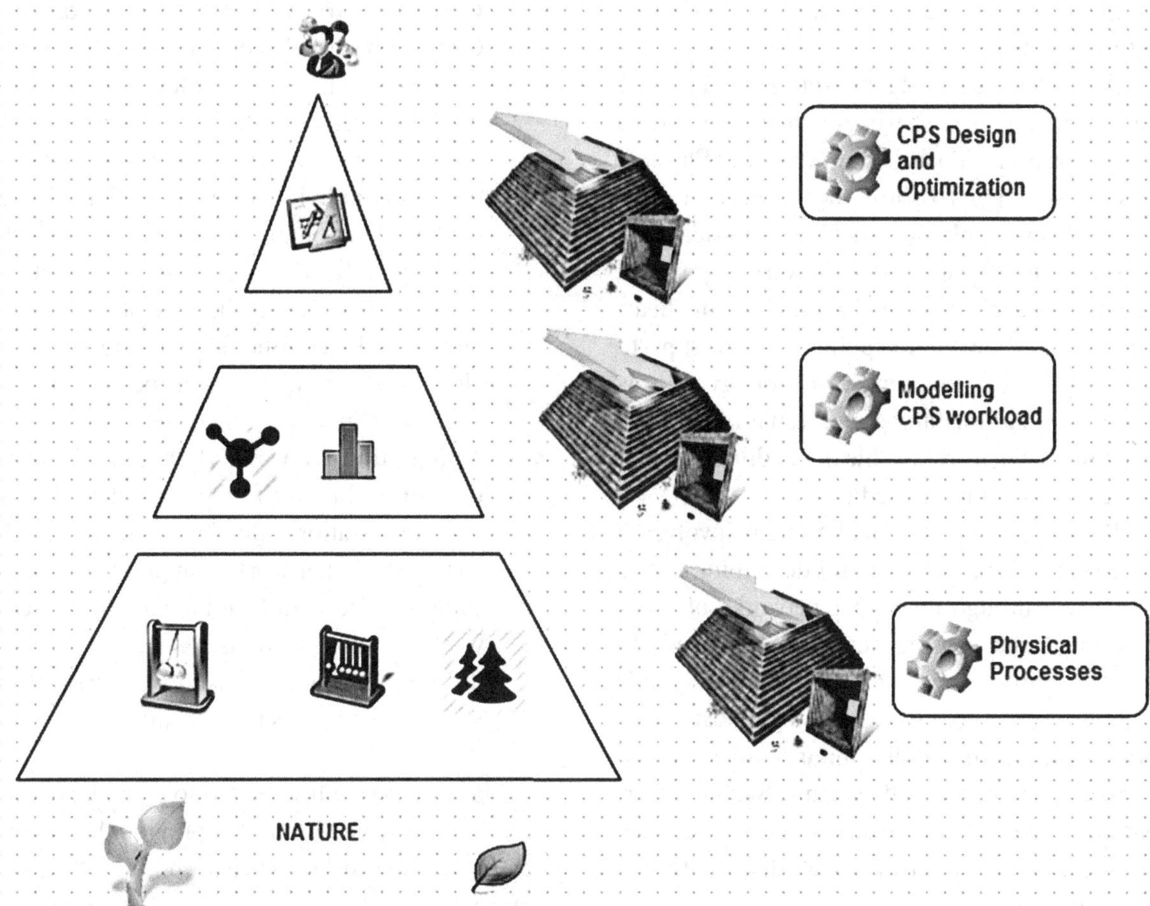

cess with the information. Over the years research companies have engineered powerful system, science, methods and tools. And on the other hand the researchers in computer science have also made innovations in programming languages, embedded system architectures, system software and a variety of powerful modelling formalisms and verification tools. These Cyber Physical System researchers aim to integrate acquaintance and manufacturing principles across the manufacturing and computational disciplines like management, interacting, social contact, concept of knowledge, software. In addition biochemical, electrical, biomedical, mechanized, physical science, software with other manufacturing disciplines to improve novel Cyber Physical System science and supplementary technology.

A huge set of physical procedures of concern to the Cyber Physical System community are summarized in the pyramid foundation (Bogdan & Marculescu, 2011) is shown in Figure 1. Physical processes are expanded through detecting, combination of information and collection which lead to dissimilar composite Cyber Physical System workload. The design of optimal Cyber Physical System architectures is enabled by accurate modelling of workloads which may improve our life.

The Cyber Physical System capacities are modelled through principal calculations that are used in future for defining important various optimization problems to the operators as similar to numerical physics which has been effective in enlightening environment. Moreover a delaying control protocol has been used to condense the traffic broadcast in sensing structure that depends on the status of data collected and also desired estimation error.

As in (Bogdan & Marculescu, 2011) Figure 1 also depicts these experiments and a numerical physics vision is positions out to Cyber Physical System strategy. To solve various current challenges that we look forward, Cyber Physical Systems have to measure and sense various physical activities like change in weather, obtaining heart rate, etc. as shown in the pyramid's lowest part.

It is critical to propose a strategy that is extremely authoritative and reliable defence structures which are capable of handling terrorist assaults and natural tragedies.

Building Cyber Physical System involves a procedure for monitoring and describing active processes through dissimilar networks of computational and sensing devices. Skill needs to bond the gap between signal processing methods and instantaneous computing to allocate self-organizing control of dissimilar wireless sensor networks and embedded systems. Such a different skill does not rely exclusively on sequence control and reductionism models that signify the standards currently.

Cyber Physical Systems surpass the established embedded systems in several phases such as safety, productivity, regularity, flexibility and forcefulness. They are characterized by an IT infrastructure controlling the effects in the physical world. Some key characteristics (Bogdan & Marculescu, 2011) of Cyber Physical Systems are summarized below:

- **System to Systems:** Unlike distinct embedded systems, normally Cyber Physical System is as a composite system, which contains several individual stand-alone subsystems. Subsequently the overall complexities of the Cyber Physical Systems are extremely higher than that of an embedded system.
- **Novel Interactions among Control, Communication, and Computation:** Cyber Physical Systems need to be vastly computerized, and every loop mechanism in the system should close at any measure. To speed up the independent operation, thus individual non-procedural issue in the control loop should be eliminated. Subsequently, the processing element is considered as a controller, the physical system, and the communication and network element is considered as a medium at the same time in the system design.
- **Application-Driven Cyber and Physical Coupling:** In this the key characteristics of each application domain is incorporated, so that the cyber world computing element should be forcefully joined with the real world physical systems. As an assumption different and great measures are critical in wired and wireless networking.

Many of the studies related to embedded systems and determinations in the previous have concentrated on the obstacles that the physical location conveys to the technical details of networking and information methods. Nevertheless, the complete possibility of the modification empowered by introducing the Cyber Physical System as an original subdivision of learning and technology provides considerable rearrangement within this field. The new approach can change complete business divisions into makers of Cyber Physical System. Developers of embedded computers agree to enlarge abilities to physical elements that could not be practically upgraded in some other way. The physical operations combine transmission and computing to improvise the way the people interconnect with the physical world, so that more profits can be conveyed by cyber-physical systems. The benefits (Bogdan & Marculescu, 2011) of using Cyber Physical Systems are:

- Makes system safer and more efficient.
- Reduces the building and operational cost of the system.
- Allows specific machineries or systems put together to design multifaceted systems which come up with different services.
- Can perform innumerable calculations instantaneously.
- Guarantees efficiency in various real world processes.
- A quick way to ensure safety in various real world processes.

While most people think of "computers" as PCs and "computing" as browsing on the World Wide Web, most of the computers in the world are components of cyber-physical systems. The recent study shows that the share of electronics in the cost of final products has been increasing dramatically. This study argues that in aerospace, self-propelled, computerization of industry, consumer electronics, telecommunications, intelligent households, fitness and therapeutic equipment, the electronics cost will be double of the total charge by the end of the century.

BACKGROUND

Cyber Physical Systems Composition

A gathering of actuators, sensors, computing stages and systems are installed to observe and/or device the material goods of physical world like an object, the plant are called as cyber physical systems.

The addition of networks into a Cyber Physical System requires that the temporal characteristics (Lin, & Stankovic, 2009) of the system be involved in the plan of the Cyber Physical Systems, meanwhile latency in network and variation in packet delay will adversely affect the scheduling of interactions among stages.

The capability to precisely allocating timestamp to any happening is severe to many Cyber Physical System applications. The actual time taken for a happening is called the timestamp.

In security based critical systems, the listed protocols are LAN network situation, wide-spread situations of Global Positioning System (GPS). To encounter the essentials of these uses, in Ethernet based systems, industry is identifying and positioning a range of skills to empower particular time stamping.

Due to fluctuations in the device's protocol stack timing, the accurate network traffic timestamp is lowered. And the effectiveness of the timer is also regulated by the operating system.

A completely developed CPS is envisioned as collection of networking elements with physical involvement and productivity as compared to other conventional embedded systems. The conception is strictly secured to the perceptions of cybernetics and measuring device networks. Further improvements in manufacturing and engineering will expand the association among the elements of physical and computational. So that there will be radical enhancement in the flexibility, independence, functionality, productivity, consistency, usability and security of cyber physical systems. This will develop the prospective of cyber-physical systems in numerous measurements, including: intrusion precision, operation in dangerous or inaccessible environments, coordination, efficiency and augmentation of human capabilities.

A large number of emerging cyber physical system applications, such as scientific exploration, military surveillance, and medical care systems, require high quality of performance to collect accurate data traces or deliver crucial data reports. These applications-specific performance requirements are important design goals of such systems. The general performance requirements include timeliness, system lifetime, and dependability. To meet these requirements on platforms of extremely limited resource, it is often necessary to jointly optimize and design network protocols.

Cyber-Physical Systems (CPS) is integration of computation with physical processes. Embedded computers and networks monitor and control the physical processes, usually with feedback loops where physical processes effect computations and vice versa. In the physical world, the passage of time is inexorable and concurrency is intrinsic. Neither of these properties is present in today's computing and networking abstractions. The foundations of computing are built on the premise that the principal task of computers is transformation of data. Yet we know that the technology is capable of far richer interactions the physical world. We critically examine the foundations that have been built over the last several decades, and determine where the technology and theory bottlenecks and opportunities lie.

Extensive cross-layer research has been done for wireless sensing systems, wireless ad-hoc networks, and other wireless embedded systems. As a general methodology, performance requirements are translated to requirements of representing metrics at different layers, for example, bit error rate at the physical layer. To meet these layered requirements, the system allocates resources to each layer and optimizes the performance. These works provide valuable results and good performance in relatively static systems, as these solutions require accurate models and estimations of parameters. However, in highly dynamic systems, the performance of these solutions may not be satisfactory due to inaccurate estimations and overhead. To address this problem, it is essential to adjust system parameters adaptively to optimize the runtime performance in dynamic systems. As control theory provides a sound foundation to monitor system performance and adaptively take actions to influence the performance, we believe that employing a feedback control approach is a key principle for the Cyber Physical System design.

A control based design (Miroslav & Radimír, 2011) for wireless networking is considered in Cyber Physical Systems. To utilize control knobs of different subsystems and layers, reflective architecture that treats control as a first class element in system design. This design provides a generic two-way interface between cross-layer and cross-node of a system for exchange of information. Architectural design abstracts the essence of control modularity so that control modules fit in the traditional layered system design without extra overhead.

Design of Hierarchical control framework for cross-layer Cyber Physical System is the reflection architecture. This architecture comprised of multiple source nodes and multiple destination nodes. In this architecture the network control on a destination node monitors the network performances of each data stream to this node and adjusts performance requirements for nodes that forward data.

The local control on every node takes performance requirements per stream as input and adaptively adjusts parameters of cross-layer network protocols. This framework adaptively adjusts network parameters cross-layer and cross-node to meet application performance requirements. Moreover, this design obtains control performances in terms of stability and transient performances. Previous solutions that are based on heuristics do not have these properties.

Cyber Physical System applications such as scientific exploration, military surveillance, and medical care systems, require high quality of performance to collect accurate data traces or deliver urgent data reports. The general performance requirements include timeliness, system lifetime, and reliability. To meet these requirements on platforms of extremely limited resource, it is often necessary to jointly optimize and design network protocols. As a general methodology, performance requirements are translated to requirements of representing metrics at different layers. However, in highly dynamic systems, the performance of these solutions may not be satisfactory due to inaccurate estimations and overhead. To address this problem, it is essential to adjust system parameters adaptively to optimize the runtime performance in dynamic systems.

The control theory provides a foundation to monitor system performance and adaptively take actions to influence the performance, employing a feedback control approach is a key principle for the Cyber Physical System design. We explore control based design for wireless networking in Cyber Physical System. To utilize control knobs of different subsystems and layers, it has been proposed a reflective architecture that treats control as a first class element in system design.

Design Constraints

Embedded systems are always well known for a sophisticated dependability and certainty standard than wide-range computing. Customers do not anticipate their CD players to crack and restart like the conventional computers. Since the usage of computer regulator has radically enhanced both the consistency and productivity of the automobiles, they have to come up with highly dependable vehicles. Cyber physical systems will not be functioning in a well-ordered situation, as the real world is not completely foreseeable. And it is required to forceful in unexpected circumstances and adjustable to subsystem malfunctions.

Compared to wide-range computing, there are possible issues that differ in the physical elements of such systems which provide protection and dependability necessities qualitatively. Additionally, physical modules are qualitatively dissimilar from elements of object-oriented instructions. Regular concepts centred on process requests and sequences do not function. This section evaluates the designing issues of such systems and precisely raises a query that existing interconnection and computing methodologies deliver an appropriate basis for CPS. It determines that it is sufficient to enhance developments in design, increasing the generalization level or legally verify the strategies that are made on present concepts. The networking concepts and computing generalizations have to be reconstructed to recognize the overall approaching of CPS. These notions will have to hold changing physical aspects and computation in an incorporated way.

Some of the Cyber Physical System challenges (Park, Zheng,& Liu., 2012; Slomka, Kollmann, Moser, & Kempf, 2011) are as listed below:

- **Real-Time System Abstraction:** It is more important to design a new model that qualifies to abstract the noticeable qualities of real time systems. Because in these systems a large amount of sensors, actuators and computing devices to exchange various types of information. For instance, the system topology of the Cyber Physical System may vigorously vary due to physical locations. Subsequently, an investigation study is required on a novel distributed real-time computing and interaction procedures that reflect the Cyber Physical System key interaction among elements. And eventually these systems provide the necessary level of operations such as protection, confidence, forcefulness, and trustworthiness.
- **Robustness, Safety, and Security:** Most of the time the physical world interaction unsurprisingly reveals a assured level of improbability due to difficulties such as uncertainty in the surroundings, possible security attacks and errors in physical devices . But it is not like in cyber systems logical computation. Hereafter, it is serious to certify complete system strength, confidence, and protection in Cyber Physical Systems.
- **Hybrid System Modelling and Control**: The major dissimilarity among physical and cyber is that the physical system progresses in real time uninterruptedly whereas the cyber system varies according to disconnected logic. As a consequence, a vigilant mix system modelling and device

mechanism is necessary for Cyber Physical System strategy, which combines the element of both the physical and cyber.

For instance, a new notional structure is required that can combine the systems of type logically event-activated and continuous-time for finishing the response control loop. In this structure, the different interval scales vary from micro-seconds to days and orders of various dimensions such as on-chip level to environmental scale should be concentrated carefully.

- **Control Over Networks:** The planning and execution of networked control of the Cyber Physical System lead to numerous tasks with respect to concerns such as computations of type time and event focused, transmission failures, unpredictable time delays and reconfiguration of the system. Precisely, strategy of network protocols in the Cyber Physical System has the following experiments such as wireless networks providing assurance of quality of service in critical missions, trade-off among control law scheme and limitations in real-time computation, associating the break between uninterrupted and separate time systems and trustworthiness and forcefulness of large scale systems.
- **Sensor-Actuator Networks:** A Wireless Sensor-Actuator Network (WSAN) is a promising region that has not been appropriately inspected, exclusively from the Cyber Physical System viewpoint. The contact between the actuators, physical elements, sensors and the processing elements should be wisely integrated into the plan of sensor-actuator systems. So far the effects of actuators and the physical details as a whole not measured in the design of a system.
- **Verification and Validation:** From the viewpoint of system verification and authentication, operating systems, elements of software and hardware and middleware are required to drive through widespread compositional processing and verification. This is to assure the requirements of overall cyber physical systems. In certain, Cyber Physical System needs to go further than the current cyber organization in relations of its dependability.

For instance, in the aeronautics industry, to create a new system the authentication process utilizes more than a half of the sources. In this field, over-design is to design a secure authenticated system which is the best known methodology. Conversely, it has become troublesome to apply the over-design approach in the complex systems with huge measure. As an importance, to design further it is required to have novel representations, tools and procedures that can combine compositional authentication and authorization of software with the other elements.

- **Control and Scheduling Co-Design:** In the community of embedded and real-time systems, control and scheduling co-design is a well-known field. But, with the initiation of Cyber Physical Systems, the issues of co-design are re-evaluated in several facets. For instance, as cyber physical systems are normally networked control systems, the consequence of the structure deferment on immovability of the system have been referred as trade-off among immovability and scheduling in real-time. The result of this investigation study is continuous control methodologies that can assurance the whole system durability with the lowest usage of the computational resource.
- **Computational Abstraction:** Physics laws, chemistry, real-time and energy restrictions, protection, possessions, robustness and safety characteristics are the physical properties that should be seized in a assessable way by predetermining concepts.

- **Architecture:** Cyber Physical Systems designs must be dependable at a meta-level and summarize a variability of physical info. To implement large-scale cyber physical systems, innovative network protocols must be planned. An original prototype can be made based on the existing concept universally indispensable, locally physical.

A set of instructions and rules used for computation is referred as a model of computation that governs the interaction, interaction, and device flow of a set of computational modules.

Hardware for a system should be designated based on certain characteristics like resisting with the environment, cooperating with the modelled physical systems and applying the control procedure. And also by considering input and output bandwidths of each component, interval from input to output, usage of power, determination measurements and charges, and some of the mechanical parameters like denial of electrical intrusion, robustness and life span. In addition to least values resulting from previous problem classifications, mechanical actuators should be skilful of generating torques and powers.

With the assistance of desktop replication tool the identified problem can be solved. If various prototypes of estimation are to be used, replication and separation tools must agree the configurations and interactions among numerous prototypes of estimation. Distinct mechanisms and subsystems need to be verified against hypothetical representations which facilitate recurrence among testing and simulation. Cyber Physical System need the combination of a dissimilar physical level and a simulated global result and control system, facilitated by reorganised and disseminated limited detecting or actuation structures. Presentations and cases of the Cyber Physical System are presented in numerous different technical capacities comprising the systems of type energy, transport, broadcastings, ecological monitoring, biomedical and genetic.

The most difficult assignment of cyber-physical system is process and control. It involves the straight collaboration of the physical sub condition with the simulated concepts used in its scheme, analysis, and confirmation.

While establishing evaluation and control strategies for cyber physical systems, there is a possibility of facing various hypothetical and hands-on complications. Between the greatest significant misplaced pieces in our present-day knowledge is a way of understanding basic architectural issues from the levels of demonstration, connection and facts.

All Local Area Network based timer management protocols challenge to measure the route inactivity among devices which if not modified will consequence in a balance between timers. Path Delay Variation worsens the accuracy of the outcomes.

A boundary timer dismisses and recirculates scheduling traffic, thereby removing connection lines. A transparent timer processes the interval as a packet that traverses the connection and delivers this data to downstream tools to correct for connection line delays.

A network connection on the data link layer links two network fragments. According to the forwarding database which has Media Access Control (MAC) or nodes IP addresses are associated to the network connection to which the system packets are sent. Recently most of the investigation studies of network are largely focusing on quality of service, IEEE 802.1p layer 2and DiffServ schemes on the IETF IP (Park et al., 2012; Slomka et al., 2011). While designing systems of type cyber-physical, regularly the real-time enforces serious issues. Nevertheless, the designing issue need to be analysed efficiently and various concepts also be re-examined.

Requirements for Cyber Physical Systems are contingent on the application area. Still all inhabiting limitations on network inactivity and path delay variation (PDV) and most necessitate deterministic calculation and interaction like for given similar inputs the system generates identical outputs.

Reflective Architecture

Dynamics found in the physical world affects the system performance, especially wireless networking performance. To address this problem, many wireless networking protocols have to be designed to bridge the gap between dynamic communication quality at the physical layer of each node and the application's performance requirements of the overall network.

Figure 2 shows system performance can be optimized by considering these vertical and horizontal constraints which is depicted in Figure 2 (Lin, & Stankovic, 2009). This requires components to strongly cooperate with each other. The conventional encapsulation of component design approach hides dependencies which do not provide enough support for optimization. To achieve better performance, components need to expose the necessary internal information and take optimization actions. Reflective architecture has a unifying mechanism for information exchange cross-layer and cross-node, supporting both traditional designs and control solutions.

The reflective architecture provides abstractions of reflective information and control. A class of reflective information is important. This information includes sensing data, performance measurements, timing, and the resource availability. On the other hand, a class of control parameters is also vital. The control parameters refer

Figure 2. Reflective architecture of CPS design

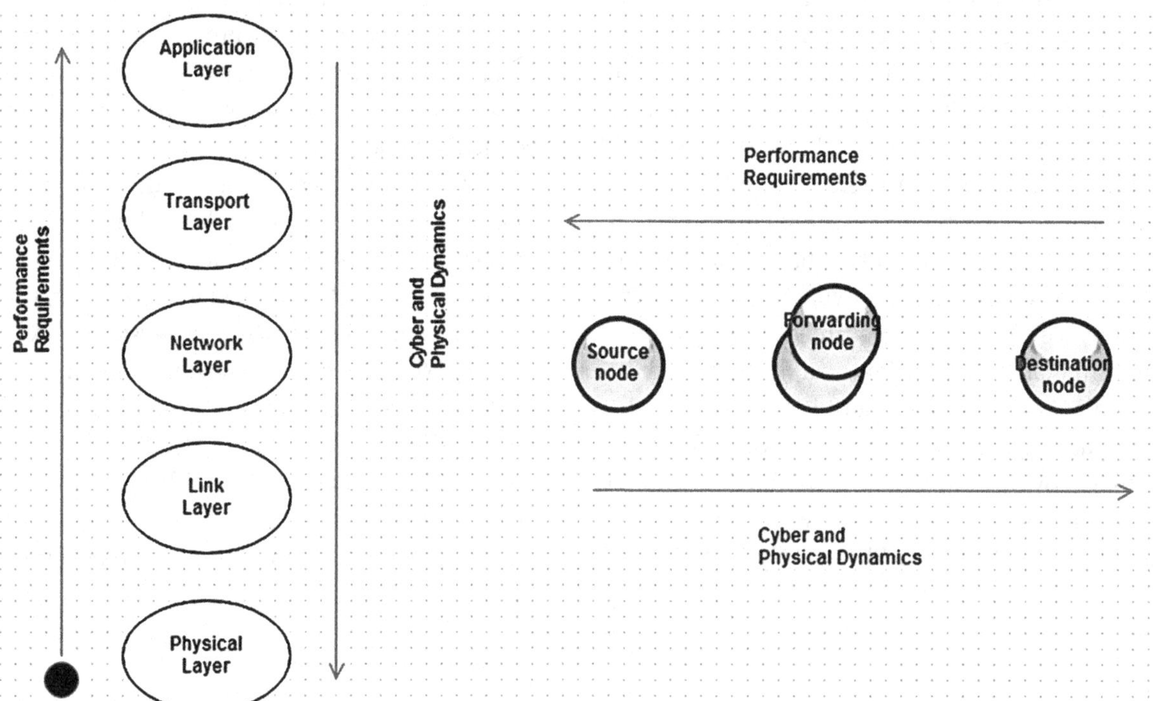

to adjustable configurations, including standard network protocol configuration parameters and specially designed control knobs.

The conventional interfaces hide the dependencies among these components, requirements and mainly focus on providing the functionality. The reflective interfaces provide the functionality relevant to dependency and requirement. The reflective interfaces also manage the possible coupled components without losing the property of information hiding. The use of reflective information for optimizing the control solutions multi-dimensionally in wireless sensor networks is the novel idea even though it is not in the case of system design. The design space is enhanced with the reflective architecture and the analysis of control-based performance is facilitated.

Control Design

The some of the important reasons for the control theory being the key technologies in the design of wireless communication are listed below are in (Lin, & Stankovic, 2009):

- The robustness and stability are the properties of feedback control theory for dynamic systems.
- The control performances such as transient performances which are necessary for Cyber Physical System designs are introduced by feedback control.
- Feedback control brings together sound analysis for system composition.

The main aim of the control design is to deal with cyber physical dynamics efficiently on the way of meeting the application performance requirements. Timeliness, reliability and less energy consumption are the typical performance requirements. These parameters are technically represented as delay, packet delivery ratio and energy cost respectively. The source nodes and the intermediate nodes of the network are accompanied with the node controllers whereas the destination nodes are accompanied with the network performance monitors and controllers.

The end-to-end performance of the data stream is measured by the network performance monitor and errors are reported after comparing them with the specified application requirements. It also calculates the desired node performance requirements based on current performance errors, costs and optimization goals and are reported to the relevant nodes along the routing path.

The critical networking parameters for modelling and control to be considered on each node are:

- The transmission power on the physical layer,
- The backup time and the number of retransmissions on the link layer, and
- The choice of forwarding links on the network layer.

The monitored performance metrics are:

- The received signal strength at the physical layer,
- The packet reception ratio and the delay at the link layer, and
- The reception ratio and delay to destination at the network layer.

The difference between the node performance requirement and monitored performance are calculated by the node controller and is used in designing the configurations of network protocols. The adaptive models of the node control are also updated.

In Cyber-physical systems, Model based design (MBD) given in (Jensen, Chang, & Lee, 2011) is a powerful design technique in which the design, analysis, verification and validation of dynamic systems is carried out based on mathematical modelling. The procedures of physical events, embedded calculations and situations are the main components of the complete model of cyber-physical system. The logical function, conventions about the location and point-to-point behaviour can be verified by testing and simulating the modelling systems offline.

A composite Cyber Physical System designed especially by coordinating unrelated subsystem is an interesting assignment. Design policy procedures that are commonly used are superior and contain measured modelling of physical structures, software synthesis, validation, verification and testing. A group of non-sequential phases but inevitably interdependent, that simplifies the advancement of an ideal Cyber-physical system is proposed. The Model Based Design (MBD) steps as in (Jensen et al., 2011) are given below.

Step 1: Problem Statement: An ordinary semantic has to be used to define the problem without using mathematical or technical terminologies. It acts as a reference for the developers, collaborators, experts, vendor and machine shops. Inventors of Safety-critical application are enormous or had better to inscribe a task plan comprising constraint succeeding, process of suggested analysis, metrics and peer review process which is of most vital. It is an essential procedure to communicate the design requirements effectively.

Step 2: Physical Model Process: In the first phase of physical modelling basic observations have to be recognized and identify relevant physical structures in which the cyber-system exist in or the physical procedures to be measured. Simulations of physical process are in the form of existent structures representations. Also the systems practice the methods of Laplace transfer functions with variance equations (Jensen et al., 2011).

Step 3: Characterize the Problem: Make parameters of types fixed and adjustable including variables to be well-ordered as different groups. Classify and distinguish the physical methods such as outline spaces, safety limitations of safety, groups of input and output, diffusion points and model behaviour. Realize the combination of physical method with calculation which includes fault conditions, point-to-point inactivity demands and response to quantization and sound (Jensen et al., 2011).

Step 4: Control Algorithm Development: Develop an appropriate control algorithm with predefined positions in which physical methods are controlled in an embedded computer. With an appropriate utilization of problem characterization, the physical dynamics can be precisely measured and controlled. The requests on inactivity, degrees of testing and quantization (Jensen et al., 2011) must be satisfied by the computational platform used. It is essential to choose the computation models before the control algorithm has to be derived. Once computational model is selected then re-examine the steps.

Step 5: Selection of Computational Models: A computational representation (Jensen et al., 2011) is defined as a group of directions used in calculation alongside with the procedures that governs the interaction, interaction and mechanism flow of a set of computational modules. The representations defined by model estimations are easy to analyse according to execution time, utilization of memory, determinism and latency.

Step 6: Hardware Specification: Choose a hardware which is capable of communicating with the modeled physical systems, go ease with the environment and able to run the control algorithm. For each component the parameters such as bandwidth involvement and production, interval from input to output, Consumption of energy, dimensional determinations and charges are to be considered. In addition, machine-driven parameters such as durability, form factor, life span and dismissal of electrical interference are also need to be considered. Though the minimum values resulting from problem characterizations are more, it is required that mechanical actuators must produce forces. In spite of inaccurate manufacturer specifications the hardware components should be tested independently. Latency, control algorithm execution time and software to connect with the hardware are requirements to be considered while selecting an embedded computer.

Step 7: Simulation: Resolve the identified problem by any simulation computing device. Simulation and synthesis tools provide a way for communication and composition, if various models of computation are used in it. In policy centred strategy, logical application and software precise design are divided into sectional elements to progress code manageability and also to condense the effect of altering hardware elements. This in turn allows the modules to be reprocessed in other perspectives.

Compare to end-to-end model, subsystems and separable components models are also more important. Component models (Jensen et al., 2011) run an assessment for construction, authentication of synthesized software and analysis. In case if no modelling tool can completely define the system, then practice the modelling device that seizes the best of its dynamics for each subsystem. Ptolemy II (Jensen et al., 2011) is a versatile tool for researching heterogeneity and also allows developers to build new computational models. Many simulation tools exist only for a few computational models which lack in providing communication between heterogeneous systems.

Step 8: Construction: To form a device agreeing to the conditions by considering the exclusions that may influence modelling. Separable modules and subsystems are to be experienced beside theoretic prototypes to facilitate reiteration among simulation and analysis.

Step 9: Software Synthesize: Instructions of synthesizers are occasionally combined into traditional simulation backgrounds to directly support the existing embedded workstation or standard program may be combined and linked to, particular design handwritten program. Compared to other implements, prototypes inscribed in Lab VIEW are easily computational through various stages without any particular design order groups or drivers.

Step 10: Verify, Validate, and Test: To test each component and subsystem individually, design simple, adjustable parameters. During hardware-in-the-loop testing computational systems are separated from physical systems. But most of the responses are retrieved from processes of physical or computational by embedded computers or Field Programmable Gate Arrays (FPGAs) (Jensen et al., 2011). To improve the previous models performance time and inactivity measurements can be used and during implementation unpredicted test results may prone to errors.

The overall behaviour of an algorithm is determined by verification and validation, based on some combinations of its inputs. Specifically state requirements of condition transform them into a prescribed arrangement for authentication and certification. Though authentication and certification are the trickiest facets in the cyber physical system design, while testing list invariants should be confirmed.

NETWORK CONTROL FOR CYBER PHYSICAL SYSTEMS

Cyber Physical System need the incorporation of a heterogeneous physical layer (Dahleh et al., 2006) and a virtual global decision and control network, facilitated by decentralized (Dahleh et al., 2006) and distributed local sensing or actuation structures. Various instances of the Cyber Physical System are presented in many different areas like force, telecommunication, transportation, environmental monitoring, genetic and biomedical systems. Currently in Cyber Physical System there exists certain complex design issues like forcefulness, performance satisfaction and expandable.

In such Cyber Physical Systems, physical world information is attained through a number of local entities like nervous system, sensor networks which can be geographically extended and of a varied nature such as high temperature, acoustic, chemical. The process and functioning needs are large-scale in character which is frequently representing the whole system in terms of aggregate properties such as degree of transitivity of an aircraft, assessment of power outage. The organization of such systems involves the incorporation between a physical layer and a cyber-layer. The physical layer contains the primary constraints of fixed architectural and physical system. The proposed information layer is addressed by cyber layer to support assessment protocols. These protocols are intended to attain globally collection of objectives. A flexible and reconfigurable information layer is designed. This system is to deal with decision system properties like energetic improbability, complication and restrictions of resource in calculation and transmission. Moreover this interrelated system is designed to be scale-dependent reflect the various stages of decision systems by converting various levels of abstractions in a hierarchical way.

For instance, consider an application connecting a group of portable sensors and representatives which has a mixture of decision layers. The decisions might be on agent's correlations, certain decisions by every agent and a universal decision by all representatives. For instance the networking layers are indexed based on time and space. Time indicates the dissimilarity in the virtual speed and space indicates the comparison of decisions on local and global surroundings.

The difficult task in cyber physical system is nothing but operation and control of the system. Because design, analysis and verification of a system, it involves the overview of cyber with the non-stop transmission of the physical reaction. Due to incompatibility between the layers cyber physical system forced to use ad hoc and informal techniques during its design. Apart from existing difficulties, cyber physical system is dependent on a combination of customary and common engineering procedures (Dahleh et al., 2006).

Due to difficulty and nonexistence of scientific and mathematical equipment's more, the three elementary components (Dahleh et al., 2006) in the plan and assessment of current and future cyber-physical systems should be:

- The model and design of a cyber-physical system is based on the development of systematic mathematical and computational frameworks. For conceptual and computational reasons, detailed models are unsuitable whereas the simplest models can be conventional.
- A high class of decision systems empowered by a flexible, reconfigurable and modular design of information architectures. There are certain queries deals with middleware; various modes of information sharing, communication network specifications, multiplexing, re-usability of multipurpose units and how embedded software is synchronized are to be answered.
- A knowledge and decision management system involves the plan of disseminated protocols. In order to obtain the specified global performance objective, these protocols provide real-time decisions based on various data sets retrieved from multiple sources. There are certain queries which report about the decision making hierarchy, interchange of data between the different levels of hierarchy, scheduling, soft-

ware verification and resource allocation. Finally to meet the required objective reconfiguration of architecture is also to be considered.

In well-defined cyber physical systems, there are numerous hypothetical and feasible complications in the methodical design of assessment and control policies. The most important issue is a basic architectural issue raise at the levels of modelling, information and interface. There are some practical difficulties which can overcome by decentralization compared to centralized approaches like bandwidth, latency, scheduling, fragility, etc. The following are few research challenges based on the components of a systematic study of Cyber Physical System:

- According to the performance objectives the modelling techniques such as design, analysis, simulation and verification are taken into account. In multi-scale or multi-resolution (Dahleh et al., 2006) approaches, explicit mechanism is essential for model management, reduction, and abstraction.
- This challenge is about the manageable techniques like uncertainty, robustness and complexity. Though there is much improvement in specific model classes like linear systems and timed automata (Dahleh et al., 2006), but still association exists between the continuous and discrete realms to focus on computational methods. In addition in the explicit real-time physical requirements certain difficulties are enforced.
- This challenge focuses on local autonomy (Dahleh et al., 2006) in the plan of constraint information structures. Limited independence is enabled in the design architecture of game theory (Dahleh et al.,2006) and the associated area of game styles pattern to provide a normal outline. This framework can be restructured with respect to changes occur in priority and environment. In game theoretical methodologies, each participant is referred as agent or an entity. This agent is capable of executing an operation and set of information. With the available information, it is believed to acquire actions to expand its effectiveness. Game forms determine the rule for multiplayer interaction and how actual information is accessible to various players at the time of their activities.
- One of the challenges focuses on the requirement of computational high-quality procedures for the plan of disseminated assessment protocols. A main motive is the nonexistence of realistic modelling of the essential system limitations. Such representations and techniques may be copied from the game theoretic or structure design technique (Dahleh et al., 2006).
- Another issue related to research challenge is a large-scale systems and statistical mechanics. Methodologies have to be developed to acquire knowledge about the approximate system behaviour based on systems space and time. These approximations may lead to fundamental limitations and system invariance characterization.
- Knowledge about the integration and the combination of limited data into a large-scale state of the system process to be identified. Though there are several difficulties technically solved, but the concepts of mathematic shapes and topology appear usual in this viewpoint (Dahleh et al., 2006).

NETWORK LATENCY IN CYBER PHYSICAL SYSTEM

Introduction

A Cyber Physical System is a compilation of actuators, sensors, networks and computing stages.

These are installed to observe and control the characteristics of relic and the object in the physical world. The important feature of Cyber Physical System is access time. Unlike established operations which yield system states in a successive manner, a Cyber Physical System must measure and in majority it manages the time intermissions among these circumstances. For disseminated Cyber Physical System, time coordination is very critical and is mandatory to sketch out an equivalent vision of physical world state and the resultant control is affected in excess of that state.

Most of the applications of Cyber Physical System contain various computing proposals which helps to interact through connections to control physical objects at its larger scope. Though the physical objects distributed are not in reality, the computational stack is allocated by networked solutions. This is to present physical separation of the application, permit more appropriate limited control or to offer redundancy. In addition to networks available in Cyber Physical System, while designing Cyber Physical Systems it includes the sequential characteristics of the network. Because packets delay variation and network latency will adversely change the period of interactions among platforms.

Various applications are reactive to Path Delay Variation (PDV) (Cardoso, Derler, Eidson, & Lee, 2011), latency, delay in continuous transmission or dissimilarities in this latency.

Role of Network Timing

The timestamp (Cardoso et al., 2011) is the physical time at which the event occurs. The capability of assigning a timestamp to an event accurately is critical to many Cyber Physical System applications. Likewise the time advancement of a Cyber Physical System is controlled according to the rate of events occur in physical time that is calculated precisely. The most frequently utilized protocols for the distribution of confined or consistent time are the Network Time Protocol (NTP) in surroundings of Local Area Network (LAN), specialized protocols for security critical systems and Global Positioning System (GPS) for wide-area situations. A very small accuracy of Network Time Protocol for promising applications is insufficient. Though the accuracy of Global Positioning System is sub-microsecond but this accuracy is inappropriate for several applications.

Safety critical systems require precise timestamps that are characteristically used to establish time division multiple access communication protocols. These protocols are used to ascertain devices with secured sampling and to interpret data to control or evaluate objectives. Systems like automotive, aircraft, safety-critical and industrial automation utilize field specific models such as CAN IEC 61158, ARINC and TTP (Cardoso et al., 2011).

In the last decade, the cost-effective, high bandwidth and the unlicensed characteristics of Ethernet made most of the computerized industry traders and other field vendors to change its transmission to Ethernet. On the other hand, Ethernet is nondeterministic and can have fundamental latency and PDV. This latency is inappropriate for many applications, if it is inaccurate. The following section considers several efforts that are in progress to allocate very less timing. This timing imposes over the connections of Ethernet in the existence of latency and PDV. The majority of these are centred on the IEEE 1588-2008 protocol (Cardoso et al., 2011).

Industrial and scientific illustrations (Cardoso et al., 2011) requiring accurate time stamps include:

- **Financial:** Adviser and other dealers connected through the interactions of Ethernet need agreement to be time stamped with millisecond precision to nanosecond correctness.
- **Audio-Visual:** The audio-video quality of Ethernet centred streaming in performance halls, residence, production and com-

mercial surroundings is timing control. Latency is not considered as an important issue in applications likes tele-surgery and computer-controlled automobile, since reaction time of visual or audio response is significant. Differentiation in latency and PDV can prevail by using appropriate storage area and reassembling in accurate time, when time stamps operate precisely at the basis.

- **Trilateration Applications:** Location's time stamping is to obtain a focused position that is retrieved from several sensors. This time stamping is received from the focused signal. Times stamping with milliseconds accurateness are needed for acoustic while localizing RF whisperers involves nanoseconds correctness.
- **Scientific:** Timing precisions at or under the nanoseconds are applied to the large Hadron Collider.
- **Power Industry:** As the industry is progressing towards the increase in grid timing accuracy, Ethernet is suitable communication protocol for both prolonged and substation transmission. The technology using grid timing is synchrophasor.
- To empower precise time stamping in Ethernet-based systems, engineering is identifying and installing a range of technologies that ensure the necessities of above said applications.

Due to timing variations in device's protocol heap, the skill to specify network congestion timestamp is lowered. And also the operating system that restricts the timer synchronization protocols usage. So the lowest level of Ethernet protocol stack holds the message timestamps for timing protocols. In addition viable silicon is used for time stamping ability, activates a physical clock and at Media Access Control or the physical level gets support from other application measures. The MAC and the network media have PHY chips in between to assist timing resolution starting from 8ns. In Ethernet-based time transfer protocol, these chips used with the specification of IEEE 1588 protocol which is basically a general one.

The clock synchronization protocols are Local Area Network dependent. These protocols attempt to compute the path latency among devices which will effect in the displacement of clocks provided it is not adjusted. Path Delay Variation (PDV) lowers the outcomes of precision. In a Local Area Network (LAN) environment, due to variations in the structure of a path and network bridges line up the Path Delay Variation occurs. The dissimilarity among forward and reverse latency is called as Path asymmetry originates with clock offset. The industry identifies two natures of devices such as transparent clocks and IEEE 1588 boundary that are used to expand the outcomes of PDV and latency on synchronization protocols.

To eliminate the lineup of connections, timing traffic is reproduced and boundary clock is ended. The measurement of time taken by a packet to pass through the connection is done by a transparent clock. These values have been utilized to rectify the delays in bridge queue that are made available to the downlink devices. To enable high precision and self-regulating clock synchronization network transfer, these devices remove the benefits of bridge queues on packets timing. Though the existence of faultless synchronized clocks at all devices, it permits each packet supply with the actual measurement of continuous interval. So they are not constructive in reducing PDV for normal traffic. To conquer the effects of PDV and latency in few applications the measured interval value is used.

According to progress and regularity of some specific synchronization protocols an attempt had been made to eliminate or lessen the effects of PDV. For instance, Kopetz introduced the time initiated Ethernet proposal by which is regularized by the Society of Automotive Engineers (SAE) (Cardoso et al., 2011).

Network Elements

A network channel combines two network fragments on the data link layer. Depending upon the forwarding database network packets are sent by way of channel that include the Media Access Control (MAC) or IP addresses connected to the bridge (Cardoso et al.,2011) .

Channels initiate Path Delay Variation (PDV) through the following mechanisms as in (Cardoso et al., 2011):

- Forwarding address database is occupied while there is excess network interchange.
- Storage area for input and output queues and packets with inconsistent processing time.
- Consecutive packets allowing dissimilar paths that exist in connected networks among multiple ways. This is common in the internet but may also be the case in Local Area Network environments during reconfiguration of mesh or ring topologies often used for redundancy purposes. This is obviously not present in star topologies.

Channels are non-predictable according to the arrangement of packets which vary not only on the order received at inputs but also on the scheduling principles and propose of the switch items. For instance, the supply order of received packets at once depends on the condition of the round-robin mechanism by applying round-robin switch items.

The Figure 3 depicts the concept of diagram in (Cardoso et al., 2011). Figure 3 shows that how PDV can also rely on the simple network topology. There will be not much of PDV when flow from machine A to B and device B to A. But in other parts of the network the PDV will be independent of the traffic, since flow is in full duplex. During point-to-point traffic only one packet will be there in a queue. This is done when devices are ready to receive all inward traffic at line rates. When a packet flow from machines D and E moved to machine F can supposed to observe PDV, since output queue at the lower bridge is filled by the above two input devices. Similarly when a common queue on an upper bridge's output port is shared, the flow from devices A to D and from C to E can encounter PDV.

In (Cardoso et al., 2011) facts related to time critical transfer with PDV and bound latency other than cycle messages are summarized. But most of the effort is ascertain on wide-area transmission. In (Cardoso et al., 2011) three key observations are made which are correct in these days:

- Maximum value for network latency is computed when there is restriction in network traffic input rate. Similarly admission control restricts the maximum number of packets which are competing for a queue by limiting PDV. Computation is based on packet length analysis, packet arrival times and destinations.
- All network layers with links with layer 2 implement restrictions on PDV and beside all significant continuous path latency.
- Traffic must be of two types such as real-time and non-real time. In real-time the latency bounds are enforced where such bounds are not enforced in traditional time traffic.

In this century, the network study is mainly based on IEEE 802.1p layer2 (Cardoso et al., 2011) quality of service as well as IETF IP-based Diffserv (Cardoso et al., 2011) techniques. These are categorization proposals which permit the bridges to forward the packets, by using IP headers and Ethernet bits. Nowadays there is no active participation of users in the process of enforcing latency bounds for instantaneous transfer.

Figure 3. PDV in network topology

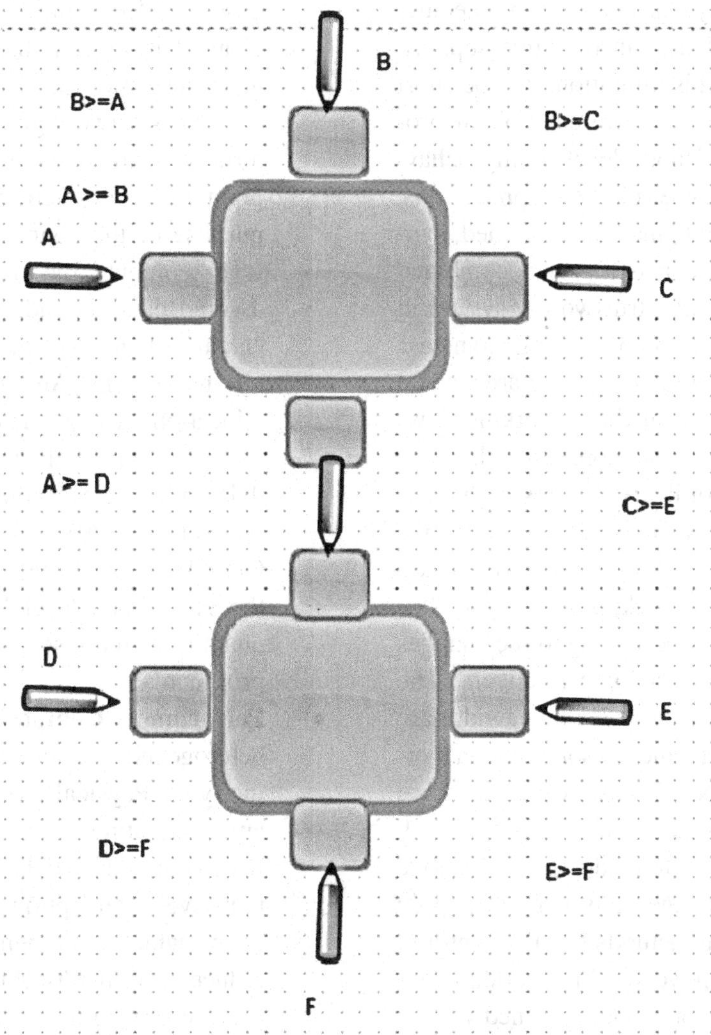

DESIGN CHALLENGES IN CYBER PHYSICAL SYSTEM

There are several issues while designing cyber physical systems in real-time. Conversely, the design issue must be carefully analysed and revise fewer of the concepts. Out of various fields in the research guidelines, following are the prospective directions presented:

- **Operating Systems:** Though operating system generate difficulty while designing real time system, it is considered as significant to maintain it. The operating system of cyber physical system is to accomplish best dependability among numerous key characteristics needed by it. It comprised of real-time, modularity, proper use of hardware or software, construction of hardware and power effectiveness. As TinyOS deal with the most of those needs, it is considered as an extensively used operating system. This operating system indicates hopeful solution for Cyber Physical

Systems. To develop instantaneous protocols and synchronization procedure, TinyOS be deficient in real-time support. In addition to this limitation, it is be short of prioritization and pre-emption in providing expected node level timing behaviour. In many cyber-physical applications, timing constraints must be esteemed, synchronized and consistent in a combined way. To construct a trustworthy system, it is required to reflect on timing guarantees.

- **Networking Protocols:** There are several issues to be dealt from the networking viewpoint and in real-time more research issues to be solved. An interesting research challenge is to allocate distributed and adaptive in the structures of synchronized multi-hop sensor. In this network, resources are allocated sufficiently according to the changes occur in physical or logical network. The resources like memory and bandwidth are allocated to dynamic sensors exist in synchronized WSNs. In many of the insecure tasks these active sensor nodes involved. As the mobile systems do not acclimatize to the system changes, it is inefficient apply static allocation methods. On the contrary, the federal adaptive synchronization is not applicable to resources-constrained WSNs. Due to its inability to react and complexity, it includes considerable measure of interaction and computation outflows.
- **Timing Guarantees:** The condition of deterministic instantaneous is assured in unstable sensor and wireless ad-hoc networks. The investigation study on deterministic assurance is to believe that the stations are error free. Though this assumption might be feasible for some cases, the real-world applications contradict this assumption. Since it has stable and high quality of wireless connections, these could be located in the regions where connections are changeable and uneven. To find a new way to describe deterministic functioning under channel insecurity, the view of real-time guarantees must be visited again. Basically a wireless network gives a delay bound deterministically and correlates an assurance point with every definite delay bound. The purpose of the connected assurance level is to compute the improbability on the assured delay bound. The delay bound is calculated in view of completed feasible retransmissions. And also to establish the allocation of the quantity of retransmissions in a given channel statistically. The delay bound corresponds to the maximum number of retransmissions whereas the Cumulative Distribution Function defines the confidence level by assured greatest quantity of retransmissions with a definite prospect.
- **Performance Compositionality:** Due to its heterogeneity, the continuous delay testing in Cyber Physical System is a composite and motivating problem. Basically established continuous delay testing obtains system-level interruption from element-level delays which is an inefficient approach. To reduce the difficulty of the continuous analysis, several refined methods apply mathematical theorems to convert a multi-element system into a single element system, thus. As in(Cardoso et al.,2011) a complete framework is described to systematically change dispersed real time structures into a single system, which is used to gather the continuous allocation of an unique system. Though the system symbolizes to initiate involvement towards functioning compositionality, the traffic model is in distributed real-time systems. On the other hand, generic traffic models apply network related mathematical formalism. This model offer combined methodologies for reducing the

multi-hop system analysis to a single-hop system. This is to verify a corresponding service curvature for the complete system.

However, there are two disadvantages (Lin, & Stankovic, 2009) in the concatenation analysis:

1. The corresponding service curvature for a known data flow depends on a difficult optimized constraint.
2. A survey on service curvature rate delay is common for modelling processes in heterogeneous Cyber Physical System applications.
    a. It is necessary to locate a reduction technique for a suitable system that is dependent on common concepts of representation for indicating dissimilar system processes and transmissions.
    b. Requirements for Cyber Physical Systems greatly dependent on the application field. On the other hand, path delay variation and delay in network include limitations so that deterministic operations can be carried out like for a specified similar system inputs, it yields the same results.

The Ethernet network procedures in progress are capable of performing undeveloped QoS endeavour based planning. The Ethernet packet times are comparable to the results of investigation study and the existence of synchronized clocks precision values. The Figure 4 (Cardoso et al., 2011) illustrates the design space. At one extreme (Uncontrolled schedule and decision), planning and access is entirely unrestrained, but in previous forms of Time-Triggered Ethernet (TTE), periodic access intervals control the scheduling.

Special connections used in TTE with Class of Service (CoS) permit three types of provisions. Using appropriate connections, Ethernet headers with QoS data show progress like QoS Schedules. A wide range of CPS utilizes survey on various combinations of end devices with planning and access control. Moreover for the bounds of PDV and delay with appropriate network connections for a wider-range of Cyber Physical System applications is needed.

To deal with the difficult design of Cyber Physical System and to allow for reasoning about a structure on dissimilar levels of construct, Model Based Design (MBD) is being approved for the expansion of Cyber Physical Systems. MBD admits for modelling, analysing and assessing system designs in various steps of the design process.

Platform Based Design (PDB) decidedly discriminate architecture with the modelling functionality. PDB concentrate on the incorporation of this representation and approves for system design assessment in conjunction with the structural design and system properties like period. In order to assess a Cyber Physical System, the point in time must be modelled.

Most of the MBD and PDB tools imagine an impracticable universal point of time in all stages. In dispersed Cyber Physical Systems, each stage has its own point of time to be illustrated by the platform regulators. The functionality of clock

Figure 4. Design space of CPS

drift is illustrated by a precise representation of platform clocks. The performance of clock coordination protocols is by present cyber-physical systems. Modelling these procedures is helpful for assessing its presentation and performance of connections for assessment. The functional behaviour is an outcome of both network structural design and network latencies. Network components of a system representation and the interval properties of hardware are used to appraise Cyber Physical Systems. Moreover a situation has been developed for relating the well-designed aspects, with the system physical properties including Ptolemy II network mechanisms.

CONCLUSION

Cyber Physical System (CPS) is an engineered system which features the combination of computations, networking, and physical processes. Physical processes are controlled and supervised by computers using networks; feedbacks are given to the computers controlling the physical process and vice versa. With Cyber Physical System, communication and computation intensely implanted in and to append novel potentials and features to physical systems to act together with physical methods.

A large number of emerging cyber physical systems applications, such as scientific exploration, military surveillance, and medical care systems, require high quality of performance to collect accurate data traces or deliver crucial data reports. Most of the time Embedded systems believed to have a sophisticated dependability and preventability measure than traditional computing. Accordingly, on disseminated real-time operations and transmission mechanisms investigation study is applied. This is to depict the way of elements interacting in Cyber Physical System and eventually supply the essential point of presentation such as consistency, protection, security and forcefulness.

As an outcome, it is required to have new representations, tools and procedures at design stage. This is to integrate comprehensive analysis of software authentication and confirmation along with other elements. An innovative network protocols must be planned for significant Cyber Physical Systems. According to the thought as locally physical and worldwide virtual, an original model can be created. Dynamics found in the physical world affects the system performance, especially wireless networking performance. To address this problem, many wireless networking protocols have to be designed to bridge the gap between dynamic communication quality at the physical layer of each node and the application's performance requirements of the overall network.

The goal of a control design is to meet application performance requirements while efficiently dealing with cyber physical dynamics. Typical performance requirements are timeliness, reliability, and less on energy consumption, representation these requirements as performance measures in terms of delay, packet delivery ratio, and energy cost

Cyber-physical systems has a controlling technique called Model based design, which emphasis on mathematical modelling to plan, analyse, authenticate and confirm energetic systems. In other words Cyber physical system model represents the pairing of its surroundings, physical methods and fixed calculation. In offline modelling systems can be practised and replicated, so that the innovators can verify their application logic, proposals about its surroundings and continuous behaviour. Designing a composite Cyber Physical System, especially with various subsystems involved is a tricky assignment. Generally it has complicated design procedures and incorporates precise modelling of physical systems, software synthesis, validation, verification and testing.

A problem has to be well-defined in a trouble-free language to work out, without using mathematical or technical terminologies. The initial act of physical modelling is to create necessary remarks. These observations are close to other important physical systems like the cyber system situation or managing the physical processes. Separate fixed constraints, amendable constraints and variables need to be managed. Physical processes need to be managed under certain conditions and develop a proper control procedure to be executed by an implanted computer.

REFERENCES

Bogdan, P., & Marculescu, R. (2011, April). Towards a science of cyber-physical systems design. In *Proceedings of Cyber-Physical Systems (ICCPS),* (pp. 99-108). IEEE. doi:10.1109/ICCPS.2011.14

Cardoso, J., Derler, P., Eidson, J. C., & Lee, E. A. (2011, June). Network latency and packet delay variation in cyber-physical systems. In *Proceedings of Network Science Workshop (NSW),* (pp. 51-58). IEEE. doi:10.1109/NSW.2011.6004658

Dahleh, M. A., Frazzoli, E., Megretski, A., Mitter, S. K., Ozdaglar, A. E., Parrilo, P. A., & Shah, D. (2006), Information and control: A bridge between the physical and decision layers. In *Proceedings of NSF Workshop in Cyber-Physical Systems*. NSF.

Jensen, J. C., Chang, D. H., & Lee, E. A. (2011, July). A model-based design methodology for cyber-physical systems. In *Proceedings of Wireless Communications and Mobile Computing Conference* (IWCMC), (pp. 1666-1671). IEEE. doi:10.1109/IWCMC.2011.5982785

Lin, S., & Stankovic, J. A. (2009). Performance composition for cyber physical systems. In *Proceedings of the Ph. D. Forum of the 30th Real-Time Systems Symposium* (RTSS'09). RTSS.

Miroslav, Š. V. É. D. A., & Radimír, V. R. B. A. (2011). A cyber-physical system design approach. In *Proceedings of the Sixth International Conference on Systems* (ICONS 2011). St. Maarten: International Academy, Research, and Industry Association.

Park, K. J., Zheng, R., & Liu, X. (2012). Cyber-physical systems: Milestones and research challenges. *Computer Communications*, *36*(1), 1–7. doi:10.1016/j.comcom.2012.09.006

Slomka, F., Kollmann, S., Moser, S., & Kempf, K. (2011). A multidisciplinary design methodology for cyber-physical systems. *ACESMB*, *2011*, 23.

ADDITIONAL READING

Koubâa, A., & Andersson, B. (2009, July). A vision of cyber-physical internet. In *Proc. of the Workshop of Real-Time Networks* (RTN 2009). RTN.

Li, K., Liu, Q., Wang, F., & Xie, X. (2009, July). Joint optimal congestion control and channel assignment for multi-radio multi-channel wireless networks in Cyber-Physical Systems. In Proceedings of Ubiquitous, Autonomic and Trusted Computing, (pp. 456-460). IEEE. doi:10.1109/UIC-ATC.2009.27

Schirner, G., Erdogmus, D., Chowdhury, K., & Padir, T. (2013). The future of human-in-the-loop cyber-physical systems. In *A distributed logic for networked cyber-physical systems*. Science of Computer Programming.

Zhang, B., Xiang, Y., Wang, P., & Huang, Z. (2011). A novel capacity and trust based service selection mechanism for collaborative decision making in CPS. *Computer Science and Information Systems*, *8*(4), 1159–1184. doi:10.2298/CSIS110225049Z

KEY TERMS AND DEFINITIONS

CPS Community: Collection of physical processes, modelling, CPS design, and optimization.

GPS: Global Positioning System.

MBD: Model Based Design.

NTP: Network Time Protocol.

PBD: Platform Based Design.

PDV: Path Delay Variation.

TTE: Time-Triggered Ethernet.

WSAN: Wireless Sensor Actuator Network.

Chapter 4
Interconnection Issues in CPS

ABSTRACT

This chapter shows the interconnection issues in different wireless networks such as ad hoc networks and sensor networks. It also specifies the need for multicast routing protocols in mobile networks, because these wireless networks are suitable for multicast communication due to its inherent transmission ability. Based on the area to be covered, mechanism used for sensor deployment, and various properties of sensor network properties, different coverage formulations have been suggested. In addition, several constructions reachable areas and their expectations along with an outline of the explanations are described. Though 802.11 planned for organization-based systems, the Distributed Coordination Function (DCF) offered in 802.11 permits mobile networks to communicate with the channel exclusive of the base location. Several performance issues related to IEEE 802.11 are revealed. This chapter identifies the main reasons for performance losses and provides solutions for the scenarios that are specific to certain issues related to CPS.

INTRODUCTION

In an Ad-Hoc Network (AHN) there are many mobile hosts which are connected with the wireless links. Each of these mobile nodes operates as both, end-system as well as the forwarder to send packets over the multi-hop ad hoc network. Ad hoc system is the a small network which can be called as a local area network, especially with part of the connection for communication purposes while some are in the closeness to the rest part of the structure. In mobile ad hoc networks each node is unrestricted to mobile and organise themselves in a random way and are freely portable around and communicate with others. The link which is shared by couple of users may have numerous routes and the broadcasting among them can be different.

Now as we saw above that the mobile ad hoc network is the temporary networks which are of independent systems with portable devices to establish a network without any centralised support. And hence the non-existence of wired structure creates numerous kinds of issues in this nature of networking. Routing is one of the issues to be considered among other issues. This simply means swapping info from one location to a new station of the interconnected structure.

Here we are talking about the AHN systems which refer to wireless structure in which all the

DOI: 10.4018/978-1-4666-7312-0.ch004

network elements are portable. When we speak about the AHN systems there is no great difference among a router and host in an ad hoc structure, subsequently all system points can be end points including the forwarder of the route.

Recently it has been noticed that many investigations are done on unicast transmission while routing. Some of the significant instances which use this technique are Temporary Ordered Routing Algorithm, the Monarch project, the MMWS project and so on.

MULTICAST PROBLEMS IN AD HOC NETWORKS

The unexplored region of AHNs is forwarding a packet and multicast channelling which is impartial. Since multicast channelling in fixed-structure is established on either soft state or hard state router, it is necessarily inappropriate for an AHN environs with unrestricted movement.

Unrestricted movement means:

- The performance of host is unrelated other hosts,
- The speed of host is unrestricted,
- Movement is also unrestricted on its way, and
- More likelihood of temporary and numerous divisions in network.

Furthermore, in many types of AHNs both energy and capacity are strictly restricted which adds to the reasons to avoid exchanging and maintaining state of multicasting. The possibility of numerous deviations in topology is challenging to utilize clustering algorithms. For low power host maintenance of hard state and recurrent selections of cluster head are more costly.

And one more significant attention of AHNs is that it should be robust and should deliver high quality of service. However multicast protocols cannot provide the highest delivery guarantees.

To overcome multicast problems in Ad-Hoc network few protocols (Anastasi, Conti,& Gregori,2004) are created such as:

1. Table-driven protocols,
2. On demand routing protocols,
3. Secure transmissions, and
4. Ad-Hoc Multicast Routing (AMRoute) protocols.

Table-Driven Protocols

One of the oldest methods of attaining channelling in mobile Ad-Hoc network is Table-Driven protocol. This protocol maintains consistent overview of the network. Routing tables are used by each node to stores the locations of other nodes in the network. This information is used to transfer data among the various nodes in the network and various mechanisms are used to confirm the creativity of the forwarding tables. One of the approved procedures is disseminating “hello”, a specific message holding address info at fixed interims of time. On reception of this message every node informs its own routing table with different positions info of other nodes joining in the network. Some of the common and popular common driven protocols are Destination Sequence Distance Vector routing protocol (DSDV), Wireless Routing Protocol (WRP), and Cluster- Head Gateway Switch Routing (CGSR).

On Demand Routing Protocols

On-demand routing protocol is another ad-on to the mobile ad hoc networking routing protocols group. With on-demand protocols, if a source node requires a route to the destination for which it does not have route information, it will initiate the process of route discovery which travels from one point to another till it finds its endpoint or to the in-between node that the direction to the endpoint. It is necessary for the receiver node to request route by sending reply to the source node to obtain an expected route to the endpoint. And ultimately when source node gets the route of the destination it uses this route to transmit data from source to target node. Some of the better known on-demand protocols are Ad Hoc On-Demand Distance Vector routing (AODV), Dynamic Source Routing (DSR), and Temporary Ordered Routing Algorithm (TORA). These protocols vary in specifying the recognized route data and storing the identified earlier route information. Here as well we may suffer some problems if the network consists of many participating nodes.

Secure Transmissions

Mobile ad hoc networks consist of two types of security messages such as data and routing. These messages are different in characteristics and essentials of security. Secure Internet Protocol is a kind of point-to-point data message. Consequently it can use the present point-to-point procedure to secure the message. Conversely, while broadcasting there will be some change in some portions of that message continuously. This is possibly cited as focal task caused by the routing communication to the ad hoc location. Normally, changeable and non-mutable types of information are transmitted by routing messages. The routing messages with mutable information are safe that it does not require any trust in intermediate node. If not it is difficult to preserve the mutable information computationally. And above, generally security will greatly decrease. The source and destination communication objective is to transmit the data to the destination safely. Every time there is no routing entry in the routing table of the node, and if it wants to transmit the data to the destination, it can implement one of the numerous procedures, such as invoking on-demand protocol's route discovery procedure or invoking processes of route discovery and data delivery in mobile ad-hoc on-demand data delivery protocol. Moreover a packet contains an endpoint IP address, ID of broadcast and a source along with a certificate A and the expiration time t2, for the security perspective. The above said information is provided in a source code public key when it joined the structure.

AMRoute

In this type of protocol robustness is emphasized even when network is highly dynamic or rapidly changing. In a specified topology it will not offer the absolute lowest bandwidth or latency securities. Mobile Ad-Hoc Networks (MANETs) comprised of relatively bandwidth reserved wireless links that are intentional to have vigorous, quickly varying, unplanned, multi-hop topologies. Due to variation in the topologies, particular nodes and collection of nodes may change continuously or disappear. For vigorous transmission over dissimilar network technologies in MANETs the TCP/IP protocol suite is expected to be used. For disseminating information to large number of nodes efficient IP multicast is needed. Here below the description of the Ad-Hoc Multicast Routing Protocol (AMRoute), is mentioned which permits to handle the IP multicast in MANETs. In MANETs the reorganizational hierarchy occur frequently related to standard fixed networks which cause unnecessary signalling overhead. And also persistent datagram loss which is the main reason why existing multicast protocols do not work well in MANETs. This happens when multicast protocols react to changes in network in addition to changes in group. AMRoute tackles this challenge by following changes in group only; and the primary unicast transmission is trustworthy for following changes in network, anyhow it is essential to do.

The important features to AMRoute that makes it effective in MANETs are:

- Sending and reproduction is only accomplished by members of a group over unicast channelling in user-multicast hierarchy.

- According to membership of group and connectivity in network, the core node changes.

The user-multicast hierarchy contains nodes as the senders and receivers of group only. Every node conscious only about its tree neighbours and transmits the data on the hierarchical connections to its neighbours. As multicast state in AMRoute is maintained only by group nodes, the non-member nodes does not assist IP multicast protocols equally it is not required by other nodes in the network. Compared broadcasting, resident multicast protocols require nodes for each source and group state at all nodes in network. AMRoute clearly saves node resources by elimination of the state in other nodes in the network. Further considerably, user-multicast tree remove the structure of tree according to the changes vigorously occur in ad hoc networks. In AMRoute at least one logical core in every group of a network is accountable for determining new group supporters and generating or continuing the multicast tree for data dissemination. This logical core is not a preset node, it can change dynamically which is considerably dissimilar from CBT core node and RT in PIM-SM since it is not the central point on the data route. The nonappearance of malfunction in single point is a MANETs essential constraint.

BACKGROUND

Technical Issues

AMRoute produces multicast dissemination tree for each group using unicast channels involving members of each group. This protocol has two key elements given in (Liu,Talpade,Mcauley,& Bommaiah,1999):

1. Tree creation.
2. Mesh creation.

The mesh and tree creation is initiated only by logical core nodes. However, according to connectivity in network and group memberships, the entire core can change. The mesh is formed by creating the both way communication channels between a couple of group associates. And finally by using the subgroup of the accessible mesh relations, the protocol occasionally generates a multi cast distribution tree.

INTRODUCTION TO COVERAGE IN WIRELESS SENSORS

Progresses in wireless transmission and Micro Electro Mechanical Systems (MEMS) have facilitated the tiny sensing devices with multi-functional, cost-effective, less energy to sense the location. Also to implement data processing and communication between two nodes in short distances.

Now coming directly to the coverage section of the wireless sensors, the coverage problem is centred on a fundamental question: "How well do sensors observe the physical space?"

The goal here is to have each location in the physical space of interest within the sensing range of at least on sensor. This sensing range of the sensors depends upon lot of factors out of which the list of few dominating factors (Fan & Jin, 2010) is given below:

1. Deployment strategy,
2. Sensing model,
3. Sensing area,
4. Communication ranges,
5. Algorithm characteristics, and
6. Sensor mobility.

In addition to these six dominating factors, failure models, information about location, time management, scalability, dynamism, adaptive are also some of the elements affected for exposure policies in wireless sensors network.

Coverage Problems

Coverage problems are mainly of three types as in (Fan & Jin,2010) (Cardei & Wu,2004)

1. Problem of art gallery,
2. Problem of circle covering, and
3. Coverage of robotic system.

Art Gallery Problem (AGP)

Here visualize that the superior desires to place the camera in the corridor such that entire passageway is resilient from thief. So basically it means that we need to place less number of image capturing devices in a polygon location in such a way that the location is observed by at least any one camera. Here arise two queries to be answered like how many numbers of cameras are required and what is the exact position to place that device?

This problem is usually modelled on a two dimensional space as a simple polygon. A simple and convenient answer to this question is to distribute the polygon into non-intersecting triangles and on all of these triangles every camera to be located. Though this problem can be answered in 2D space perfectly in polynomial time, but when it is extended to further dimension it is disclosed as NP-hard problem.

Circle Covering Problem (CCP)

Main objective of CCP is to reduce the range of the circles which can entirely cover the specified range for an agreed number of matching circles. Some query rises like how to organize matching circles on the level that can completely covers the range? Though few methods offer limited number of circles, no method has been found universally so far.

Robotic System Coverage (RSC)

The many-robot systems are mainly covered by three types of structures. The blanket coverage is a first type of coverage in which the entire detection area is expanded by the immobile organization of sensors. The barrier coverage is the next type of coverage scheme in which likelihood of unobserved diffusion through the obstacle is reduced by immobile organization of nodes. The sweep coverage is a last type of robotic system coverage which is almost all corresponding to the relocating obstacle.

All of the above said issues are relevant to the coverage issues in wireless sensor network like to check whether region is observed and covered adequately. These consequences also deliver some hypothetical circumstances to the exposure issues. However the answers of these issues are not openly related to WSN because of dissimilar conditions. For instance, in AGP a camera can capture boundlessness space except there is some hindrance, whereas detecting device has the highest detecting range. Further, the change in the topology and disseminated style of WSN also restrict use of solution of these difficulties.

Coverage Schemes

Depending upon the objectives and applications of exposure area, the coverage schemes can be categorized into three kinds: Coverage with respect to area, point and path is shown in Figure 1 as in (Cardei,& Wu,2004). The brief summary of above categories is mentioned below.

Area Coverage

Here the key factor of the sensor network is to cover or observe a region which is collection of all the space points within the sensor field and each of the region need to be monitored as in Figure 1(a). Some of the schemes of area coverage are mentioned below.

Energy-Efficient Random Coverage

It is an important issue in WSN, caused by resources run on battery. Devices that preserve energy resources have a straight impact on the network performance. During the network performance, it will sense the functions of nodes and send data to the sink. Network performance is also referred as time interval. Due to interferences like less power resources, few nodes may become unavailable or extra nodes might be deployed. To overcome this issue, sensor nodes are made active and redundant nodes are put in the sleep state for a longer period.

Connected Random Coverage

Node connectivity is a key issue in WSNs. A strong connection is established in a network, when any active node transmits the information with any other active node. To do this, intermediate nodes are used as relays. Once the sensor nodes are deployed, they form a network. In this network information is gathered by these nodes and sends back to controllers or data sinks. The main focus is to utilize less number of operational nodes to keep up the coverage area with a proper connectivity. Usage of less number of functioning nodes reduces power utilization and the network performance. This can be more effective, if the communication range is at least double of the working sensing range. If the transmission range is too high, then there are more chances of getting interferences. Then the communication range is set as twice the sensing range to guarantee a strong connectivity.

Deterministic Coverage

According to researchers, a less amount of sensing devices are positioned in a specified range, the coverage for sensing can be covered. The detecting region is a circle with a radius (r). And the radius ranges between the sensing and communication should be equal. In this scheme, a connected component is created by joining circles in a sequence. This sequence should be in such way that the space between two contiguous circles is r. To cover a specified area, it is required to fill with a line of r-circles with radius r (1.8660) among them. Similarly alternative circle is added to interconnect all other similar r-circles. By doing so, the sensor network is connected in a coverage area.

Node Coverage as Approximation

To monitor a wide area, a huge sensor network is deployed. In this dense sensor network, the coverage area is estimated by the sensor locations depicted that area. To do so, we require a Connected Dominating Set (CDS) comprised of active sensor nodes. CDS is constructed using a distributed and localized protocol, which was discussed in Wu and Li paper as marking process. If the transmission range of any adjacent nodes is different, then those nodes are called as coverage nodes. The coverage nodes are actually not connected, which are also referred as gateway nodes. These gateway nodes are used to form a CDS. By maintaining the CDS property, a trimming procedure can be used to decrease the scope of coverage node set. The trimming process is referred as pruning process. According to Dai and Wu, a pruning rule is created called pruning rule K. Using this rule, a exposure node can withdraw from its state, if it is neighbor node set is covered collectively by coverage nodes. Additionally, the nodes covering the neighbor node set always have higher priority while connecting. A constant approximation ratio is ensured by pruning rule. According to marking process rule, the CDS can be locally maintained, when sensors change its state like on or off.

Point Coverage

Here the main aim is to cover locations of links group that needs to be observed. This arrangement emphasis on finding correct position of sensor nodes, where assure well-organized coverage application for partial quantity of immovable links as in Figure 1(b). The following is an approach for sensor placement exposure methodology such as random point coverage and deterministic point exposure.

Figure 1. a) Area coverage; b) point coverage; c) path coverage

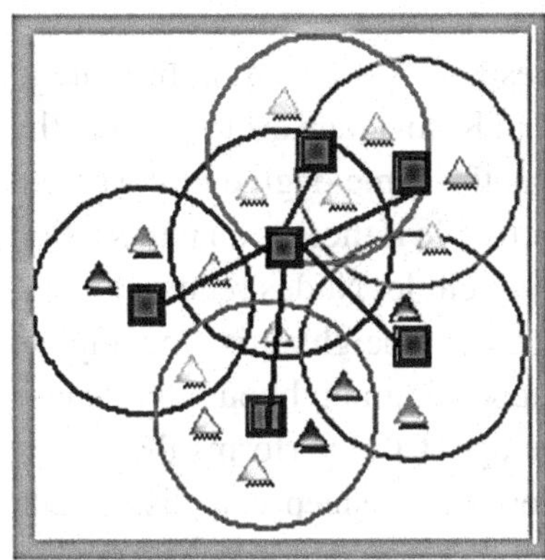
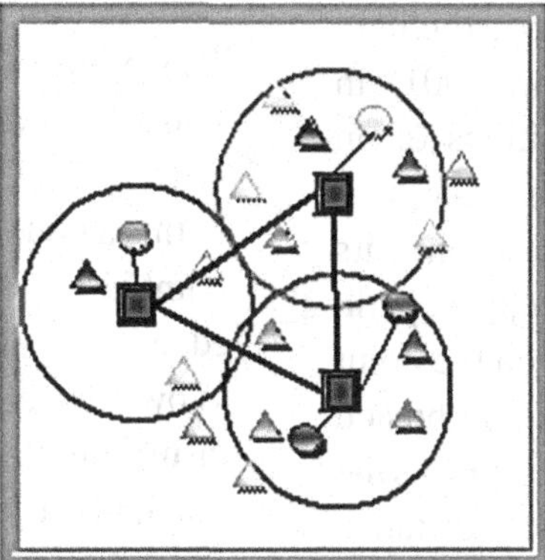
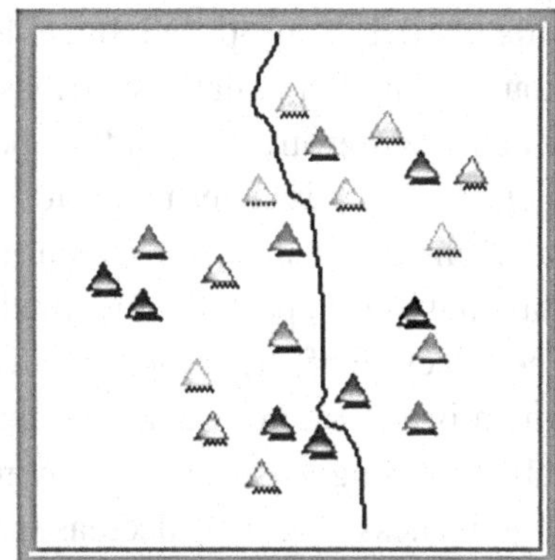

Random Point Coverage

In the previous studies, it has been shown that this type of coverage is applicable to certain application such as military. In this a restricted number of nodes with the recognized position that must to be examined. Huge amount of sensing devices are distributed in a random fashion to monitor its neighbour's performances. These nodes nearer to its destination transmit observed info to a dominant connection of that coverage. To implement this each sensor node has to monitor it is target node. In this way every sensor is able to watch all destination nodes which are covered in its sensing region. During this process the set of sensors are divided into disjoint sets to increase the lifetime of sensor network. These disjoint sets helps in covering all destination nodes. Random point approach continuously makes the disjoint sets active, so that for a specified interval only one set can be active. In this way all purposes are observed by set of sensors. This technique increases the time duration between the two activations to limit a maximum number of disjoint sets. The overall power of all sensors is increased by reducing the active sensor's time by a fraction. The separate sets are demonstrated as isolated set covers so that each cover set observes all the objective nodes. It has been proved that disconnect set exposure problem is NP-complete. This set cover computation can be solved using mathematical integer programming design of type mixed.

Deterministic Point Coverage

This approach is only possible in responsive and approachable locations, where a set of sensors are explicitly positioned. Main objective is to fix up a less quantity of nodes and their position such that all locations are reachable and the associated sensors are placed. The situation arises when all sensor nodes have the identical detecting range. The detecting range almost equals to the broadcast range with a performance ratio 7.256. The coverage and connectivity is maintained by creating a least cost spanning tree. This tree maintains targeted points along with sensor node locations.

Path Coverage

Here the objective is to lessen or expand the likelihood of unobserved penetration through the region. This is also referred as barrier coverage shown in Figure 1(c). In this scheme the path start and end points are selected from top and bottom limit lines of the area. The path selection is based on the following barrier coverage models.

Barrier Coverage Model

This model is proposed by (Meguerdichian, Koushanfar, Potkonjak, & Srivastava,2001) in which the starting and ending positions of an agent (sensor) is determined to sense the sensors. The agent node movement determines its maximal breach path and maximal support path. The selection of any sensor is based on the point which is nearest in distance. In maximal breach path, assuming sensor nodes are homogeneous the effectiveness of sensing decreases as the distance increases. It has been observed from researches that maximal breach path is depicted through Voronoi diagram and maximal support path is depicted through Delaunay triangulation lines. These diagrams are generated by assigning every segment with equal weight with the closest sensor node with segment length. Basically the path computation is done through breadth-first-search and applies binary search to identify or calculate the closest node distance. In (Li et al.,2004) a distributed algorithm is proposed, which computes the path distance using relative neighbourhood graph. Mainly the maximal support path can be used for consuming less energy and finding a shortest path distance. When sensor nodes are randomly placed, then the probability of dissemination in a path is close to zero. This type of coverage problem is mostly discussed in the context of random as well as grid-based sensor networks.

In addition to this there are different schemes used for sensing the nodes are coverage configuration protocol, adaptive self-configuring sensor network topologies, optimal geographical density control, k-neighbours constrained coverage strategy, random independent scheduling, connected dominating coverage set, lightweight deployment-aware scheduling, low-energy adaptive clustering hierarchy.

The more often applied schemes are mentioned below.

Coverage Configuration Protocol (CCP)

This protocol uses K-Coverage eligibility rule to sense the nodes. In K-coverage every point in the sensing circle has the same degree of coverage. In this a node is eligible if there is an intersection point in its sensing circle. Nodes require knowledge about its sensing neighbours. Incomplete knowledge about sensing neighbours will cause insufficient coverage. CCP performs the transition in three states such as sleep state, listen state and active state.

Adaptive Self-Configuring Sensor Network Topologies (ASCENT)

In this each node examines its interrelation and adjusts to its involvement in the network structure with multihop. This topology is centred on the calculated functioning region. The region in which a node gestures when perceives excessive packet loss and request for extra nodes in the area to link the network to transmit communications. When packet loss occurs due to collisions, and then reduces its duty cycle. It investigates the location of native transmission and does not intersect the multihop forwarding, till it has the provision to do so.

Above all the area coverage problem is mostly considered in coverage problem. In wireless sensor network region, the sensor nodes covered are less with the low energy consumption.

ISSUES IN IEEE 802.11

The association of qualified engineers named as Electrical and Electronics Engineers institute is committed to progressing high-tech invention and quality. IEEE introduced IEEE802.11 standard in the year 1997. IEEE 802.11 is a set of standards with physical layer which are formed and maintained by IEEE LAN or MAN committee which is referred as IEEE 802. These standards are used in communication networks like Wireless Local area Networks in 2.4, 3.6, 5 and 60 GHz frequency ranges. Many of the home-based networks use 802.11a, 802.11b, or 802.11g standards for wireless communication. Basically these standards come up with the Wi-Fi range wireless system products.

The 802.11 group practices basic protocol which contains sequences of one way communication modulation procedures on air. The widely held are those well-defined by the protocols of type 802.11b and 802.11g that are revisions to the unique standard. Though the standard 802.11-1997 was the principal wireless networking standard, 802.11a was broadly pursued by 802.11b and 802.11g. A novel multi-flowing modulation procedure is 802.11n. Further standards in the group such as c to f, h, j are service modifications and additions or adjustments to the earlier necessities.

The frequency bandwidth range for 802.11b and 802.11g is 2.4 GHz ISM band. This is available in the rules and regulations of US Federal Communications Commission of Part 15. Due to the choice of this type of frequency bandwidth, because of this choice of frequency band, irregularly 802.11b and 802.11g devices may get affected from preventions from electronic ovens, battery-operated telephones and Bluetooth devices. 802.11b and 802.11g limit their intervention and vulnerability to intrusion by the methods of signalling type are Direct Sequence Spread Spectrum (DSSS) and Orthogonal Frequency-Division Multiplexing (OFDM) (Chaudet, Dhoutaut, & Lassous,2004) correspondingly. Instead of using 2.4 GHz ISM frequency band, the standard 802.11a practices the 5 GHz U-NII bandwidth throughout the universe to supply at least 23 non-intersecting channels in which nearby stations intersect. The advanced or inferior frequencies may be recognized have better or worse functioning reliant on the situation.

Country to country the division of the broadcasting frequency spectrum consumed by 802.11 fluctuates. According to the FCC Rules and Regulations of Part 15 permits 802.11a and 802.11g devices in US to be operated without a license. The channels one through six in 802.11b and 802.11g uses frequencies the lies in the range of 2.4 GHz incompetent broadcasting band. According to Part 97 of the FCC Rules and Regulations, authorized incompetent radio operatives may control 802.11b/g devices by sanctioning improved output power but not profitable content or encoding.

Let's look at a simple situation of mobile networks established on IEEE 802.11 wireless communication. It consists of a sequence of forwarders and all of them lie in the neighbour's carrier sensing zone. Each sender creates transmitter-recipient duo that tries to direct some data frames to one recipient in its broadcast region regularly. This setup contains the three pair's fairness challenge and permits studying particular fairness concerns of the IEEE 802.11 channel access procedure. An interesting phenomenon can be simulated, based on the definite number of duos in a sequence with its similarity. It introduces powerful modelling, by basically considering the possibility for a forwarder to direct data while its neighbours are delaying. To equals with the replications totally, this approach advances to a non-sequential structure of equations. And also it permits to investigate both insignificant and very huge chains. According to asymptotic behaviour and few parameters, fairness challenge in a sequence is analysed. In a lengthy sequence, well-intentioned asymptotic fairness of the IEEE 802.11 channel allocation mechanism can be observed. Through a presentation, the way to improve the fairness in a sequence of three duos can be depicted.

While 802.11 is intended primarily for networks with substructure centred, the Distributed Coordination Function (DCF) (Chaudet et al.,2004) provided in 802.11 permits cells to approach the broadcasting channel without the necessity of a base station. Consequently, findings in wireless multi-hops systems which is referred as ad hoc networks frequently depends on the usage of the IEEE 802.11 standard for the layers of type physical and MAC. Though, for the past few years, the use of 802.11 in ad hoc networks has been called into question. Different scenarios show serious performance issues. The performances presented by 802.11 are often small and straight impact the performances of higher layers protocols.

This protocol outlines access layers of type physical and medium. This standard has initially been considered for handling base station in networks; it contains a disseminated channel approach protocol, called the Distributed Coordination Function (DCF) that requires no base station. With the DCF, ad hoc networks can rely on 802.11 as soon as a routing protocol is provided.

Utmost of the designed protocols for ad hoc networks believe that 802.11 are used on low layers. But some works have put under light a certain number of implementation issues arising with 802.11 used in an ad hoc context that lead to the following question: Is IEEE 802.11 really well suited for ad hoc networks? All the works on the subject accuse the DCF mode. But every investigation processes its particular situation and there is no effort that reviews all challenged implementation problems. Furthermore, some findings assess 802.11 via particular functions and it is demanding to separate the performances of 802.11 from the ones of higher layers.

The IEEE 802.11 DCF is division of the Carrier Sense Multiple Access with Collision Avoidance (CSMA/CA) category (Chaudet et al.,2004). Emitters have to check for the free channel so that collision can be avoided while sending the frame. All the frames are queued and dequeued frame has to wait for a small time period called Distributed Inter Frame Space (DIFS) (Chaudet et al.,2004). After DIFS the frame will be sent through the medium which is idle. If the medium is eventful during DIFS then the sender creates a contention window using randomly generated back off interval. If the medium still idle the mobile waits for DIFS by decrementing back off time slot by slot. During this interval if a medium is busy, then the process is stopped. After a new DIFS the process will be resumed later with the remaining number of back off slots. The frame is successfully emitted when the back off reaches zero.

The above mechanism is not to avoid every collision, but it minimizes the collision probability. The sizes of the contention window of emitters are doubled whenever collision occurs. During this process the same frame is re-sent with the same process as per the above mechanism. If collision happens again, as defined by the standard when the contention frame size reaches its maximum size, it is doubled (Chaudet et al.,2004) . The frame is dropped after several (fixed) numbers of retransmissions. The contention window size is reset during retransmissions as well as successful transmission of a frame.

Every single unicast frame has to be accepted, as collision discovery is impossible due to the half-duplex feature of the wireless routes. For every successful frame receiver has to wait for a Short Inter Frame Space (SIFS) (Chaudet et al.,2004) interval and then sends the response. Compared to DIFS, SIFS has shorter interval in order to provide importance to responses over data frames. The absence of response from SIFS is treated by the emitter as a collision and the frame is retransmitted.

Subsequently, acknowledgment frames are as essential as data frames. To prevent unexpected congestion of acknowledgments a fixed time called Extended Inter Frame Space (EIFS) is used instead of DIFS. During EIFS emitters sensing a signal on the medium of an 802.11 frame unable to decode the frame contents which will defer their transmission, when the channel becomes laze. This scheduling is adequate to protect acknowledgment transmission and much higher than DIFS. Basically EIFS wait to receive an error-free frame and it cancels this time during EIFS.

To avoid hidden nodes situation Request To Send (RTS) (Chaudet et al.,2004) and Clear To Send (CTS) (Chaudet et al.,2004) is used to exchange information so that two autonomous senders concurrently direct a frame to the equal recipient. The emitter has to check for a free medium by sending RTS frame to initiate the process of transmitting a frame. The transmission begins by receiving a CTS frame from the receiver, if there is no interference during transmission. During this transmission both sender and recipient identify these frames and reserve medium for it. Once the frame is identified till the end of the transmission the medium is set as busy. This process is called Virtual Carrier Sense (Chaudet et al.,2004) .

Figure 2 summarizes a part of these operations as in (Chaudet et al., 2004). This figure represents the MAC operations between three nodes which are connected in a shared range. Node A starts its transmission by sending a frame when a medium is free. This frame can be emitted after a DIFS period so that acknowledgment can be received from node B. Now node A emits another frame which will be enqueued. Node A appeal a back off, If a previous transmission was taking place. In the above figure a back off of 2 slots is drawn and node C desires to direct a frame to B parallel. Once the medium becomes free, it emits a frame before the DIFS is elapsed. When node A and node C emits at the same time, then collision occurs at node B. As no acknowledgment is sent back, the contention window is doubled so that both emitters re-emit their frames. Node C successes the case this time and stops its emission by decrementing node A back off by two slots. Once the Data acknowledgment is exchanged, node A restarts the back off procedure with its two continuing slots.

Performance Issues

Implementation analysis of IEEE 802.11(Chaudet et al.,2004) standard is simulation based and helps to realise the behaviour of the MAC layer in spite of physical layer simplification. In most of the cases designed models are helpful in understanding the fully connected or synchronized networks than analytical models. Though experimental conditions and results are difficult to analyse but the performance analysis of this standard is more reli-

Figure 2. IEEE 802.11 protocol operation

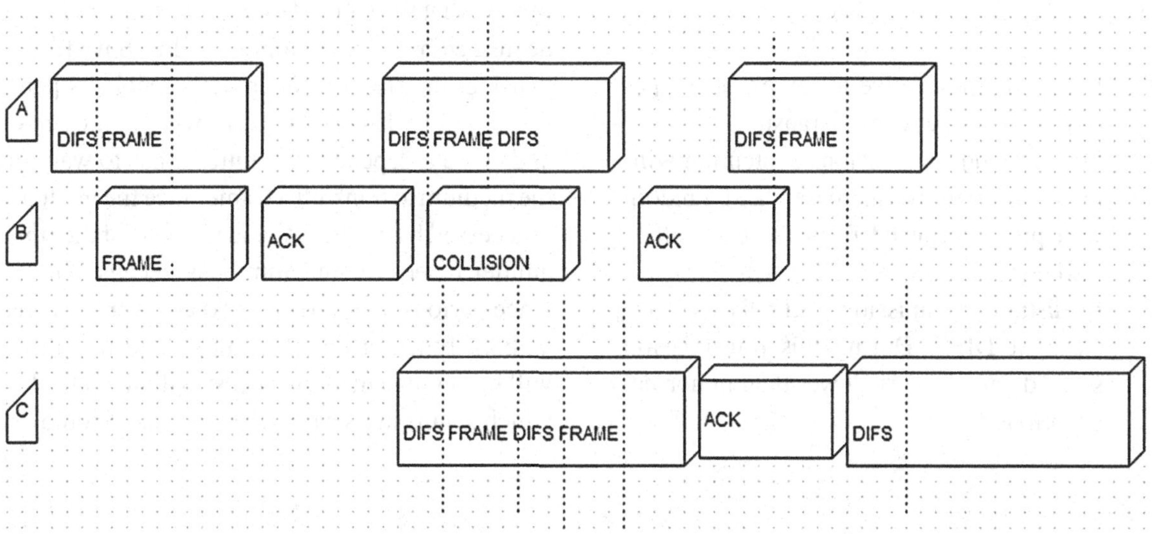

able through experimentations. The performance issues of 802.11 can be classified in three main categories (Chaudet et al.,2004):

- For all the mobile nodes involved in this will have decreasing throughput from its configuration results. The overall throughput decrease is due to inefficiency of network capacity.
- In long term fairness issues (Chaudet et al., 2004) some of the flows wait for a medium access for a long period where as whole channel bandwidth is captured by other flows.
- In short term fairness issues (Chaudet et al., 2004) the flows are emitted by burst which is a result of its configuration.
- Till the medium capacity is full performance issues do not appear. In ad hoc networks the medium capacity becomes full when shared and unusual radio medium exists in certain applications like video streaming, file transfer etc.

In 802.11 DCF there are several reasons that prevent an emitter for regaining the receiver medium in standard situations. The throughput decrease classified into the following three categories (Chaudet et al., 2004):

- If a medium is active for an extensive period then emitter cannot transmit.
- Due to frequent collisions contention window size will be increased and random wait phase retrieved from the back off is also be long.
- In distant transmissions EIFS is used instead of DIFS. During this transmission static delay phase is slower than in normal situations.

The network topology represented in the Figure 3 as in (Chaudet et al., 2004) regroups all types of basic configurations that lead to performance issues. In this figure there are three different communication lines used. The solid lines represent the direct communication between two mobiles at a high rate. Dashed lines represent used as communicating link between two mobiles with the rate 2Mb/s. This communication links unable to use the full capacity due to signal quality whereas the carrier sensing links between mobiles represented by dotted lines. In other words when a mobile senses medium as busy it means another mobile is emitting a frame. To streamline the process the mobile nodes considered to be in the carrier sense range. In this range when any mobile node emits a frame, EIFS approach is triggered. In reality these two zones are similar but not exactly the same. Various types of performance issues occur based on the active flows in this network.

Figure 3 depicts the 802.11 performance issues in three situations as in (Chaudet et al., 2004) such as busy medium, long random wait and long fixed wait.

Busy Medium

In this 802.11each emitter sends one frame at time so that throughput of each node is gradually decreased by slowest emitter. In the above figure consider the flows from emitters-receivers pairs such as C-D, E-F and G-H in which emitters C and G are independent. Emitter E has to wait for the medium to transmit a frame since the medium is accessed by emitters C and G. Most of the time emitter E sees the medium busy because the silence periods of emitters C and G never coincide as both function independently. Due this there will be derange medium access with the ratio 1:2 which results in a severe fairness issue. Moreover

Figure 3. Performance issue configurations of Ad-Hoc network

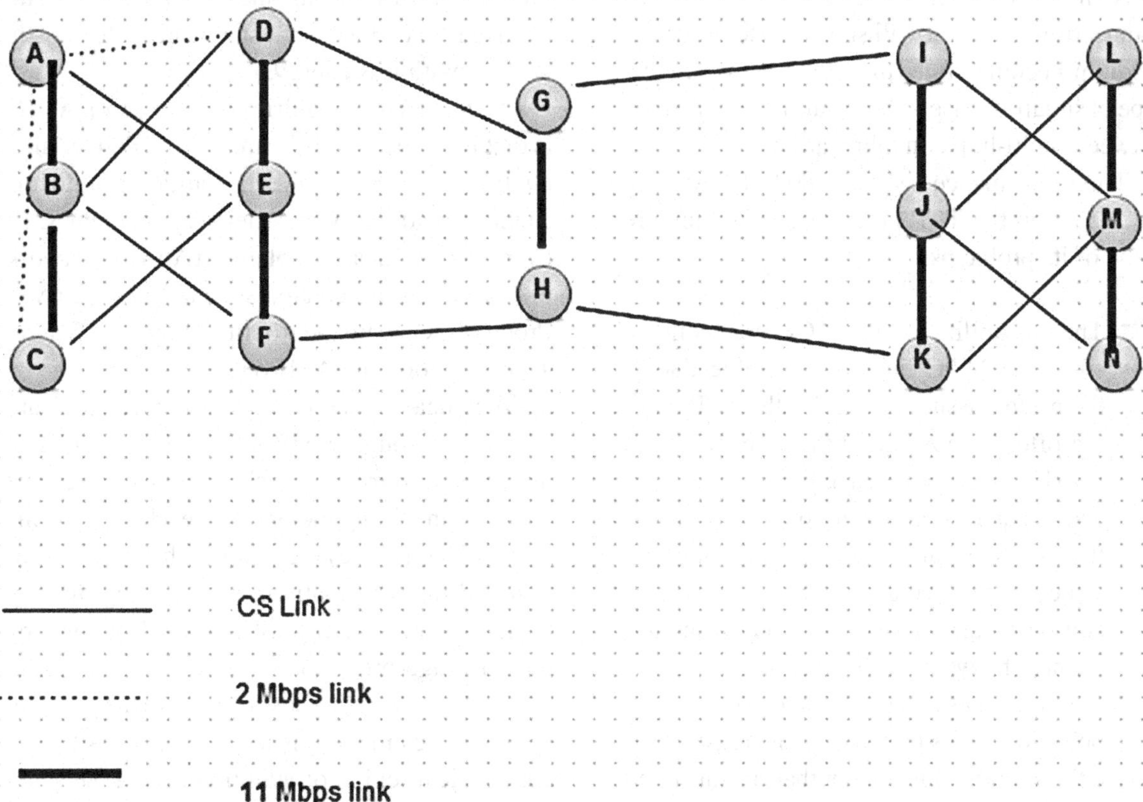

when there is a flow from E to F there is very less chance of medium access compared to other two emitters.

Long Random Wait

The emitter doubles the contention window size when it does not receive an acknowledgement and waits longer than other nodes. Though exchange of RTS-CTS solve the hidden terminal problem but still faces fair medium access in the long term (Chaudet et al.,2004) . In the above figure the exchange of RTS-CTS create active flows from K to L and Q to L. Emitters K and Q collide at L while transmitting the frames till its back offs allow successful RTS transmission. Either of the emitters succeeds in transmission as the other emitter is restricted by CTS to decrement its back off. The successful emitter resets its contention window to avoid the re-occurrence of collisions while accessing the medium. If the process of RTS-CTS is not active then the emitter freely emit the frame based on frame size as frame fit into a back off interval l(contention window size not increases). When the RTS-CTS mechanism is applied the emitter able to reserve the medium so that CTS can be emitted during the time. The medium share issue occurs if the CTS is not recognized by an emitter.

Long Fixed Wait

In this nodes have to wait for EIFS to prevent acknowledgements congestion received from distant receivers to distant emitters. While performing, the back off time is not decremented to identify a frame. In the above figure though flows from M-N and L-Q are active, emitter don't recognize frames from L. But it will start transfer once the medium becomes free. In ad hoc networks this type of situation arises when routing is performed between multi-hop communications.

The performance issues of 802.11 have also an impact on the TCP protocols. Following are some of its problems:

- The instability of the TCP connections: since the MAC links are unstable due to the present issues of 802.11, the TCP flows are often stopped and have to restart with the slow-start phase each time.
- The inequality between some TCP flows: the TCP mechanism increases the fairness issues encountered with 802.11 in some configurations, what results in a strong unfairness between the TCP flows.
- Lastly, fairness issues often lead to a bursty behaviour. This provokes an increase in the delays, and a high jitter that are unsuited to multimedia or real-time applications or even interactive applications.

CONCLUSION

In an Ad-Hoc network (AHN) there are many mobile hosts which are connected with the wireless links. Each of these mobile nodes operates as both, end- system as well as the router to forward packets over the multi-hop Ad-Hoc network. In ad hoc networks sending packet and multicast routing is an impartially unfamiliar region. Subsequently multicast transmission in static network depends on either hard state or soft state routers, as it is necessarily inappropriate for an AHN situation with unrestrained movement. Furthermore, in many types of AHNs inadequate capacity of storage and energy consumption, this increases to the reasons to prevent switching and preserving multicast state. Also numerous vagaries in topology make it challenging to relate clustering procedures like management of hard state and recurrent selections of cluster head are too costly for host with less energy.

And one more significant concern of AHNs is that it should be robust and should deliver high quality of service. However multicast protocols cannot provide the highest delivery guarantees. To overcome multicast problems in Ad-Hoc network few protocols are created such as Table- Driven Protocols, On demand Routing Protocols, Secure Transmissions and AMRoute.

Technical issues related to multicasting are discussed through. AMRoute produces multicast dissemination tree for each group using unicast channels involving members of each group. This protocol has two key elements such as tree formation and mesh formation. Now coming directly to the coverage section of the wireless sensors, the coverage problem is centred on a essential query: "How well do sensors observe the physical space?" The aim here is to have each position in the physical region of attention within the sensing range of sensor at least. This sensing range of the sensors depends upon few dominating factors such as deployment strategy, sensing model and area, communication ranges and sensor mobility.

The performance issues of 802.11 have also an impact on the TCP protocols. Some of its problems are the instability of the TCP connections, the inequality between some TCP flows which increases the fairness issues encountered with 802.11 in some configurations, what results in a strong unfairness between the TCP flows. And lastly fairness issues often lead to a bursty behaviour.

REFERENCES

Anastasi, G., Conti, M., & Gregori, E. (2004). IEEE 802.11 ad hoc networks: protocols, performance and open issues. In *Proceedings of Mobile Ad Hoc Networking*, (pp. 69-116). Academic Press.

Cardei, M., & Wu, J. (2004). Coverage in wireless sensor networks. In Handbook of sensor networks, (pp. 422-433). Academic Press.

Chaudet, C., Dhoutaut, D., & Lassous, I. G. (2005). Performance issues with IEEE 802.11 in ad hoc networking. *IEEE Communications Magazine*, *43*(7), 110–116. doi:10.1109/MCOM.2005.1470836

de Morais Cordeiro, C., Gossain, H., & Agrawal, D. P. (2003). Multicast over wireless mobile ad hoc networks: Present and future directions. *IEEE Network*, *17*(1), 52–59. doi:10.1109/MNET.2003.1174178

Fan, G., & Jin, S. (2010). Coverage problem in wireless sensor network: A survey. *Journal of Networks*, *5*(9), 1033–1040. doi:10.4304/jnw.5.9.1033-1040

Liu, M., Talpade, R. R., Mcauley, A., & Bommaiah, E. (1999). *AMRoute: Adhoc Multicast Routing Protocol* (Technical Report, 1999). Academic Press.

Meguerdichian, S., Koushanfar, F., Potkonjak, M., & Srivastava, M. (2001, July). Coverage problems in wireless ad-hoc sensor networks. *IEEE Infocom*, *3*, 1380–1387.

ADDITIONAL READING

Ahamed, S. R. (2011). Review and analysis of the issues of multicast routing in ad hoc networks: A novel study. *International Journal of Engineering Science and Technology*, *3*(4).

Jia, W. (2011, July). Coverage enhanced algorithm using artificial potential force. In Intelligent Control and Information Processing (ICICIP), 2011 2nd International Conference on (Vol. 2, pp. 969-972). IEEE. doi:10.1109/ICICIP.2011.6008395

Kimm, H., Engle, A., & Lee, F. (2011, February). Broadcast analysis of spanning tree flooding algorithm for mobile ad hoc networks. In *Proceedings of the 5th International Conference on Ubiquitous Information Management and Communication* (p. 85). ACM. doi:10.1145/1968613.1968714

Li, M., Wan, P. J., & Frieder, O. (2003). Coverage in wireless ad hoc sensor networks. Computers. *IEEE Transactions on*, *52*(6), 753–763.

Obraczka, K., & Tsuduk, G. (1998, October). Multicast routing issues in ad hoc networks. In Universal Personal Communications, 1998. ICUPC'98. IEEE 1998 International Conference on (Vol. 1, pp. 751-756). IEEE. doi:10.1109/ICUPC.1998.733066

KEY TERMS AND DEFINITIONS

AMRoute: Ad hoc Multicast Routing Protocol.

AODV: Ad- Hoc On-Demand Distance Vector Routing.

CDS: Connected Dominating Set comprised of active sensor nodes.

CGSR: Cluster- Head Gateway Switch Routing.

DCF: Distributed Coordination Function.

DIFS: Distributed Inter Frame Space –small time period for frame to wait.

DSDV: Destination Sequence Distance Vector Routing Protocol.

DSR: Dynamic Source Routing.

TORA: Temporary Ordered Routing Algorithm.

WRP: Wireless Routing Protocol.

Chapter 5
Cyber Physical Internet

ABSTRACT

This chapter explores the concept of the Cyber Physical Internet (CPI) and discusses the design necessities of it. In addition, it provides the restrictions of the present networking concepts to satisfy these necessities. The structural design of protocol stack for CPI has an extra layer Cyber-Physical Layer (CY-PHY Layer) to offer a conceptual description of the properties and type of cyber physical information. To enable standard communication between heterogeneous systems, Cyber Physical System-Interconnection Protocol is used. This protocol is mainly designed for special CPSs, which require overall instruction and performance guarantee for cyber physical interaction. The main objective of this protocol is to offer CPSs heterogeneity at three different levels: function interoperability, policy regulation, and performance guarantee.

INTRODUCTION

At the point when the web was initially presented, the motivation behind web was to inter-connect machines to impart the computerized information enormously. Then again when the embedded systems started, the target was to control system parts under continuous requirements through sensing devices usually at low to medium scales. Today, the advancement of the Information and Communication Technology (ICT) (Koubâa & Andersson, 2009) gave rise to the paradigm of Cyber-Physical Systems (CPS).

In the most recent two years, a progressive change has begun from stand-alone, independent embedded systems to cyber-physical systems (CPS). The units liable of this progressive change are Technical advancements in sensing, computing, and networking (especially profoundly embedded sensors and Wireless Sensor/Actuator Networks (WSANs)). Combination of computation, networking, and physical dynamics make the Cyber-physical system in which embedded units are arranged to sense, observe and control the physical world (Xia, Ma,Dong, & Sun, 2008).

The integration of physical procedures with the processing is old enough. The Cyber Physical Systems which are in use today are more complicated and diminutive scale in size when compared to the predicted or foreseen Cyber Physical Systems without bounds. The enormous networking of embedded computing devices like sensors and actuators is origination of the progression (Xia et al., 2008).

DOI: 10.4018/978-1-4666-7312-0.ch005

The projected change that CPS will introduce with this progression is the way of interaction with the physical world as similar to the Internet which changed the way the people interact with each other. Network need to integrate the computing devices which are distributed geographically and physical elements and hence, network plays a major role to enable extraordinary or exceptional communications between the physical world and human beings. Additionally, it is clear that WSANs serve as a backbone of the network in different CPS (Xia et al., 2008).

The vision towards large-scale distributed computing systems (Koubâa & Andersson, 2009) is currently evolving to be a new topic for research and development, where computation and environment are integrated and no more differentiated. For this, there is a need to coordinate outside physical information and techniques with computations for purpose of dissemination and universal control of the surrounding environment. Actually, embedded computing systems are fundamentally reliant on their surroundings where they are installed through sensing physical courses of procedures (Koubâa & Andersson, 2009).

The new prerequisites of enormously organized embedded systems are successfully fulfilled by the traditional embedded systems as computing gets to be progressively incorporated into our environment. Alternatively, the universal organization is being provided by the Internet to enable the information sharing and recovery.

Nonetheless, Internet applications have been determined by the need to share the legitimate data on the huge scale (Koubâa & Andersson, 2009) gave the mapping between the physical environment and the coherent data has not been considered in the outline of those applications. Accordingly, the convergence of the Internet with embedded systems is an imperative point of reference for empowering huge scale distributed computing systems that are firmly coupled with their physical environment.

As an initial move towards this union the Radio-Frequency Identification (RFID) based systems (Koubâa & Andersson, 2009) have empowered the idea of system of physical entities, which is generally referred as Internet-of-Things. RFID has been well-thought-out as the key engineering for Internet-of-Things (IoTs) (Koubâa & Andersson, 2009).

Alternatively, the Wireless Sensor Networks (WSNs) standard has developed as an alternate option to networks of physical actions, which upholds the control and observing of physical occurrences in environment through sensing. Some different choices have considered the utilization of sensor-based cellular phones for observing regular things through cellular networks. These methodologies come into the idea of Cyber-Physical Systems (CPS), which are the systems installed in extensive land territories and normally comprise of extensive number of distributed computing devices firmly coupled with their physical environment.

BACKGROUND

CPSs Components

CPS allows us to add capabilities to physical systems, by merging computing and communication with physical processes. The benefits of CPS are:

- Safer and more efficient systems,
- Reduce the cost of building and operating systems, and
- Build complex systems that provide new capabilities.

Figure 1 represents the main components of cyber-physical systems.

The boundary line amid CPS and Internet-of-Things has not been evidently distinguished as both ideas are determined analogous from two autonomous groups despite the fact that they have

Figure 1. Large-scale cyber-physical systems components

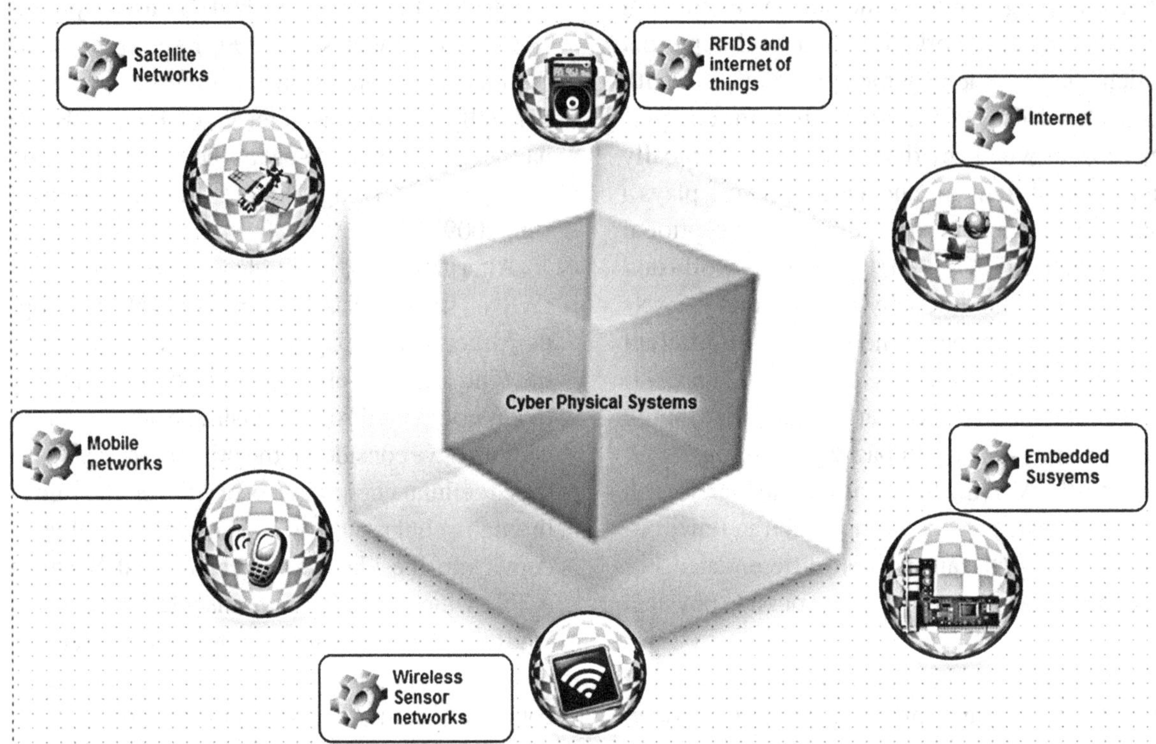

continuously been narrowly allied. The merging of CPS and Internet-of-Things has turned into genuine certainty with the development of the 6LoWPAN. This merging permits to utilize the Internet as a strong base to sensor systems, also to embed with RFID systems (Koubâa, & Andersson, 2009).

As of now, the CPSs are distributed and are working as private systems, where each network implements particular undertakings identified to the location where it functions. The inspiring mission in the outline of CPS is the way how to permit the interconnection and interoperability (Koubâa & Andersson, 2009) of all these distributed networked embedded systems into a solitary vast scale network that fulfills all obliged prerequisites.

In a forthcoming CPS, as indicated in Figure 1 an expansive number of embedded, potentially mobile computing devices will be interconnected through WSANs, constituting different independent subsystems that give certain services to end clients (Xia, et al., 2008).

A CPS may be made out of various subsystems. Worldwide data sharing is attained by associating WSANs to the Internet. For example, in a cyber-physical city, there may be various cyber physical subsystems for personal health awareness, smart home, intelligent transportation, support of facilities, and open security. CPS will basically extent all through in fields of science and designing, for example, industry, farming, health awareness, building, military, security, ecological science, biology, and topography, and in addition our regular life (Xia, et al., 2008).

WSANs assist CPS as the interface between the cyber system and the physical system. Sensors assemble data about the physical world, while actuators respond to this data by executing proper activities upon the physical world. WSANs empower cyber systems to observe and control the conduct of the physical world. Accordingly, the performance and even ease of use of CPS will vigorously rely upon the outline of these WSANs. With pervasive CPS, the quality of life is enhanced by the improved communication with the nature's domain in which we live.

Design of Cyber Physical Internet (CPI)

CPS is a society-scale system in which a fault tolerance has to be built in. All the data collected from the sensor-actuator systems in CPS need to be processed efficiently. For this, there should be Techniques to ensure the results can be visualized easily by users.

Throughout the demonstrating process of an extensive scale complex systems (Koubâa & Andersson, 2009), it is constantly paramount that intended models guarantee the best trade-off amidst their distinctive necessities. The history says that the real systems that spread out into the business don't generally satisfy the goals of the hypothetically anticipated models. IEEE 802.11 (Wi-Fi) and IP (Internet protocol) are the two most popular standards that embed this conviction flawlessly. These two standard conventions are generally known to be somewhat poor as far as productivity and Quality-of-Service (Qos) are considered. A few advances have been proposed for IP, (for example, Integrated Services, Differentiated Services, and so on.) and also for Wi-Fi (e.g. IEEE 802.11e) to upgrade their performance. Regardless of effectiveness and lack of QoS, these two conventions have been extensively and rapidly spreading from the time of their release.

Alternatively, more complex protocols like X.25, ATM or HyperLan have been outlined with more caution to accomplish higher productivity and better QoS, yet did not improve an excessive amount of space in the financial market. It creates the impression that there is a hole between how new systems are required to work and how they do work truly. The reason is that the visualization of the business sector stakeholders is not the same as the vision of scholarly scientists.

Therefore, it could be effortlessly perceived that, in reasonable terms, the modeling paradigm is to rapidly plan, realize and put-into-business modest results that (Koubâa & Andersson,2009):

- Just work,
- Fulfill basic requirements, and
- Can be patched to plug new functionalities or to improve their behaviors.

As the reconsidering of the current processing establishments to assemble huge scale CPS was not viable, taking benefit from the legacy infrastructure to accomplish the substantial scale CPS goals appears to be beneficial. Consequently, the investigation determinations ought to concentrate on the system integration methodology for empowering expansive scale CPS, which is known as the Cyber-Physical Internet. Interoperability is the important challenge to construct substantial scale heterogeneous cyber physical systems. Furthermore, specifications of CPS in the coordination methodology of the current systems ought to be contemplated.

IP is the standard protocol which plays the important part in the forthcoming Cyber-Physical Internet. IP has been thought, since the conception of the sensor system prototype, as being incompatible with the necessities of sensor-based networks. In any case, this idea has been newly reconsidered and with the rise of 6LoWPAN that implants Ipv6 on top of the IEEE 802.15.4 as a substitute to Zigbee Network Layer. IETF 6LoWPAN Working Group has won the challenge and 6LoWPAN turns into a severe contender to Zigbee as it permits to flawlessly consolidate the world of sensor system with the Internet, which Zigbee is not fit to. On the other hand, if 6loWPAN wins regarding high level of interoperability with current systems, it's effectiveness with regard to energy and real time assurances must be acceptable. Actually, the design goals of 6LoWPAN are prone to put more concentration on interoperability and embedding with the Internet instead of average necessities of sensor systems. Enhancing the trade-off between those configuration targets remains a research challenge (Koubâa & Andersson, 2009).

In the real-time the design of cyber-physical systems usually imposes a serious challenge. Hence, the issue should be cautiously investigated and certain perceptions should be reconsidered. Even though there are numerous favorable exploration ways in the real-time field, a section of possible directions is given below (Koubâa & Andersson, 2009):

Operating Systems

It is vital that operating systems backs real time anyway. It actuates added design intricacy. The principle test is to accomplish an ideal stability between a few imperative characteristics required by a CPS operating system, comprising modularity, compelling equipment/programming part, hardware abstraction, energy proficiency, and real time. The most broadly utilized operating system, Tiny OS, signifies a guaranteeing answer for CPS as it addresses the greater part of those necessities. Conversely, the deficiency of real time backing characterizes a severe impediment in Tiny OS for developing real time protocols and synchronization mechanisms.

The deficiency of anticipation and prioritization in Tiny OS is a principle handicap for giving anticipated timing behavior at node level. In numerous cyber physical applications, where timing demands must be considered, reliability and real time are highly coupled. It is in this manner essential to take timing certifications into account for building reliable systems. Actually, the absence of real time in Tiny OS has stopped the release of standard IEEE 802.15.4 protocol stack for both open-ZB and TKN realizations. The performance of the IEEE 802.15.4 has been much solid when executed over ERIKA, a guaranteeing real time operating system for embedded units (Koubâa & Andersson, 2009).

Networking Protocols

From the networking point of view, real-time forces few difficulties which are yet open to investigate. One of the exciting research issues is to allocate the sufficient distributed and adaptive resources in synchronized multi-hop sensor networks by considering physical/logical alterations in the network. In synchronized WSNs, Resource (memory, bandwidth) allocation to dynamic sensor nodes which are a part of serious responsibilities is considered to be more proficient.

The utilization of static distribution strategies is not proficient for profoundly dynamic and mobile systems as they don't adjust to the network changes. Alternatively, the centralized adaptive synchronization instigates a substantial quantity of computation and correspondence overheads, which truly can't work in resource obliged WSNs, because of its complicated nature and non-responsiveness. Henceforth, new methodologies are to be discovered for handling resources for synchronized and mobile multi-hop WSNs in a distributed, effective, transparent, and more particularly real time way (Koubâa & Andersson, 2009).

Timing Guarantees

The procurement of deterministic real time assurances in volatile wireless adhoc and sensor systems is considered as a disputed problem. Majority of them which are managing deterministic assurances consider that the channels are fault free. This hypothesis may be right for extremely uncommon and amazing cases, where wireless connections are exceptionally steady and of a high quality. The greater part of current reality applications negate this supposition, since most of the wireless connections are basically found in the gray region, where connections are very flexible and unbalanced.

The idea of real-time promises must be reconsidered. Novel procedures to describe deterministic routine under channel vulnerability must be established. Guaranteeing that a wireless system deterministically gives an interval bound would not make sense. One fascinating characterization is to relate a trust level with each one assured delay bound. The goal of the related trust level is to enumerate the vulnerability on the assured delay bound (Koubâa & Andersson, 2009).

Performance Compositionality

Heterogeneity makes the end-to-end delay exploration in CPS is an intricate and exciting issue. Fundamentally, system level delay is derived from the component level delays on the basis of the traditional end-to-end delay exploration. This form of prototype is recognized to be ineffective. More refined strategies use structure hypotheses to change a multi-component system into a one-component system, consequently decreasing the unpredictability of the end-to-end exploration.

A complete schema is presented to methodically convert distributed real-time systems into a single system, which is utilized to induce the end-to-end schedulability of the original system. Despite the fact that these works signify a developer commitment towards performance compositionality in distributed real-time systems, their traffic model (focused around the schedulability hypothesis) is fairly limited to intermittent/an occasional streams and consistent execution times (i.e. most pessimistic scenario execution time), which is insufficient standard for demonstrating heterogeneous CPS applications (Koubâa & Andersson, 2009).

Data Aggregation

The existing Internet protocol layers make an aggregate deliberation on the way of information to be handled. Conversely, numerous CPS applications are not intrigued in the information itself yet they are noticeably intrigued in complex requests about the physical world. It is feasible for a client to demand that every sensor conveys its sensor interpretation and afterward calculates the result which is focused around each one of those sensor interpretations. In any case, such a methodology produces a massive quantity of data traffic something that (Koubâa & Andersson, 2009):

1. The necessary time to attain the output of the query is increased, and
2. Energy of sensor nodes is wasted.

Carrying out data transforming inside the system, for instance permitting routers as well to process incoming packets before forwarding, can lead to noteworthy changes conversely. This is commonly known as information aggregation, content based network, and in-system transforming or information refining system. Despite its marking, three imperative issues stay for the utilization of such a methodology in Cyber-Physical Internet:

Query Language Specification

A language which can be used by the clients to describe their queries and input to the network is required to be outlined. As of now, marginally altered versions of SQL are being used in the communication process of wireless sensor networks. In any case, the altered versions of SQL are not adequately communicative. For instance, in a particular state where client is required to identify whether a path is without ice or not, it is challenging for a sensor node to perform the operation and process the signal provincially effectively by utilizing SQL. One of the solutions for this could be installing a device driver on a sensor node to behave as a virtual sensor. Computation by the virtual sensor is depending on physical sensors.

For example, the output of a virtual sensor is a Boolean value. Hence, the output would be "true" if it senses ice near to it otherwise the output would "false". Formerly, queries which are depending on the virtual sensors are in SQL. A software package referred as "Global Sensor Networks" comprises a support of virtual sensors. Nonetheless, this package must be executed on a gateway which combined with wireless sensor network instead of sensor nodes themselves (Koubâa & Andersson, 2009).

Query Planning and Optimization

Research group of databases has made a broad study on query processing of SQL queries. The basic thought is to reduce the cost of a query and hence query optimization procedures are being introduced in order to determine the path of realizing the query which can reduce its corresponding cost.

The cost of the query processing is dominating when compared to the cost of disk access or CPU processing. The limited bandwidth of the communication channel is the major bottleneck of the data aggregation in CPS. Hence, it mostly required to reduce the cost of query processing using optimization techniques. This is significant because:

1. Details about the (wireless) structure of the network and intervention interactions among nodes are required so as to make parallel transmissions possible.
2. A selected MAC protocol is used to perform some operations (like MIN, MAX) effectively. The client's query is to be decomposed into operations by the query optimizer being aware of the potentiality.

Data Integrity

The interpretations of sensor need to be accurate so as to put a query. Common end-to-end encryption/validation procedures are not sufficient as the data aggregation permits routers to alter the payload of the data. Consequently, guaranteeing data integrity need to be vital role of the network (Koubâa & Andersson, 2009).

The feasibility of carrying out research is growing at the crossing point of the logical and physical domains. This progression is inspired by three basic developments that have extraordinary consequences on the forthcoming computer science as a discipline. These developments are (Abdelzaher, 2006):

- **Moore's Law:** It infers improved contraction and reduced price of hardware, prompting its steady explosion.
- **The Widening Human/Machine Bandwidth Gap:** Despite the fact that computing turn out to be more rapid and more pervasive according to Moore's law, the human data processing ability and human populace progress much slower. Over time, this prompts an expanding hole between the capacity of computing devices to gather data and the capability of people to expend it. In this way, human interest in data accumulation and transforming will get to be progressively more negligible and at progressively larger amounts of reflection. Computing devices will cooperatively require turning out to be more self-governing to evade the human bottleneck. This suggests that they will need to have their method for cooperation with their surroundings with dynamically less human intervention. As it were will figuring be more self-sufficient as well as progressively more inserted. This suggests that they will need to have their own particular method for collaboration with their

environment with dynamically less human intercession. At the end of the day will registering be more self-sufficient as well as progressively more inserted. Alternatively, computing is not only autonomous but also more embedded. (Abdelzaher, 2006)

- **The Cost of Lack of Communication:** Every time the lack of communication or information need to pay highly. For example, the more information from relevant sources improves the output of optimization and decision making. This prompts a major inclination for:
    - Worldwide interconnection of the thriving upcoming independent embedded devices, and
    - Cost of communication to be reduced.

The above three key patterns proclaim the development of ubiquitous, progressively independent, globally interconnected embedded systems with their own particular method of communication with the physical world. Applications may include (Abdelzaher, 2006):

1. Calamity response networks,
2. Intricate real-time control networks (such as power-grid control),
3. Environmental sensing networks to discover environmental phenomena at an extraordinary spatial and temporal granularity, and
4. Personal sensor networks. A basic question that arises is one of architecture. Specifically, what are the reusable middleware components, network protocols, and system services, at various levels of abstraction, that can form layered, distributed software architecture for cyber-physical computing? Is the existing networking infrastructure sufficient?

There are certain queries which are needed to be answered like whether existing distributed middleware frameworks will meet the needs of cyber-physical applications. To answer this question, the deficiencies of current software systems and networks are needed to be explored when applied to cyber physical systems.

To provide security to a system, it is necessary to prevent systems from attacks. These attacks require adequate mechanisms for communication security such as encryption and authentication and eliminating possible covert communication channels. A secretive channel might be defined as an implemented, unlawful indicating channel that permits a client to secretly break the safety rule and observe needs of the system (Farag, Lerner, & Patterson, 2012). Oftentimes, covert channels are eliminated by identifying them and preventing their creation at the communication endpoints Nonetheless, network security is not the main focus of this work, and we rely on the standard practices and techniques to secure communication in CPSs.

Intrusions can be launched by a malicious entity, such as system operators, having physical access to the controller which has some advantages over network attacks such as the ability to acquire side-channel information. Embedded controller peripherals are compromised to gain access to the controller and exploit its vulnerabilities. For example, a system operator having certain access rights can deceive an industrial control system by deliberately entering misleading operational instructions. Many external attacks against embedded controllers can be launched without human intervention to circumvent the controller's legitimate operation or leak classified information. Most external threats targeting a CPS exploit existing vulnerabilities of the system and the inadequacy of perimeter security defenses.

A computation platform is composed of several layers of abstraction, including application software, middleware, OS and device drivers and the hardware or physical layer. The hardware abstraction layer may incorporate processors, memory, and I/O peripherals where each one of these components is associated with a hierarchical computation model and a specific implementation. Although this view of a computation platform reduces the complexity of the engineering design problem, it increases security concerns about potential vulnerabilities associated with each layer of abstraction.

External threats targeting CPS computation elements and controllers include software and hardware attack. Previously, cyber-attacks have targeted the software stack of computing platforms by exploiting various software vulnerabilities such as buffer overflow and format string to execute the attacker's malicious code. Recently, hardware attacks have increased because of their ability to evade detection by the top layers security defenses, and the power gained by controlling the most privileged layer in the computational platform.

A serious threat to CPS embedded controllers' results from the incorporation of untrusted elements and components. One example of internal threats is a Trojan horse, a malicious inclusion or alteration to the system to do assured activities and functionalities not caught by the design requirements (Farag et al., 2012). Trojans execute a predefined malicious operation and are deliberately developed and included into a system by an entity participating in the system production flow. Thus, Trojans are serious threats to the CPS embedded controllers as they aim to disrupt the physical system. On the other hand, other system vulnerabilities can be inadvertently created by developers which can be later discovered and exploited.

A Trojan relies on system internals to conduct its functionality without the need for external activating triggers. Often times, Trojans can evade detection by most perimeter security measures such as firewalls and intrusion-detection techniques which are primarily developed to counter attacks from external sources. Trojan effects on the host platform can be partitioned into:

- Modify the functionality of the target device,
- Modify device specifications and parameters to reduce reliability,
- Leak information, and
- DoS.

Trojans can be classified based on their layer of inclusion into Hardware Trojan Horses (HTHs) embedded in the hardware components and software Trojans associated with any layer of the software stack. Recently, HTHs have gained an increasing interest from the security research community because of their potential to conduct more powerful attacks without being detected using software security solutions.

FUNDAMENTAL LIMITATIONS AND IMPORTANT RESEARCH CHALLENGES

To address the deficits of current systems, various challenges are dealt by globally interconnected networks of embedded devices (ex: Mobile). These challenges are discussed below in detail:

Networking Challenges

The present design of Internet is not capable of accommodating different of physical data sources, distributed computing elements, and actuators

The current design is enhanced for point-to-point correspondence. In fact, the fundamental deliberation of TCP is a reliable point-to-point association. Interestingly, upcoming independent systems of embedded devices will be fixated on data synthesis as the crucial system persistence. This is an immediate result of the incorporation of an expanding number of embedded devices, (for example, sensors) in the Internet and the expanding need to promote data abstractions to bridge the human/machine gap as specified previously. Data synthesis as the essential system persistence obliges an alternate protocol stack that may take motivations from distributed database design, information mining, control, and sensor systems. A basic investigation is to define network architecture in a manner that upgrades it for distributed data fusion and recovery rather than point-to-point correspondence (Abdelzaher, 2006).

Computing Challenges

New models and standards are required for distributed cyber physical computing. Past distributed computing standards (and current middleware systems that execute them) have endeavored to extract away scattered communication, giving backing to location transparency and concealing correspondence subtle elements. Conversely, forthcoming cyber physical computing standards will require:

1. Abstract scattered enormously simultaneous communication with the physical world.
2. Signify the exterior environment appropriately for the developer. Processing that fulfills the above necessities, naturally immersive computing.

For instance, the abstraction of logical entities that relate to physical objects in the environment might be disseminated by the upcoming object-oriented (naturally immersive) programming system. The current condition of the physical objects is to be summarized by the logical entities. This exemplification needs to shroud complex points of interest about state estimation in a distributed noisy domain, and complex distributed protocols for physical entity tracing and disambiguation. New distributed middleware and underlying hypothetical establishments are required to back such standards (Abdelzaher, 2006).

Programming Language Design Challenges

The more concentration of the forthcoming cyber physical applications will be on information synthesis. Minimum of two different skilled developers are required to build the application. They are:

1. The developers who can implement distributed information synthesis flawlessly and develop signal processing algorithms.
2. The programmers who are capable of developing control systems and decision systems which are more complicated, highly independent and require high-level information to alter the entities of the network.

The existing programming languages are not appropriate for both the requirements. In a perfect world, the reflections of the upcoming programming languages for cyber physical computing ought to spin straight around environmental components (like physical entities, actions, accomplishments and information sources). These languages must have unequivocal backing for the representation of vulnerability as first class deliberation.

Case in point, there may or may be a typical object in an object-oriented language. Interestingly, an object that characterizes an external entity, (for example, traced vehicle) may be connected with a certainty level that depicts how probable it is that this object really exists in the outside world. New programming languages must be intended to help these required deliberations (Abdelzaher, 2006).

Software Engineering Challenges

The enhanced interconnection of heterogeneous data systems and the expanded dependence on distributed data processing provide more open doors for functional and timing lapses because of integration of increasingly more number of components into complex data handling systems. The enhanced software robustness is a great concern of latest software engineering training. Though, it is more concentrated on centralized or clustered systems. The new challenges due to distribution are imposed in enormously distributed embedded systems in the fields of software engineering and in real-time assurances. Guaranteeing convenience and robustness of such systems in the vicinity of bugs, programming related failures, and complex timing communications will be one of the basic concerns of cyber physical computing (Abdelzaher, 2006).

Data Management Challenges

The enhanced independence of forthcoming systems infers that information mining and machine learning procedures will assume a vital part in such systems to recognize data patterns, identify complicated distributed signatures of measures of concern, and by and large perform without human help. This has critical consequences on the outline of network protocols and programming abstractions. Reusable machines will be required to manage information administration procedures in lossy, perhaps versatile, inadequately organized situations (Abdelzaher, 2006).

Privacy and Security Challenges

In forthcoming cyber physical systems, the security concerns must be satisfied and security ought to be guaranteed. The communication with a distributed physical environment builds the threats (e.g., the potential physical harm because of a security rupture) and provides new chances (e.g., the utilization of physical information to legitimate nodes or identify intruders). Protection and security instruments must be an essential fraction of the upcoming models and not an after-thought (Abdelzaher, 2006).

Promising Innovations and Abstractions

Taking signal from the accomplishment of the web and given the progressively distributed nature of the imagined, implanted, self-governing, cyber physical systems, layered design is required to structure the improvement of forthcoming systems. Wide-region test beds, for example, GENI may demonstrate influential for research with cutting edge cyber physical processing protocols. The operation of the cyber physical system distributed "protocol stack" will be more extensive than that of general communication stacks. It may incorporate the novelties and deliberations (Abdelzaher, 2006).

An Information-Centric Protocol Stack

Impending systems will emphasize around raising data abstractions beside communication pathways (from sensors to purchasers). Subsequently, raw information that enters the system will be slowly changed over to noteworthy abnormal state application-particular data that may be utilized for prompt action or learning.

Adaptable backing is required for system storing and in-system transforming. The stress on information storage and synthesis as essential system procedures obliges reconsidering of basic system protocols, for example, those for congestion control. Case in point, in a system of storage nodes that perform transforming on live and stored information, a basic resource becomes storage size (and CPU power) rather than just communication bandwidth. "Congestion" ought to thusly consider exhaustion of these resources, which is not essentially the same as transmission capacity overutilization (Abdelzaher, 2006).

Environmentally-Immersive Middleware

Services are needed for simple structure of complex information fusion principles actualized by the system for higher-level applications. No less than two distinctive information combination purposes ought to be backed. The principal is to recognize and consistently signify physical environmental entities from distributed sensory signatures. The second is to gather and trace distributed entity state. New object-oriented middleware is required to help entities that characterize elements in the physical world (Abdelzaher, 2006).

Integration Analysis Tools

Software such as schedulability analyzers and basic design instruments required to be built to authorize and break down distributed end-to-end system characteristics of complex cyber physical systems, for example, their timing, security, dependability, and robustness to disasters.

The primary need towards cost-effective distributed cyber physical system outline and advancement is to create and coordinate the aforementioned protocols, middleware administrations, and devices into a typical architecture with layered, reusable, secure, deficiency confining segments. In this respect, a 5-year milestone may be a GENI-based execution of such architecture, and a 10-year point of reference could be making an interpretation of it into a typical state of practice on a new Internet and its supporting administrations (Abdelzaher, 2006).

Since several problems associated with common security research challenges, RETC-CPS (Run-time Enhancement of Trusted Computing - Cyber Physical System) protection scheme is applied. RETC-CPS is supported by prototype developments illustrating scheme efficacy. Problems are as listed below:

1. Securing a reconfiguration control of a dynamically reconfigurable system containing untrusted components. Validating various update requests issued by untrusted components and authenticating update contents delivered via open communication channels is a challenge associated with this problem.
2. Tolerating Hardware Trojan Horses (HTHs) in third-party IP cores used in CPS hardware platforms.

Detecting anomalous behavior of untrusted components treated as black boxes and enforcing appropriate countermeasures in response is a challenge associated with this problem.

3. Mitigating cyber threats to process controllers containing untrusted components.

Detecting erroneous behavior introduced by potential cyber threats and preempting their effects to preserve the controlled physical process stability is a challenge associated with this problem.

These are the security challenges commonly arise in computing platforms containing untrusted software and hardware components.

A major challenge associated with any security solution is evaluating it not only in terms of performance and overhead, but also in terms of trust and security. The security architectures are evaluated by presenting specific threat models, developing test benches generating these models, and validating the RETC capability to mitigate these threats. The presented threat models are associated with either state-of-the-art cyber threats or novel zero-day attacks. The RETC-CPS protection scheme is also evaluated in terms of performance degradation, induced overheads, verifiability, automation applicability, trust locality, and attainable trust.

PROTOCOL STACK ARCHITECTURE

CPS is a combination of numerous and distinctive systems that observe physical objects and events, including WSNs, systems that depend on RFID, cellular telephones, and so on.

Forthcoming enormously networked embedded systems need latest principles for attaining interoperability. The challenge is to establish a global network that interconnects all cyber physical systems and gives a plug-and-play service to the clients in a totally transparent manner. Hence, it is important to reconsider the present networking deliberations to guarantee an overall interoperability of cyber physical systems. This necessity forces the design and the advancement of latest consistent protocols for cyber physical systems. Considering the properties of nature's domain, where the CPS will be installed, these protocols have been intended.

The design of the cyber physical Internet tended to the fundamental limits of protocol stack model of IP and the WSN. Along these lines, it is important to offer an enhanced protocol stack model for CPS that additionally coordinates the characteristics of the physical environments. Figure 2 represent the potential reference architecture for the CPI (Koubâa & Andersson, 2009).

The architecture of protocol stack for CPI ought to incorporate an extra layer, the Cyber-Physical Layer (CY-PHY layer), which gives a theoretical depiction of the properties and nature of cyber physical information. This layer ought to give the set of protocols to unanimously exemplify information in an integrated and organized way. Moreover, the CY-PHY layer ought to give services to protocols of lower layer to support an effective cross layer design of the core application and communication protocols. This implies that protocols of all layers need to adjust their conduct as per the data gave by the CY-PHY layer.

For example, in the perspective of health care monitoring, the data gave by the body sensors will have a noteworthy effect on the performance of the set of protocols intended for this application. Actually, based on the category and the way of cyber physical information, numerous progressions may be forced in the protocol layers, specifically:

Physical Layer

The information from the CY-PHY layer can prompt modification in few characteristics of

Figure 2. Protocol stack architecture for CPI

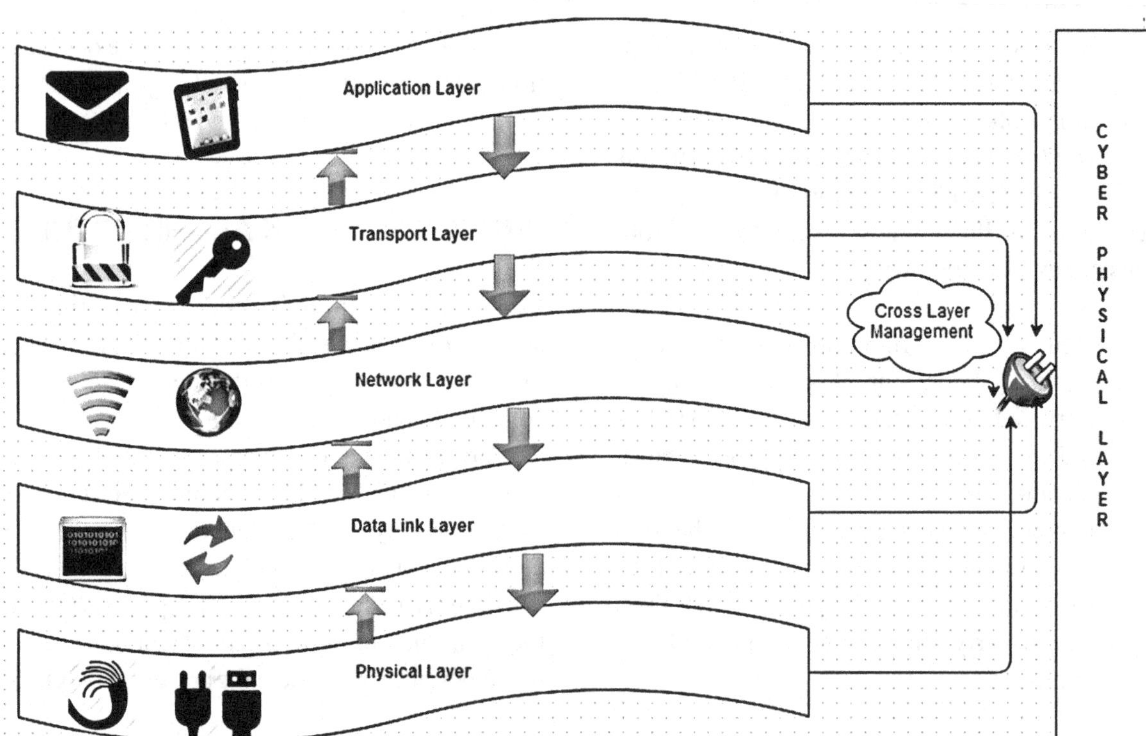

the physical channel, for example, the channel frequency range and the modulation pattern relying upon the prerequisites of the cyber physical information. It might be considered that some frequency ranges could be assigned for significant cyber physical communication utilizing powerful modulation techniques. There have been extraordinary developments in radio technologies with the design of software radios and cognitive radios, which offer better adaptability to adjusting radio features to the client necessities (Koubâa & Andersson, 2009).

Medium Access Layer

The MAC layer offers various functional approaches like synchronous or asynchronous and services for protocols of higher-layer, distinctive levels of Quality-of-Service (QoS), energy management services (e.g. duty cycle) and so forth (Koubâa & Andersson, 2009). In CPS, the vibrant behavior of the environment will fundamentally affect the functional behavior of the MAC layer, which must be versatile to the CY-PHY information.

For example, the choice to change from synchronous functional approach to unsynchronized approach (or the other way around) or the adjustment of the duty cycle must be determined by a CY-PHY layer. This might be attained by certain current innovations like the IEEE 802.15.4 protocol, which provide the signal-enabled mode (synchronized) and the non-signal empowered mode (unsynchronized) in its MAC layer. This collaboration between the MAC layer and CY-PHY layer is exceptionally vital to empower a close-loop control of the QoS coordinated with the status of the monitored environment (Koubâa & Andersson, 2009).

Network Layer

The Network Layer gives routing and data aggregation services. The cross-layer cooperation between the Network Layer and the CY-PHY Layer is important to characterize the ample routing techniques and data aggregation tools. For instance, the aggregation procedures capacities utilized for handling temperature data would be totally dissimilar from those utilized for accelerometer or bio-medicinal sensory information. Furthermore, the choice of the routing system or the factors influencing a given routing protocol may rely on the type of the information and furthermore from the status of the environment (Koubâa & Andersson, 2009).

Transport Layer

Transport protocols have not been broadly explored for CPS, despite the fact that it is of a fundamental significance to point out distinctive degrees of reliability pertaining to the end-to-end transfer of information. This commonly suggests three traditional assignments in the transport layer comprising (Koubâa & Andersson, 2009):

- Reliable transport,
- Flow control, and
- Congestion control mechanisms.

The Internet as of now provides the connection based TCP and connectionless UDP transport protocols for providing ensured and best-power services, correspondingly. These protocols are not appropriate for CPS applications, which elevate the requirement to consider about new transport protocol that adapts up to the prerequisites and possessions of CPS. Designing reliable transport protocols without the necessity to send back acknowledgements to the source nodes to elude obscuring the system with expanding control traffic is a true challenge with respect to transport protocols.

Application Layer

The application layer is in charge of transforming information and mining valuable data as for the application goals. One of the primary difficulties is to give typical distributed signal processing procedures for every impending CPS applications. This will support the improvement of CPS applications and diminish the time-to-market and cost (Koubâa & Andersson, 2009).

CPS INTERCONNECTION PROTOCOL

More extraordinary persistent cyber physical systems are evolving, for example, mobile tracing and health care system, ecological observing systems, and building maintenance control frameworks as the wireless communication and embedded computing expertise have begun to advance. In these frameworks, heterogeneity is a central investigation issue. To empower standard communication among these frameworks, novel communication paradigm CPS-IP is suggested with a system integrated in it. The objective is to aid the production of systems where there is a coordination of countless physical information sources, actuators, and computing components. It is moderately altered from the Internet Protocol which is intended for a huge scale, broadly useful systems.

CPS-IP is intended for exceptional persistent CPS systems developed on significant framework which needs worldwide guideline and performance confirmation for cyber physical communication. The innovation of the design is that it discourses heterogeneity of CPS systems at three separate levels (Lin, He, & Stankovic, 2008):

- Function interoperability,
- Policy regulation, and
- Performance assurance.

Introduction

Cyber physical systems are made by consolidating advances from numerous diverse fields, for example, remote sensor systems, embedded systems, control theory, and real-time systems. Conversely, the majority of the key innovations in these fields are frequently free from each other. The absence of communication backing for systems constrains the blast of study and technology. To empower collaboration among discrete systems, it is crucial to outline a standard communication paradigm that addresses the vital concerns for cyber physical systems.

Developing cyber physical systems have three exceptional requirements that oblige an upgrade of interconnection protocols:

1. **Resource Constraints:** Many of the components that are utilized in cyber physical system avoid the usage of complicated IP-type protocols because of their inadequate memory, ability to compute and dynamism.
2. **Special-Purpose Constraints:** The cyber physical systems are introduced for significant applications which have strong connection with physical phenomenon together with mobility. Such applications need powerful frameworks and real-time responses. There are additional spatial-temporal obligations also. IP as universally useful protocol do not address these problems.
3. **Function Interaction Constraints:** There is a unique two way data exchange in cyber physical systems: every subsystem gives information and control interfaces to cyber physical association. Decentralized and distributed control loops might be framed amongst distinctive subsystems. Along these lines, it is vital to have a unique persistent open outline for interconnection of cyber physical systems.

CPSs Interconnection Protocol (CPS-IP)

The data-oriented communication paradigm, CPS-IP is built for cyber physical systems. Connecting two heterogeneous CPS subsystems flawlessly is the main objective of CPS-IP. CPS frameworks oblige distinctive levels of extraordinary persistence help other than negligible interconnection. Thus, a structure is proposed which is integrated with CPS-IP. The innovation of the methodology lies in a three level design (Lin et al., 2008) as shown in Figure 3.

The function operability which needs the adaptable and reliable composition of heterogeneous parts and subsystems jointly at the technical, syntactic and semantic level is the basic level objective of the design. The CPS-IP is intended to accomplish this objective. It is an abnormal concept, afar negligible network that empowers an exceptional persistent open design for operation interoperability among CPS subsystems (Lin et al., 2008).

The strategy guideline which needs that specific standards are adapted at heterogeneous components of CPS frameworks claimed by distinctive vested parties to guarantee performance and asset imparting, protection and security is the second level objective of the design.

The third-level objective of design is the execution affirmation which obliges uniform performance through diverse subsystems irrespective to the heterogeneous physical and system environments. The initial phase to address this challenge is an exceptional system, merging distributed response control and reflective interfaces (Lin et al., 2008).

Design of CPS-IP

CPS frameworks ought to have an extraordinary persistence open framework outline to operation interoperability with the criticalness given to the cyber physical communication. To attain this objective, distributed correspondence paradigm

Figure 3. CPS levels of heterogenity

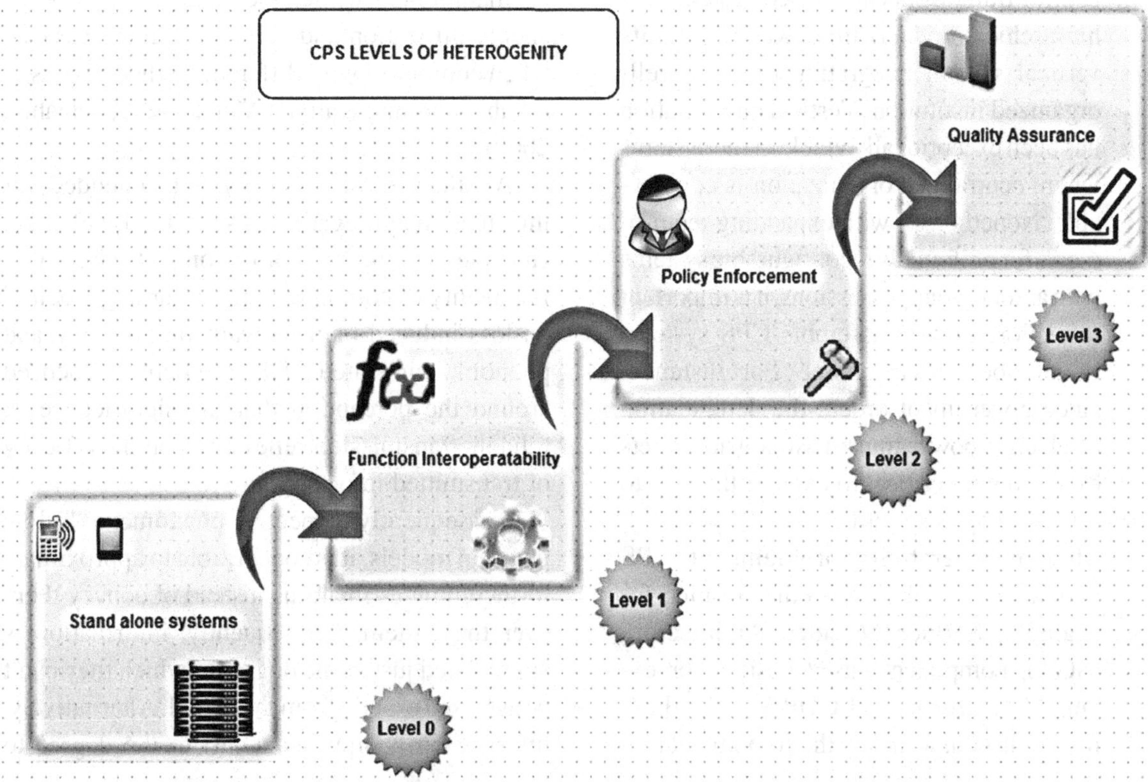

is suggested. The current results in the web and in distributed framework innovation can't be utilized specifically for three significant reasons (Lin et al., 2008):

1. Primarily, the Internet is usually viewed as a general purpose system. A single technology which is used to integrate everything is IP. High-level of differences and adaptability, which is precisely the configuration objective of the Internet is permitted by general purpose systems. Alternatively, CPS systems are considered as system with distinctive persistence. Because of security, strength and lawful issues, it would tolerate substantial threat to construct national power grids and worldwide gas pipeline frameworks on top of a general purpose structure. This extraordinary persistent feature presents the requirement to design an abnormal state deliberation over the simple network as delivered by IP technology.
2. The conventional distributed sensing and control frameworks are sealed system with hierarchical ownerships, which permits vertical system integration through well-organized institution. Vertical coordination has been exceptionally viable in the systems where centralized organization is conceivable. Nonetheless, with expanding requirements for profoundly reconfigurable systems with autonomous possessions, it is important to explore how to assemble CPS systems in an open environment. For instance, since government orders the deregulation of electric power transmission grid, it gets exceptionally critical to explore the way to assemble open systems.
3. The interoperability problems of CPS systems are unlike from other results, for example, Service Oriented Architecture (SOA), component based design, for example, JavaBeans and CORBA. All these results discourse mostly the communication between the computing methods with no attention on cyber physical communication. The significant innovations of CPS-IP are in (Lin et al., 2008):
    a. Robust and secure CPS-IP control,
    b. Transparency in information exchange and control loop formation, and
    c. Resolvability in the CPS structure.

TRANSPORT PROTOCOL SERVICES

A new transport protocol is utilized for information gathering within sensor networks that observes physical phenomena. In a system with flexible channel settings, this protocol adjusts transmission reliability depending on the essentialness of transmitted spatial-temporal information to the reestablishment of the phenomenon. Information whose oversight produces a higher estimation faults are communicated with added consistency. The protocol aggregates information from nodes to the base station giving a consistent expected estimation fault while essentially decreasing the energy utilization and communication overhead when contrasted with different methodologies to reliable communication (Ahmadi & Abdelzaher, 2009).

Another transport protocol is intended for information aggregation in sensor networks that characterizes the level of (incomplete) unwavering quality of communication regarding a bound on loss-induced fault in evaluating the physical phenomenon stated. The protocol is focused around the perception that the significance of reliable transmission relies on upon the efficacy of transmitted information.

Subsequently expected phenomena follow physical models, it is conceivable to approximate forthcoming estimations instead of convey them over the system. Consequently, information is appreciated just to the degree to which they can't be assessed exactly from the model. Alternatively, information is significant just to the degree to which they diminish model approximation fault. Transport protocol limits the general incorrectness of sensing the physical environment in an untrustworthy system. The anticipated fault limit might be selected by the client. A zero-fault protocol indicates a fully reliable transmission.

Improving transport to the exclusive features of sensor systems has gotten a great deal of consideration in past. There are numerous reliable sensor system protocols that ensure conventional end-to-end packet delivery. Likewise, there have been earlier efforts to present new unwavering quality semantics for information transport in observing applications. These former methodologies have two significant shortcomings like:

1. Have just restricted information of the actual significance of an information packet from the application point of view, and
2. Usually depend on response from the recipient to adjust the number of packets transmitted. The second problem is a result of the chief, and forces communication overhead on the system.

There has been a great deal of work in sensor systems on versatile testing of a physical environment to give a faultless estimation with the least number of samples. Additionally, numerous works address information lessening utilizing forecast models. Specifically, these plans transmit data just in the event that it can't be acquired from physical models exactly.

The main contrast between information lessening strategies and protocols is that these protocols consider reliable communication and henceforth the choice as to which packets are to destroy is totally up to the protocol. Conversely, a reliable medium is not expected and just impacts the packet delivery possibilities where channel fatalities eventually determine the transmission of packets. This stochastic quality presented by an unreliable medium has not been tended to in any information lessening procedure (Ahmadi & Abdelzaher, 2009).

Another transport protocol for wireless sensor networks that uses an indicated bound on approximation lapse as a metric to define the quantity of data to be reliably transmitted. It is referred as cyber-physical in light of the fact that it considers the physical significance of packets holding spatial-temporal measurement information. The primary thought is to favorably retransmit and thus improve the likelihood delivery of packets that considerably enhance reestablishment of the approximated phenomenon. This is possible without worldwide data while accomplishing the global limited fault necessity. The protocol attains the anticipated approximation fault with the minimum energy utilization without response from the base station or without nodes being synchronization. Prevention of response is imperative on the grounds that it diminishes communication overhead and permits the protocol to be connected to extremely vibrant phenomena, where the former is not a noble sign and response system can't effortlessly alleviate (Ahmadi & Abdelzaher, 2009).

The protocol is realized in Liteos on Micaz motes and thoroughly assesses its behavior through test-bed tests. It is experimentally exhibited that the protocol surely gives the demanded reliability. At the point when the protocol is looked in contradiction of packet level reliability, response dependent, and transport protocols that are not reliable, this protocol demonstrates that an incredible measure of energy is saved at the cost of generating a minute fault in the result.

The transport protocol is intended to run on top of a system comprising of a set of sensors and a base station installed to observe a physical phenomenon. It is supposed that sensors perform evaluations and send the estimations to the base station for processing. Transmitting monitoring data reliably to the base station is the purpose of the transport protocol. Since numerous WSN routing protocols are based on tree structure, it is supposed that packets could be routed up and down the tree established at the base station. On the other hand, the protocols can effort with any common routing protocol by upholding tree data in transport layer. The routing layer starts the transmission at intermediate nodes as similar to the destination (Ahmadi & Abdelzaher, 2009).

Numerous monitoring sensor systems are intended to reestablish a physical phenomenon at the base station. Each perception from any specific sensor at a particular time is signified as a sampling point in space and time. In the transport layer, if the wireless link fails to receive the update message, then the transmission reliability is adjusted focused around the measure of approximation fault added. The probable value of approximation fault is utilized as the reliability metric. Alternatively, if the approximation fault is ensured to be limited by an anticipated constant at any time, then the transport protocol is said to be reliable.

It is connection-oriented protocol where each connection includes a part of contributing nodes in the network and helps gathering information from these nodes to the same base station. Similar to the other transport protocols, the connection is established using listen and connect procedures. The sensors which are participating in observing on the given port initiates the connect procedure whereas the base station initiates the listen procedure (Ahmadi & Abdelzaher, 2009).

Ports are represented using port numbers and are helpful in discriminating the applications that are being executed on the network. The approximation fault and the tolerable value of approximation fault that the protocol must ensure need to be specified by the base station during the initial stage of connection setup. Additionally, the model parameters which are to represent the physical model of the phenomenon are also provided by application sometimes. The linear Auto-Regressive Moving Average (ARMA) models are supported by the protocol. The transport protocol supposes deliberately varying information if it is provided with a model.

The transport layer offers a particular send procedure for sensor information, called send information, to send spatial-temporal evaluations to the base station. The spatial-temporal data payload has a particular format: It holds a cluster of estimations each preceded by a header including a timestamp, a data type ID, and sampling rate (Ahmadi & Abdelzaher, 2009).

Case in point, payload can hold all the readings from the temperature sensor of the node during a particular period of time. While utilizing this procedure, a somewhat distinctive kind of the estimations may be sent back by the receive procedure at the base station. On the other hand, the aggregate difference is ensured not to surpass the estimation of the tolerable approximate fault defined in the listen call. Regular send function is also provided with a specific end goal to send other subjective information (e.g., send control data). Its payload is transmitted with 100% reliability. At the end, the base station closes the connection using close function.

Enumerating the significance of a packet and organizing the transmissions to limit the global approximation fault is the primary challenge in the design of a cyber physical transport protocol with energy effectiveness. The principle objective is to preserve the energy with no communication overhead. Besides, the design ought to have the capacity to handle common packets with 100% reliability. A probabilistic transmission approach must be selected utilizing neighborhood choices to ensure the consequential fault in anticipated value sense (Ahmadi & Abdelzaher, 2009).

CPI can be defined as the physical world merging with the virtual principal to an Internet of things, data and services. CPS is embedded systems, using sensors, monitor, and collect data from physical processes, like:

1. Steering of a vehicle,
2. A production line,
3. Human health functions, and
4. Energy consumption.

The systems are networked making data globally available. Software applications can directly interact with events in the physical world, e. g. in autonomous driving, intelligent manufacturing, or smart health and energy systems.

The functionality and the affordability of automobiles, medical apparatus, domestic appliances, production plants, airplane, etc., are significantly enhanced by the embedded hardware and software systems. New fields of research and new commercial platforms will be started by interfacing these systems to a virtual environment of globally networked services and data systems. Cyber Physical Systems have the capability of turning into a problematic innovation, are multidisciplinary and exceed traditional industry sectors.

Future CPS will contribute to security, effectiveness, ease and human health, and help resolving crucial difficulties of general public, for example, the ageing people, inadequate resources, versatility, mobility or the transferral in the direction of renewable energies (http://www.eitictlabs.eu/fileadmin/files/docs/Action_Lines/Cyber-Physical_Systems.pdf).

The cyber physical systems have computations which are profoundly embedded and communications with physical processes. The time-scale of physical methods and computation methods are fundamentally diverse. Physical methods may influence the cyber component in unpredicted means. Appropriateness, protection, reliability, security, confidentiality, and flexibility all yield on an alternate eccentric.

CONCLUSION

The way the humans communicate with the physical world and the way they control it is changes by the cyber physical systems. Zero-vitality structures and urban communities, great profit cultivation, near-zero locomotive victims, never-ending life helpers, medical care irrespective of the location, circumstance conscious physical critical infrastructure, outage free power, and safe migration from unsafe zones are yet some of the numerous societal profits that CPS will offer.

CPS is a society-scale system in which a fault tolerance has to be built in. All the data collected from the sensor-actuator systems in CPS need to be processed efficiently. For this, there should be Techniques to ensure the results can be visualized easily by users. IP is the standard protocol which plays the important part in the forthcoming Cyber-Physical Internet. IP has been thought, since the conception of the sensor system prototype, as being incompatible with the necessities of sensor-based networks. In any case, this idea has been newly reconsidered and with the rise of 6LoWPAN that implants Ipv6 on top of the IEEE 802.15.4 as a substitute to Zigbee Network Layer.

It is vital that operating systems backs real time anyway. It actuates added design intricacy. The principle test is to accomplish an ideal stability between a few imperative characteristics required by a CPS operating system, comprising modularity, compelling equipment/programming part, hardware abstraction, energy proficiency, and real time. The most broadly utilized operating system, Tiny OS, signifies a guaranteeing answer for CPS as it addresses the greater part of those necessities. Conversely, the deficiency of real time backing characterizes a severe impediment in Tiny OS for developing real time protocols and synchronization mechanisms.

From the networking point of view, real-time forces few difficulties which are yet open to investigate. One of the exciting research issues is to allocate the sufficient distributed and adaptive resources in synchronized multi-hop sensor networks by considering physical/logical alterations in the network. In synchronized WSNs, Resource (memory, bandwidth) allocation to dynamic sensor nodes which are a part of serious responsibilities is considered to be more proficient.

A language which can be used by the clients to describe their queries and input to the network is required to be outlined. As of now, marginally altered versions of SQL are being used in the communication process of wireless sensor networks. In any case, the altered versions of SQL are not adequately communicative. To address the deficits of current systems, various challenges are dealt by globally interconnected networks of embedded devices

Forthcoming enormously networked embedded systems need latest principles for attaining interoperability. The challenge is to establish a global network that interconnects all cyber physical systems and gives a plug-and-play service to the clients in a totally transparent manner. Hence, it is important to reconsider the present networking deliberations to guarantee an overall interoperability of cyber physical systems. This necessity forces the design and the advancement of latest consistent protocols for cyber physical systems. CPS-IP is intended for exceptional persistent CPS systems developed on significant framework which needs worldwide guideline and performance confirmation for cyber physical communication. The data-oriented communication paradigm, CPS-IP is built for cyber physical systems. Connecting two heterogeneous CPS subsystems flawlessly is the main objective of CPS-IP.

A new transport protocol is utilized for information gathering within sensor networks that observes physical phenomena. Another transport protocol is intended for information aggregation in sensor networks that characterizes the level of (incomplete) unwavering quality of communication regarding a bound on loss-induced fault in evaluating the physical phenomenon stated. One another transport protocol for wireless sensor networks that uses an indicated bound on approximation lapse as a metric to define the quantity of data to be reliably transmitted. The transport protocol is intended to run on top of a system comprising of a set of sensors and a base station installed to observe a physical phenomenon. It is supposed that sensors perform evaluations and send the estimations to the base station for processing.

REFERENCES

Abdelzaher, T. (2006). Towards an architecture for distributed cyber-physical systems. In *Proceedings of the 2006 National Science Foundation Workshop on Cyber-Physical Systems*. Academic Press.

Ahmadi, H., & Abdelzaher, T. (2009, December). An adaptive-reliability cyber-physical transport protocol for spatio-temporal data. In *Proceedings of Real-Time Systems Symposium*, (pp. 238-247). IEEE. doi:10.1109/RTSS.2009.45

Farag, M. M., Lerner, L. W., & Patterson, C. D. (2012, June). Interacting with hardware Trojans over a network. In *Proceedings of Hardware-Oriented Security and Trust* (HOST), (pp. 69-74). IEEE. doi:10.1109/HST.2012.6224323

Koubâa, A., & Andersson, B. (2009, July). A vision of cyber-physical internet. In *Proc. of the Workshop of Real-Time Networks* (RTN 2009). RTN.

Lin, S., He, T., & Stankovic, J. A. (2008). CPS-IP: Cyber physical systems interconnection protocol. *ACM SIGBED Review*, *5*(1), 22. doi:10.1145/1366283.1366305

Xia, F., Ma, L., Dong, J., & Sun, Y. (2008, July). Network QoS management in cyber-physical systems. In *Proceedings of Embedded Software and Systems Symposia*, (pp. 302-307). IEEE. doi:10.1109/ICESS.Symposia.2008.84

ADDITIONAL READING

Aissa, A. B., Abercrombie, R. K., Sheldon, F. T., & Mili, A. (2012). Defining and computing a value based cyber-security measure. *Information Systems and e-Business Management, 10*(4), 433-453.

Akella, R., Tang, H., & McMillin, B. M. (2010). Analysis of information flow security in cyber–physical systems. *International Journal of Critical Infrastructure Protection, 3*(3), 157–173. doi:10.1016/j.ijcip.2010.09.001

Dahleh, M. A., Frazzoli, E., Megretski, A., Mitter, S. K., Ozdaglar, A. E., Parrilo, P. A., & Shah, D. (2006), Information and control: A BRIDGE between the physical and decision layers, *NSF Workshop in Cyber-Physical Systems.*

Lee, E. A. (2006, October). Cyber-physical systems-are computing foundations adequate. In Position Paper for NSF Workshop On Cyber-Physical Systems: Research Motivation, Techniques and Roadmap (Vol. 2).

Lee, E. A. (2008, May). Cyber physical systems: Design challenges. In Object Oriented Real-Time Distributed Computing (ISORC), 2008 11th IEEE International Symposium on (pp. 363-369). IEEE.

KEY TERMS AND DEFINITIONS

ARMA: Auto-Regressive Moving Average (ARMA) is a linear model supported by CPS protocol.

CPI: Cyber Physical Internet.

CPS-IP: CPS Interconnection Protocol to interconnect heterogeneous CPS subsystems faultlessly.

CY-PHY: Cyber-Physical Layer an additional layer which gives conceptual description of the properties and type of cyber physical data.

HTH: Hardware Trojan Horse is a threat embedded in the hardware of a system.

RETC-CPS: Run-time Enhancement of Trusted Computing - Cyber Physical System.

RFID: Radio-Frequency Identification.

SOA: Service Oriented Architecture.

Chapter 6
Network QoS in CPS

ABSTRACT

Wireless Sensor Actuator Networks (WSANs) perform a vital role in CPS. This chapter describes the key features of WSANs and the necessities of QoS provisioning in the perception of cyber physical computing. Network Quality of Service (QoS) is one of the research issues that is focused on in wide way. To address the challenges identified, a feedback scheduling framework is explained in the latter part of this chapter. It is a difficult task to satisfy end-to-end QoS requirements in CPSs. To overcome this, a model-driven middleware called NetQoPE is used to protect the application designers from the complications of programming at lower level CPU and by streamlining network QoS mechanisms. The chapter shows how in applications of CPS NetQoPE offers QoS guarantee.

INTRODUCTION

Quality of Service (QoS) is a network service obtainable for a particular network transfer based on available dissimilar technologies and the specified utilizations can come upon its service requirements. QoS force essential processes of network connections and the ability to control the accepted traffic. The principal goal of QoS is to provide priority including dedicated bandwidth, controlled jitter and latency during interactive traffic and absence of characteristics. QoS methods used for potential campus industry applications, networks service provider and Wide Area Network (WAN) to supply the vital blocks of building. There is no specific description for QoS. But from the communication point of view, there are several definitions that describe time independent technical characteristics for transmission of data. A promising set of connections can afford QoS assurance for Continuous Media (CM) data transfer with delay and bandwidth.

QoS for networks is a wide range of industry oriented regulations and procedures. Network QoS is applied in critical applications to ensure great performance quality. Network supervisors can utilize QoS methods with the existing resources capably and also used to obtain an expected stage of service passively or equipping their networks.

When the network traffic behaves uniformly then it is referred as network quality. The best endeavour of network is given to the network transmission with no assurance for interruption, distinction in delay, consistency or other

DOI: 10.4018/978-1-4666-7312-0.ch006

implementation characteristics. In most of the applications to have a good service provision, the management of the necessary bandwidth functioning is acceptable. However, the consequence of an application with one bandwidth implementation is deprived or improper for other applications. In Quality of Service, quality means applications and customer requirements are crucial compared to other users. In other words management of traffic needs an improvement. The Quality of Service is an innovative area in the field of the networking. There are more services that are given to the users. The quality of those services is very essential in the field of networking.

Applications with various continuous functionalities are Cyber physical systems (CPS) such as intelligent buildings, security systems, network control, self-reliance medical devices and systems. These applications operate in resource constrained location and have untrustworthy Quality-of-Service (QoS) needs focused by the physical location changes in which they function. In the area of the CPS, the computer networking or parallel and distributed systems and other packet-switched networks, the mechanized transmission submits to resource condition management procedures rather than the service quality that is being achieved. Quality of service is the capability to afford diverged precedence to data flow, customers or to confirm performance certainty to a data stream. Quality of service assurance is important if the network facility is inadequate in fixed bit rate applications like real-time multimedia broadcasting such as Voice over Internet Protocol (VoIP), web based apps and Internet Protocol television.

In the CPS, either protocol with QoS or connections structure may consent on a traffic convention with the function software and hold back network nodes capability like in a session founding stage. The accomplished performance of a node like delay and speed of data is observed throughout this phase. And also vigorously manage network nodes scheduling priority. Throughout the slash down stage, it may discharge the detained reserve ability.

The Quality of Service is not maintained by process or network. By offering best connections above the network effort by providing great facility is a substitute to compound QoS control method. In a likely high traffic stack, it is satisfactory. The requirements for QoS procedures reduce the consequent absence of network jamming.

In CPS the Quality of Service is measured as quality with different classifications relatively directing ability to retain property. Quality of service occasionally directs to the level of quality of service, i.e. the definite examine excellence. Elevated QoS is frequently confused with a great accomplishment level or attained examine quality such as low latency, low bit error and high bit rate possibly.

A different and questionable meaning of QoS based on the CPS, the process of application layer used such as broadcasting video and telecommunication services, is necessities on a calculation that replicate or expects the personally qualified quality. In this situation, QoS is a suitable growing outcome on subscriber consent of all flaws disturbing the service. Other terminologies with the same meaning are the Quality of Practice (QoP), in a personal business concept "customer perceived performance" and the required "degree of satisfaction of the user" or the targeted "number of happy customers".

BACKGROUND

Network QoS Management

The objectives and strategies of QoS are established and assessed by the QoS regulation. A widespread approach implies the subsequent steps:

- Remote network MONitoring (RMON) probes are the network based devices that assist in deciding the descriptions of network traffic. Also, the proposed QoS applications should be base lined with respect to reply time.
- Once the features of traffic have been acquired, QoS techniques should be arranged and improved QoS should have an application to be intended.
- Evaluate the results by testing the response of the targeted applications to see whether the QoS goals have been reached.

Advancement in technical areas of embedded computing, ubiquitous sensing and wireless transmission are foremost in a growth of engineered systems production that are referred as Cyber Physical Systems (CPS). Still more issues to be focused from the point of CPS, as this vision becomes a reality. An extended investigation study is required in the organization of network quality of service (QoS) in this emerging area. CPS view Wireless Sensor and/or Actuator Networks (WSANs) as an indispensable fragment of it.

In Network, the QoS management can be based on the policies. The network design is a most significant part in developing a CPS. In this segment, we initially observe the salient characteristics of networks and then examine the QoS requirements. The QoS can be implemented to different types of networks.

Wireless Sensor Actuator Networks (WSANs) are an emerging a novel invention of CPS network that features co-existence of CPS networks and actuators as in (Xia, 2008) (see Figure 1). In

Figure 1. Wireless sensor actuator networks

WSANs, based on the type of an application there may be a necessity to quickly reply to sensed data. Additionally, to provide exact actions, sensor data should be relevant at the time of acting. For this reason, the issue of real-time communication is very important in WSANs since actions are performed on the environment after sensing occurs.

An innovative conversion from unconnected self-reliant embedded systems to Cyber Physical Systems (CPSs) has originated. Methodological progress in computing, detecting and networking, mostly extremely embedded CPS association and wireless CPS networks or wireless actuator networks (WSANs), are accountable for this direction. As Cyber-physical systems unite networking and calculation with the physical motions, implanted devices are arranged to observe, detect and manage the physical environment. Since the amalgamation of calculation and physical operations is not innovative, CPS is considered to be the field yet to be discovered.

Current Cyber Physical Systems are less significant in dimension and difficulty compared to the predictable CPS of expectations. Primarily the transformation comes from considerable association of embedded processing devices such as CPS networks and controllers. This envisioned exchange of CPS will depict how there is interaction with the physical surroundings as internet perform the operation of exchanging data with one another. Networking will become a critical issue as there is a need of combining computing devices disseminated in nature and physical elements. To assist exceptional communications between individual and the physical world, WSANs will be implemented in a variety of CPS to serve as a primary network communication.

Network quality of service (QoS) supervision is a concern with the Cyber Physical Systems network design. CPS will be planned and assembled as dynamic contribution instead of building as a particular producer with directional restrictions on all boundaries. The fundamentals and manufacturing values deal with modularized and exposed CPS. Cyber Physical Systems need sufficient answers to these challenges from the incorporated perception of changes, instantaneous computing, control and transmission.

Network Characteristics

The primary objective of QoS is to present high service provision for the functions. These functions are required to make sure latency management, adequate bandwidth, controlling variations and fall of data loss. Table 1 expresses these network features (Xia, 2008).

The networks are broadly classified into two types: Local Area Networks (LANs) and Wide Area Networks (WANs). The WANs are also referred to as extended-haul networks. WAN measures the likelihood of the network being available to the users but sometimes network not available due to scheduled maintenance. Any network that is related to the CPS based on the QoS will have the characteristics which are closely related to QoS provisioning.

Following are a standard set of network characteristics used in grid applications and services.

- **Geographic Distribution:** It shows the difference between any two types of networks that are dispersed in nature. A LAN is constrained to a restricted to a area with an exposure of few kilometres, but WAN extend over greater space with an exposure of several thousand kilometres. For that reason LANs

Table 1. Network features managed by QoS

Network Features	Explanation
Bandwidth	Measurement of bit rate at transmission carried by the network.
Latency	Data transmission delay from source to destination.
Jitter	Variation in a packet transit delay.
Reliability	Proportion of packets rejected by a router.

provide services within the specified area where as WANs offer the services worldwide.

- **Data Transmission Rate:** Compared to WANs data transmission rates in LANs are to a large extent. The LANs data transmission rates vary from 0.2Mbps to 1Gbps. On the other hand, broadcast rates in WANs vary from 1200 bits per second to some extent over 1 Mbps.
- **Error Rate:** Normally LANs are less tolerant to data broadcasting errors than WANs perform. In general bit error rates are in the series of 10-8 to 10-10 with LANs as conflicting in the series of 10-5 to 10-7 with WAN.
- **Communication Link:** LANs uses widespread transmission links such as perverse set, fibre optic lines and coaxial wires. Conversely in WANs depending on the location that is disseminated physically over a huge geographic region the transmission links are used. The communication links used in WANs are means of communication, satellite stations, and microwave networks and these links are comparatively time-consuming and untrustworthy naturally.
- **Ownership:** Due to restricted topographical exposure, LAN is possessed by a particular group. Typically WAN designed by interconnecting various groups of LANs. Therefore LANs cost and complications of preservation and managerial are considerably lesser than of WANs.
- **Cost of Communication:** Comparatively the total communication costs of a LAN are lesser than of WAN usually. The key reason for this is error rates are low, forwarding procedures are easy and managerial and preservation costs are less. As the transmission channel is possessed by a particular group, the data transmission cost is insignificant in LAN. WAN has high data transmission cost as the transmission channels are of types leased line connections or other transmission lines such as phone routes, microwave networks and satellite stations.

The key factor is to classify numerous categories of network dimensions. Agreeing to the system characteristics, it assesses the network object on which it has been taken. This is a concept that had been applied in various grid systems which is necessity for the exchange of available dimensions. The considerations about system dimension description are retained in a collective glossary to ease it. In Grid Observing and Location Services, collective scheme is enabled to define network observing data and thus support to discuss manageability concerns among the wide varieties of network dimensions consumed amongst the locations of a grid.

The Network Measurement Working Group (NMWG) establishes functioning of network by concentrating on active and present dimensions applied. This section describes those measurements to define the regular terms. In grid applications the regular and novel measurement approaches are not defined properly. On the other hand, it enlightens the limitations and advantages various approaches of measurement. Due to restricted access at the hosts some of the tools of measurement are inclined while designing it.

The IETF Internet Protocol Performance Metrics (IPPM) working group is strongly associated with the working group of network measurement. These work groups focuses mainly on the designers of network procedures and ways to acquire measurements that are defined. Our objective is to find a complete system that can apply all types of measurements in practice and also considers the tools and applications of grid. The IPPM can be implemented wherever it is achievable.

In the grid environment, the NMWG is involved to improve appropriate schemes to empower the explanations that are to be available and recovered. It's a belief that the characteristics and entities of grid measurement community get a support of NMWG. However, there is an expectation that necessary modifications may be centred on the involvements acquired from the NMWG's effort and other applications centred on this order. Nets that distribute certain features of both LANs and WANs are usually denoted as Metropolitan Area Networks (MANs). The MANs regularly cover a broader geographical zone than LANs. MANs objective is to correlate LANs that are placed in a whole town or urban area. MANs frequently use coaxial wires and microwave connections as transmission links.

The Basic need for QoS-enable applications is to expect the development of ability constraints and be capable to indicate these necessities into the web. The separate service approach of admission control is required for the core network, so that it can specify the existing capacity situations to the structures of network access. The admission control uses admission-decision systems which comprised of service capacity and the existing net stack. The strategy factors of this network might agree to the prevention level of different admission determinations to meet high importance necessities of facility.

The signal and intervention part of QoS ranges into the inter-field area, where two or more repair suppliers jointly want to discuss adequate capability outlines and service associated access. In inter-domain routing protocols QoS covers the calculation of mutual settlements and includes the constraint to enhance QoS qualities too. The apparatus and operational methods are preferred to support this inadequately stated functionality to remain.

In a network management organization, it is promising to implement each energetic device inside a network so that element-by-element view cannot be easily converted to continuous view of function service presentation.

The main personalities of the networks with regard to the QoS are the portability, distinct collection, statelessness, navigation and cooperative channels. Any QoS explanation assumed must contain these features to a minor or larger scale.

QoS Requirements

The future vision is for wireless sensor/actuator networks (WSAN) turn into persistent in day today lives such as in residence, workplace and vehicles. They assure to change the approach things are managed in the physical world, just like the Internet transformed the world. Eventually, the contributed universal information is accomplished when it is linked with the Internet. To fulfil the various applications of service desires, WSANs are motivated to maintain QoS supply which is a practical tendency.

CPS familiarize with application by nature. Hence, the networks have to offer QoS hold up to fulfil the service desires of applications objective. From a customer point of view, the detailed necessities are located on the primary network connections of QoS applications in reality. For case, CPS networks at a suitable time inform the incidence of a fire to actuators in a fire handling system (Xia, 2008). QoS requirements differ from one application to another. For instance, in a safety-critical control system there is a huge delay while transmitting the data from the CPS networks to actuators. Moreover packet loss will not be allowed during the sequence of transmission. But packet loss is acceptable for any system which has the temperature insider an office. Conceptually assurance is given to provide fully satisfied service requirements for a system assumed. QoS is characterized based on the factors such as reliability, rightness, robustness, availability and security in the specified networks. There are certain parameters of QoS which are used to measure the processes such as variation in packet transit, performance of the system, interruption and rate of packet failure (Xia, 2008).

- **Throughput:** The active amount of data flow moved inside a assured interval of time is termed as throughput. In few situations it is stated as bandwidth. As the throughput of the network goes high, then will have the better performance of the system. The nodes which produce high speed data streams (Xia, 2008) like camera sensor nodes require high throughput to transmit images. The WSAN throughput is maximized to improve its resource efficiency.

- **Delay:** It is an elapsed time between the packet starting from the base node and the packet delivery at the target node. During this transmission the delay is calculated with respect to queuing, switching and propagation of a packet. WSANs transport the data packets in real time to the delay-sensitive applications. A real-time system is not a high-speed computation or communication (Xia, 2008) system but it will execute its process in a timely manner.
- **Jitter:** Variations in delay are generally referred as Jitter. When packets are transmitted consecutively then it experiences the difference in queuing delays.
- **Packet Loss Rate:** It is a network dependent parameter. The probability of packet loss during the packet transmission is referred as Packet Loss Rate. Usually packet loss occurs due to obstruction, improper connectivity or error bit rate.

As network performance depends on the fundamental transmission protocols applied. The transmission rules of network are well known and have the structure comprised of layers of type physical, data link, network, transport and application. Particular consideration has been given to navigation and transport protocols of Medium Access Control (MAC). In CPS based networking various efforts had been made to support QoS with the expansion of transmission protocols. WSANs routing and transport protocols are still considered as existing open issues related to QoS-aware MAC. Transmission protocols are planned to support QoS in networks for the service differentiation. This can be done by considering CPS networks and actuators heterogeneity that are concerned with the CPS. Due to this, the transport and navigation protocols of QoS-aware MAC vastly designed for WSNs are inappropriate for WSANs. Though CPS has different applications for each application it requires dissimilar QoS requirements. But the existing technologies of networking cannot offer unrelated QoS to dissimilar utilizations.

To assure a better service level, transmission protocols designed for WSANs should be able to identify the service constraint of data transfer. For a future a standard service is considered as a best-effort service. Therefore it is essential to have original QoS procedures to be leveled on top of the active networks. In CPS to develop QoS-aware network communication protocols and to optimize the network performance, an effective cross-layer design is required. More work can be done using this design like the ordering of transfer at lower levels might be connected with the implementation of function at the application layer. WSANs are a novel invention of CPS associations whereas Wireless Sensor Networks (WSNs) has an infrastructure in which passive information is gathered. When CPS is involved, WSANs are vigorous that it facilitates cyber systems to observe but also control the behaviour of physical humanity.

QoS Enforcement

QoS motivated resource supervision is used to support and provide QoS. While assigning resources, the resource control system needs to consider application's QoS requirements along with resource availability and resource control policies to be used. Whenever irregularities appear in a system reallocate the resources to support QoS and need to monitor QoS parameters also. The system must check for reliable QoS parameters before allocating resources to it. QoS parameters change dynamically and transferred between different layers, whenever there is change in the system. These layers move into dissimilar types of deals like certain, best-endeavour or analytical. As a result the application is determined when there is no intervention. Once the resources are allocated, the resource supervisor assurances the continuous accessibility of the allotted resources and also QoS mechanisms at each layer. This can be done only if resources accessibility and dynamic parameters are monitored effectively. The active parameters are measuring the workload process and network traffic and detecting variations in the QoS parameters. The application is notified about the level of change like gradual decrease in the QoS and the resource supervisor cannot make changes in resource allocation to rearrange collective resources to assure allotments. The application handlers are invoked to change application's QoS level to new level or to decrease it by a level.

QoS for CPS

In the future, Cyber Physical Systems composed of mobile computing devices will be connected through WSANs. This large number of embedded devices offers services to end users by establishing various independent systems. Universal data is shared by linking WSANs with the Internet. A CPS is defined as a collection of various subsystems. Cyber-physical city is an example for interconnection of different cyber-physical subsystems such as dedicated health care treatment, intelligent home, intellectual transport, maintenance of facilities and communal protection. Cyber Physical Systems are widespread in our daily life and in the disciplines of engineering and science such as manufacturing, farming, health care treatment, construction, armed forces, protection, natural science, ecology and geology (Xia, 2008).

Figure 2 as in (Xia, Ma, Dong, & Sun, 2008) depicts the physical topology of a Cyber Physical System. In CPS, WSANs act as a crossing point among the physical and cyber system. The physical

Figure 2. Physical topology of CPS

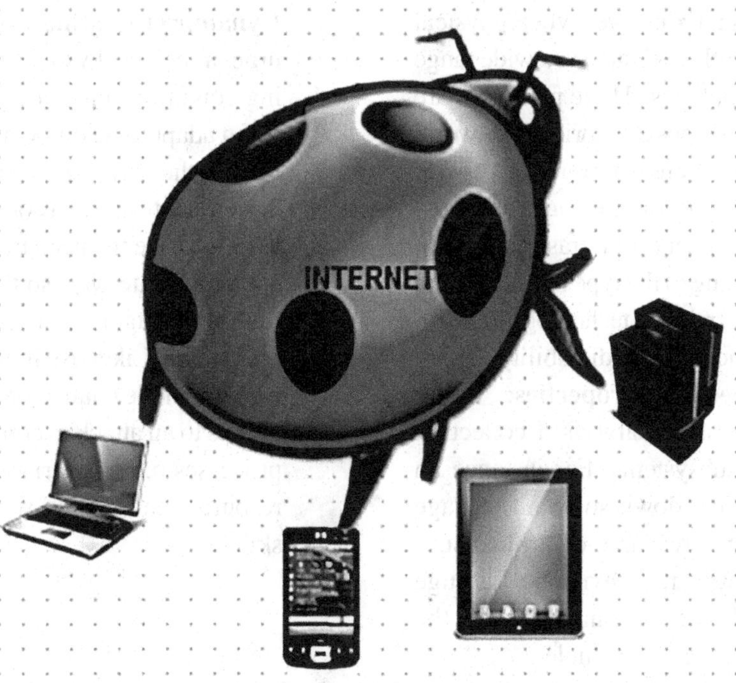

world data is collected by sensors, while actuators carry out reasonable actions by responding to this physical world information (see Figure 2). WSANs allow cyber systems to observe and control the behaviour of the physical world. Subsequently, the performance and functionality of CPS is always depending on the plan of these WSANs. The quality of life can be enhanced communicating with the environment with the help of ubiquitous CPS.

Cyber Physical Systems are measured by their intractable requests for Quality of Service (QoS), such as expected continuous latencies, scalability and correctness. Cyber Physical Systems provides QoS requirements to organize flawlessly and modify the connections utilize to host the CPS. And which engrave crosswise in various levels of networks, middleware, and operating systems. Cyber Physical systems combine with the values of Aspect-Oriented Software Design (AOSD) (Xia et al., 2008) to deal with the complicated configuration issues.

Following are the (Xia et al., 2008) allotted by Cyber Physical Systems for the development of complicated issues in the lifecycle growth and maintenance:

- **Heterogeneity:** Extensive cyber physical systems frequently executed on a wide range of computing policies. These platforms are interrelated by various categories of networking tools with different resources of QoS. Cyber physical systems are constructed using dissimilar elements of infrastructure that changes according to the type of operational platform and correlation technology to maintain its efficiency and predictability.
- **Deeply Embedded Properties:** Cyber Physical Systems are always a collection of implanted subsystems. For instance an anti-padlock slow down software manage system develop a resource-controlled subsystem. This system is division of a huge cyber physical function which controls the largely functioning of a vehicle.
- **Simultaneous Support for Multiple QoS Properties:** Many machine-driven and human control critical systems are replaced by Cyber physical software controllers. Concurrently these regulators must hold various demanding QoS constraints as well as real-time requirements. The real-time requirements are related to availability, low latency and bounded jitter, fault dissemination or retrieval across boundaries, protection requirements, proper confirmation and approval of physical requests, inadequate weight, power utilization and memory trace.
- **Large-Scale, Network-Centric Operation:** In disconnected and standalone configurations, it is not viable to organise the cyber physical systems scale and complexity. To overcome this, in different range of networks the functionality of cyber physical systems is partitioned and distributed. For example in an urban bio-terrorist evacuation capability networks connecting command and control centres with bio-sensors are used. This network is vastly distributed to collect data from police, hospitals and urban traffic management systems using bio-sensors.
- **Dynamic Operating Conditions:** In a significant cyber physical systems the operating conditions change dynamically so that it can adapt to resource management strategies for the successful process of the system. According to civilian contexts, power outages emphasize the need to identify failures in an appropriate way, so that it adapt in real-time to maintain mission-critical power grid operations. Likewise in military contexts, a mission mode change or loss of functionality due to an attack in combat actions. These processes require variation and continuous resource reallocation with mission-critical skills.

QoS Specification for CPS

As per user requirements an application constraint of QoS are represented in conditions of elevated level factors. Each system layer has dissimilar QoS specification which is used to specify QoS procedures at every layer. Following are the levels of system (Balasubramanian et al., 2010):

- Network and transport protocols,
- Set of network connections,
- Middleware,
- Tasks of operating system such as arrangement, resource supervision, and practical support,
- Disseminated platforms like devices, CPU, recollection, or storage areas, and
- Application.

QoS design includes requests for:

- **Performance:** To create resource commitments potential performance characteristics are needed.
- **Synchronization:** Describes the required level of coordination between associated services, measures or flow of data.
- **Level of Service:** To maintain performance commitments, it is needed to specify the degree of resource commitment.
- **Cost of Service:** As per user's price the level of service to be acquired.
- **QoS Management:** According to QoS restriction the level of QoS to be accepted and event with the scaling processes.

Basically QoS desires are measured to check whether they can be happened. For example, if a requested stage of service is not delivered then before scheduling it's process the user has to check whether there is gradual decrease at a certain level or not.

A middleware with QoS supports the required Distributed Real-time and Embedded (DRE) (Balasubramanian et al., 2008) systems with network QoS. A model-focused element middleware framework referred as Network QoS Provisioning Engine (NetQoPE) (Balasubramanian et al., 2008; Balasubramanian et al., 2010). NetQoPE protects some of the applications with network QoS approaches by:

- Identifying network QoS requests per-flow,
- Implementing admission control decisions and resource allocation, and
- Imposing network QoS per-flow at runtime.

NetQoPE is used to offer network QoS guarantee to continuous application stream. NetQoPE without changing its programming model offer a discriminated level of functioning in network to a stream of every application. This method gives flexibility in controlling the network-layer processes.

Cyber Physical Systems are powerful combination between the system's computational and physical elements. Nowadays cyber physical systems can be established in various areas like processes in chemical, civil communications, aerospace, automotive, force, health care, industry, transportation, amusements and domestic devices. Worldwide the software reliability has happen to a worldwide topic of interest, as there is increased rate of software failure. Consequently, an additional care has been taken to emphasize the significance and determination of the digital computing system's reliability. Dependable digital computing system states the system competence in terms of comprehensive capacity services. These services are mainly associated with the management, consistency, protection, accessibility and assessment of a system. As there is much interest in the determination of the software in any field, the attention towards the dispersed real-time system dependability also rises.

Cyber-Physical Systems limitations which are essential include:

- Non-existence of tools and recognized illustrations are competent of communicating and combing various perspectives and features. This take account of several concept layers of prescribed representations which are nonexistence in physical procedures. These processes retrieved from different levels of data compilation order and investigate its cross-layer.
- Security significant and insignificant functionality is isolated due to limited methodologies. And also for protected configuration of their operations during human-in-the-loop process.
- Capability to think about the information exchange among physical restrictions of CPS and QoS.

A novel software expansion technique with a part of involvement is an Aspect-Oriented Programming (AOP). Systems could be divided into various intercutting techniques and use AOP methods to design independently. Quality of Service (QoS) and system performance are directly related to each other. QoS modelling require aspect-oriented specification approach and UML and prescribed techniques are utilized in the aspect-oriented QoS modelling approach.

Model Driven QoS Provisioning Engine

A model driven component middleware structure is referred as Network QoS Provisioning Engine (NetQoPE) (Balasubramanian et al., 2010). NetQoPE organises and set up operations in DRE systems and implements its network QoS characteristics by means of multistage approach. The specific four stages are solutions of design time, prior to deployment, solutions of arrangement and runtime solutions shown in Figure 3 as in (Balasubramanian et al., 2010).

The four stage (Multistage) architecture of NetQoPE includes the following elements to systematize the process of QoS provisioning in CPS applications (Balasubramanian et al.,2008; Balasubramanian et al., 2010).

- **The Network QoS (NetQoS) Specification Language:** It is a Domain-Specific Modelling Language (DSML) (Balasubramanian et al., 2010) which maintains measurement of design-time with network QoS necessities (Balasubramanian et al., 2010) such as delay in data flow and bandwidth. Application programmers are allowed for operations in which it is applied rather than using dissimilar bandwidth and delay. NetQoS streamlines the application arrangements in circumstances with the dissimilar network QoS desires which has diverse bandwidth needs.
- **The Network Resource Allocation Framework (NetRAF):** It is a structure of middleware-based resource allocator. During pre-deployment time NetRAF (Balasubramanian et al., 2008) uses the network QoS measurements as input that is obtained by NetQoS. As a consequence QoS provisioning requirements direct the primary network QoS approach during deployment time (Balasubramanian et al., 2010). NetRAF lessens the overhead runtime and simplifies admission control processes at pre-deployment time. This is effective if it provides application-transparent and resource allocation per flow.
- **The Network QoS Configurator (NetCON):** The deployment-time configuration of the middle containers is delivered by network QoS configurator. This configurator is based on the middle-ware. Whenever an application performs some remote operation, NetCON adds flow-specific identifiers such as software component Differentiated

Figure 3. Four stage architecture of NetQoPE

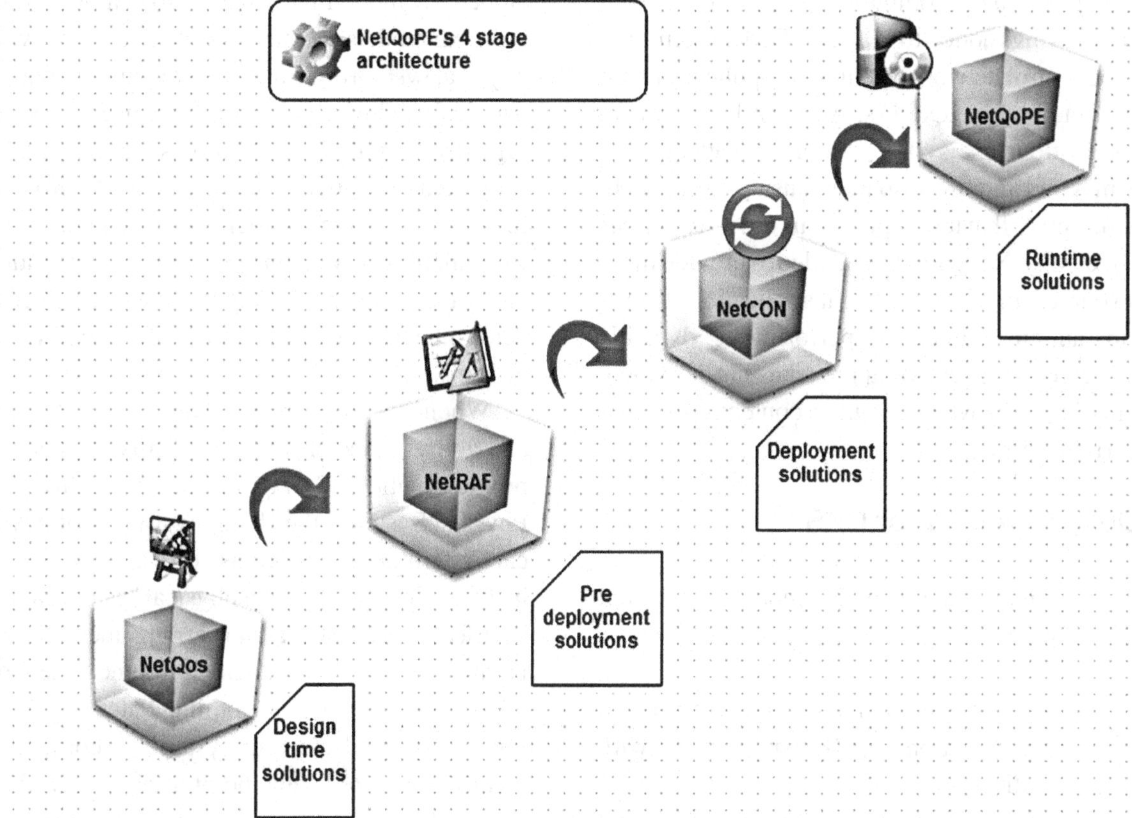

Services Code Points (DSCPs) to IP packets during execution. Container-mediated and application-transparent abilities are used to implement network QoS at runtime. During this period DRE systems permitted by NetCON to control the organized routers of QoS services by not changing application source code. As depicted in Figure 3, the NetQoPE's each stage output is used as next stage input. In turn it helps to systematize the DRE applications operation and arrangement with the backing of network QoS.

To allocate network resources properly in applications with network QoS requirements, NetQoPE uses domain-specific modelling languages. Deployment specific QoS requirements need not be modified, but it can reuse the software to apply business logic approach in the different perspectives of deployment. The application code of network QoS procedures are to be programmed to find out whether the network resources accessible to meet the needs of QoS. To simplify validation and adaptation in the deployment of application, NetQoPE provide these capabilities in resource allocation approaches beforehand.

NetQoPE's has tools of model-oriented arrangement and constitution to support applications with network QoS context-specific settings (Balasubramanian et al., 2010) to configure the fundamental component middleware. A runtime middleware framework NetQoPE applies these settings in the programming model of applications without any modification. Applications need not to change its way of communication, as the network QoS settings added to it. In few DRE systems the allocation of network resources to applications are restricted by NetQoPE's. As open DRE system applications use system resources inadequately, it may not require resources during runtime. In assumption that few applications use its resources effectively, NetQoPE is extended to provide more resources. In mission-critical applications to provide anticipated network performance, dynamic resource management approaches are provided. This happens when resource contention occurs during runtime.

QoS Modelling for CPS

A widespread QoS processing model constructed into a system includes:

- The generalized QoS framework construction
- An application's QoS requirements with specification
- Mapping between QoS requirements and resources
- Preferred QoS behaviour with QoS approaches

The cyber-physical systems have wide range of minuscule like pacesetter to extensive like the nationwide energy grid. The computer based devices are power of economic sources and exists everywhere. In CPS it is difficult to find out whether computational characteristics are outcome of computer programs or physical processes, because CPS is a system with the combination of information and physical processes. Real or Continuous time models are given more importance in scrutinize time-related such as meeting the objective and practical scheduling. The embedded system uses time models for demonstrating sequential description of the physical location to which it is interrelating.

Cyber Physical System uses real-time and embedded modelling language to deal with various time models. To meet the challenges of cyber physical system design, its heterogeneous models and design flow abstraction layer need to be re-organized. Modelling and representation of CPS are essential challenges in research. It is difficult to develop a reliable integrated model which is a combination of cyber and physical characteristics. Aspect-oriented modelling is a suitable choice to determine the various attributes of cyber physical systems.

Whenever software concepts such as stability and convergence are raised as an issue then the programmatic QoS adaption outspreads. In Cyber Physical Systems, the changing aspects of physical system are specified as software parameters by QoS. The stability of a physical system cannot be affected due to the ad hoc arrangement of QoS parameters which are difficult to tune. The QoS adaptation software is nothing but a regulator for an arranged discrete system. According to control structure's view point to plan, reproduce and analyse the QoS variation software refined tools are required.

Textual code based of abstraction is offered by programmatic QoS adaptation methods. In CDL-based adaptation policies require changes manually which lies in the most of the part of cyber physical system. Ensure that all changes are reliably made in a system. Vigorous changes occur in the behaviour of a system due to the development of crosscutting properties. The crosscutting property is nothing but like in surveillance distributed system communication bandwidth is altered according to the policy transformation.

The performance and characteristics of certain scheduling algorithms decides the QoS provisioning. These algorithms fixed in nature. Sometimes QoS provisioning depends on communication protocol also. These executions provide fixed QoS with the flexibility of tuning. Subsequently, any QoS adaptation includes structural adaptation during runtime. In turn this switching process is extremely difficult and impossible in few cases like improper closing down and regenerating of nodes. During structural adaptations some issues like situation management and broadcast, transitory improvement and eminence increase occurs. Because of these issues there will be no backing from the programmatic QoS adaptation. In all categories of software development Object-Oriented Programming (OOP) has been considered as leading programming approach. The focal point of is to divide the problem into several modules find a modular solution to summarize the system performance. Though the basic elements of Object-Oriented Programming are intercutting techniques that are distributed across methods, but these concerns cannot be easily captured in a method. OOP be unsuccessful to distribute a forceful and result being extended to handle these intercutting techniques.

Aspect Oriented Programming (AOP) (Zhang, 2012) is a new approach to separate the crosscutting concerns into modules. It constructs on Object-Orientation (OO) but concentrates on few topics that are not focused by OO. AOP approach is to divide the task into well-designed mechanism as well as aspectual elements called aspects. An aspect is defined as a small part of crosscutting the well-designed mechanism. These components are designed to specify the state and behaviour to change the multiple classes into reusable sections. Some of the examples of aspects are allocation, classification, concurrent, fault acceptance and management and fault acceptance. The intercutting problems are summarized into an aspect, so that a solution can be proposed by AOP. And to construct a ultimate system it combines major components of the software structure with the weaving method. The incident of managing several intersecting plan requirements is in the group of intercutting techniques, which are well adopted by aspect oriented techniques.

Hence, aspect oriented programming (AOP) methods are applied in the structural design of system to attain a modularity level that is unachievable through established encoding practices. It is required to evaluate and classify these intercutting techniques incident in active system performance to follow that hypothetical assumption. In aspect oriented languages, the crosscutting concerns can be resolved and yield system structural design that is more sensibly consistent. It is subsequently feasible to measure and estimate the gain of handling AOP to the structural design of system.

UML is a general purpose modelling language which is used in a various domains of software engineering community. Hence, it is very important from the research point of view towards aspect-oriented real-time system modelling method. But there is a difficulty rises that how a real-time system model can be expressed as an aspect in terms of real-time feature. A concurrent structure model which is based on UML and Real-Time Logic (RTL) is an aspect-oriented method.

To detail the timing possessions of ongoing systems Real Time Logic (Zhang, 2012) is produced as a first order predicate logic. This investigation of timing properties conveys a consistent strategy for the determination of both relative and absolute timing of actions. Fundamentally RTL hold the timing prerequisites of real time systems to restrict the features of first-order logic. To signify the relationship between actions of a framework and their times of happening, RTL includes a solitary un-deciphered binary occurrence function, indicated by @. With this, RTL is believed as a development of integer arithmetic without product operation. Generally RTL equations are Boolean blends of uniformity and imbalance predicates of standard integer arithmetic. The contentions utilized within these are integer valued statements including variables, constants and applications of the represented by a symbol @. The associated propositional formula is used to compute the correctness of a real-time system.

The comparative and fixed period assets of CPSs are used to represent Extended Real Time Logic (ERTL) (Zhang, 2012). This mathematical representation used for the demonstration and examination of CPS. However, these systems are the combination of persistent variables and separate incident dynamics. The augmentation presented by ERTL facilitate the modelling of system performance are series of activities that are part of computing system environment referred as physical entities and the sequential group of the computing system executable tasks. Thus provision has been given to use formal notation in different phases of software development.

Another representation of UML specification is an Object Constraint Language (OCL) and it is not a replacement of any formal languages exists. But OCL is to mention the necessity of object constraints that cannot be considered in graphical diagrams. These diagrams are representation of communication between the components and the constraints. OCL can be tested without any system execution because it is an expression language. The QoS properties can be represented effectively since OCL can be specified by the grouping of pre-requisite, post-conditions and constant. Moreover QoS attributes and QoS actions are represented by the class member variables and the methods respectively. The transformation of system QoS parameters can be tested before and after the calls so that the parameters can be monitored at a specified time intervals.

QoS concern is referred as a cross-cutting concern, since it is dealt in many parts of the system. Intercutting techniques can be defined as techniques with large amount of several objects or components. Intercutting techniques need to be separated and sectionized, so that the components effort in various arrangements needs no change of code. The objective of having code is to link the component with its appropriate configuration. Basically this code will be dispersed all over the element implementation and linked with the additional code of the component. To save the module programmers from implementation and to have a vigorous change in component implementation modularizing is required. Aspect oriented programming is a different approach for segmenting crosscutting concerns. Intercutting techniques can be modularized as per its feature and later it can be expanded into the code using AOP.

POSSIBILITIES AND CHALLENGES IN INTERNET QoS

Several efforts have been taken over the years to support end-to-end QoS at different network layer protocols. This is to meet the network QoS necessities that are applied in various applications. In many of the research and development happenings main attention is given to Internet QoS. In the perspective of cyber physical processing, WSANs do not apply QoS approaches due to its characteristics. Moreover WSAN is a region in which QoS support is unexposed. As sensors and actuators are part of WSANs it cannot be referred as WSNs.

Possibilities of Internet QoS

Following are the main characteristics of WSANs that challenge QoS provisioning (Xia et al., 2008).

Resource Constraints

The sensor nodes in WSNs consume less energy and of fewer cost small devices. These devices are operational with a restricted facility of processing data, power of battery, broadcast rate, and recollection (Xia et al., 2008). For instance, MICAz is a wireless measurement system designed by from Crossbow Company. This system is has Atmel ATmega128L 8-bit micro regulator with the clock frequency of 8 MHz, flash program memory of size 128KB and EEPROM of size 4KB. Moreover it is allowed with a limited data transmission rate of 250kbps along with a constraint on bandwidth availability and different frequency range of wireless channels. In WSANs it is impractical to exchange or renew the arranged sensor node batteries. So the power management is considered as an important issue. Compared to sensor nodes actuator nodes generally have more energy and has durable processing and transmission facilities. Allocation of resources in sensor and actuator nodes is inadequate.

The network QoS may affect by the inaccessibility of processing or transmission resources which are limited. For an illustration, in WSAN when nodes want to transmit information they have to contend for restricted bandwidth frequency provided by the network. As a result few of the data transmissions come across huge delays and occasioning in short scale level of QoS. In WSAN data packets are interrupted before it reaches its end nodes because of inadequate memory. Therefore, it is significant that in WSANs the available resources should be utilized efficiently.

Platform Heterogeneity

Sensors and actuators have dissimilar resource limitations as discussed above. These are dissimilar in computation and communication capabilities due to its various design methods and objectives. In a wide-range of WSANs each subsystem has its own methods relevant to networking and hardware. Because WSANs has limited associated set of rules with accessible commercial inventions with varied types. Hence this policy with dissimilarity makes the system demanding to choose properties of interconnected systems. Therefore, in many circumstances utilization of resource is very minimal and also policy with dissimilarity become demanding for the nodes to perform transmission among them practically and consistently.

Dynamic Network Topology

The sensible devices in WSNs are immobile whereas actuators in WSANs are portable. Many of the applications like intellectual transport, war in urban area, supported living, assessment of universe and controlling animal consider portability as a fundamental necessity. New sensors or actuators are supplemented while executing some actions. The method of energy management changes the status of a node from or to the inactive mode. Due to drained battery level few nodes may expire. These factors are the main reason for WSANs to keep changing its network structure. WSANs utilize essential dynamics to necessitate QoS procedures operate in active and changeable surroundings. In other words, according to available resources while processing WSANs must be easy-going and accommodating. For case in point, a network should be able to assure practical and consistent transmission even though a transitional node expires. This is possible only by progressing acceptable protocols and processes.

Mixed Traffic

Sharing the identical WSAN, inducing both episodic and continuous data requires diverse applications. This feature will become more remarkable, as the scale of WSANs grows. To observe and control the data, some of the sensors produce physical elements episodic measurements. In the meantime, other sensors are arranged to sense precarious events. For illustration, sensors are placed in an intellectual home to observe temperature and lighting variations. While certain sensors are accountable for recording actions like arrival and departing of a person. Additionally, discrete sensors used for dissimilar types of physical elements like high temperature, dampness, situation and swiftness. These measurements are used with different features like sampling rate and message size to produce movement data flows. This feature of WSANs demands the maintenance of service distinction in QoS controlling.

Challenges of Internet QoS

To accomplish QoS assistance in WSAN, the above encounters have to be concentrated. There are several open issues which also pose as a challenge for QoS, outlined below:

Service-Oriented Architecture

The concept of Service-Oriented Architecture (SOA) has been widely used in the domain of web services. Though capabilities of SOA are not explored in WSANs, but it has been effectively used in the various part of the technology. SOA is an architectural style (Xia et al.,2008) comprised of conventional of services that are used for making subsystems of complex systems. To provide functionality SOA is represented as model which further can be divided into different reduced modules. SOA facilitates compatible services unprotected by particular systems, when possibility of prototype and structural design development change in the incorporation of systems. The systems that provide compatible services are accessible systems and interrelated systems with less cost and swift (Xia et al., 2008). This is mainly used for WSANs QoS provisioning that are combined as extensive cyber-physical systems that are used for executing various applications in different platforms. Though categorizing and identifying services are essential for developing SOA in WSANs, still many queries have to be answered in this regard. The queries are related to categories of services, functionality and properties of each service, performance requirement and difference between sensor and actuators nodes while identifying services.

QoS-Aware Communication Protocols

It is necessity to design communication protocols that provide heterogeneity between sensors and actuators during communication. This is to have a QoS support in WSANs efficiently. Because of this purpose the WSNs protocols used in transference, channelling and MAC with QoS-aware are not appropriate for WSANs.

Communication protocols should support service differentiation which is an important component of QoS. Though cyber-physical systems with WSANs comprised of various functions, knowingly each may have different QoS requirements. Noticeably, present-day wireless networking technologies like Zigbee and Bluetooth cannot offer a range of QoS for multiple applications. Hence, the design of WSANs communication protocols is to identify each type of service requirement. From a practical viewpoint, the QoS service would be consistent for the anticipatable future (Xia et al., 2008). Optimizing network performance can be effectively done using cross-layer design. Hence this design can be combined for the improvement of QoS-aware transmission protocols in WSANs. For instance, the association of traffic priority and application performance is done at lower layer and application layer respectively.

Resource Self-Management

The most significance of QoS provisioning is resource management which is helpful in obtaining QoS levels. This point is true since resources of energy, processing and transmission of CPSs are restricted. The higher level of QoS requires more resources like memory size, CPU time, force and bandwidth. WSANs expanding complexity, vigorous feature, and varying environments in which it operate, have management of resource as demanding. The self-management technologies are required to overcome the above mentioned challenges to indicate that the structure will come across issues related to resource controlling in a self-directed way. Resource manager adjust the resources according to variations in resource availability to optimize the QoS efficiently. Due to the less availability of resources the resource management overhead should be lessened. Distributed methods have to be discovered to maintain scalability.

Feedback scheduling is a better way to utilize it. This scheduling approach suggests a feasible method to resource management in an adaptable and changeable situation by applying fixed control theory and methodology. It has been showed that in an easily changing situation feedback scheduling provide resources under insecurities. To offer QoS assurances to realize the self-management of resources, WSANs are expected to use this implementation in it. By using control theory the prospect of the system can be enhanced. Still research analysis remains to find the way the control problems are correlating with the resource management.

QoS-Aware Power Management

The major issue of WSANs is energy conservation. The period of unleashed sensor and actuator nodes is strongly controlled by the accessible battery power. To extend the lifecycle of network the energy consumption of WSANs nodes has to be limited. This is due to the powerful energy of wireless communication than sensing and computation in WSANs. The computations in actuator nodes consume more energy, because the existence of problems is gradually dense in computations. Consequently, the actuators should reduce its utilization of CPU energy by applying the energy scaling methods vigorously.

In many cases diminishing exploitation of energy and exploiting QoS are two incompatible necessities. For example, trustworthiness can be enhanced by expanding determined amount of retransmissions that are admissible or using maximum energy stages of transmission. But in both the cases more energy will be consumed. Therefore, transactions must be carried out between optimization of QoS and energy maintenance. Then the problem develops by rising a query that during runtime how to make these transactions and is it possible to discover a combined performance metric that is used to optimize the energy efficiency and QoS either online or offline.

The power management procedures are different for actuator and sensor nodes based on the QoS requirements and its network topology. Thus the development of various abilities of sensors and actuators are exploited through QoS. In the same way based on the type of traffic same node may be assigned with different transmission power levels. To reduce the usage of energy in sensor and actuator nodes, computation is used in network. This is to decrease the traffic load with the improved computation in each involved node. However, for QoS-aware power management the wireless channels present the essential and non-deterministic unlimited challenges.

Supporting Tools

The important task of WSAN is to link the cyber space with the physical world. Discrete-time systems are referred as cyberspaces and continuous-time systems are referred as physical world. The progress of replication and devise tools of this integrated system are used to estimate the WSANs QoS performance procedures. A question rises that is it possible to develop a service-oriented architecture based tool. If so then it is necessary to develop services to implement the programming technologies and also it is required to have a wide-spread research and development for standard test beds and prototypes. With the help of these supporting tools innovative set of rules, procedures and processes can be developed for QoS organization implementation.

Feedback Scheduling as a Solution

The above mentioned challenges are difficult. A feedback scheduling framework as in (Xia et al., 2008) (see Figure 4) is an illustration response for overcoming several concerns outlined above. A feedback scheduling technique of firmed feedback control theory and technology is considered for providing a methodology to independent resource management in self-motivated and inconsistent situations. Feedback scheduling is efficient of controlling ambiguities in resource accessibility by inevitably adapting to forceful changes (Xia et al.,2008).

The accomplishment of WSANs QoS support through resource self-management using general feedback scheduling framework is shown in the above figure. The fundamental role of the feedback scheduler is to maintain a desired QoS level by adjusting particular scheduling parameters of appropriate traffic flow. According to the diagram 4 certain QoS parameter such as system output is the controlled variable, the manipulated variable is nothing but adjustable scheduling parameters and the set-point is the required value of QoS parameter (Xia et al., 2008). Basically the design of the feedback scheduler is based on control theory and facts to improve the expectedness of the CPS. A well-made feedback scheduler often move the resultant QoS to the planned theme (Xia et al., 2008), when unexpected change occurs in resource accessibility such as rise in traffic load. This technique can be applied in each node exclusively so that it can be reachable.

CONCLUSION

Quality of Service for networks is a wide range of industry oriented regulations and procedures. Network QoS is applied in critical applications to ensure great performance quality. Network supervisors can utilize QoS methods with the existing resources capably and also used to obtain an expected stage of service passively or equipping their networks. The principal objective of QoS is to offer dedicated bandwidth, controlled jitter and latency. QoS methods used for potential campus industry applications, networks service provider and Wide Area Network (WAN) to supply the vital blocks of building.

A huge number of issues have to be focused before this vision becomes a reality. The management of QoS for Network in this latest field require widespread efforts of research. In CPS wireless sensor and or actuator networks (WSANs) is considered as an important subsystem.

Figure 4. Feedback scheduling network

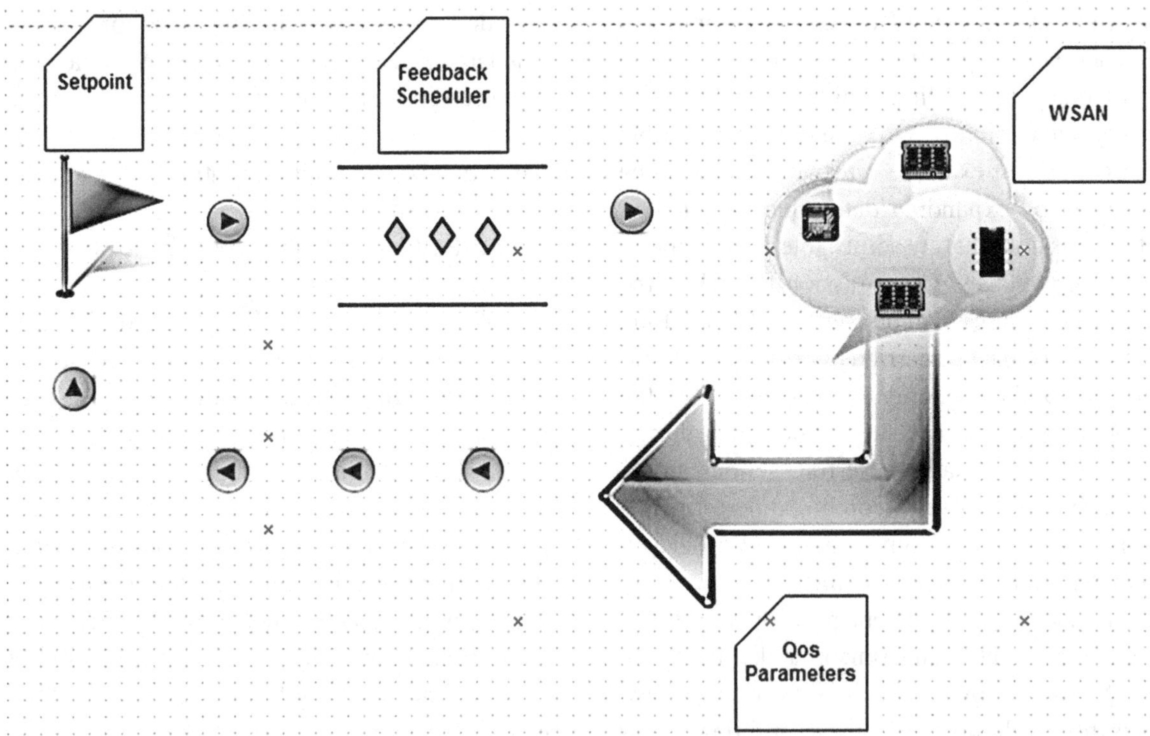

Network characteristics managed by QoS is bandwidth, latency, jitter and reliability. CPS by character is application-oriented. Therefore, the networks have to offer QoS hold up so as to assure intended applications with service requirements. From a customer point of view, the detailed necessities are located on the primary network connections of QoS applications in reality. For case, CPS networks at a suitable time inform the incidence of a fire to actuators in a fire handling system.

QoS requirements differ from one application to another. For instance, in a safety-critical control system there is a huge delay while transmitting the data from the CPS networks to actuators. Moreover packet loss will not be allowed during the sequence of transmission. But packet loss is acceptable for any system which has the temperature insider an office. Conceptually assurance is given to provide fully satisfied service requirements for a system assumed. QoS is characterized based on the factors such as reliability, rightness, robustness, availability and security in the specified networks. There are certain parameters of QoS which are used to measure the processes such as variation in packet transit, performance of the system, interruption and rate of packet failure.

As per user requirements an application constraint of QoS are represented in conditions of elevated level factors. Each system layer has dissimilar QoS specification which is used to specify QoS procedures at every layer. Possible levels of system network and transport protocols set of network connections, tasks of operating system such as arrangement, resource supervision, and practical support, disseminated platforms like devices, CPU, recollection or storage areas.

Cyber Physical Systems are measured by their intractable requests for Quality of Service (QoS), such as expected continuous latencies, scalability and timeliness. Cyber Physical Systems provides QoS requirements to organize flawlessly and modify the connections utilize to host the CPS. And which engrave crosswise in various levels of networks, middleware, and operating systems. Cyber Physical systems combine with the values of Aspect-Oriented Software Design (AOSD). Due to the existence of actuators and sensors WSANs can to be considered as WSNs. The important features of WSANs that contest with QoS provisioning are restrictions in resource allocation, topology of self-motivated network and varied transmissions. These challenges have to be realized to have QoS support in WSAN. There are several open issues which also be considered as a challenge for QoS.

REFERENCES

Balasubramanian, J., Tambe, S., Dasarathy, B., Gadgil, S., Porter, F., Gokhale, A., & Schmidt, D. C. (2008, April). Netqope: A model-driven network qos provisioning engine for distributed real-time and embedded systems. In *Proceedings of Real-Time and Embedded Technology and Applications Symposium*, (pp. 113-122). IEEE. doi:10.1109/RTAS.2008.32

Balasubramanian, J., Tambe, S., Gokhale, A., Dasarathy, B., Gadgil, S., & Schmidt, D. (2010). *A model-driven QoS provisioning engine for cyber physical systems*. Academic Press.

Xia, F. (2008). QoS challenges and opportunities in wireless sensor/actuator networks. *Sensors (Basel, Switzerland)*, *8*(2), 1099–1110. doi:10.3390/s8021099

Xia, F., Ma, L., Dong, J., & Sun, Y. (2008, July). Network QoS management in cyber-physical systems. In *Proceedings of Embedded Software and Systems Symposia*, (pp. 302-307). IEEE. doi:10.1109/ICESS.Symposia.2008.84

Zhang, L. (2012). Aspect-oriented development method for non-functional characteristics of cyber physical systems based on MDA approach. *Journal of Software*, *7*(3), 608–619. doi:10.4304/jsw.7.3.608-619

ADDITIONAL READING

Das, S. K. (2010, October). Multimodal sensing in mobile and cyber-physical systems. In *Proceedings of the 3rd workshop on Mobile video delivery* (pp. 1-2). ACM. doi:10.1145/1878022.1878023

Lin, S., & Stankovic, J. A. (2009). Performance composition for cyber physical systems. In Proceedings of the Ph. D. Forum of the 30th Real-Time Systems Symposium (RTSS'09).

Wang, E. K., Ye, Y., Xu, X., Yiu, S. M., Hui, L. C. K., & Chow, K. P. (2010, December). Security issues and challenges for cyber physical system. In *Proceedings of the 2010 IEEE/ACM Int'l Conference on Green Computing and Communications & Int'l Conference on Cyber, Physical and Social Computing* (pp. 733-738). IEEE Computer Society. doi:10.1109/GreenCom-CPSCom.2010.36

Xia, F., Tian, Y. C., Li, Y., & Sung, Y. (2007). Wireless sensor/actuator network design for mobile control applications. *Sensors (Basel, Switzerland)*, *7*(10), 2157–2173. doi:10.3390/s7102157

Zhang, L. (2011). QoS Specification for Cyber-Physical Systems. In Advances in Computer Science, Environment, Ecoinformatics, and Education (pp. 329-334). Springer Berlin Heidelberg.

KEY TERMS AND DEFINITIONS

AOSD: Aspect-Oriented Software Design which deals with the complicated configuration issues.

DRE: Distributed Real-time and Embedded systems.

NetCON: Network QoS Configurator is a middleware-based network QoS configurator.

NetQoPE: Network QoS Provisioning Engine is a model-driven component middleware framework of network QoS.

NetRAF: Network Resource Allocation Framework is a middleware network QoS resource allocator.

NMWG: Network Measurement Working Group focuses on existing and currently used measurements to determine network performance.

QoS: Quality of Service.

RMON: Remote Network Monitoring is a device used in network QoS management.

Chapter 7
CPS Security

ABSTRACT

Information security can be efficiently provided by the sound structured information and a set of specialized experts in the field of IT and CPS. The interconnection among the systems in the CPS imposes a new challenge in providing security to CPS. A concise study of CPS security is given in this chapter. The problem of secure control systems is also indentified and defined. The way the information security and control theory guards the system is explored. The security of CPSs can be enhanced using a particular set of challenges, which are also described later in this chapter. The resistance to malicious events is strengthening as cyber physical systems are part of critical structures. The CPSs are time sensitive in nature, unlike the distributed system where a little amount of delay is acceptable.

INTRODUCTION

The most significant integration element in today's information centric enterprises is the modern information technology systems. The information technology systems facilitate the proficient determinations of the enterprises which exist for the persistence of the business related goals. The trio of confidentiality, availability and integrity defines the traditional IT security. These elements of the trio are neither mutually exclusive nor tailed in isolation. They will be considered in balance according to the needs of the business enterprise (Conklin, 2009). There is a need for security in cyber physical systems and the balance of the three elements of the trio varies from the system to system and is purely based on the information flow behaviour of the system being protected.

The traditional security, confidentiality and integrity are more concerned when compared to the availability. Hence, the controls drive towards the technology development for protecting the confidentiality and integrity even at the cost of availability if needed. The adaption of these existing controls to the CPS environment neither is sufficient, suitable nor supports the goals of the organization.

As there are different levels of information systems in the enterprise, it is appropriate to provide the security or protection to information according to their level and this becomes the main objective of an information security system. Providing security in this fashion will be effective also as there is no need to utilize resources in providing security for the information which is having less importance and they can be utilized more

DOI: 10.4018/978-1-4666-7312-0.ch007

efficiently to protect the most important information. As there are different levels of information, similarly there are various levels in threats also. For example, secret military, navy information is having high protection profile when compared to the accounting information of the same enterprise. Here, it can be observed that the protection of military information is based on confidentiality whereas protection of accounting information is based on integrity.

The availability and strong integrity are the essential requirements of the cyber physical systems. This makes these systems different from the traditional IT systems in many firms. The central IT security system must apply what it knows and the better approaches of the traditional IT security when it attempts to protect the cyber physical systems for the first time (Conklin, 2009). This methodology is loaded with problems inappropriately. These problems are:

- The precise needs of CPS security in the enterprise are not addressed.
- The different terminologies of the two communities, traditional IT and CPS obstructs the passing of requirements and capabilities between them when there is an attempt to communicate needs.
- Even though the central IT security is aware of the needs and requirements, the desired levels of protections cannot be achieved as their traditional tool sets are not sufficiently equipped.

The gap between the CPS and security whether the communication is proper or not because of the mismatch between central IT security and CPS needs. This gap raises and avoids communicating the required level of security knowledge to the CPS group that is in need of specific security requirements.

The systems whose physical infrastructure elements are controlled with the help of information technology are referred as Cyber Physical Systems (CPS). The researchers in the fields of technology, business and social sciences are gathered in a recent NSF sponsored workshop to survey the needs of future research in the field of CPS. It was identified that the problems related to the security of CPS is not just in the technical domain but also in the domains of process and the people (sociological, psychological and political). These multiple domains influence the solutions of the security problems.

The dissimilarities between the two groups, security and CPS technical are better addressed by training. The training can also facilitate better communications between security and CPS technical. The comprehensive training and education programs to support both the groups in the requirements and capabilities of communication are much more needed than the simple awareness of the issue. The central IT functions including security are required to communicate with the elements of the enterprise which they support. Most of the organizations have already addressed this issue previously. Generally, while dealing with the IT organizations, instead of giving more sight of supporting and enabling role to business related, the concentration will be IT centric which is a big flaw.

When the systems related to finance become online, the security and performance concerns are more significant from the business side of the enterprise. The view of such systems varies from the IT security systems. As the business critical systems are integrated with the IT systems, communication issues play a significant role. Similar challenge is also posed with respect to CPS.

The significance of business communications is a moderately new and developing area relative to the university programs in IS/IT/CS. Even though the university programs are long-standing enough, they are considerably concentrated only on IS/IT/CS principles irrespective of the specifications of the enterprise objectives. Much more improper result would yield if the same survey is repeated with respect to the CPS specific information. This needs to change as the age of IT Enterprise-CPS integration has arrived and education needs to properly prepare the future workforce. Development, improvement and circulation of educational material are a time-consuming, expensive task, and much like typical project documentation – left as a fatality of budget and resource constraints.

The result is the one which has proven to be very expensive in enterprise ERP system integration efforts and given the nature of CPS would be wise to avoid in the future. So the development and dissemination of training and education materials is one of the clear effort required for secure CPS enterprise integration. This will at least address future workers and management pursuing graduate education.

The presently existing workforce is allied with the second feature of training and awareness and is already in place and operational on CPS. It takes time for the effect to come into existence and change the near term if new ideas are to be brought only after the critical mass enters graduate school where they may be exposed or new hires. Hence, the awareness of senior executives is the solution. This solution will open the lines of communication with the help of in-house training efforts. This educational flaw of both sides: CPS and security personnel can be addressed by planning the intensive and motivated meetings rather than as classroom training.

The meetings should address both fundamental and also specific ideas and the same must be available as materials. The elements that need to be addressed in the fundamental concepts of meetings are vocabulary differences between the communities and the priorities in the application of the triad are rearranges by the assistance from the meetings. The best practices like "How do I secure it steps" are yet to be fully developed.

These best practice elements (Conklin, 2009) are a challenge because:

- CPS elements are not designed to be secured across open networks.
- The imbedded base is huge, preventing sweeping change-outs.
- The life of CPS elements is in decades, not years like traditional IT elements.

The financially viable verdict on security placement on the network side of the house is made as it is becoming a very challenging task in providing security to these kinds of systems. The lack of technology to provide security at different levels appropriately is causing a break in the faster growth of this. As the growth is slow, it is still in its initial stages only when compared to other IT security systems in the enterprise. The silver bullet solution in CPS security cannot be found as there no such solutions in traditional enterprise IT security itself. Depending on the requirements of a particular system, the corresponding level of security is provided by aggregating the collection of tools, processes, techniques and procedures over time. The research projects which are carried out at a corporate lab or university are presently taken a shape of the tools and systems which are being used in the traditional IT security systems. Niche solutions are the point solutions to particular problems. While the capabilities are enhanced or the components are amassed, these point solutions are enlarged to obtain larger solutions. In CPS environments, the same methodology is repeated and then has become a recognized need and market to drive the innovation.

Cyber-physical systems (CPS) are at a crisis. Trademark CPSs with multi-loop administration comprises of device controllers, plant-level disseminated association and system-wide Supervisory control And Data Acquisition (SCADA) (Pal, Schantz, Rohloff, & Loyall, 2009) mechanisms are encouraged by business sector constrains as well:

- The possible numbers of divergent systems (e.g., control and business) are connected to each other to form an internetworked organization of systems straddling extensive geographic areas.

- Employ the general purpose computer hardware and software for dealing with the information and off-the-shelf networks (occasionally connecting public infrastructure like the Internet) for communication purpose.
- End-users and clients are authorized additionally with sequence and control.

This drive resulted in replacing the defensive and purpose built interfaces for typical CPSs with the more interfaces and well known novel dependencies among interrelated subsystems. In an open and organized situation, the permissions of the users and supervisors to access the ordered and control surfaces intensify the impact of erroneous or malicious events. The level of risks is very high as the cyber physical system of systems is plays a critical role in the today's dangerous national infrastructure. In addition, CPSs cannot admit the delay or unavailability for few seconds as many of the scattered systems (e-commerce or logistics preparation systems). Hence, CPSs must obey the requirements of the timing very strictly weather it is during the normal operation or during the improvement process. Providing security for the typical distributed information systems is quite simple when compared to the security provision of internetworked and strongly connected CPSs.

It becomes tedious or may not possible to detect attacks accurately and so it may not be feasible to avoid or eradicate the threat of all attacks at an early stage when a number of independent cyber security issues attack simultaneously in a new situation and hence require many more extra added challenging necessities.

There is a substantial progress in many technical fields with the effort of developing supporting versions of distributed information systems based on these hypotheses. Additional challenges need to be faced in order to transfer these successes and develop survivable cyber physical systems. Examples of security issues (Conklin, 2009) that are further aggravated in the context of CPS security include:

- **Data Interpretation:** The data in large volumes of low-level is used to determine the security state of the CPS. This data includes both the cyber and physical aspects of the CPS. But this might be incomplete or imperfect.
- **Information and Control Sharing:** The individual systems, operators and users belonging to various groups to perform different jobs that may also play contrasting roles and responsibilities constitute in an internetworked system of systems. The sharing of information and control authority in this context effectively.
- **Containing Compromises:** The system-wide impact of cyber-level concessions or licence exploitation by malicious actors is reduced within the individual subsystems.
- **Maintaining Timeliness:** The properties of the base system need to be guaranteed round the clock and during all kinds of situations like good working condition, when under malicious attacks, and even when the intrusion or overhead is induced by the defence mechanisms.
- **Validation:** The vibrant defensive activities of the CPS need to be validated such that it is permitted to be used in applications where safety is significant.

The discussion of these challenges is carried out elaborately and introductory or basic ideas are presented to step ahead. Here, instead of reflecting the importance or difficulty, the ease of exposition is highlighted.

BACKGROUND

Security Control for CPS

The abilities of computing and communication are cohesive with units of monitoring and control in the physical world by the Cyber Physical Systems (CPS). In general, CPS consists of a group of agents like sensors, control processing units, actuators and communication devices as a network (Cardenas, Amin, & Sastry, 2008) as shown in Figure 1.

There are many applications of CPS being used at present such as Supervisory Control and Data Acquisition (SCADA) systems and their role is increasing day by day with the involvement of wireless embedded sensors and actuators to build various new applications in the fields like medical devices, smart structures and autonomous vehicles.

Most of the applications of CPS are very sensitive to safety. This sensitiveness towards the safety states that the damage or failure caused to the physical system which is being under operation is

Figure 1. Distributed controllers
A1, A2, A3 -> Actuators, S1,S2,S3,S4 -> Sensors, C1,C2,C3 -> Communication Devices.

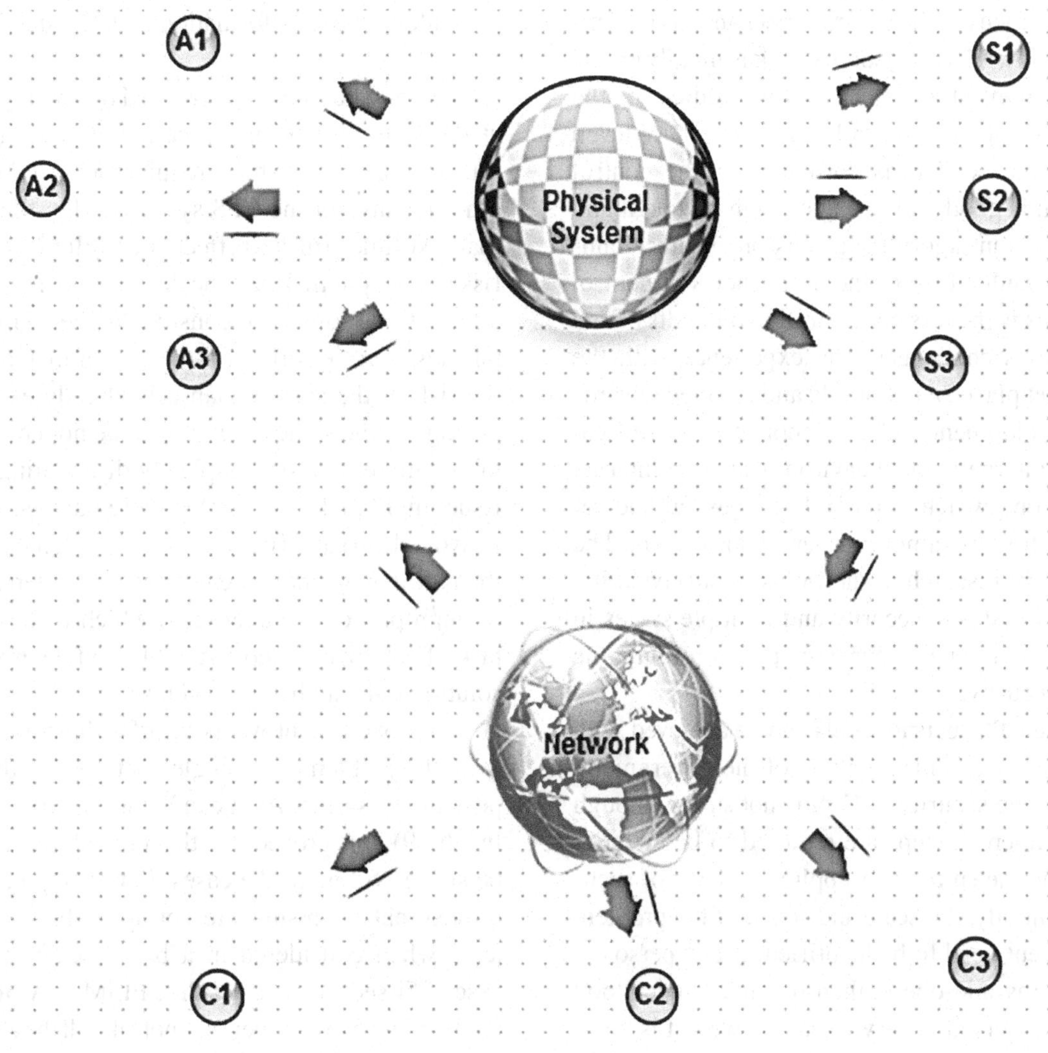

very serious and irreparable and also it affects the people depending on the corresponding physical system. Various important functions in national critical infrastructures such as oil and natural gas, electric power distribution, water and waste-water distribution systems and transportation systems are performed by SCADA systems. A noticeable affect would be there on the health of the public, may lead to large economic losses and safety if there is any disturbance or interruption occurs in these control systems.

Even though some measures are being taken to avoid malicious cyber-attacks and random failures towards CPS systems like SCADA, still there is a vigorous requirement in the improvement of these efforts to improve the reliability of the CPS.

The focus of the security mechanisms in computer network or sensor network is mainly on the way to prevent the attacks but not addressing the way to make the control system operation even under attack. The performance of the control system is good and strong enough on tough and fault-tolerant algorithms against precise uncertainties or faults. One of the deficiencies of control systems is the less concentration on faults due to malicious challenger. The experience with the Internet played a major role and directed towards the development of CPSs. Among the most efficacious internetworked environments, the Internet is the one which is possibly successful and remained as an example of user empowerment. The extensive research in the fields of survivability, control systems, security and multiple stages in research of cyber-security helped in refining the CPS security.

The CPS security goals can be achieved with a major involvement or role of the government. Today, the security in CPS is not strong enough and numerous steps are required to be taken to provide the suitable or applicable level of security. Initially, the scale and scope of the problem statement need to be identified. If any person is unhealthy and obese, then it can be understood that the person is very fat and is weight is more than what it need to be. The challenge to treat this kind of patients is to make the person healthy using safe methods and directions. The abrupt decisions cannot be taken like cutting and removing the fat and supposing the patient to tolerate.

Similarly, the change from the weaker CPS security to the stronger needs four elements (Conklin, 2009):

- The present situation's scope, reasons, and scale are to be identified.
- The anticipated effect in quantifiable terms to be identified.
- The path from the present situation towards the required situation is determined.
- The process of measuring the improvement along the transformation is determined.

These issues are highly related to a policy and at the same time every issue has its own cost-effective allegations that are interconnected with other features of the CPS systems. The solution may take time to make it effective and eliminate the risk of the system. But if the decision is made and a suboptimal solution is considered, then it might take less time, effortless at the cost of increasing the risk of the system than it is already experiencing. At the same time, it must be noticed that taking more time or completely discounting the issue might make the system more damage with unavoidable risks. Today, most of the elements of the risk management are not easy to understand or appropriately compensated which makes the task of achieving a most suitable middle ground solution to be a phenomenal task.

The government wants to offer the solutions to all the problems in a single document within a possible less time. As it can be analysed (Conklin, 2009), it is proved that this procedure cannot be successful in all the cases. For example, it is proved that the results are not up to the desired level when considered in a broad scale in the case of IT security and acts like FISMA. A single comprehensive document cannot take all the above four points into consideration and address them properly. The elements of the CPS play a major role in determining the scope, scale and the reason for the present situations of CPS security. As the API defined some basic standards for the oil, gas and some similar other industries, similarly NERC has defined some standards for the electrical system and expended significant resources in account of the same. The requirements and terminologies of an industry vertical are personalized by each of these standards.

Security Issues

The design of the algorithms which are used in CPS for management and inference purpose need to gratify some of the definite functioning goals like closed-loop steadiness, safety or the optimization of a performance function. Instinctively, the main objective of the security system is to protect the cyber infrastructure from the malicious attacks and at the same time securing the operational goals of the cyber system.

It is not the case that only the operational goals are to be dealt by the security. Nevertheless, non-operational goals also need to be handled by the security. For instance, if the estimations gathered by the sensor system hold touchy private data we must guarantee that just approved people can get this information.

Integrity (Cardenas et al., 2008) alludes to the dependability of information or assets. An absence of trustworthiness brings about trickery (Cardenas et al., 2008) when an approved gathering accepts false information and accepts it to be genuine. Uprightness in CPS can subsequently be seen as the capability to keep up the operational objectives by avoiding, locating, or surviving misleading assaults in the data sent and accepted by the sensors, the controllers, and the actuators.

Accessibility or availability (Cardenas et al.,2008) refers to the capacity of a framework being open and useful upon interest with absence of appropriate outcomes about Denial of Service (Dos) (Cardenas et al., 2008). While in most workstations a short-term Dos assault may not trade off their administrations (a system may work typically when it gets accessible once more), the solid ongoing imperatives of numerous cyber physical systems present new difficulties. For instance, the DoS on the sensor estimations may make the controller not able to avoid the system and substances around it from the damages which are irreversible if an essential physical process is not stable enough in open loop.

The prevention of the information collected by the sensor networks, the instructions forced by the controllers, and the actuators substantial activities from the DoS attacks and making them to endure by preserving the operational goals is the main objective of the availability in CPS.

The capacity to keep up the data furtively and securely from illegal clients is referred as confidentiality (Cardenas et al., 2008). The data is disclosed or revealed with the lack of confidentiality and subsequently, the data can be accessed by the illegitimate users.

The utilization of CPS in business applications has the probable danger of disregarding a clients' security even evidently harmless data like estimations of humidity may uncover personal data which is very sensitive.

Furthermore, the federal regulations like Health Insurance Portability and Accountability Act (HIPAA) must be obeyed by the CPS when used for medical systems (Cardenas et al., 2008). This makes the protection of the patient's data mandatory.

Making the state of the physical system free from the opponent inferring by listening to the channels which are in the communication process of sensors, controllers and actuators indicates that the confidentiality is maintained in CPS.

Despite the fact that one of the major properties in CPS is confidentiality, it is believed that the ongoing research in methods for imposing confidentiality is not influenced with the addition of a real time automated decision making and a physical system.

CPS Abstraction

This section describes a novel group based programming abstraction for cyber physical systems (CPS) (Vicaire, Hoque, Xie, & Stankovic, 2012) referred as 'Bundle'. A Bundle generates balanced collections of sensing devices when contrasted with alternate abstractions of programming. Then again, past deliberations concentrated more on Wireless Sensor Networks (WSN) and they lack to address the major features of CPS. By increasing the range of programming and enabling the support to compound systems of systems instead of single WSN; Bundles permit the programming applications to connect various number of CPSs which are being supervised by remarkable domains of organizations and mobility is maintained both inside and point to point CPSs. The actuators which are represented as a significant component of CPS can also be grouped by the Bundles with ease as it performs the same on sensors. Mixed strategy like notes, laptops, PDAs and actuators based on the requirements of the applications is supported by the Bundles. Bundles permit to employ the same actuators and sensors in various applications simultaneously. Bundles consider the present associates' reaction to build the probable methods or systems for feedback control by dynamic enrollment upgrade and necessities reconfiguration. Java is used to implement the idea of Bundle as it is certain that it is simple and shortens the programming. The number of applications used to build code for Bundles design, its comprehensive realization and to approximate its performance is 32. The diagonally-network applications that encase complex sensing and activation rationale, various mobile nodes and input control systems are included in this set. The number of lines of code in every application is approximated to be 60.

The business systems such as customer management and billing, personality plant control systems which are mostly autonomous in nature are connected to each other and organizations which are manifold in nature are broadened with the help of next generation CPSs. Similarly, various kinds of users with their respective necessities, authority to access the data, various operators and controlling interfaces need to be supported (Conklin, 2009). The recommendation to gather and communicate the large volumes of information is considered to be as compensation to the requirement to control data stream across organizational limitations, and to counteract unlawful imparting and utilization of quick data and control surfaces.

The Second debate is prompted from this: how the data is shared efficiently and how the dependability in systems of internetworked organization is controlled where the autonomous systems, workers and clients of various organizations being their correct positions and performing their respective tasks without breaking the policies of corresponding organization and narrow needs?

For a particular sample, consider that the medical machineries in patient rooms in a clinic are integrated by the CPS. The CPS also controls medications and restorative mediation into patients' bodies in addition to the production and maintenance of up-to-date report of a patient. The records of the patients can be accessed in various locations by various people like doctors', hospitals, the people who buy the medicines, the people who sell the medicines, researches, etc., but the level of access cannot be same for everyone. The accessibility to the control surface is made standard by accumulating all various set of rules that are applicable together. Obviously, it is not acceptable that various subsystems form an open internetwork with the CPS. Alternatively, developing a system that proposes a tailored stovepipe for every instance of imparting and interoperation is unfeasible and software engineering terrible. When the various external subsystems which coordinates with each other can have just the confirmation that is specific for them, then how is it possible for anyone to outline or design and bring an internetworked system into operation?

Further it is noted that the similar problems in the cyber realm are purely dealt by developing the cross-domain and federated solutions (Conklin, 2009). The relevance of these solutions in the context of CPS is foreseen. On the other hand, federated control can be made possible only by future research only. The apprehension of the federation in the solutions of sequence management is connected to data administration. Even in the present solutions of cross-domain, it is assumed that the environment is prohibitive regarding accessible interconnections among domains and regarding the requirement to have the knowledge which may not reasonable for CPSs.

Containing Compromises

The unpredictable consequences might be experienced by individual subsystems which are composed to offer ample control and security within themselves. In general, the people will utilize anything more when its price is less and hence the demand will increase. Similarly, in the electric grid environment the terrible situation might rise if the price is made varying; there is a chance that the power consumption by the users might increase and leads to a new record instead of minimizing the existing or sometimes it may even cause a brownout. This kind of steps to capture the desired pricing data would be taken generally by an intruder to activate an offensive; the reserved or secret data is revealed out to public or phishing gateways by deceiving and interacting with the unsuspicious users. At the same time, it is also a risk to have the utility control smart systems in users' homes as there is a chance of the dripping or leakage of the users private data by the conceded utility systems. There is also another risk that the utility systems might control the other smart devices at home in an offensive manner (Conklin, 2009). Subsequently, the effect of cyber level compromises on the systems to be minimized or malicious attackers exploitations within isolated subsystems to be privileged is stemmed as the third challenge.

As a prospective way forward, it is eminent that use of a survivability design incorporating numerous intersecting discovery skills and control provinces with hypothetically overlapping control hierarchies has shown with significances in the environment of information systems. The transformation from cyber realm to the physical realm can be realized only with the help of further research, particularly, when a cyber-component is cooperated and maltreated by a malicious challenger, and to develop technology and design techniques to diminish and vigorously confine the cyber-based interdependent control surfaces that expurgated across organizational and subsystem limitations. The physical features of the system can be protected by upgrading the detection mechanisms used in survivability designs. At the same time, it is required to upgrade the semantics of containment also (Conklin, 2009). Perhaps in the domain of cyber systems when a system is corrupted, its network access is blocked and such activities require more synchronization with the physical world activities like load shedding.

There will be an extensive growth of the Cyber Physical Systems (CPS) in the near future. The diversified actuation and sensing may be included in the future CPS. Numerous numbers of applications are permitted to be realized at the same time with the backing of services. Inter and intra network mobility is also supported by the CPS services (Vicaire et al., 2012). These services hold the properties of availability and maintainability.

A novel CPS infrastructure can be built with the combination of actuators and wireless sensor networks. Similarly, many communication systems of systems can be developed with the integration of cell phones which are based on sensors with the body networks. Innovative thoughts and concepts are required to convert this visualization into conventional. These new concepts must make the programming easy and simple, various actuators and sensors of heterogeneous networks to form a group, and the management of these groups dynamically during the existence of mobility and feedback control (Vicaire et al., 2012).

The scenario discussed below can be considered to understand the requirements more clearly. The houses of two neighbors named Sita and Gita set up their houses using WSNs in order to monitor the motion. A collaborative application is also installed by both of them in their houses which supervises and informs them if any robbery is happened while they are present in the house. The indication is given using an alarm which will be with them (Vicaire et al., 2012). Some of the crucial considerations to be taken in this case are:

- Various types of devices are being used in the application.
- The actuators referred as alarms and the sensors from both the houses are grouped.
- Both inter and intra network mobility is supported. This indicates the movement can be from one room to the other in the house or outside.
- The alarm sound is based on the resultant functioning of sensors and the application is used to just indicate the happenings in the house during their absence.

A distributed design is developed by the present cluster based generalizations to guarantee energy and bandwidth effectiveness. The nodes combined in the form of groups depending on one of various parameters like connectivity of radio, geographical location, top-level influence or pertaining to the applications proximity. They are designed to work with the applications that can be executed on autonomous networks and so, there are some definite constraints while making use of them for CPS. The sensors from various networks or sensors that move only inside the network cannot be formed as group. The sensors are to be reprogrammed by the new applications. On the other hand, it is not so easy and simple to develop applications with them. Further, forming the actuators in to groups is not upheld by any of them. These restrictions and constraints are tackled and the existing group based abstractions are made comprehensive by a Bundle. The main attention is towards making the resource constrained actuators and sensors to be simple i.e., the centralized base station takes the control of application logic from them. The logic is maintained to be similar irrespective of the number of applications using the sensor (Vicaire et al., 2012).

The subsequent are the main characteristics of a Bundle which provides a dominant idea:

- Ease of programming that helps in developing the applications for CPS succinctly;
- The sensors and actuators from diverse systems and clients are grouped together;
- The sensors and actuators movement in the intra and inter network can be supported by updating the membership of them dynamically and;
- The same set of sensors and actuators are permitted in more than one application simultaneously.

The below are the main focal points of this concept:

- The enhancement of the present group based abstraction is a novel centralized group based abstraction and is referred as a Bundle. It includes some of the significant abilities like programming across systems, updating dynamically and automatically and maintain actuators.
- An assessment with 32 single and multi-system applications to show the straightforwardness and compactness of programming with Bundles, its value of supporting versatility and its worthy energy overhead.

Security Objectives and Threat

In CPS, the design of the algorithms which manage and assess the system should be in such a fashion that they gratify definite set of goals like closed-loop strength, security or the optimization of a given function. Intuitively, the provision of security to these functional goals from the malicious attackers attacking the infrastructure of cyber network is the main objective of the security system. At the same time, the non-operational goals also are required to be managed by the security system. For example, if the private or confidential data which is sensitive has been estimated by sensor network, then appropriate measures must be taken such that this sensitive and confidential data can be accessed by authorized persons only (Cardenas et al., 2008).

Availability, safety, maintainability, reliability, and integrity can be considered as the properties of dependability. Confidentiality, authentication, non-repudiation, and authorization can be considered as the properties of security. There is a chance of affecting both the properties of dependability and security by an attack. Some of the effects may go beyond the limitations of violating the above specified properties and such possible effects are to be determined and given an exceptional consideration. Altogether, a particular Unmanned Aerial Vehicle (UAV) is having numerous dissimilar cyber attacks (Yampolskiy, Horvath, Koutsoukos, Xue, & Sztipanovits, 2012). The assessment of the appropriateness of DFD-based methodology for the CPS liability is the primary objective of this study. Hence, the attacks which highlight the complex interactions of cyber and physical are identified and a mixture of them only is presented below.

The groups of all the displayed attacks are formed depending upon the component which they influence and/or under utilization. A literary explanation is given for each and every attack. An acronym of an attack which is depending on the name of the attack is used to identify and discriminate the attacks from each other. Additionally, it is also specified that the possibility and which of the dependability and security properties may get violated by the attack and at the same time attack's stride impact is also determined.

Security Goals

In general, the system which holds the three abilities given below is referred as Cyber Physical System (CPS):

1. Ability to sense the physical world (e.g., ability of estimating the distance between the car ahead and self),
2. Ability to decide (e.g., to know what to do next. whether the car to be accelerated or decelerated), and
3. Ability to do an activity in the physical world (e.g., able to put brakes, clutch etc.).

The internetwork of CPSs with the cyber world is progressing and simultaneously, the communication among CPSs, and the communication between the CPS and the Internet or the control stations is increasing. This may give a chance for the cyber attacks to affect the CPSs. Simultaneously the role of various types of CPS in our day to day life is progressively increasing. For sample, different models of modern aeroplanes and cars, every variety of unmanned vehicles, different crucial infrastructures and finally smart homes which lead to smart cities. This dependability on the CPS makes the functioning of CPS to be more cautious and to be proper and perfect. Hence, the damage to CPSs and its defective behaviour is not tolerable. The defenceless nature and weakness of CPS towards cyber attacks and the significance of CPS in our life is making CPS as an appealing target. The amount and recurrence of such attacks develop consistently. In the meantime, the inspiration of enemies, complicated nature of performing attacks, and the attack results contrast among known occurrences.

For example, in 2000 the Maroochy Shire Council's sewage control framework in Queensland, Australia, is the source of flooding of its close-by locations. This attack was executed by a terminated employee as an effort to impose his rehiring. An alternate conspicuous case is the Stuxnet, which has prompted the physical harm of centrifuges at an Iranian uranium advancement plant while concealing the attack behind the long ago recorded status information.

The CPS must be tolerant enough to survive against Cyber and physical attacks and hence the reliability of CPS is enhanced. The development of a successful CPS security system obliges that the potential attacks on CPS could be uncovered and surveyed in a methodical way. The present public exploration is prevailed over either by handy illustrations focusing the liability of particular systems against attacks similar to how electronics of a present day vehicle might be negotiated or by general depictions of conceivable methodologies and important research fields like categorizing the entry points of the attacker.

To evaluate the weakness of CPS, the lost relationship in the dynamic dissection is connected to an extensive variety of CPS in an efficient manner. Consequently, it is needed to assess the applicability of security susceptibility investigation strategies decided in computing systems and networks on CPS. The efficient investigation of cyber attacks in opposition to CPS is surveyed through Data Flow Diagrams (DFD). A few levels of DFD are utilized in order to echo the communication between cyber and physical in CPS. Below is an outline for Extended DFD (XDFD) that can be utilized for the CPS vulnerability evaluation efficiently.

Let us consider AscTec Hummingbird quadrotor UAV shown in Figure 2. The two rationales are given below which indicates why it suits perfectly on cyber-physical attack taxonomy:

1. It is straightforward enough to perform manual exhaustive investigation.
2. It holds the characteristic of structural components of the more intricate systems, for

Figure 2. AscTec Hummingbird
(http://www.suasnews.com/2010/09/1892/mapping-inside-a-building-using-a-multirotor/)

example, numerous processors, remote communication sections and bus communication.

The Asctec Hummingbird comprises of a central part and four booms. The central part itself consists of all the electronics in addition to the battery. The four engines and propellers are connected at the nail clippings of the booms. The four engine controllers are spotted on the booms as well (Yampolskiy et al., 2012).

There are two control units in the electronic control of the Hummingbird. They are High-Level (HL) and Low-Level (LL) processors, and four specific engine controllers. The manager of the Humming bird has rights to re-program the HL processor. The SDK provided for download in the trader website gives basics and excellent point to start with in order to implement the applications to a particular client.

Two pins which are dedicated to the booting process are connected physically to facilitate the burning of new software into the HL flash. i.e., overwriting of flash is physically secured and obliges physical contact to the fittings. Consider the case for this investigation when it is not needed, i.e., it is conceivable to overwrite the code without physical access to the unit. The LL processor code is encoded and not supposed to be changed by the client.

Synchronous Serial Port (SSP) is used for the communication between HL and LL processors internally. HL processor and the four engine controllers are not connected to each other either physically or logically. Rather, all the commands are communicated to the LL processor by the HL processor. The LL processor completes the inferring process of these commands. Then the engine controllers receive the commands from the LL processor in sequence. Both the domains of cyber and physical recognize the communication between the UAV's and the external world. The communication with the remote control (R/C) and/or workstation is permitted for both the HL and LL processors in the domain of cyber. This communication is made by means of Zigbee remote interface.

Let us consider probable three distinct hardware:

1. The Zigbee module can be accessed by the HL processor only.
2. The shared bus can be used if the same Zigbee module is to be used in the communication process by both HL and LL.
3. The two communication modules for which these two processors have access are different.

A number of LEDs and beeper are used to indicate the different actions to the operator under physical announcement. For example, in the case if the battery charge level is getting to be excessively low, the beeper is utilized to indicate the same. If a Lithium-Polymer battery is utilized, this is particularly essential in light of the fact that it could be irreversibly damaged or even blast in the event if it releases underneath 9 Volt during the air travel.

Three different cases which are analysed:

1. The LEDs and the beeper can be accessed by the HL processor only.
2. The same LED and the beeper can be accessed by both the processors.
3. The signalling devices to which these processors have access are different.

The aforementioned depiction reflects communications throughout the operation of the quadrotor UAV. To reflect all conceivable communications, additionally communication between UAV and a computer is also to be considered throughout the period of preservation. The booting process of AscTec Hummingbird's HL processor is to be carried out when two pins which are dedicated for this process are interconnected physically and to transfer and burn the new flash code to the AscTec Hummingbird's HL processor.

Here, two cases are considered:

1. The execution of code of the HL processor is stopped and it is essential for such a boot methodology, and
2. The execution of code of HL processor can be carried out while the connection is being established with the external computer and it is not essential for boot methodology.

It might be more usually used in more compound systems like cars for accessing the monitoring data which makes this second mode an exciting one.

Attacks

A broad idea of CPS is depicted in Figure 3 (Kisner et al., 2010). The sensor estimations are characterized by 'a' and control commands sent to the actuators are symbolized by 'b'. There are two components in a controller: the control algorithm and the estimation algorithm. The control power is chosen based on the given present approximation using the control algorithm. The physical system state is followed using the estimation algorithm.

Figure 4 gives the description to various attacks to CPS (Kisner et al., 2010).

In Figure 4, fraud assaults are symbolized as X1 and X3, where the fake data a ≠ a' or b ≠ b' from (one or more) sensors or controller is sent by the challenger. The fake data may comprise: an erroneous estimation, the inaccurate time when the estimation was reasonable, or the wrong sender id. The challenger can initiate these assaults by acquiring the secret key or by negotiating a few sensors (X1) or controllers (X3). Dos assaults are symbolized as X2 and X4, where the challenger stops the controller from accepting sensor estimations. To initiate Dos, the challenger may congest the communication channels, negotiate with nodes and stop them from transmitting information, and assault the routing protocols (Kisner et al., 2010)

The exterior physical attack which is in a ready state or a straight attack which is in opposition to the actuators is symbolized as X5. Besides detecting these kinds of attacks, solutions cannot be determined in the algorithmic perspective. Consequently, it is deliberately required to stop or avoid the cooperation of actuators and other immediate assaults against the physical network.

Despite the fact that these attacks are all more destructive, consider that a threat reluctant challenger will initiate cyber attacks X1-X4 in light of the fact that:

Figure 3. CPS abstraction

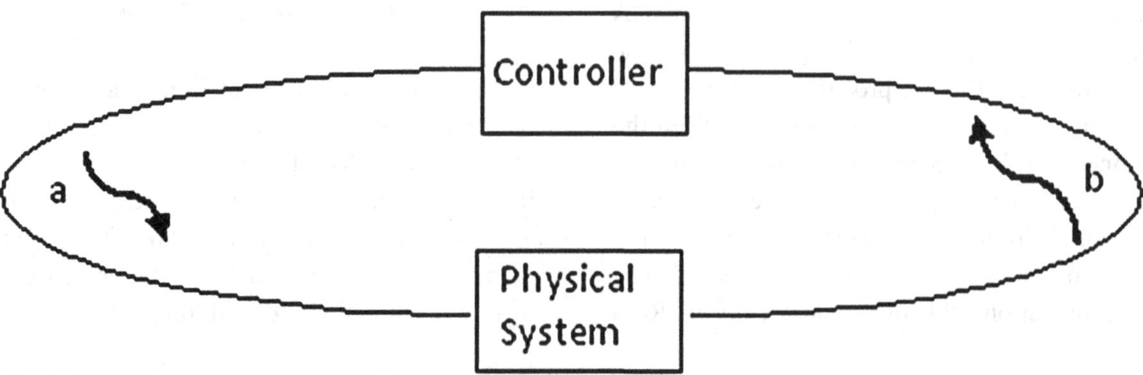

Figure 4. Attacks

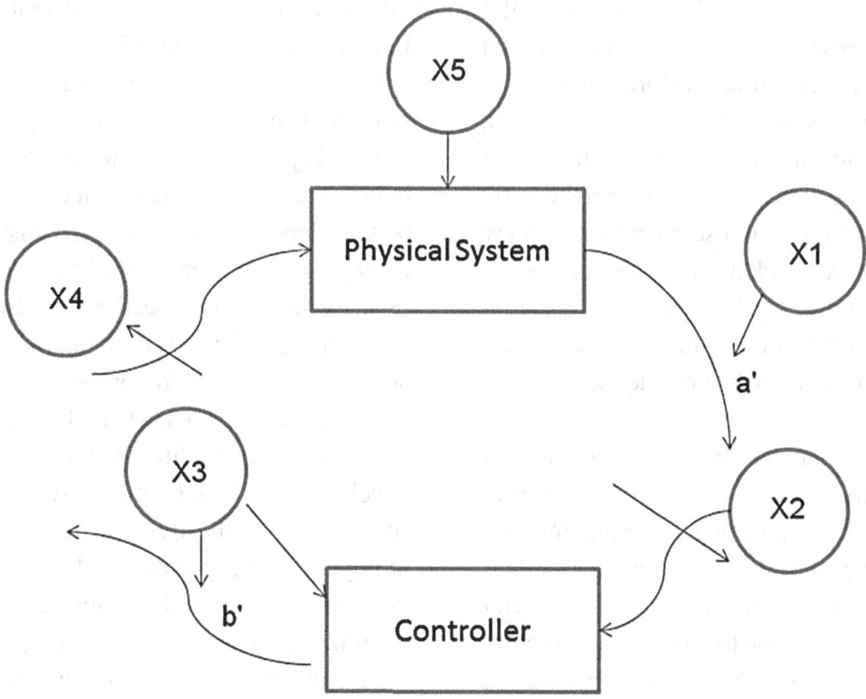

1. It is more complicated to recognize and accuse the culprits,
2. It is not physically precarious for the attacker, and
3. The attacker may not be controlled by geography or distance to the network.

CPS Security Framework

Spurred by the ever-growing availability of online services and resources, threat models are becoming a moving target, constantly evolving. As an end result, the same security techniques so as to were sufficient a decade, or level a few years ago, can prove inadequate today. In particular, recent advance in polymorphic attacks and the increasing volume of zero-day and under attack threaten to overwhelm protection mechanisms. As attackers are finding new ways to gain right to use to networks and systems, so defense mechanisms must find new ways to guard them.

Adaptive security mechanisms can be converted into a necessity rather than an option for coping with the 'affecting target' nature of cyber threats. Such mechanisms will present effective threat discovery and prevention capabilities, while minimizing the price of security.

An adaptive security mechanism implies educating the behavior of a system or its threat model. In this method, attackers can target the learning phase itself; hence the planned self-sanitization mechanism aims to sense and removes malicious activity from the learning process humanizing its quality. Moreover, it has been proposed to enhance the security mechanisms with a self-calibration segment that can be employed in conjunction with the sanitization performance resulting in a fully automated protection cycle. These techniques can be applied in an online fashion to ensure that the resulting mechanisms return changes in the system's or attackers' actions resulting in a self-updating process.

The race between the attacker and protector for gaining access to the protected system is one of the skills in sequence and resources. A well-equipped attacker, armed with intimate information on the confined system as well as extensive resources, can still challenge attacks that change the learnt behavior. To cope with this possibility, a theoretic framework is proposed to use an enhanced view of global network attack activity" as opposed to the single site view. By leveraging the location uniformity of collaborating sites, a more precise model of an attacker's behavior and purpose can be provided.

The security and liability in cyber physical systems are represented based on a network control theory which is guaranteeing for characterizing both data infringement in the cyber world and their effects on elements in the physical world. After an inspiration of the control-theoretic structure (Xue, Roy,Wan, & Das, 2012), the following are deduced:

- The warning of how effortlessly a conscious enemy can recognize system elements from noisy neighborhood estimations.
- A meaning of liability as an effect measure for a conscious or expected opponent.
- Exchange of the complex transaction of security and liability thoughts in risk/instability investigations for cyber physical systems.

SECURITY CHALLENGES

The approach of low-powered embedded wireless sensor networks has prodded the realization of new applications at the interface between the present reality and its advanced sign (Anand et al., 2006). Emulating this pattern, the cutting edge Supervisory Control and Data Acquisition (SCADA) framework is relied upon to substitute conventional information collection – a distributed system of Remote Terminal Units (RTU) or Programmable Logic Controllers (PLC), with units as wireless sensors. The sensors security properties must be thoroughly studied and realized before these intelligent systems are installed in critical places like power plant life, emergency rooms etc. Current knowledge has been to apply on the customary security model and procedures to sensor systems: as in expected nature's domain, the objective has been to be concerned for physical substances: devices, relations, packets and finally networks.

Sensors have elite attributes that warrant novel security contemplations: the geographic conveyance of the devices permits an attacker to physically keep nodes and learn secured key material, or to intrude or infuse messages; the organizational character of sensor systems and their protocols which maintains route allow the attacker to figure out where the root node is located (Anand et al.,2006).

Perhaps above all, numerous sensor systems depend on replication (emulated by accumulation) to exactly obtain ecological data even with defectively aligned and untrustworthy devices. This result in a central difference between a physical message in a sensor system and a logical unit of sensed data: very less data about the real environment can only be collected if only single sensor is used to read a message, while a message holding a total or accumulation of readings may uncover significantly more.

These attributes open the way for a completely new security ideal model that recognizes that there is a key difference between physical and legitimate messages in order. What's more additionally it concentrates is on how to minimize the association between the two to limit chances for trade off. At this point of research, we enrol the challenges for sensor systems – security hindrances that, when succeed, move us closer to installing them in extensive numbers for observing and securing critical infrastructures.

Security Challenges and Research Agenda

Measuring Confidentiality

The message secrecy and validity in sensor systems are proposed to be handled with the use of computationally economical cryptographic strategies according to the numerous surveys.The trouble of guaranteeing privacy and legitimacy is not, however wholly to the energy imperatives forced on sensors. A numerous small processing devices which are intended to physical capture are the components of a sensor system (Anand et al., 2006).

The trade-off between the sensors and their corresponding keys need to be any crypto system. In any case, the trade-off of few nodes may not bring about an aggregate misfortune of security. Instead of giving high-stake assurances about confidentiality or safety, there is a requirement for giving probabilistic certifications regarding trade off. Characterizing measurements and models for various protocols logical level data protection and security properties is the first challenge (Anand et al., 2006). Assuming that few nodes may be conceded and quantifying the risk may be one of the conceivable solutions for this issue.

Context Obfuscation

A perspective is required for a sensor value to have importance (Anand et al., 2006). This is important to comprehend where and when the value was documented. On the other hand, if the when and whereabouts of one interpretation are known, it may be probable for an opponent to derive an extraordinary arrangement in connection to different readings which are adjacent to each other. Hence, sensor systems should be having knowledge about these metadata and their obligation in security. Subsequently, the categorization of cost-effective plans for concealing sensor system control is the second challenge (Cardenas et al., 2008).Conceivable results may be focused around transfer messages at consistent intermissions, disassociating an impression from a physical occasion by adding an arbitrary delay to message broadcast, or adding spurious messages to veil the appropriate send times (Anand et al., 2006).

Secure Aggregation

In sensor systems where collection (Anand et al., 2006) takes place at intermediate nodes, it is impractical to do end-to-end encryption from sensors to the base station in light of the fact that every node must have the capacity to perform operations with the information. The standard security principle that the system ought not to be trusted and that all messages ought to be encoded and unscrambled at the source and destination is incongruent with the combination. Disappointingly, the option of believing each connection between the sensor and the base station is unappealing. To develop new cryptographic methodologies that permit the collection of messages while guaranteeing sufficient security is the third challenge (Anand r et al.,2006).

Topology Obfuscation

Accumulation of information by the intermediate nodes prompts a non-uniform dissemination of data among nodes. consequently assaulting a leaf node in a tree-organized system picks up little impact (Anand et al.,2006) (for interruption) or data (for overhearing); assaulting a node close to the root picks up huge impact and data about the collective value. For eavesdropping, there is an exciting third instance of attacking nodes amidst the tree: intermediate nodes perform enough accumulation to make up for wrong sensors, yet their values may be local enough to uncover private information. Veiling the routing infrastructure of the sensor system is the fourth challenge (Anand et al.,2006). On the off chance that an enemy can assault a couple of selected nodes, the noticeable procedure is to compromise sensors (and their keys) that coherently exist in high esteem positions in the routing tree.

Scalable Trust Management

In the area of sensor systems, trust administration (Anand et al.,2006) is the issue of recognizing which nodes are real, trustworthy and which are not reliable. The number of nodes that can be considered, energy limitations, and the trouble in re-creating the trust lead to comprise the physical threat.

When sensors are installed, all exclusive challenges are related to trust administration in sensor systems. Hence, creating "lightweight" key controlling system and dissemination structures which are applicable for large-scale sensor networks is the fifth challenge (Anand et al.,2006). Because of breathing space obligations, it is difficult to specify all the proposed key administrative frameworks in this exploration.

Aggregation with Privacy

Contrasting to conventional figuring stages, end clients who are recognized by sensor nodes have little capability to place an approach. For instance, clients can utilize anonym zing proxies to ensure their privacy while searching the Internet. On the other hand, the end client has no information as to the level of data divulgence, and must have faith in the choices made by the sensor system while being sensed by a sensor. Designing networks with security assurances is a difficult job as sensing is a reflexive action which can be performed without the awareness of the client which is being sensed. Creating novel privacy procedures to deal with such necessities is the sixth challenge.

Illustrative Example Application Scenarios

Sensor systems could be installed to observe and ensure power grids and shipping infrastructure. In such a network, it is important to guarantee that the testing values gathered be vigorous (Challenge 3) and the level of vigorousness be enumerated so that suitable level of control might be worked out (Challenge 1). Precluding the challenger from getting the knowledge about the state of the system would include concealing the timing and topology (Challenges 2, 4). Every sensor will be expected to be dynamic for a certain lifetime in an extensive SCADA system. The probabilistic framework of network activity and the resources at every node are used to predict the lifetime. Such a model is used to characterize the scope offered by a sensor node and consequently, to devise renewal methodologies to supplement dead sensors (Anand et al.,2006). Given an extensive number of sensors, some of which are occasionally supplanted, administration of encryption keys might be very troublesome; accordingly it turns out to be important to create lightweight, secure trust administration keys (Challenge 5) that allows expansion and evacuation of sensor nodes. The Personally Identifiable Information (PII) is being gathered by many applications of sensor network. Such applications are:

- As a measure of embedded of sensors, the people who are in buildings are being sensed for calamity attentiveness or power savings.
- Observing the actions or happenings of the elder people so that they can be safe at home.
- Checking or sensing vehicles.

Along with challenges 1-5, there is additionally a need to ensure the protection and in few cases verify secrecy in few applications like Fasttrak on the highway transponders in vehicles.

CONCLUSION

New strategies are gravely required for demonstrating and determining dangers and vulnerabilities in cutting edge cyber physical systems, that can represent the mixture and combinative nature of both the system progress and the dangers/instabilities themselves. In this chapter, a network-control-theory structure for demonstrating security and liability in cyber physical systems, which is guaranteeing for demonstrating both data infringement in the cyber world and their effects on the progress in the physical world, is presented.

Data Security is a field of IT that has a strong collection of information, and a unit of specialists with substantial knowledge in securing IT systems. Cyber Physical Systems (CPSs) additionally have a compelling assortment of information and a qualified team of experts that have been effectively handling systems for a considerable amount of time. These are two different groups that would profit from cooperating to each other relatively in a hierarchical administration structure.

As systems get interrelated among them it becomes a new challenge of securing CPS. New innovations will be required, yet much could be picked up from the current facts, in the event that it is appropriately imparted between these two groups.

A key integration component in today's data driven endeavours is the advanced data engineering systems. Ventures exist with the end goal of business related objectives and the data engineering systems empower productive deliberations in quest for those objectives. Conventional IT security deliberations have been characterized around the triad of privacy, reliability and accessibility. What is frequently ignored in this improved perspective is that these three components are not fundamentally unrelated or sought after in segregation, yet survive in a specific stability as characterized by the business needs of the undertaking. Similarly, cyber physical systems have the requirements of security also, and the same triad might be utilized though with one preventative note; the equalization of the three components may be diverse relying on the way of the data stream connected with the particular system being secured.

It can be observed that in the conventional security system, reliability and confidentiality are given a high significance, with accessibility being managed a part of lesser significance. This has prompted the improvement of innovation and controls that are determined by the need to ensure reliability and confidentiality, even at the cost of accessibility. Basically it is neither suitable nor useful to the objectives of the organization by attempting to acclimatize these current controls to the CPS environment.

Offering the proper levels of security to information and their systems depending on the responsibility in the venture is the target of a data security exertion. In the same way that a venture would not use resources to secure data that has no quality, they are required to consume suitable levels of resources to ensure things depending on worth to the undertaking. The security for these data resources is against particular risks which differ by quality. Secret military information has distinctive assurance profiles than the accounting system information in the same firm in terms of confidentiality. One of these is built emphatically in light of privacy and the other on trustworthiness.

The integrity and accessibility are the very strong necessities of Cyber Physical System. This has a tendency to make these systems diverse from customary IT systems in numerous projects. Hence, it better to apply the existing and better approaches of traditional IT security as a first reaction to protect these systems by the central IT security system. Tragically, this methodology is overloaded with issues. Initially, the particular security needs of the CPS components are not addressed. Second, regardless of the fact that there is an endeavour to impart requirements, the two groups, conventional IT and CPS have distinctive terminology and this obstructs the communication of necessities and facilities between the groups. In conclusion, regardless of the fact that the Central IT security system completely comprehended the needs and prerequisites, their conventional tool sets are not capable to give solutions for attaining the required levels of assurance. This discrepancies between central IT security and CPS, whether appropriately imparted or not, has prompted a gap in which security thinks CPS ought to be controlled and CPS does not trust security. This leads to the communication gap between group with the best security awareness and the group that has particular security needs, i.e. the CPS.

Cyber Physical Systems (CPSs) are the systems where information technology is integrated with the physical infrastructure components with the end goal of controlling the components of physical infrastructure. The researchers in the fields of technology, business and social sciences are gathered in a recent NSF sponsored workshop to survey the needs of future research in the field of CPS. One of the intriguing discoveries and purposes of exchange was that the issues connected with the security of CPS rested not just in the technical domain but also in the domains of process and the people (sociological, psychological and political). Additionally, these multiple domains are influenced by the solutions of the security problems also.

REFERENCES

Anand, M., Cronin, E., Sherr, M., Blaze, M., Ives, Z., & Lee, I. (2006). Security challenges in next generation cyber physical systems. In *Beyond SCADA: Networked embedded control for cyber physical systems*. Academic Press.

Cardenas, A. A., Amin, S., & Sastry, S. (2008). Secure control: Towards survivable cyber-physical systems. *System*, *1*(a2), a3.

Conklin, W. A. (2009). Security in cyber-physical systems. In *Proceedings of Workshop on Future Directions in Cyber-Physical Systems Security*. Newark, NJ: Academic Press.

Kisner, R. A., Manges, W. W., MacIntyre, L. P., Nutaro, J. J., Munro, J. K., & Ewing, P. D. et al. (2010). Cybersecurity through real-time distributed control systems: Oak Ridge National Laboratories report. *ORNL. U. S. Atomic Energy Commission*, *TM-2010*(30), 4–5.

Pal, P., Schantz, R., Rohloff, K., & Loyall, J. (2009, July). Cyber-physical systems security-challenges and research ideas. In *Proceedings of Workshop on Future Directions in Cyber-Physical Systems Security*. Academic Press.

Vicaire, P. A., Hoque, E., Xie, Z., & Stankovic, J. A. (2012). Bundle: A group-based programming abstraction for cyber-physical systems. *IEEE Transactions on* Industrial Informatics, *8*(2), 379–392.

Xue, M., Roy, S., Wan, Y., & Das, S. K. (2012). Security and vulnerability of cyber-physical. In *Handbook on securing cyber-physical critical infrastructure* (pp. 5–30). Boston: Elsevier. doi:10.1016/B978-0-12-415815-3.00001-7

Yampolskiy, M., Horvath, P., Koutsoukos, X. D., Xue, Y., & Sztipanovits, J. (2012, August). Systematic analysis of cyber-attacks on CPS-evaluating applicability of DFD-based approach. In *Proceedings of Resilient Control Systems* (ISRCS), (pp. 55-62). IEEE.

ADDITIONAL READING

Karim, M. E., & Phoha, V. V. (2014). Cyber-physical systems security. In Proceedings of Applied Cyber-Physical Systems (pp. 75-83). Springer New York.

KEY TERMS AND DEFINITIONS

Availability: Ability of a system being accessible.

Confidentiality: Ability to keep information secret.

HIPAA: Health Insurance Portability and Accountability which orders the protection of patient's data.

Integrity: Trustworthiness of data or resources.

PLC: Programmable Logic Controllers.

RTU: Remote Terminal Units are wireless sensing devices.

SCADA: Supervisory Control and Data Acquisition is a wireless embedded system.

Security: Deal with non-operational goals.

UAV: Unmanned Aerial Vehicle a aircraft without human pilot.

WSN: Wireless Sensor Network is a collection of sensor nodes.

Chapter 8
Security Issues of CPS

ABSTRACT

As cyber physical system security is not satisfactory, the security of a particular infrastructure depends on both internal and other related vulnerabilities. Communications between components in the cyber and physical realms lead to unintentional information flow. This chapter describes the difficult communications that occurs between the cyber and physical domains and their impact on security. Assailants may be competent to initiate exclusive attacks to cyber physical systems. There are several types of attacks that affect the interactions between the cyber and physical devices, which might be in a passive way or in an active method. Even though the communication provides authenticity and confidentiality, a few attacks form some threats against ad hoc routing protocols as well as location-based security systems. It has been said that many attacks modify the activities of the targeted control system.

INTRODUCTION

Since decades, the focus of vital foundations and modern control systems is Cyber-Physical Systems (CPS), but then there have been definite instances of machine based attacks. CPS, in any case, is getting more helpless against machine assaults for some reasons. The basic discussion is about the requirement to build challenging models for CPS. At that point, it is recognized that a number of new and basically diverse issues being experienced in the case of CPS as contrasted to well-developed IT security. The depictions of the risks that may appear are required for a systematic investigation of the security of any system. Mounting a challenging model is an approach to comprehend the likelihood of the issue and evaluate the threats. The resources and the inspiration of some possible aggressors will be depicted now. Computers may be compromised anywhere by the cybercriminals and they can locate then even in control systems. These attacks may not be focused on. The goal of these attacks is not damaging control systems; however they may cause adverse reactions: the function of the control system which is infected with malware may be improper (Cardenas et al., 2009).

Today, the security of control systems is an active research field. Yet, from a research perspective, nobody would have expressed the novelty and the basic diversity of this field in contrast to traditional IT security. The product fixing and the property of not being suitable to rapid upgrades are the features distinguish the

DOI: 10.4018/978-1-4666-7312-0.ch008

security of control systems from the traditional IT security. For instance, overhauling a system may need months to prepare the process of making the system offline. Consequently, it is financially hard to defend the suspension of the operation of an industrial computer all the time to establish new security patches. Some security patches may even abuse the official recognition of control systems (Cardenas et al, 2009).

Nowadays, it is far away from an ultimate idea even though the criticalness of security has been defended with many latest reviews. SearchNetworking.com has made Network Report Card analysis and found that the major concern of 47% people who participated in survey is towards network security. The problems like corporate notoriety, aggressive position, and financial growth are strongly associated with security. According to the eMarketer analysis, the violation of computer security is causing an average of $10 billion thrashing for every year (Haque & Ahamed, 2006). The security is described as "The protection of information assets through the use of technology, processes, and training" by Microsoft. The essential attributes of security is usually portray in terms of CIA (Confidentiality, Integrity, and Availability). The inability to access the data by an illicit user is guaranteed by the attribute "Confidentiality". Maintaining the data to be secured and accurate and avoiding the intervention of an illicit user is described as "Integrity". Whenever the legitimate uses need the data, it is made accessible – "Availability". Pervasive security is described as the security in pervasive computing. Besides the features and necessities of computer security, few new liabilities and security cracks are launched in pervasive computing because of its exclusive features when compared to computer security. "Numerous, casually accessible, often invisible computing devices, frequently mobile or embedded in the environment, connected to an increasingly ubiquitous network infrastructure composed of a wired core and wireless edges" is described as pervasive computing. Pervasive computing is the intellectual adolescent of Weiser. The computation is integrated with the environment by this visualization and noticeable communication between the computational units and the users is guaranteed. It can thought as the converse of virtual reality. These days, pervasive computing is demonstrating its convenience to use and degree in every perspective. The coming era of computing technology is made appropriate for several circumstances like the battlefield, hospital and the home with the availability of, and incredible progress in pervasive devices like PDAs, tiny sensors, smart phones, etc. In fact, pervasive devices build a collaborative space where various units are interconnected and support each other to conquer few demands associated with ability. This turns into the way to accomplishment and prompts imparting of data and resources. The disadvantage is that this gives chances to steal and hack. At times, it appears that an open invitation is being given for dynamic and reflexive eavesdroppers because of the features of the pervasive circumstances. Pervasive computing has still to resolve the security issues by keeping in mind that the end goal is to expand the convenience and range scope of situations that can profit from this system.

BACKGROUND

Limitations of CPS

Cyber Physical systems are being implemented in various industrial sectors from medicine to steel factories. The applications of CPS are huge and much wider than that of IT solutions. Building CPS is a very challenging task, it requires intelligent circuits to be first designed and built. These circuits will then be setup in various public infrastructures. How secure and reliable these systems are, is however a different question. The circuit designers can build the best reliable circuit according to the test cases they have. But in truth no system or module is perfect and 100 percent reliable. The real test for each system comes when it is set up in a public atmosphere. the environment provides the best and the worst conditions for the system thus testing it and sometimes providing some extra ordinary conditions to which the system is not capable or built to respond.

Also another limitation to building CPS is resources. Unfortunately the technology of building perfect control systems that can react on their own and make decision without any human help. The technology for building autonomous systems is however not yet perfected.

It can be argued that the resource needed 25 years back are not the same that are needed now. Earlier efficiency was the major need for such networks and systems. But now higher importance is given to robustness and predictability of the system. Since these systems are built for a long term of duty it is necessary that the resources that are used for their building can work for long periods of time. From the nut bolts to microprocessors that are used in the system, everything should be built taking into thought the term for which the system will be used.

In the past decade, the computer networks attacks have turn out to be powerful. Even though some of the control networks are harmless previously, currently they became more susceptible against malicious attacks. As the control systems are the heart of numerous discriminating infrastructures, the penalty of an effective attack on control systems might be more dangerous than on any other systems. Subsequently, breaking down the security of control frameworks is an emerging concern. In the control and confirmation group there is a critical collection of effort on networked control, stochastic framework check, powerful control, and fault-tolerant control. Recent literature did not tend to concentrate on many significant security concerns for control systems. For instance, despite the fact that the modes of failure are much corresponded at the time of attack, it is expected that the autonomous failure is caused. This expectation is due to deficiency in the analysis. Alternatively, the majority networked control work accept that the failure modes pursue a given class possible distributions. Nonetheless, an actual aggressor has no motivations to pursue this implicit distribution, and may attack in a nondeterministic way (Saurabh, et. al, 2009).

For instance, with a specific end goal to guarantee a 50 year manufacture cycle for a fly-by-wire airship, an airplane maker is compelled to buy, at the same time, a 50 year contribution of the microchips that will run the embedded programming. To guarantee that approved ongoing execution is continued, these chips should all be produced on the same production line from the same masks. The systems will be not able to profit from the following 50 years of innovative progress without again doing the (tremendously pricey) validation and certification of the product. Clearly, effectiveness is almost superfluous contrasted with consistency and assurance is hard to accomplish without solidifying the configuration at the physical level. Obviously, something isn't right with the software deliberations being utilized (Lee, 2006).

Security Concerns in CPS

Cyber Physical systems (CPS) have been made to play a central role in the working of various infrastructures and industrial control systems. Their use in such important parts of today's modern world has made them more vulnerable to attacks by malicious and corrupted attackers. Although at the beginning of the decade the computer based attacks (Cardenas et al.,2011) were few in number, but recently the number has started to increase. It is required to prevent such attacks by setting up models to detect intrusions and prevent them from happening, also models are needed to help the system respond and recover from these computer attacks.

The detection of these attacks can be done by first outlining and finding out the weaker points of the system and strengthening them. It involves scanning the whole security of the system from time to time to assess the risks and monitor them. Such a model is called an adversary model.

Security of the most CPS has been mostly been compromised due to disgruntled employees. Many attacks such as the attack on Maroochy shire Council's sewage control system in Queensland, Australia in 2000. The offender of the attack was an ex–employee of the contractor company that had established the control systems at the sewage plant (Cardenas et al., 2011). Such incidents are needed so that we can take stock of the biggest security concerns i.e. insiders. These people provide malicious attackers backdoor entry and vital information of the systems. It is important to take notice of insiders because even if the whole system is completely isolated from public networks the attackers can still cause harm to the system.

Apart from other limitations for security of CPS, is to understand how the attacker will move and work if he gains an access to the systems. By understanding this we can predict how the system will be affected and be one step ahead of the attacker. We can set up small traps around the system network where it is high probability the attacker will move to first after gaining entry to control systems.

Current CPS such as various industrial control systems is not yet intelligent enough to detect any intrusion on their own. By building intelligent system using detection algorithms, which will take into account the changes in the sensor value and the data change in other control devices output values to alert the system administrators of an intrusion in the system.

Also by building resilient systems, the systems may be well capable of detecting and protecting itself from attacks by changing control commands thus preventing the intruder any chance to manipulate the data from the control devices.

Since a successful attack cannot be ruled out successfully, it places more importance on the detection and recovery aspects of the security of CPS. Traditionally the intrusion detection systems are used to trace the path of the attacker through the system. But a need for real time intrusion detection system is necessary since it can sense the interferences in real time by observing the abrupt and sudden changes in the sensor values and other devices on which the system is dependent. Also most importantly current systems cannot detect the affected node and isolate it from the other part of the network thus decreasing the severity of the attack.

A good example of CPS implementation is the power grid systems that have been implemented across the United States of America. These grids represent a distributed form of cyber physical system that has become an important part of life for the current generation. It is a well- known by past history that blackouts for large amount of time can cause economic and safety chaos and inconvenience to many people. The dependency of various daily use devices and comforts on electricity makes the impact of blackouts all the more severe.

The seriousness in effect of force power outage on our life is growing constantly as the power distribution grid turn out to be more consistent and more robotized and with increasing population it is becoming necessary for automated networks to distribute power to prevent human error. Current standardization processes include the implementing the new IEC 61850 protocol that will substitute the present DNP alternates and other protocols. The 61850 standard is used for setting up the interaction console amid substations that supply power to, *e.g.*, parts of acity and the control centers that handle power distribution in the region to maintain the equilibrium between supply and demand. This has led to a growing need and deployment of automated substations to amplify the effectiveness and decrease the maintenance overhead. But automation of such systems makes them more susceptible to power outages as they are now perceived as targets of a well-organizedcyber-attack, power outages can happen also when a distributed control system malfunctions.The effect can be long lasting or small if measured in time factor, they can be fatal economically or have an effect on human lives, if the substation is affected the whole area that it services will be affected. If the substation is connected to other substations and the problem spreads then the affected area can increase. This severity can be different if the problem is created by malicious attackers or there is a genuine malfunction of the components.

The integration of extensive sensing, communication, computation and control with the physical systems is referred as Cyber Physical Systems (CPS). The applications are in different fields like transportation, energy, civil infrastructure, manufacturing, aerospace, chemical processes, etc. Most of the applications are sensitive towards safety. The Internet which is highly available and affordable with economical technology for communication makes infrastructures of that kind more vulnerable to cyber security risks (Mo,& Sinopoli, 2009). The typical functionality of the society is based on the infrastructures like power grid, telecommunication networks etc. So, this may lead to influence the national security. Serious issues like considerably slowing down the financial system of the country, the environment or loss of human life may arise due to any thriving attack. Hence, ensuring the safe functionality of CPS is significantly vital role of CPS security.

The investigation group has recognized the vitality of tending to the challenge of devising secure CPS. The effect of attacks on the cyber physical frameworks is tended in. Consider two conceivable classes of assaults on CPS: Denial of Service (Dos) and deception assaults. The Dos assault avoids the exchange of data, typically either control inputs or sensor readings between subsystems, while the deception assault influences the information trustworthiness of packets by altering their payloads. Deception attack is lacking behind when compared to DoS attack because it is trickier to indentify these deception attacks and are sufficiently tended to. In a later stage, a technology is built up to identify a specific kind of deception attack. A considerable study is made in order to examine, identify and handle failures in CPS. The influence of accidental packet drops on estimator performance and on controller, numerous failure detection algorithms in dynamic systems is examined (Mo,& Sinopoli, 2009). Robust control is a objective to design controllers that operate appropriately under tentative parameter or obscure aggravations, is appropriate to a few CPS circumstances. On the other hand, a vast extent of the survey except that the failure is either irregular or amiable. Alternatively, a sly aggressor can cautiously outline his attack method and betray both detectors and vigorous controllers. Subsequently, the pertinence of failure detection algorithms is flawed in the vicinity of a smart attacker (Mo,& Sinopoli, 2009).

Currently regular Ethernet is being used to deploy DNP and future 61850 standards. The whole deal associations with control focuses are regularly committed lines and, henceforth, are viewed as protected from cyber attacks. This can be made as a safe hypothesis, but this does not totally rule out the security issues the substations have. Since most of these substations are unmanned an attacker can physically access the substation. Also substations that are manned can be attacked by targeting insiders for vital information regarding the working of the substation and passwords etc. Physical admittance inside a substation (or via local wireless preservation link at a substation) could permit attackers to influence power devices. Very basic amount of protection can be provided by encrypting the TCP layer of the protocols involved. However, the messages that have ongoing prerequisites can't be taken care of by TCP. These messages remain tremendously helpless against assaults as they can't simply be encrypted specified that packet transmission happens at the link layer in present results. An alternate issue is postured by the intricacy of distributed systems of substation units that exchange sensor data and individually choose actuator controls. Certain malfunctions at this level may bring about loss of equipment and the formerly portrayed outages.

The US has reported that there have been attacks on various control systems throughout the country and atleast one successful attempt has been reported.

It is an instantaneous requirement for the study on the protection of discriminating infrastructure inside the power grid to contradict cyber physical attacks and distributed control issues that may bring about more enduring outages.

SECURING CPS

Problems and Risks

The Cyber Physical Systems have two dimensions. The first is the system's computational elements, whereas the second is the physical elements. In cyber physical systems both the elements are tightly coupled, where they coordinate and work together in unison. The preludes of such systems are the embedded systems, where the main concentration is on the computation features rather than the physical features. This type of advanced systems pose a new set of problems, risks associated with the problems and consequences of the system being very unpredictable and unknown.

The cyber physical systems have been in the centre of the industrial infrastructure, be it the electric grid, or sewage control system or the safety critical nuclear powerhouse management system for a long time, even then we have experienced problems and attacks against the cyber physical systems.

The threats and the vulnerabilities in the Cyber physical systems may be attributed to the shift of control from manual labor to automated systems. They can be categorized into two sets. It may be due to the errors and software bugs in the increasing complexity of software's, or it may be a malicious attack against the system by attackers who intentionally want to create chaos.

An additional property of control systems that is generally specified is the continuous prerequisites of control systems. Control systems are self-governing resolution building agents which require formulating resolutions instantaneously. As accessibility is an overall investigated issue in data security, continuous accessibility gives a stricter operational environment than most traditional IT systems (Cardenas et al, 2009).

All in all, data security has build well established technologies and configuration standards (confirmation, access control, message integrity, separation of privilege and so on.) that can help us to avoid and respond to attacks against control systems. Nevertheless, explore in computer security has concentrated generally on the security of data. Analysts have not measured how assaults influence the estimation and control algorithms and at last, how assaults influence the physical world. In spite of the fact that the current instruments of data security can give fundamental components for the security of control systems, these systems alone are not sufficient for the exhaustive safeguard of control frameworks. It is possible to realize the consequences of an attack provided the communications of the control system with the physical world should be reasonable. Till now there is no study on how an enemy would choose a technique once it has attained unapproved access to some control system devices. New attack recognition procedures need to be proposed: if the control or sensor information is being corrupted then attacker can be recognized by observing how the physical procedure ought to act focused around the control commands and sensor estimations (Cardenas et al., 2009).

It has been observed that numerous agent-based pervasive computing applications, talks about several scopes of security for a particular environment named Multi Agent System (MAS). Additionally, it also characterizes a security model named Buddy where a security characteristic has been conveyed among all the nodes and every node attempts to defend its neighbor. Hierarchical models are more inclined to be assaulted by malicious attacker. If a particular agent or group of agents keep up the security emphasizes in hierarchical architecture, it is much less demanding to find and infiltrate them. In the Buddy model, every agent accounts the vicinity of its nearest neighbor or buddy through a token passing system. While confronting threat, every agent will request for assistance from its buddy.

Every agent will perform as 'Token Sender' at one time and as 'Token Receiver' during other time. At the point when an agent accepts a token in a predefined time limit, it will come to know that its buddy is in proper condition. Else it identifies an issue and relay a global message to distinguish the situation. Every agent in the network gets an opportunity to relay from time to time (Haque & Ahamed, 2006).

The increase in the vulnerabilities in the cyber physical systems is due to the following reasons such as technology development and evolution and malicious purpose (Cárdenas et al., 2008).

Technology Development and Evolution

- **Automation:** The computers control everything from the initialization, integration, testing, and the working. The physical controllers usually controlled by manual labor are being replaced by embedded operating systems and micro-controllers. Due to additional functionality and complete autonomy of the system, there is an increase in the complexity of the foundation of the software which attributes to more flaws in the conception.
- **Distributed:** To enhance the efficiency of the cyber physical systems, the remote access to all the components connected in the network is being provided. The networks may be corporate networks or even internet. The cyber physical systems which need to be isolated are not as secluded as necessary.
- **Reusable Software Components:** In the recent years, reusability is playing an importantrole in cyber physical systems. Earlier, proprietary components used to be developed which were applied to the purpose of a specific application. The bugs if any in the commodity IT systems may creep into the final systems. Ultimately, all the threats are inherited by the components.
- **Open Design:** The software engineers are divided upon using whether going for an open design or a closed design. A closed design decreases the vulnerabilities, while an open design allows the testers to debug the system and remove any threats.
- **Increasing Size and Functionality:** The systems are allowed to add new features which allow the possibility of new vulnerabilities and threats.

Malicious Purpose

- **Large and Highly Skilled IT Global Force:** More and more people are becoming proficient in technological skills due to the IT boost. Therefore a larger group of people are trying to hack into systems and finding and exploiting vulnerabilities and threats in cyber physical systems.
- **Cyber Criminals:** There are a lot of prebuilt hack tools which provide direct functionality to hack into systems. There are a lot of malicious software like worms, virus and Trojans which creep into even industrial level architecture undetected, which compromises the system. Less computer-skilled people also have admittance to a number attack instruments and cybercrime systems.

A paramount explanation for cyber crime is extortion (Cárdenas et al., 2008).

- **Disgruntled Employees:** Disgruntled employees are presently the significant source of focused computer attacks against cyber physical systems in huge industrial network (Cardenas et al., 2009).

In November 2001, a wireless radio, a SCADA controller and control software was stolen by a 49-year-old VitekBoden and release up to one million liters of sewage into the river and coastal water of Maroochydore in Queensland, Australia. The sewage leak was considerably large. Nearly, 500 meters of open drain in housing area is polluted and gushed into a tidal canal. Significant resources are deployed to clean up the spill. As a result VitekBoden was sentenced to two years in jail. (https://www.tofinosecurity.com/why/Case-Profile-Maroochy-Shire).

- **Militants, Activists, Terrorists:** Are another potential threat (Cardenas et al., 2009) to cyber physical systems. The word 'Cyber Physical Terrorism' refers to two elements: cyber physical systems and terrorism. Thus Cyber Physical Terrorism could be defined as the premeditated attack against computerized systems which effect in aggression in opposition to noncombatant goal by sub-national groups or clandestine agents.
- **Nation States:** Most military powers (Cardenas et al., 2009) are researching future attack innovations, including cyber attacks against the physical framework of different countries. For instance, some national authorities state that electric grid in US has been infiltrated by spies. A few others say that a logic bomb caused a gas pipeline blast in Siberia which affected the economy of Russia during the cold war in 1982.

Differences between CPS Security and Traditional IT Security

It is evident that the security of cyber physical systems during latest years, require to be novel and in a broad sense distinctive in this area from an research perspective contrasted with traditional IT security.

Cyber Physical Systems have a characteristic that distinguishes with IT security, which is programming fixing and repeated revisions, which are not appropriate for cyber physical systems. If there should arise an occurrence of updating a system, it obliges months of preparation of take the system to inactive state and this way is financially hard to support suspending the operation of a industrial machine on a usual base to install new security patches (Cardenas et al., 2009). Some security patches may even abuse the affirmation of cyber physical systems.

A major issue in determining the interruption is the presence of versatile enemies that will endeavor to sidestep the detection process; hence, consider an enemy that thinks about our inconsistency detection process. A traditional methodology is considered in the models by expecting an effective assailant with information of the definite linear model that utilize i.e., environment A, B, and C, the factors, and the control command indicators. Such an effective aggressor may be impossible in a few situations, yet need to test the versatility of the system to such an assailant to ensure security for an extensive variety of attack situations. The objective of the assailant is to bring the weight up in the tank without being discovered (i.e., raise the weight while keeping the fact he controls beneath the subsequent threshold. There are three sorts of model assaults, for example, surge assaults, inclination assaults and geometric assaults. In flow attacks model assailants need to do greatest harm when they get access to the system. In a bias attacks model assailants attempt to change the system unconnectedly by including some challenges over a substantial duration of time. At long last, in geometric assault models aggressors attempt to change the conduct of the system unconnectedly at the start of the assault and afterward augment the harm after the system has been stimulated to a more ineffective state.

In a latest story, on March 7 of 2008, an atomic power plant was unintentionally shutdown on the grounds that a workstation used to observe chemical and analytical information from the plant's business affiliation rebooted after a product redesign. At the point when the machine rebooted, it reset the information on the control system, bringing on security systems to badly decipher the absence of information as a drop in water tanks that chill the plant's radioactive atomic fuel poles.

Real time necessity is another property of cyber physical systems that is typically detailed. The cyber physical systems should be capable of taking real time resolutions. Hence they need to be as independent resolution making agents. While accessibility is an overall contemplated issue in data security, real-time accessibility gives a stricter operational environment than most conventional IT systems.

Additionally, huge industrial cyber physical systems have a lot of legacy systems. A few investigation exertions have attempted to give trivial cryptographic procedures to guarantee information integrity and secrecy. The latest IEEE P1711 standard is intended for giving security in legacy serial connections. Including some low level of security is finer to having no security by any means; then again, the vast majority of the deliberations accomplished for legacy systems ought to be considered as fleeting results. For appropriately securing significant cyber physical systems the fundamental technology must fulfill some basic performance necessities to permit the usage of well tested security mechanisms and technologies.

All the functionalities of the cyber physical systems are not highly discriminating with the traditional IT systems. In contract with the enterprise systems, cyber physical systems demonstrate less complicated network dynamics like infrequent alteration in servers, static topology, constant number of users, general communication patterns, and finally minimum number of protocols. Thusly, realizing system intrusion detection systems may be less demanding than in traditional endeavor systems.

ATTACKS AND ITS CONSEQUENCES

Aggressors might be capable to initiate exclusive attacks to cyber physical systems (i.e., attacks that are not feasible in traditional IT systems). There are several types of attacks that affect the interactions between the cyber and physical devices which might be in a passive way or in an active method.

Types of Attacks on Cyber Physical Systems

As in (Wang et al., 2010), Figure 1 depicts the types of attacks to CPS which are summarized.

Eavesdropping Attack

This a passive type of attack in which the opponent interrupts the information transferred by the system. Basically eavesdropping perceives the system process but does not affect the functioning of the system. CPS is vulnerable to this attack during the traffic measurement such as data monitoring in sensor networks is interrupted during supervising phase. Eavesdropping disrupts the personal data transmitted in the system such as like patient's fitness grade information. In Figure 1, attack 4 and attack 8 represents this type of attack on process of data gathering and selecting control demands respectively.

Figure 1. Types of attacks to CPS

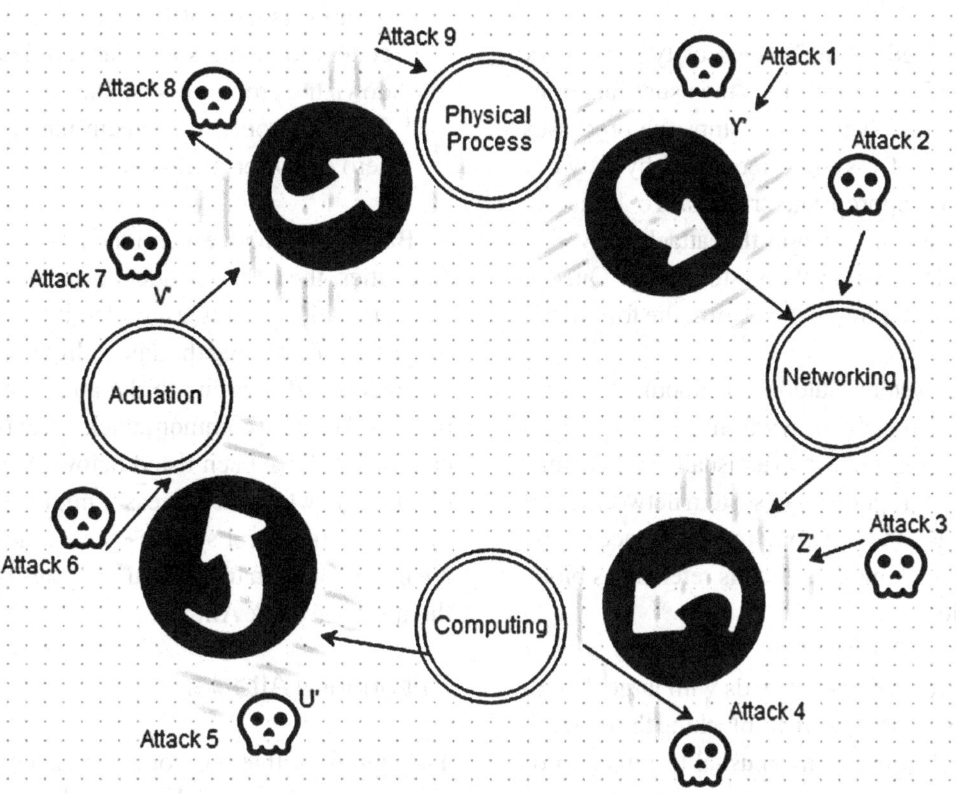

Compromised-Key Attack

In this a key is an undisclosed code to understand the protected data. Once an aggressor gets this key then it is considered as compromised key. With the help of compromised key, attacker has an opportunity to communicate in a secured way without any intervention of sender or receiver. Now the attacker easily modifies the data and able to calculate other keys to have an access to other secured resources or for secured communications. However the process is challenging and resource oriented, it is feasible for an attacker to acquire the compromised key. Attack 9 shown in Figure 1 is to obtain the sensors to perform engineering task opposite way. In other words an attacker reveals the secret information exclusively or acts as a sensor node to endorse other sensor nodes in obtaining keys.

Man-in-the-Middle Attack

In this attack fake communications are driven to the operator in the form of positive or negative fake messages. This in turn make the operator to perform some task when it is not required or not to perform action as if everything is fine when a task actually to be carried out. In Figure 1 attack 1, attack 3, attack 5 and attack 7 are of this type. Attack 7 sends V' for system modification where it is not an actuate command. When an operator tries to correct the problem by following usual methods, then it results in adverse. There are several amendments and review of control data which could affect the system processes.

Denial-of-Service Attack

This is referred as DoS attack of type network attack. The DoS attack stops the usual functioning of a system. This attack stops the processes or responses of a system requested by network resources or appropriate traffics. To limit the usual services of network, this attack delivers a large data by making the system busy. Once it gets access to CPS, it will perform the following:

- Make system shutdown by flooding the sensor network by heavy traffic,
- Cause system to stop unusually by transmitting improper data to system networks, and
- Restrict the network resources access by system elements which is referred as block traffic.

In Figure 1, attack 2 floods with large data to the whole sensor network by blocking the network flow. Attack 6 performs unusual termination of actuation process by transmitting improper data to actuators in the network.

Characteristics of Adversaries

The following are the some of the main types of potential adversaries given in (Wang et al.,2010):

- **Skilled Hackers:** They are experienced developers who find weaknesses of software to misuse it by writing a code for it.
- **Disgruntled Insiders:** These intruders such as contractors, employees or business people may not have enough knowledge of intrusions because their aim is to retrieve system data or to cause system loss through unauthorized access which is a cyber-crime.
- **Criminal Groups:** These people create a threat by launching an attack on a CPS.
- **Nation-States Terrorist Group:** This group gets help of insiders or experienced coders to create some capabilities to slow down the process of critical CPSs facilities. This is to obtain the main targets such as aero or power-grid systems in a country.

Based on the above mentioned adversary characteristics, the CPS defenders can develop some threat model or strategies to identify and resolve the attacks. Protecting the data rich cyber physical systems is difficult due to the above mentioned reasons. The most common attacks on cyber physical systems have been listed below. A latest sort of attack, in which an aggressor might be capable to initiate to control systems (i.e., attacks which are not possible in traditional IT systems), one of them is (Anwar & Ali, 2012):

Resonance Attacks

The aggressor that has compromised a few sensors or controllers will drive the physical system to oscillate or alter at its analytic recurrence

Jamming the Communication Attack

Specialists evaluate the security of Cyber Physical Systems through exploratory assessment of two separate segments in target tracing applications; in the first segment they survey the effect of low level jamming assaults on junction properties in diverse target tracing situations. In the second part they evaluate the intelligent jamming attack strategy in which an assailant intends to amplify his incentive depending on different jamming assault strategies and activities.

Integrity Attack

The attacker desires to agitate the system by infusing external control inputs and false sensor evaluations to initialize this kind of attack (Anwar & Ali, 2012).

Numerous reports have been examined on security of cyber physical systems, which may emerge excessively exaggerated; the way that a client can acquire unapproved benefits in a control system ought to be considered fatally. The Maroochy Shire event in 2000 demonstrated a few of the impacts that assaults can have (Cardenas et al., 2009).

The way of attacks on smart grid could be extremely diverse from that on communication systems, for example, the Internet. The aim of an aggressor may not be simply attaining unapproved data; a challenger could in principle disable the power grid by assaulting the Energy Management System (EMS) which gathers information from remote meters and generates approximation of system states at the interims of about 15 minutes. In the event that an enemy can hack into the power grid and produces false reading information, the energy management at the control center may be deceived by the state approximator, conceivably producing incorrect conclusions on possibility investigation, dispatch, or actually billing. In this section, the effect of vindictive information assault on smart grid, state approximation and contradict evaluations against such assaults (Kosut, Jia, Thomas, & Tong, 2010).

There is a difference amid the traditional "terrible information" because of common reasons (meter breakdown, correspondence blackout, and topological inaccuracy) from malevolent information infused by a challenger. The later may be attentively intended to amplify the effect of assault and avoid revealing. While the issue of terrible information discovery has been well investigated over a long time, the impending harm of malignant information assault has just been explored in recent times.

The conditions under which the challenger can subjectively disturb the state approximator without being identified by the traditional terrible information identification are acquired. The dispute exhibited in can actually be made much stronger: if a challenger can control adequate meters and if there is no former distributions on system states, no indicator will ever have the capacity to recognize a precisely designed malevolent information attack (Kosut et al., 2010).

SECURITY PROBLEMS IN CONTROL SYSTEMS

Computer based frameworks that control a physical process is referred as control systems. They portray a wide mixture of IT based frameworks associated with real world. In light of their applications they are classified as Process Control Systems (PCS), Supervisory Control and Data Acquisition (SCADA) frameworks and Cyber-Physical Systems (CPS). The majority control systems have a set of networked agents comprising of: sensors, actuators, control processing units, and communication devices (Cárdenas et al., 2008).

Fundamental designing of a control system is as follows. It comprises numerous layers. In the primary layer the physical segment is joined with sensors and actuators. The real world quantity is sensed by sensors and this quantity is changed to digital value by actuators. This digital value is then prepared in control system for working and producing the output. The central processing devices referred as programmable logical controllers are associated with the sensors and then actuators. The real time information is transmitted between the process controllers and operator systems by the control system. The workstations are utilized in the fields like supervisory control, arranging the physical infrastructure points. The larger amount is the site producing operations, which is responsible for production control, advancing the methodology, and maintaining the history of a procedure (Cárdenas et al., 2008). Cases of control systems are shown in Figure 2.

Basic threats to control systems are many. Since the replacement of physical controls by microprocessor and embedded operating systems are going on thus increasing the complexity and implementation flaws, which are often unsecure to control systems

Working of control systems employs high field of networking therefore are subjected to all kinds of network risks. In networking high security has to me maintained to prevent unwanted loss of data, confidential information and system hacking and faults.

In the specific instance of SCADA systems, flourishing assaults objective is to change the expert station view of the environment adjusting the semantic of the data. In the meantime the aggressors need to reduce the exploitation of software and hardware. This is carried out by misleading some of the nodes. Conventional intrusion detection systems almost not work against these kinds of attacks.

The linear traditional estimation methods focused around models of the environment are utilized in detection. The structural properties of the system are affected by the physical attacks. Both the sensor and control information are affected by the integrity attacks. Hence both the physical attacks as well as the integrity attacks need to be detected. Nodes sense the environment and convey the sensed data to the expert station that performs aggregation and analysis of information. The expert station will figure out

Figure 2. Control systems applications

the approximated state of the network by taking the sensor information into account. Decisions or control is determined based on these approximations. Both sensing and control information are transmitted using communication networks and are accordingly subject to denial of service (Cardenas et al., 2009)

The designing of the control system is open-sourced so any attacker can easily access and take out the necessary information. However open designing is useful because the bugs can be easily fixed here. The officials operating control system, because of its open sourced interface can get easily and quickly fault resolved without much time being wasted and without any data loss. But still the debate among the organizations is still active regarding closed and open design. The equal numbers of advantages and disadvantages, pros and cons have still put the final solution and law whether to use open design or to employ closed designed control system in the industry, on stay.

The population is growing, so the area of functionality of the control system is also expanding. Control systems work environment is expanding, so the large numbers of users are also expanding. Therefore larger set of individuals can now discover and produce array of assaults for computer-based systems. Another most dangerous threat to control system is Cybercrime. Cybercrime involves the people who are having less computer knowledge also have admittance to a numerous attack instruments and cybercrime networks. The reason behind people involving behind cybercrime is the extortion. The crime helps them make money. Money which they can earn on the surge of safety of people, money which they earn leading to loss for an organization.

One of the attributes of pervasive security is to reduce collaboration with the client. Accordingly, the data being gathered about the client remains practically transparent from clients' perspective. To build psychological fulfillment for the client, criticism may be an important part. It will enlighten the client about the alteration of information and to whom and how it will be utilized. On one side the client participation in security guaranteeing components is to be reduced; on the other, pervasive units are required to be served by numerous context oriented data including location, character, circumstance, time, and so forth., where in a few cases client contribution is required. The issue of adjusting security with client collaboration is constantly there (Haque & Ahamed, 2006).

A vital undertaking for encouraging the administrator's feedback is its data awareness. Study on human-workstation cooperation for enhancing the responsiveness of the administrator is a main exploration challenge. Other than recuperation with a human on top of it there is similarly a requirement for automatic recuperation. Since CPS use self-governing, real time decision making procedures for controlling the physical world, assaults may present new difficulties for the design and analysis of secure systems. Fundamental thoughts are from control hypothesis, for example, reconfiguration or fault-detection and separation, to design self-governing and real time detection and reaction procedures for wellbeing basic applications that oblige constant feedback (Cardenas et al., 2009).

The important information which is often subjected to get loss by the attack on the control system is being described now. The first one is the policy, the prototype which every host has on his system. It is this policy and prototype which sets rules how the resources are going to be visible and used by any person who operate that system. There are along with general policies, some special policies are also there on the usage of some specific resources. These policies are very much have to keep safe and are often the target of attackers. Apart from these, policies on the usage, access of resources, the information about the location of the control system, location of the resources. An asset may insist some particular trusted areas as a prerequisite for attaining the service. An asset may be accessed by remote clients although others may have entry limited to their area (Haque & Ahamed, 2006). Therefore not only the access methods are to be kept safe, also the resources with the most importantly the resources carrying the information about the location of the control systems.

The attackers while attacking often look first for the connection mechanism. The connection mechanism defines the prototype, how the control systems are connected to each other.

Data incorporates a connection mechanism and its security, bandwidth, packet routing, and so on. Likewise, it incorporates data about the devices being utilized as a part of communication amid the client and the environment.

Recent Threats to Control Systems

The cases of the threats to control systems recently have increased. Maroochy Shire Council's sewage control system in Queensland, Australia after installed in January 2000. After the installation, the problems started increases as alarm was not ringing at required time. In 2000 the Interior Ministry of Russia stated that attackers had stopped brief control of the system controlling gas streams in regular gas pipelines. In 2008 a young person in Poland utilized a changed TV remote control to control the switch tracks of trams. As a consequence, a death poll of 100 people, when drivers of the trams lost their control over the trams (Cárdenas et al., 2008). There are many cases of accidents happening in past all over the globe which have led to the discussion on this severe security issue on control systems.

Feeling the need to develop and take measures to control and reduce the increasing threats on the control systems all over the world, various organizations have worked on the security reforms. ISA (a society of industrial automation and control systems) is involved in emerging a security standard ISA-SP 99 which helps in safeguarding manufacturing and industrial control systems. Many other industrial sectors like chemical, oil and gas, and water have made the committees which are recently evolving programs and standard for safeguarding their infrastructure from attackers, preventing information about location, resources, prototypes, etc. to flow. The department of energy in a foreign country has also controlled security efforts by launching the national SCADA (Supervisory Control and Data Acquisition) test bed package and by emerging a 10-year framework for securing control systems in the energy sector. This program prevents control system from being attacked and developing false issues. The energy demand is keep on increasing (because of growing population) therefore every country wants to keep their control systems in energy department safe and secure.

In Simple and Secure Resource Discovery (SSRD) (Haque & Ahamed, 2006) analysts projected a trust model. Here a trust estimation of 1.0 denotes ample reliability and 0 denotes absence of reliability. Another node with no former knowledge of communication gets a trust estimation of 0.5 demonstrating neither reliable nor unreliable. Here the feature trust is depending on the service and has the features of reflexivity and transitivity. Every vendor or supervisor of a device holds a table which shows the security level needed by each of the accessible services. The range of security level needed by an administration is from 1 to 10. The resource supervisors additionally preserve an alternate list named 'service trust', which depicts the trust identified with every available service for all the neighboring nodes. At whatever point an appeal for service is received, this table is utilized as a look up table. Threat is an essential parameter that is required to portray in keeping up security. This is particularly dangerous for the situation when a choice must be made about conceding opportunity to an obscure element that does not have appropriate suggestion; the related plausible hazard needs to be figured.

Here threat has been considered as the likelihood that a communication will prompt a disastrous circumstance. Threat valuation model is developed which will be implanted in the threat approximator initially mines characteristics which are then grouped and the Average Loss Rate (ALR) is computed. Mahalanobis distance is utilized in defining the resemblance among vectors. Later the Risk Probability (RP) of a communication is determined. This model contrasts from other static models in light of the fact that it has the ability to vigorously compute the threat component for a new collaboration (Haque & Ahamed, 2006).

Context-Aware Security Framework

A context is a collection of environmental states and settings that controls the systems or application's performance in which event occurs (Wang et al., 2010). The following Figure 3 as in (Wang et al., 2010) depicts the concept of context-aware security framework. This security-relevant context comprised of various security quantities such as authentication, encryption, key agreement protocol, access control and so on.

A context-aware security system is a security mechanism for CPS can change according to the physical environment with the help of context coupling. There are four types of context such as system context related to CPU, Wireless network status, etc., user context related to Location, Medical History, Emotion, etc., physical environment context related to Temperature, Lightning, Weather, etc., time context – Time. This framework mainly focuses on security significant context to prevent the system information from illegal access and alteration to support privacy, reliability and accessibility.

The general workflow of context-aware security framework is represented through health care example. In a health care CPS the surgery doctor is ratified to have admittance to patient's records. When the doctor is inside the hospital he can easily retrieve the patient's information, at the same time while the doctor is in roaming,

Figure 3. Context-aware security system

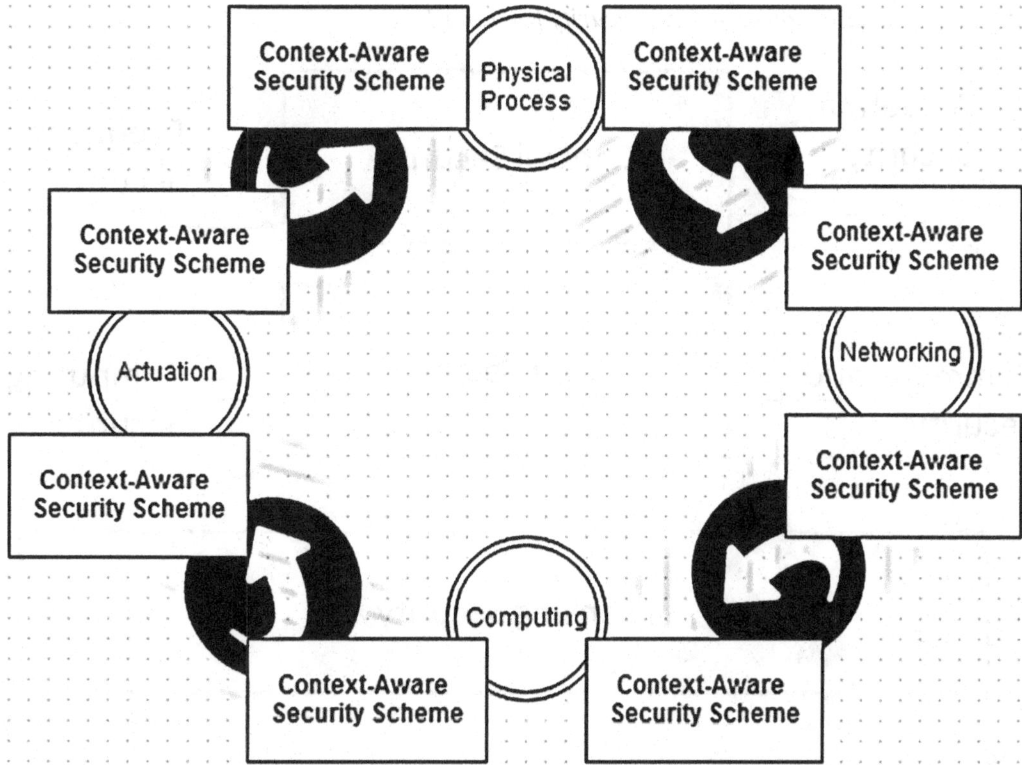

the sensing data shows his/her location as outside the hospital. When the doctor wishes to use the information then the operation of admittance control is combined with the modified context and access is denied. This framework is divided into three aspects (Wang et al., 2010) shown in Figure 4 for CPS such as sensing security, cyber security and control security are described below.

- **Sensing Security:** To obtain the objective of secure sensing a Trust Platform Module (TPM) (Wang et al., 2010) is implemented. TPM supports trusted boot to measure the code boot time through cryptographic hash function. This is to be done before loading each section of code and it uses ARM11 processor to improve the security level of system by restricting security parameter to a chip. The sensor node platform comprised of ARM11 chip, external memory flash and SDRAM, transmitter (Zigbee), temperature sensor and power supply activated by battery. Hence the information is secured from the sensors to the verifiers with secret keys and preventing the platform from attacks.
- **Cyber Security:** It is a combination of communication security and computing security. As CPS is to form a network for information synthesis, it requires a context-integrated communication protocols design for security. These protocols are used to secure CPS communication (both inter and intra) from interferers (active) and eavesdroppers (passive) challengers. The processed and collected data is stored for future access and secured from illegal access. In spite of available context-aware schemes related to key, authentication and privacy protection management to secure data CPS platform requires context-aware encryption, digital signature and access control solutions.

Figure 4. Main aspects of context-aware security framework

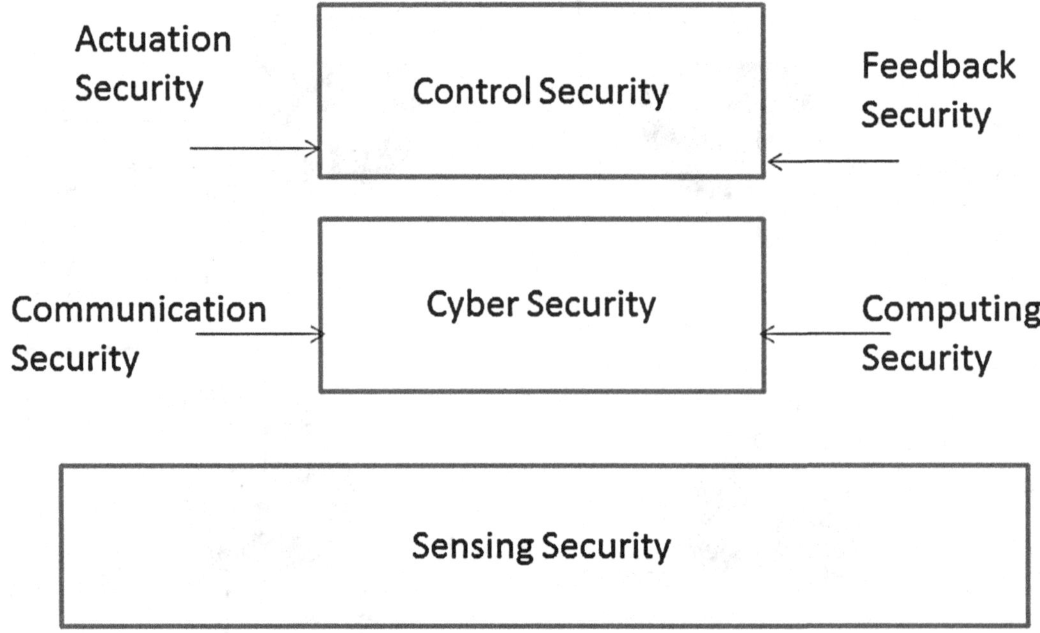

- **Control Security:** It is a combination of actuation and feedback security. Actuation security checks whether suitable approved actuation had been taken place or not. Feedback security is to check whether the feedback for actuation performed is protected by control systems of CPS.

Basically security solutions concentrate on data security but still it has to provide security from several attacks on CPS.

Context-aware privacy protection and encryption scheme restricts the eavesdropping of user's information. Context-aware mutual authentication protocol solves the realism issues like man-in-the middle attacks whereas context-aware access control resolves the illegal access of data. To have more security context-aware keys management scheme execute CPS related applications using keys management and context-aware intrusion detection identify invalid interference and prevent DoS attacks in CPS.

CONTROL SYSTEMS AGAINST MALICIOUS ATTACKS

Control systems are computer-based systems that monitor and control physical processes. These systems represent a wide variety of networked information technology (IT) systems connected systems are also called Process Control Systems (PCS) (Cardenas et al., 2011), Supervisory Control and Data Acquisition (SCADA) systems (in industrial control or in the control of the critical infrastructures), Distributed Control Systems (DCS) (Cardenas et al., 2011) or Cyber-Physical Systems (CPS) (to refer to embedded sensor and actuator networks).

The guaranteeing of the availability of services only to legitimate clients by a security mechanism is specified as secure discovery. The traffic is required to be synchronized by including the details like owner of service, type of service and so on by the system when there is a demand for a service by the clients. At this step, 'Secure Delivery' guarantees that the service demanded by the client will be offered in the obliged way. That implies the service, on the path to the client, ought to be safe from any forging or altering (Haque & Ahamed, 2006).

The system is required to maintain the updated list of available services. This will help in offering a particular service to a client when there is a demand. Availability indicates that the service is available to provide. Control systems are typically made out of a set of networked agents, for example, Programmable Logic Controllers (PLCs), and specialized gadgets. For oil and gas industry use incorporated control systems to handle refining functions at plant sites, Observe streams, container levels, or stress in storage tanks; and control the combining chemicals to the water (Cardenas et al., 2011).

In this encompassing and in light of the fact that the amount of devices could be truly tremendous, it is extremely hard to identify the physical device with which communication is being taking place. For this we require a protected communication channel alongside device validation. Again the solicitation for making this trust channel is coursing through the imparted, problematic wireless channel. As a methodology to tackle this issue, it has been projected to utilize GPS and other area tracing systems for identifying the exact area of the communicating device. At the same time, it is known that GPS doesn't work inside structures and a possible area tracing system which is pertinent for small pervasive devices is still in the stage of exploration (Haque & Ahamed, 2006).

Numerous control applications could be named as safety – significant: their malfunction can result in hopeless damage to the physical system. SCADA systems, specifically, carry out essential operation in national significant foundations, water and waste-water management, and transportation systems. Additionally, they are at the center of health –care devices, and transportation administration. The disturbance of these control systems could have a huge effect on public health, security and lead to expansive financial damage (Cardenas et al., 2011).

Control systems, nonetheless, are presently at an advanced stage of danger to computer attacks on the grounds that their weaknesses are progressively getting uncovered and accessible to a constantly developing set of persuaded and exceptionally talented assailants. Stuxnet captures schedules to study, compose and find obstructs on a Programmable Logic Controller (PLC). By capturing these solicitations, Stuxnet is capable to adjust the information transmitted to or reflected back from the PLC without the administrator of the PLC ever realizing it (Cardenas et al., 2011).

Research on malignant information attack from the viewpoint of a challenger who must make a tradeoff amid incurring the greatest harm on state approximation and being recognized by the EMS at the control center is being carried out. The thought of Attacker Operating Characteristic (AOC) is characterized that portrays the tradeoff between the possibilities of being distinguished vs. follow-on (additional) mean-square error at the state approximator. Subsequently the issue of ideal attack is devised as diminishing the likelihood of being discovered subject to creating the Mean Square Error (MSE) to amplify beyond a predestined level. Discovering the attack with the ideal AOC is unmanageable, regrettably. A heuristic that permits to get attacks is presented. These attacks are that with least assault power spillage to the detector while amplifying the mean square error at the state approximator beyond a predestined goal. This heuristic lessens to an eigenvalue issue that could be resolved even while disconnected from the net (Kosut et al., 2010).

The objective of the worm in a Windows is to hunt for WinCC/Step 7, a sort of programming used to program and observe PLCs. They are commonly customized with a stepping stool logic program: logic conventionally used to design control procedures for boards of electromechanical communications. If Stuxnet is not able discover the software in the contaminated windows machine, it will not do nothing; be that as it may, on the off chance that it discovers the software, it taints the PLC with an alternate Zero-day exploits, and afterward redevelops it. Stuxnet additionally endeavors to conceal PLC modifications with a PLC toolkit (Cardenas et al., 2011).

CONCLUSION

Some interesting features that these systems have when compared to conventional IT systems are recognized and projected some new research difficulties focused around the physical models of the methodology being controlled. The identified exploration difficulties are for the most part vague and hope that forthcoming research in these fields can give an added level of security to control systems. At that point, an upgraded security and detection methods for power system against pernicious information attacks are presented. The power system can be made safer from any pernicious cyber physical information attack with the reconstruct data structure and equivalent enduring test, which does not require any physical exertion contrasting with the results in the literature. In the event of access control, the system is focused around the part and characteristics of the client. Again this benefit of getting to framework assets and services is unpredictable which relies on upon the time, circumstance and other relevant data. Here the client needs to belief the pervasive computing environment comprising the resources and services accessible. In the meantime the framework needs to guarantee the characteristics and access privileges of the client. In spite of the fact that numerous access control mechanisms have been produced for a number of particular situations, a typical structure which works in all situations with equivalent proficiency is required.

REFERENCES

Amin, S., Cárdenas, A. A., & Sastry, S. S. (2009). Safe and secure networked control systems under denial-of-service attacks. In Hybrid systems: Computation and control (pp. 31-45). Springer Berlin Heidelberg. doi:10.1007/978-3-642-00602-9_3

Anwar, R. W., & Ali, S. (2012). Trust based secure cyber physical systems. In *Proceedings of Workshop on Trustworthy Cyber-Physical Systems*. Academic Press. Retrieved from http://www.cs.ncl.ac.uk/publications/trs/papers/1347.pdf

Cardenas, A., Amin, S., Sinopoli, B., Giani, A., Perrig, A., & Sastry, S. (2009, July). Challenges for securing cyber physical systems. In *Proceedings of Workshop on Future Directions in Cyber-Physical Systems Security*. Academic Press.

Cardenas, A. A., Amin, S., Lin, Z. S., Huang, Y. L., Huang, C. Y., & Sastry, S. (2011, March). Attacks against process control systems: risk assessment, detection, and response. In *Proceedings of the 6th ACM Symposium on Information, Computer and Communications Security* (pp. 355-366). ACM. doi:10.1145/1966913.1966959

Cárdenas, A. A., Amin, S., & Sastry, S. (2008, July). Research challenges for the security of control systems. HotSec.

Haque, M. M., & Ahamed, S. I. (2006). Security in pervasive computing: Current status and open issues. *International Journal of Network Security*, *3*(3), 203–214.

Kosut, O., Jia, L., Thomas, R. J., & Tong, L. (2010, August). On malicious data attacks on power system state estimation. In *Proceedings of Universities Power Engineering Conference* (UPEC), (pp. 1-6). IEEE.

Lee, E. A. (2006, October). Cyber-physical systems-are computing foundations adequate. In *Proceedings of NSF Workshop on Cyber-Physical Systems: Research Motivation, Techniques and Roadmap* (vol. 2). NSF.

Mo, Y., & Sinopoli, B. (2009, September). Secure control against replay attacks. In *Proceedings of Communication, Control, and Computing*, (pp. 911-918). IEEE. doi:10.1109/ALLERTON.2009.5394956

Wang, E. K., Ye, Y., Xu, X., Yiu, S. M., Hui, L. C. K., & Chow, K. P. (2010, December). Security issues and challenges for cyber physical system. In *Proceedings of the 2010 IEEE/ACM Int'l Conference on Green Computing and Communications & Int'l Conference on Cyber, Physical and Social Computing* (pp. 733-738). IEEE Computer Society. doi:10.1109/GreenCom-CPSCom.2010.36

ADDITIONAL READING

Burmester, M., Magkos, E., & Chrissikopoulos, V. (2012). Modeling security in cyber–physical systems. *International Journal of Critical Infrastructure Protection*, *5*(3), 118–126. doi:10.1016/j.ijcip.2012.08.002

Hu, Y. C., Perrig, A., & Johnson, D. B. (2003, April). Packet leashes: a defense against wormhole attacks in wireless networks. In INFOCOM 2003. Twenty-Second Annual Joint Conference of the IEEE Computer and Communications. IEEE Societies (Vol. 3, pp. 1976-1986). IEEE. doi:10.1109/INFCOM.2003.1209219

Lee, E. A. (2007). Computing foundations and practice for cyber-physical systems: A preliminary report. University of California, Berkeley, Tech. Rep. UCB/EECS-2007-72.

Wesson, K. D., Humphreys, T. E., & Evans, B. L. (2012, October). Position Paper: Secure Time Transfer for CPS. In *NSF/NSA National Workshop on The New Clockwork for Time-Critical Systems*.

KEY TERMS AND DEFINITIONS

Cyber Criminals: Hack the system directly with the help of hacking tool.

Disgruntled Insiders: Intruders provide loss to systems.

DoS: Denial of Service is a type of attack.

EMS: Energy Management System which collects data from remote meters and produces estimations of system states.

Militants, Activists, Terrorists: A possible threat to CPSs.

PCS: Process Control Systems.

Resonance Attacks: Compromise sensors or controllers to change the physical system.

Skilled Hackers: Skilled hackers misuse software to change the code.

Chapter 9
Interoperability and Communication Issues in CPS

ABSTRACT

Cyber physical systems involve multi-domain models during the development process of the design. This chapter focuses on integrated design methodology that provides reliable relationships between various system models of heterogeneous types. Each model is linked with the base architecture over the abstraction of an architectural view framework. From quadrotor perspective, this framework compares system models from different domains. Present methods lack in modeling, analysis, and design of CPSs due to nonexistence of an integrated framework. To overcome these difficulties, an architectural level system model is defined to capture the structural interdependencies. A base architecture for the complete system is described in this chapter to confirm the structural reliability the model elements and components present in it. The usefulness of this process is exemplified in the quadrotor air vehicle.

INTRODUCTION

An ample diversity of computing environments is evolved with the progress in the information technology. The group of different networks connected to each other is referred as heterogeneous networks and at the same time interoperability among these networks is plays a vital role. The integration of computational and physical elements is called as cyber physical systems. Smart home, transportation, health care, etc., are the areas where the cyber physical systems can be applicable. As different networks can be integrated as heterogeneous networks, similarly various CPS networks can also be integrated to form a global CPS network. The interoperability and the communication among various components in the CPS are guaranteed by the middleware framework. The middleware is able to deal with various protocols of different devices in the communication process.

BACKGROUND

System Models

Many different province models are utilized in the development process of the Cyber Physical Systems (CPS). The required architecture can be developed using the runtime base architecture

DOI: 10.4018/978-1-4666-7312-0.ch009

which behaves like a skeleton structure of the architecture and the structural, semantic mapping between the elements of the model and the objects of the system.

The model based development approach can also be used to build complex cyber physical systems using models during the development process of the system. Different frameworks are possible to be developed with preferred features of the system. Either the cyber elements or the physical systems can only be represented but it is not possible to represent both using the particular modeling framework. Ex: The physical processes can only be represented but it is not possible to represent the computation or communication elements using the differential equation models. Similarly, the concurrency and control flow in software can be represented using the discrete formalisms like process algebras, which cannot represent the continuous phenomena in the physical world. Hence, multiple models are required to complete the design and development of the heterogeneous elements in CPS.

The architecture of the system is used to provide the details of structural representation at high level of abstraction and also the designers are allowed to perform the tasks like functionalities to various elements, the estimation of the compatibility of different elements, the tradeoff among different quality attributes like performance, maintainability and reliability. The better approach for developing a system is to build the relationships among different model at the architectural level instead of transforming one model into the other or introducing a universal modeling language. The structure and the relations among different elements in a system are confined in the architectural approach exclusive of the effort to realize all the particulars of any specific model. The base architecture for CPS is illustrated using the CPS architectural style. The STARMAC (Stanford Testbed of Autonomous Rotorcraft for Multi Agent Control) (Bhave, Krogh, Garlan, & Schmerl, 2010), quadrotor is given as a case study. A set of connected concerns are symbolized using a group of architectural perceptions which also help in characterizing the architectures. The components and connections of a system are represented as an annotated graph in the Component and Connector (C&C) perspective model (Bhave et al., 2010). In this model, the main computational and physical elements are represented as the components, the pathways among various communications and physical elements are represented as connectors and properties of the elements are represented as annotations.

The whole CPS cannot be depicted based on the existing C&C architectural styles even though they concentrate mainly on software and computational infrastructures. The systems base architecture is the runtime representation of the complete CPS. All the cyber components, physical components and connectors constitute in the base architecture of CPS which can be treated as an illustration of the CPS architecture style. The type of information and the physical quantities that flow among components need to be communicated by the base architecture. Hence it should have the required information in order to perform the task correctly and appropriately. The suitable connectors characterize the relations among various physical variables and communication system among the components. The confirmed necessities and system provisions are used to construct the base architecture of a new CPS all through the design phase. The models of the system, old credentials, the system designers' awareness and the existing system are used to infer the base architecture of the legacy CPS. In both the cases, the progress in the design of the CPS leads to the advancement in the base architecture during the development process of the system.

The relation of the architectural views to the base architecture is demonstrated using the various systems like real time, multi-loop feedback, and embedded systems. The aerial vehicles are permitted to perform the autonomous operation using the test algorithms which are developed based on the STARMAC quadrotor platform. The body frame of the aircraft is surrounded with the four rotors symmetrically which are used for actuation. The inertial measurement unit, sonar, and the Global Positioning System (GPS) unit are the elements of the sensor suite in the vehicle. It is realized as a hierarchical system where two levels are involved as low level attitude controller and a high level position controller. The reference routes to be followed by the quadrotor are generated by the remote Ground Station Controller (GSC). The flight is manually controlled by joysticks which are the elements of GSC. A serial link is used to provide the communication between the two onboard controllers. The UDP protocol is utilized to administer the interactions between the PC and GSC over a Wi-Fi network.

Multi-Domain Models of CPS

The base architecture for the quadrotor which is built based on the STARMAC. As the CPS is an integration of physical process and the cyber elements, similarly the complete runtime architecture is designed. Models of multiple domains are utilized to depict and perform the analysis of CPS. Only few requirements of the base system are concentrated by each model. The different views of the STARMAC quadrotor as the physical, software, control design and hardware is represented using four different models in (Bhave et al., 2010) is shown in Figure 1. In practice, each model or any analysis tool are developed as a group of communicating components or modules. The specific formalism under the basic design of the tool explains the structure of each model with syntax and semantics. The structure of the model is also referred as its architecture. At any level of generalization, the models of the system to be integrated and relation among these models are to be described.

The abstractions and modifications of the base architecture are the architectures of the systems which are characterized in the architectural view. The dependencies in the midst of the various models are determined, administered and the jointly limiting design choices are estimated based on the well-defined relations between a view and the base architecture. The outcome of different investigations and the designs are maintained in the base architecture which behaves as a storehouse in this case to precise the interdependencies. The individual relations to the base architecture of the system are analyzed which enables to provide the

Figure 1. Multi-domain models of a CPS

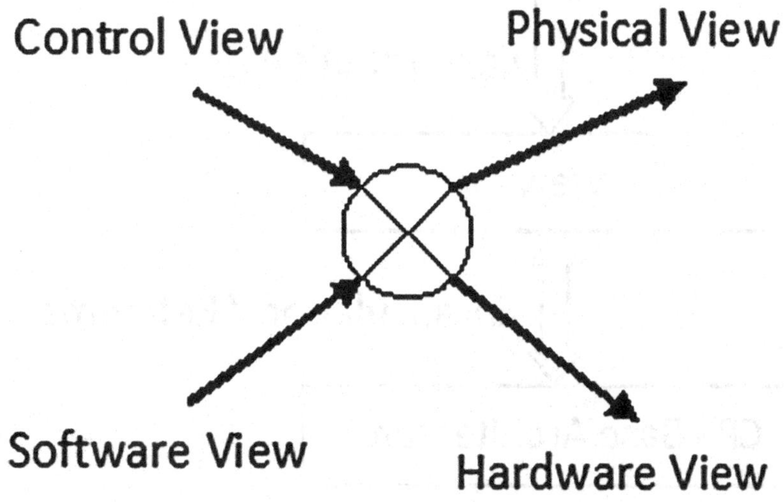

causes related to the mappings among different models. The details of mappings among heterogeneous models of CPS cannot be presented by the existing tools. To realize the impact of one view over another by the design choices or investigations is usually unfeasible. Hence this is characterized as a crisis for architectural modeling. From the structural point of view, the nonfigurative details that arc inappropriate for a specific scrutiny of a resultant architectural model are documented as a report in the architectural view.

The concept of base architecture and the informal definition of architectural view are formalized based on the following definition (Bhave et al., 2010):

Definition 1:

A tuple <C_V, R^M_V, R^V_{BA}>: Is used to represent an architectural view V for a modeling formalism M, where:

C_V: The component connector of the architectural view V whereas the modeling formalism identifies the category, limitations, and semantics.

R^M_V: Is a mapping which shows how the components of the model are related with the components of C_V.

R^V_{BA}: Is a relation that associates elements in C_V with elements in the BA.

The association among the views, system models and the base architecture conceptually in (Bhave et al., 2010) is shown in the Figure 2. Commonly, there will be no one-to-one association between the model components and the base architecture elements. RMV abstracts the components of the model or is a one-to-one mapping. A collection of simple elements is integrated into single component in the view and a "componentized" version of the model is built successfully. The particular modules and connectors of the view are assembled and are related to the subset of the components of the base architecture by the system architect based on the improvement relation, R^V_{BA}. The system architect defines only a subset of the associations while the remaining associations are derived depending on the semantics of the fundamental view. The acceptable

Figure`2. Relationship between models and the BA through views

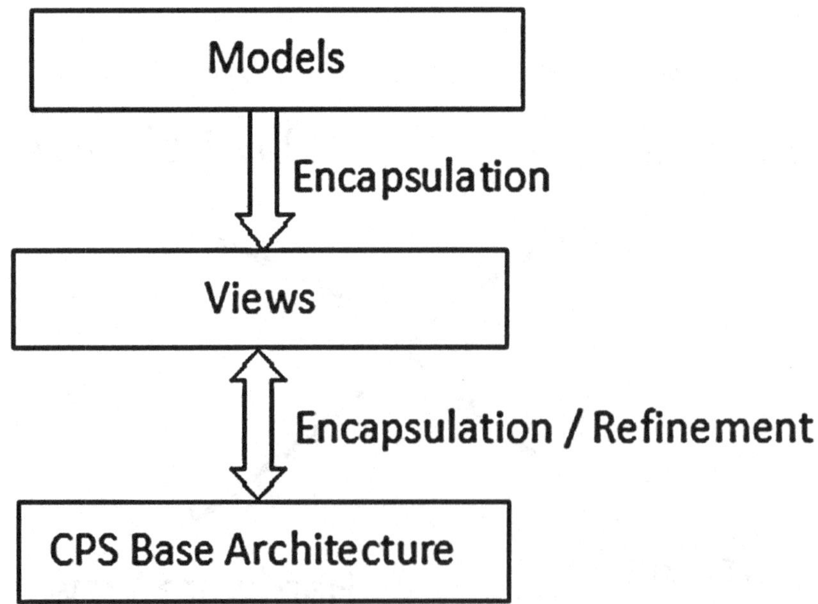

mappings are one-to-many which is also referred as encapsulation and many-to-one which is also known as refinement. The unknown conflicting connections among the encapsulated components may arise due to many-to-many relations, hence they are permitted. The structure produced from an encapsulation process on the components of view is referred as encap-view (Bhave et al., 2010). Similarly, the structure based on the encapsulation process on the elements of the base architecture is known as encap-BA (Bhave et al., 2010).

MapleSim is used to model the physical dynamics of the quadrotor from the primary ideology. Similarly, Simulink is used to model the dynamics of the vehicle from the present control system.

Control View

The quadrotor system is inspected as a signal flow (Simulink) model in the control engineer's point of view. The Robostix subsystem of the Simulink model is used to depict the position controller element of the base architecture and the emphGumstix subsystem of the simulink model is used to depict the attitude controller element of the base architecture. The STARMAC dynamics block, 3DM blocks, Superstar II are used to signify the vehicle dynamics, IMU sensors and GPS correspondingly.

Simulink is used in the construction of the control view. In the control view, each component is represented using a top-level Simulink block and the connector is represented using a single line among the components using R^{M}_{V}. The semantics of the fundamental signal flow of Simulink Meta model are used to derive the semantics for the control view. Ex: Since the signal is used to depict the connector in the control view, the only connector in the control view can be related to semantically alike connectors connecting two components in the base architecture using R^{V}_{BA}. The four cyber physical connectors linking the attitude controller and an encapsulated component of the base architecture are mapped to a single connector linking the Robostix and Starmanc of the view.

The Robostix, GPS and Gumstix elements of the control view are integrated as one macro component. The position controller, GPS, and attitude controller of the base architecture are integrated as a single element. Macro element of the control view and single element of the base architecture are associated with each other.

The subsequent state might come up when many-to-many mapping among macro elements is permitted:

In the macro element of the control view, a contradictory connector presented linking Robostix and GPS might be masked.

Hence, this type of connectors might not be able to determine when some form of consistency verification need to be carried out on the control view and the base architecture.

Process Algebra View

The behavior of the Finite State Process (FSP) (Bhave et al., 2010) is modeled using process algebra. The collection of event traces referred as processes are represented in terms of event patterns. Each transition of a system corresponds to as an event in a trace. Generally, the activities of cyber elements are confined moderately sound by FSP, at the same time the summary of continuous dynamics are used to depict the physical elements. The ancient process of FSP can illustrate the activities of the entities which are the components in the FSP view. The events are used by the processes to communicate with each other, the communication is represented as a connector between two FSP components, and FSP process is used to explain the protocol which is used by the communication.

The dynamics of the quadrotor is summarized and the association between the ground station and the position controller is concentrated by the FSP specification of the quadrotor. Each unit of the view is associated with the FSP process by generating the process algebra view. The process of sending the set points to the position controller, PC by ground station controller, GSC is defined by the ground station process which is associated with the Gnd_Station (Bhave et al., 2010) element. The process of reaction of the ideal closed loop quadrotor against the position set points is defined by the position controller process which is associated with the Quarotor component. The communication protocol between the Gnd_Station (Bhave et al., 2010) and Quadrotor is described by the FSP process which is associated with the connector which links the Gnd_Station with the Quadrotor.

There are two different kinds of connectors as below:

- A wireless UDP is characterized by a lossy connector whereas the wireless TCP is characterized by a lossless connector.
- The performance of the whole system is evaluated and can be compared based on the protocol among the links since there are several connector protocols.

The process algebra is associated with the base architecture. Single Quadrotor element of the view is encapsulated with the physical components in the base architecture and this encapsulation is depicted by the abstraction of vehicle dynamics.

Physical View

The rotors apply the forces and torques to the vehicle frame and based on which the dynamics of the vehicle are depicted in the physical view.

The vibrant performance of the whole system architecture can be characterized formally by means of the CPS style. Modelica language is used to realize the model of quadrotor dynamics. The formal correlations involving the exertion and flow variables of all connected component's ports are utilized to term the semantics of the CV. The set of components in the physical view are associated with subset of the elements in the base architecture.

Logic Model: Modeling CPS with Coroutined Co-Inductive CLP(R)

CPS exhibits four different features like executing distinct calculations, concurrency, deal with continuous quantities and run forever. The physical systems are controlled by the hybrid automata which also communicated with CPS. A comprehensive set of real valued variable in the finite state automaton define a hybrid automaton. The evolution laws denoted as differential equations are used to tag the states of the automaton. Based on the law associated with each state, its variable values vary continuously with time. The invariant condition that must be satisfied by the control till when it is associated with the location is also appended in the tag of the location. The guarded sets of assignments are tagged to the transitions of the automaton. When the guard is true, the transition is activated and the values of the variables are modified based on the assignments. Each transition is tagged with a labeling function. The initialization of the system is described by a set of feasible values.

Reactor Temperature Control System

It is a conventional paradigm of the Cyber physical system. Reactor core (Saeedloei,& Gupta, 2011) is one of the elements of this reactor temperature control system and is controlled by two control rods. The temperature should be maintained between the minimum and maximum threshold values. The temperature is decreased when it goes beyond the maximum threshold value with the help of one control rod. If any of the control rods is not available, then it is not possible to reduce the temperature. Hence, the reactor needs to be shutdown. Prevention measures must be taken to avoid the situation of shutting down the reactor.

The timed automata/pushdown timed automata can be converted to co-inductive CLP(R) (Saeedloei,& Gupta, 2011) programs. The set of transition rules are used to depict the timed automaton/pushdown automaton system, where clock constraints and stack actions are associated to each rule. The hybrid automata can be handled using this system with enhancement. In this case, the logic programs are depicted as hybrid automata, the uninterrupted quantities are used to signify the physical quantities and lastly, constraint logic programming models the limitations forced by the transitions. The non-terminating aspect of the hybrid automata is modeled using the co-inductive logic programming. By permitting the co-routine, the concurrency among hybrid automata can be handled.

Continuous or real time quantities can be reasoned with the solution based on the constraints over the existent by extending the Logic Programming (LP) (Saeedloei & Gupta, 2011) to Constraint Logic Programming (CLP) (Saeedloei & Gupta, 2011). The calculations over the combination of both the continuous and discrete quantities are permitted using CLP. The whole system can be depicted and demonstrated using CLP(R) (Saeedloei & Gupta, 2011) when the real time features are articulated as constraints besides the additional physical dynamics of the real time systems/CPS. The speculative sets, dynamic calculations, and unrestrained structures can be easily identified by the powerful technique referred as co-induction. Logic programming can be enhanced co-inductively. The maximum secure end based calculations are offered an operational semantics by Co-inductive LP (Co-LP) (Saeedloei & Gupta, 2011). Demonstration and confirmation of the Kripke structure properties and the automata that recognize infinite strings can be carried out indirectly using co-inductive LP. It is possible to elegantly utter the continuous realization of CPS by means of Co-LP.

The integral and incorporated constraints like freeze, etc., are used to recognize the co-routine facility of logic programming. When the required constraints are satisfied, setting up of the Prolog objectives is treated by co-routine. The binding of the variable is the mainly regularly employed clause in the Prolog. Once the binding process of the variable is completed, the goal which is used to depict the changes made on synchronized letters is programmed.

The comprehension of Reactor temperature control system based on the logic programming is exemplified below:

Modeling the Reactor Temperature Control System

The minimum and maximum threshold values of the reactor temperature control system are initialized. The way the changes takes place in the variables during the period for which the system stays back in a particular location is determined by solving their respective differential equations. By estimating the time when the maximum threshold temperature is reached by the reactor, the time at which the transitions add1 or add2 (Saeedloei & Gupta, 2011) take place can be estimated. Similarly, the time at which the transitions remove1 or remove2 (Saeedloei & Gupta, 2011) take place can be estimated by determining the time at which the minimum threshold temperature is reached by the reactor.

The set of transition rules enhanced with clock operations, progression laws, and set of limitations related to the security and invariant states are expressed by means of respective predicates. By means of logic programming, co-inductive and co-routine predicates, the three hybrid automata of the system are recognized as a set of transition rules. The controller automaton is realized with the execution of the corresponding predicate repeatedly, at the same time rod1 and rod2 are fed with suitable synchronization letters. The simultaneous implementation of all the components of the reactor temperature control system is characterized using the three arguments. The three arguments are:

- Record of synchronization letters with their respective timestamps which are delivered to the two rods and are created by the controller.
- Wall clock time initially.
- Parameter of the system (safety of the system).

The initial condition of both the rods depends on the initial wall clock value. The parameter which guarantees the safety of the system can be determined when the whole system is implemented as a co-inductive co-routine CLP(R) program.

The interesting properties of the system can be verified by posing queries when the system is realized using logic programming. The complete state space of a program can be discovered using backtracking method by making use of the ability of logic programming.

If the verification process need to be carried out on property P, then notP is considered as the proof of contradiction is used. i.e, if it is proved that notP fails concerning the logic program that depicts the system, then it is implied that P is succeeded. Otherwise, the counter example is provided stating the reason behind the failure of P.

Cyber-Physical Systems: Workload Modeling and Design Optimization

The cyber physical systems are developed by continuously and increasingly integrating the computation, communication and control systems. The physical processes that are a part of CPS are monitored and controlled by the wired or wireless networks which are associated with each other. The computational models are developed for the precise embedded applications by the society of embedded systems. Including the time-based and feedback-based control (Marculescu & Bogdan,2011) in the programming model is one of the objectives besides launching a reliable communication among computational elements. The direct communication involving the system and the physical world is feasible when the embedded systems computational paradigm is generalized using the above mentioned objectives of the CPS. Some of the CPS applications that are different from the traditional networked embedded systems are VANET which includes vehicles as nodes and simulated the movement of the vehicles, groups of bacteria in the process of delivery of drugs and in the process of analysis. The necessities of the CPS to be satisfied are safety, security, reliability, low power consumption and performance. A new science of networks and multidisciplinary systems which integrates heterogeneous type of networks and technology together is required to satisfy these multifaceted constraints. Certainly, linear control paradigms workload modeling cannot depend on the traditional approaches.

The quantity of data processed for every unit of time transferred among different CPS nodes is referred as CPS workload. This CPS workload influences both the local constraints and macroscopic metrics. Buffer utilization can be considered as a local constraint whereas CPS throughput can be treated as a macroscopic metric. In general, the workload needs to be sent to data centers consistently in carry out additional analysis and conclusion purposes. Hence, the spatial and temporal features of this workload need to be considered while taking a decision corresponding to the dimensions and topology of a specific wireless network. The traffic of any type may catastrophically cause the critical information to be deferred or drop which in turn may disable the ability to take a decision on the size of communication buffers among the sensors or data centers in a network. As bio-implantable (Marculescu & Bogdan,2011) devices are related to the life of the patients, the features of the workload produced by these devices cannot be neglected. Hence, the CPS design and optimization processes should consider the specific workload features as one of the important aspects.

Main Characteristics of Physical Processes

The temperature, speed, humidity, heart rate, etc., are the physical parameters that need to be measured by some of the CPS components. Such components are illustrated as a set of concurrent processes that have the ability to communicate with each other and alter themselves to modified environmental conditions. A vibrant system activities needs to be stimulated in such physical processes as they need to react to a variety of exterior conditions. The operation or performance of the traffic behavior or weather conditions will hardly ever be stable. Otherwise only for a short duration of time, they can be stable. The self-similarity and dynamic nature are the features of the physical processes irrespective of their complex behavior. The heartbeat is depicted as an electrical activity (Marculescu & Bogdan,2011) using an ECG. There are four parts in the ECG (Marculescu & Bogdan,2011): atria depolarization as P wave, ventricles re-polarization as T wave, ventricles depolarization as QRS complex, and inter-ventricular septum re-polarization as U wave. The R wave in QRS complex is more perceptible and evident when compared to the other waves as there will be more number of muscles in the ventricles in comparison with atria. The details about the heart rate changeability are supplied using R-R interval which is defined as the variation between two successive R waves. The identical average irregularity is noticed during the initial stages at different intervals and subintervals and is represented as a self-similar behavior. The deficiency or inclination of trailing the self-similarity indicates a high probability of congestive heart failure in the viewpoint of a physician. During the process of analysis of system behavior, there is a need to replace the derivatives of fractional orders by the integer order derivatives. The regularity of unusual events is confined by the kurtosis which is defined as the ratio between the fourth order moment and the standard deviation of a probability distribution.

The local fractal exponent is used to represent the physical process at any point of time. A higher order moment study is required to appropriately exemplify this kind of actions as it is already proved by nonzero kurtosis that the built-in non-stationary data do not fit well by the Gaussian approach. Similar behavior is displayed by several additional physical processes in the past. The impact of industrial pollution on climate changes can be evaluated using the Cloud Condensation Nuclei (CCN) (Marculescu & Bogdan,2011) which is measured using CCN spectrometer. It indicates that the clouds echo more solar radiation when CCN exhibits elevated concentration of atmospheric measurements which may lead to more irregular temperature variations on the earth's plane. Dissimilar communal impact is exhibited by different geophysical processes as every day average wind speeds with their self-similar behavior during various time scales. The time scale of the impact of the human footprint and the climate changes in the earth's atmosphere is larger whereas the time scale of the impact of the everyday average wind speeds is very low as days or probably minutes. Certainly, the different kinds of traffic are affected extremely and instantly with the details about the wind speeds, the movement of the clouds and the rain formation. The different predictions can be made only when the required data can be gathered and interacted with the capability of the CPS.

Modeling Challenges

Models play a vital role in the design process of the model driven development. The system design is progressed and the requirements for the system are formed by the models. The design defects are identified as a result of simulation and analysis when compared to prototyping. Under certain conditions, models enable the automated or semi-automated processes to be produced. All the present modeling languages and structures are concentrated by the intrinsic heterogeneity and complexity of CPS.

The models of physical processes, computation platforms, software, and computation networks are the components of a CPS model. There exist a feedback loop between the physical processes and the computations. The major challenge is to provide reasonable reliability to model such system which requires incorporating software engineering, control engineering, sensor networks, etc. Furthermore, several heterogeneous components are included in the models. The central focus is on the composition semantics.

The fuel management subsystem of the aircraft Vehicle Management System (VMS) (Derler, Lee, & Sangiovanni-Vincentelli, 2011) is utilized in order to demonstrate the CPS challenges. Ptolemy II is an environment for modeling and simulation for heterogeneous systems. The components of VMS which communicate by means of ports are depicted using an actor-oriented design approach by Ptolemy. Hence, components behave as actors in this approach. So, actors/components communicate with each other. The Model of Computation (MoC) (Derler et al.,2011) characterizes the rules of communication among actors. The director which is a section of a model or sub-model specifies and realizes MoC in Ptolemy. A particular hierarchical model is a model which integrates more number of directors where divergent MoCs are implemented by each director. Every director of a model governs a particular section referred as its domain. There are various established and new MoCs like discrete events, finite state machines, process networks, continuous time, synchronous reactive and numerous range of dataflow that can be realized by the directors involved in the open source Ptolemy software distribution. Hybrid systems are modeled using the continuous time models and the domains which are discrete as in the case of FSM or DE combined as a hierarchical composition. There will be many fuel tanks, different valves, sensors, pumps, switches, pumps, etc that are operational in the modern aircraft. The crucial function of the systems which are based on the fuel is to provide the fuel to the engines consistently. Balancing the system by allocating the weight on an aircraft, the optimizing the performance and the provision of engine coolant to the system are the next important functions of similar systems. The tanks which feed engines obtain the fuel from the collector tanks. The fuel is transported among storage tanks in order to sustain the center of gravity of the vehicle. The heat produced for the period of the flight uses fuel as a heat sink.

Some of the chief challenges of modeling are:

- Solver reliant, Zeno activities, or non-determinate,
- Maintaining consistency of model elements,
- Avoiding disconnection among model elements,
- Modeling communications among the functionality and realization, and
- Modeling scattered behaviors.

HETEROGENEITY

The development of the mathematical models of the systems under design is referred as Model Based Development (MBD) (Rajhans & Krogh,2012). Then, appropriate tools are utilized to verify the developed models with respect to the requirements of the design. The redesign or redevelopment can be avoided and the time and cost for this process can be saved using MBD approach as the errors can be detected before the completion of the system design or prototypes. Models of different kinds are developed and evaluated for most of the trivial systems. Now the problem of heterogeneity occurs to assure the reliability of the heterogeneous models without a complete single modeling formalism and to integrate the outcomes of the authentication from various formalisms to deduce the system level properties.

The tight coupling among the computational elements, communication networks, and physical dynamics the heterogeneity becomes inbuilt in cyber physical systems. Consider the cooperative intersection collision avoidance system for stop sign assistance and a vehicle is waiting on a small road to traverse all the way through the traffic of a big road by the side of stop sign controlled junction. The velocity and location of the approaching vehicles are perceived using cameras, sensors, and magnetic induction loops and these values are delivered to the decision system by means of wired or wireless networks. Then the decision system computes the safe gaps and eliminates the involvement of human decisions. This is the main objective of the cooperative intersection collision avoidance system. All features of this difficult heterogeneous system cannot be modeled using single high quality integrated formalism. Using a single model for the verification purpose of the system accuracy is an intractable problem.

Different formalisms are used in the development of various models to make appropriate at the best to satisfy divergent features of the complete design is implicated in the model based development of CPS. Tools like MapleSim and Modelica use the casual equation based models as general formalism in the aim and study of CPS to model the fundamental physics of a system. Similarly, the tools like Simulink are used to model signal flow model which is appropriate for control design and recreation; tools like Labeled Transition System Analyzer (LTSA) (Rajhans & Krogh,2012) are used to model the labeled transition systems and finite state machines which are appropriate for communication protocols and decision logic; tools like SpaceEx (Rajhans & Krogh,2012) are used to model hybrid dynamic systems or automata which is appropriate for realizing the integrated actions of continuous dynamics and discrete mode switches theoretically; tools like OMNET++, NS-2 are used to model the network simulations which are appropriate for performing the analysis on the communication network in terms of parameters like packet loss, throughput, delay, latency, etc.; tools like Spin are used to model software which are utilized in performing the verification process of the decision logic implementation. The design and study of complex systems and heterogeneous models required to be performed by various skilled engineers and hence required a wide range of expertise.

Heterogeneous Verification

The fundamental system is explained using the models and the requirements. A method is to be developed to evaluate the related sets of actions is the basic step in realizing heterogeneous models and requirements simultaneously using a general structure. The action associations are used to develop the framework such that the accurate semantic heterogeneity is maintained by permitting the various models and requirements to make use of many dissimilar kinds of action formalisms. The set of specific type of all feasible actions is represented as an action formalism B. The actions could be of any kind like event traces, hybrid traces, continuous paths, I/O relations as there are no limitations.

Definition (Behavior Relation) (Rajhans & Krogh, 2012):

A behavior/action relation is a relation $R \subseteq B1 \times B2$, where B1 and B2 are behavior/action formalisms. A relation R maps the behavior of B1 to the behavior of B2.

The specification formalism is used to implement the requirement which is a logical statement. Any kind of specification formalism may be utilized as there are no limitations. The Kripke structures (Rajhans & Krogh,2012), automata, different temporal logics, or English language also can be used to specify the requirements. Provided that the semantic analysis is unambiguous in terms of related behavioral formalism, any language can be used to inscribe the requirements. If the requirement is satisfied for all the behaviors in behavior formalism, then it is said to be semantically analyzed in the particular behavior formalism. If a particular requirement S2 is satisfied by the behavioral formalism in the semantic analysis and another requirement S1 which is weaker than or can be inferred from S2, then it implies that the requirement S1 also satisfies the behavioral formalism in the semantic analysis. A group of models of a specific kind are referred as a modeling formalism M. As similar to behavior formalisms, the modeling formalisms can also be of many different kinds like hybrid automata, casual equation based models, transition systems, signal flow models, etc. A modeling formalism has different models as an element and a model can be as an element of particular formalism. The semantic analysis of a model M is the set of actions that a model M permits and are defined by a given behavior formalism.

Definition (Heterogeneous Abstraction) (Rajhans & Krogh, 2012):

If a model M2 is a subsection of a model M1, behavior formalism B1 corresponds to model M1, behavior formalism B2 corresponds to model M2, and then by definition of heterogeneous abstraction, the behavior relation $R \subseteq B1 \times B2$, maps at least one matching behavior in behavior formalism B2 of model M2 for every behavior from behavior formalism B1 of model M1. The set of safe actions permitted by the requirements will not be violated by the set of behaviors of the model M. Either the formal methods like theorem proving or semi-formal methods like organized state space discovery are required to be utilized on every feasible occasion in order to set up this kind of entailment as there are no limitations on the kind of technique chosen by the system designer.

SYNCHRONIZATION METHODS

The system which need to assimilate the cyber systems and physical systems utilize the concept of cyber physical systems. The technology related to the computing and communication is utilized by the cyber components and the physical processes are controlled by physical components. When the physical processes are controlled using computers and computers interact among them over a wireless or wired network, then both the systems described above are integrated by CPS. The reliability and safety are the exceptionally significant features of CPS as it affects the physical world. The collective CPS characteristics of the system need to be realized in order to assure that the cyber components perform well by means of the substantial progress and belief and declare that the performance of CPS is secure and trustworthy. High variety of technology is used by smarter car safety assistance systems in order to avoid accidents with the availability of present well-built sensors, computation capabilities and communication abilities. As the model of CPS is universal, applications from different domains may arise in various ways. It is very difficult to identify the domains which are not influenced with the concepts of CPS. The design of systems in many domains can be enhanced in numerous characteristics due to emerge of modern technology as CPS applications proliferate. However, there are many challenges which will be introduced by CPS besides its advantages which need to be handled efficiently. As cyber components are integrated with the physical elements by CPS, it combines the continuous effects with the discrete and similarly, both the continuous and discrete dynamics are incorporated with the hybrid systems which are well-known mathematical models. In general, the digital controllers and the discrete control decisions provide the discrete dynamics and the physical process components of the CPS provide the continuous dynamics. Even though hybrid systems are efficient in many aspects, all the features of CPS cannot be modeled using the hybrid systems. For example, the hybrid models ignore the effects of distribution of CPS. The model using hybrid systems cannot confine the growth of the multiple hybrid agents together.

Hence, the discrete dynamics, distributed dynamics, and continuous dynamics are involved in the development of distributed hybrid systems. The certification and analysis of distributed hybrid systems is possible but it very big challenge which is lasting since long time. On the level of technical implementations, the tools, theories and technologies are integrated. For example, the technology commencing the mechanical design, computer programming methods and sensor development are integrated and many more technologies need to be integrated to design, investigate and realize the CPS. The methods which require performing the design, analysis, and understand CPS might include the mathematics, electrical engineering and control.

It is not amazing that in heterogeneous environment, the solutions for the different parts of various problems in divergent CPS are integrated using different tools of varying strengths. The arithmetic data, generalization, initiation, repetition and differential equations required to be handled by the persistent arguments. To prove automated theorem, several methods or skills like fixed point procedures, computer algebra are integrated by Keymaera (Platzer, 2010). CPS combines numerous approaches from various disciplines like mathematics, electrical, mechanical and computer science engineering. The cumulative challenges of CPS are dealt by the collective effort of the disciplines specified above. The combined work in the system design based on CPS is definitely dominates the system design which is based independently on either cyber features or physical features.

A Logical Approach to CPS Verification

Providing mutual solutions for the collective or integrated problems is a very big challenge of CPS. Logical approach solutions (Platzer, 2010) are suggested for the challenges related to the CPS verification.

The verification approach is based on mathematical foundation and logically strong for hybrid systems. The two significant features such as relative entity and reliability can be acquired by performing the analysis on the theoretical properties in detail. Various numerous applications like verification of collision freedom in flight collision avoidance maneuvers, verification of a distributed car control system and collision freedom of the cooperation protocol for the European train control system utilizes the above mentioned logical verification method which is realized using the verification tool called Keymaera(Platzer, 2010). The various features vary from perfect world dynamics to distributed system models or from inherent communication with estimations to precise communication. There are many applications which have complex, secure, significant, spatial, temporal conditions, regions divided into various parts dynamically and accepts changeable number of members.

Various mathematical features comprising linear dynamics, distributed dynamics and nonlinear dynamics are involved in the fundamental system models. A high-quality variety of usability is verified by considering the suppleness of models because of above specified range of various features.

NETWORK PERFORMANCE

The sensors, networks and inaccessible computation are integrated in the environment of a physical system by cyber physical systems. QoS sensitive cyber physical systems concentrates on the group of wide area which is inspired from the integration of synchrophasor data and the real time smart grid applications. The measurements of the electricity grids which are sampled using the new sensors known as Phasor Measurement Units (PMUs) (Arya et al.,2011) are distributed as flow which is to be sent consistently to various synchrophasor applications in a synchronized way. The North American Synchrophasor Initiative (NASPI) [4] categorizes the QoS necessities of the synchrophasor applications into a group of various levels. The QoS requirements are to be satisfied while constructing any network and are a challenging issue. The networks are made fascinated because of the scope as given below:

The required QoS by the concurrent and distributed architecture is to be maintained beyond simple point-to-point QoS (Arya et al.,2011) which need to be related to the application requirements.

It is significant to disgrace the performance elegantly for the period of the overloads or dangerous actions while amplifying the sampling rates and making more PMUs to be active and deliver the data stream in an application specific manner.

The advantages of layering and point-to-point QoS are incorporated in the CPS-NET (Arya et al.,2011) which is developed as a flexible three layered architecture. During excess or heavy loads, the data streams of in-network and particular application are permitted to be combined. The basic QoS which related to a particular path is offered at the bottom layer. The synchronized distribution and donation abilities are offered at the middle layer are combined with the data streams of traffic engineering transversally multiple lower level paths and trees. During network overload, the performance is degraded slowly using the application specific aggregation by the distributed stream processing infrastructure which is offered by the top layer. The complete PMU data is delivered from the publisher to the subscriber under the low load conditions while the top layer is inactive. But the complete PMU data might not be delivered under the heavy load conditions of the network because of its insufficient ability. Hence, the performance is degraded under the heavy load conditions in an unexpected way as the system responds to the heavy load only by discarding the data randomly.

During the heavy loads, the load is reduced gracefully by dropping some of the packets in the case of applications like multimedia, video streaming, etc. but still maintains and retains the data; however the expected quality is not reflected. Similarly, the fine degradation of synchrophasor applications is attained during the period of heavy loads using the application perceptive in-network aggregation functions. In particular, the co-optimization of higher layers is activated by the lower layer of the three layer architecture for the period of overload to perform the aggregation of data and application related filtering. The data aggregation and the filtering mechanisms that are preferable are stated by the subscribers at the time of subscription to a particular content. At the same time, the preferred mechanisms could be applied to which kind of data and at which preferable timeframes are also stated. If a convenient API exists, the aggregation and filtering functions can be expressed at the best by the application writer.

The summary of information related to the network, assignment and composition of operators is as a part of the distributed stream computing system (Arya et al., 2011) whereas the stream programming language is used to represent the declarative view.

The reliability is enhanced using Cooperative Preamble Sampling Medium Access Control (CPS-MAC) (Khan & Karl,2011) protocol with the help of the gain of overhearing and is dependent on the preamble sampling and Cooperative Communication (CC)(Khan & Karl,2011). All the packets or messages are received by a node in its range of reception even though they are not intended for it and actually are sent to the other nodes because of overhearing. The packets which are not intended for it need to be discarded particularly in the case of dense networks or sensor networks as the energy gets wasted and hence this is considered to be a challenging task. On the contrary, the CPS-MAC improves the probability of overhearing a packet up to 1-hop and 2-hop purposely. So, using CPS-MAC protocol, each node obtains two similar packets in the case of 2-hop neighbors, where one is the original copy is from the source and other copy is the duplicate from the 1-hop cooperating node. The technique known as Maximum Ratio Combining (MRC) (Khan & Karl,2011) is used to integrate both the copies of the same packet in order to recover the original packet most probably in the case of 2-hop neighbor. The CPS-MAC is permitted to fight against channel fading with the benefit of spatial diversity. With all the features, CPS-MAC is able to improve the reliability without wasting any extra energy. A simple network with maximum 2-hops can be considered as a 3 – node network which are represented as source, partner and destination. This can be extended to any number of nodes and the proved to be scalable. The dense network traffic is formulated when all the nodes in the network create traffic. The channel contention can be proficiently handled by CPS-MAC. The CPS-MAC performs better in heavy traffic conditions when compared to low traffic conditions.

The neighboring nodes are awakening with the use of preamble sampling and the packets or data is forwarded from node to node in the direction of destination in the case of relaying MAC protocol. Throughout the process, the performance of the sensor nodes is influenced because of the two parameters. One of the parameter permits the transmission power of the sensor nodes to be adjusted based on the state of the battery and the required lifetime. Hence, various transmission powers exhibit varying reliability and varying energy utilization of the network. Other parameter permits the frequency of sensing events to vary the load dynamically.

Virtual Network Platform Architecture

The data transmission and dispensation on real network is maintained by virtualized network platform and is used to administer large scale CPS proficiently. The communication among different CPS service groups is supported using the virtual network platform. The guaranteed link, safety and QoS are required in the case of large scale CPS. The environment of different services of CPS can be made simultaneous with the help of virtualization. One of the virtual networks is isolated from the other networks and will not be affected by the other virtual networks because of the property of network isolation in (Ahn & Yoo, 2012) is shown in Figure 3. The different devices and controllers

Figure 3. Isolation scheme

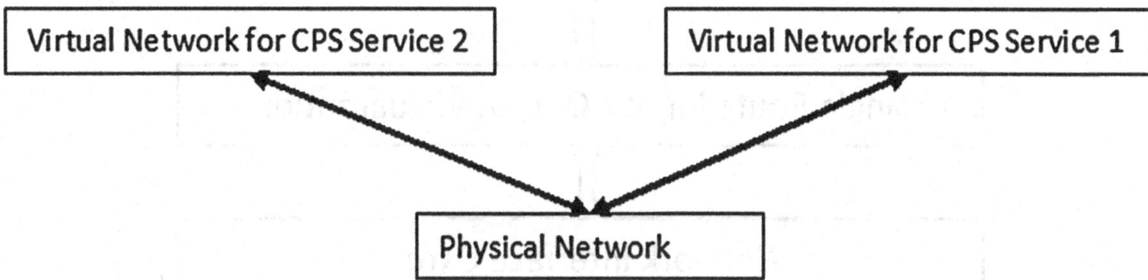

are supported by the effective available network bandwidth distribution and management with the use of performance isolation. Virtual routers are managed and numerous isolated virtual networks are generated using virtual network platform which depends on Xen (Ahn & Yoo, 2012) as shown in Figure 4.

The independency of each virtual network is guaranteed with the reliability of specialized CPS which is approved by isolation. Quality of service is optimized for each CPS services and secured using isolation. On a physical network, virtual routers help to support numerous virtual networks by the system. VLAN ID, Virtual LAN ID and tunneling method (Ahn & Yoo, 2012) are utilized to isolate the numerous virtual networks from each other. The reliable communication among sensors, controllers and devices is made possible by the virtual network platform with the advantage of network isolation. The independent service is provided to the CPS data in the isolated virtual network. Hence, the contamination like hacking or attacking from illegal authority is diminished and the intrusion by each other will not take place.

The fast and flexible virtual network must be produced by the virtual network platform architecture as shown in Figure 4 which behaves as a base architecture in developing virtual networks and are available from anywhere anytime among CPS controllers. Bandwidth is assigned dynamically to each virtual network and hence, it indicates that the isolated performance is offered by the virtual network platform. The BCN technique of Intel VM, virtual channel bonding and priority based bandwidth control are three ways to employ performance isolation.

Figure 4. Virtual network platform architecture

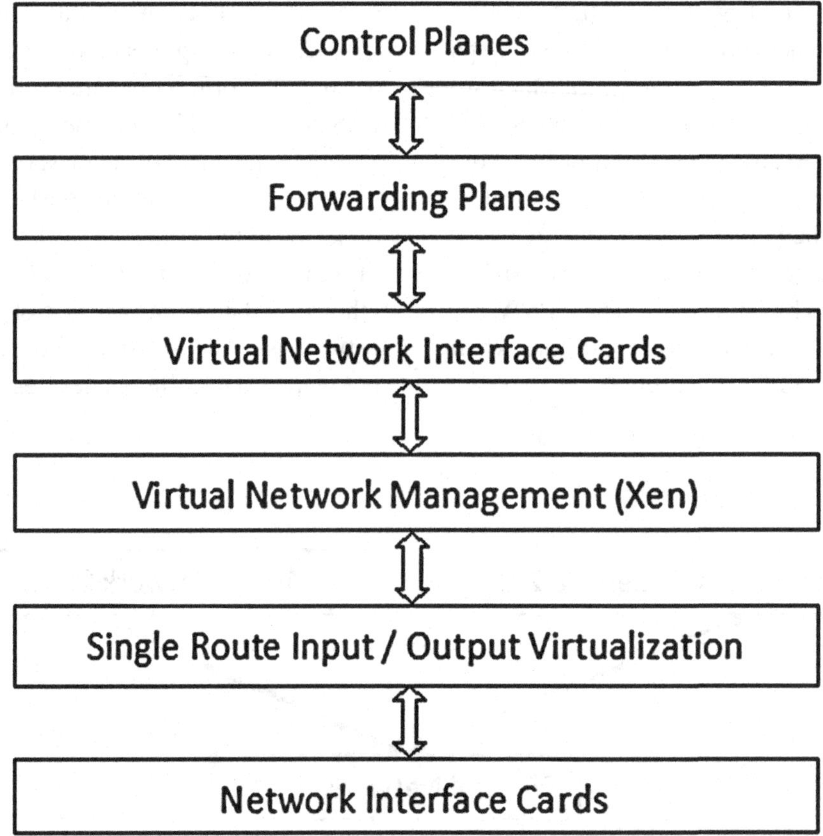

As the performance of the network in terms of stability is optimized, it has the ability to maintain controlling devices in a synchronized fashion. Rarely, uniting the accessible bandwidth permits the virtual network to exhibit better performance. The performance of the virtual network platform in CPS is uncertain even though it has important characteristics like flexibility and scalability. The Single root I/O virtualization (SR-IOV) (Ahn & Yoo, 2012) and Graphical Processing Unit (GPU) (Ahn & Yoo, 2012) are functioned along with the system in order to improve the performance of virtual network platform. Several features of CPS like safety, performance optimization, flexibility, and security are assured by the virtual network platform.

CONCLUSION

The system which is an integration of computation and physical processes is referred as Cyber Physical Systems (CPS). The physical processes are supervised and managed by the embedded computer networks in which the physical processes and computations affect each other via feedback loops. Hence, the joint dynamics of computers, networks, software and physical processes are needed to be analyzed to facilitate the design of such systems.

The general purpose computing is a challenging and vital task in CPS. The time taken by a process to complete its job is considered as a concern of performance instead of suitability in the case of general purpose software. When a task consumes more time in completing its process, it does not mean that it is not suitable but it indicates it is less convenient and hence less important. To say that the CPS is operating successfully and acceptably, the time taken by a process to complete its job plays a very important role. There is chance of many things to perform its task at the same time in the case of CPS. Many things which may occur simultaneously are the elements of the physical processes whereas these are sequentially ordered in software processes. In contrast, the processes of the physical world are hardly ever procedural. As there are more number of simultaneous processes in the physical processes, coordinating the actions which affect the processes, computing and managing the dynamics of these parallel processes is challenging task. As a result, concurrency is an essential parameter in CPS. The in-built sequential semantics are required to be associated with the fundamental concurrent physical world and this is the main technical challenge in analyzing and designing the embedded software. The realization of the models and the association among these models plays a significant role in cyber physical systems. The dynamics are main part of the models and the how the system state is developed in time. The static information about the structure of a system is characterized using structural models. These structural models are equally important as dynamic models to design the system. There are many benefits in functioning with models as they have strict properties. Models define certain things as explained below: as the model produces the same outputs always however the number of times the same inputs are provided, it is stated as deterministic. Any physical realization of a system cannot be possibly defined as deterministic. If the details which are required are only excluded, then it is referred as a good abstraction. The good abstraction of the physical system provides the self-assurance to perfectly characterize the physical realization of the system. In the embedded systems where the human lives are endangered because of failures require such enormously important self-assurance. The behavior of the systems in the physical world is realized by the analysis of models of the systems.

The power grids are sampled using sensors like synchrophasor and deliver these measured values to various grid applications like voltage monitoring, visualization, state estimation, etc. The sampled data need to be transmitted consistently to the intended applications with low delays as the sampled data are QoS sensitive. The performance of the system need to be gracefully degraded and the stream the data delivery according to the particular application when there are heavy loads in the network or when the grid crisis requires the amount of transmitted to be high.

At the time of heavy loads, particular application in-network aggregation of synchrophasor data streams is permitted by flexible 3-layered network architecture, CPS-NET. The fundamental path definite QoS is offered by the lowest layer. The synchronized distribution and donation abilities are offered at the middle layer are combined with the data streams of traffic engineering transversally multiple lower level paths and trees. During network overload, the performance is degraded slowly using the application specific aggregation by the distributed stream processing infrastructure which is offered by the top layer. In particular, the co-optimization of higher layers is activated by the lower layer of the three layer architecture for the period of overload to perform the aggregation of data and application related filtering.

The simple stream processing programming model and the theoretical information about the placement, network, and composition of operators is provided to the user. The performance of the synchrophasor applications can be gracefully degraded by CPS-NET architecture using a voltage stability monitoring smart grid application.

The multiple models from various domains are required in devising cyber physical systems. The associated structure and the semantics of different models can be compared using the dynamic base architecture of the system using a combined depiction. The concept of an architectural view is used to associate each model to the base architecture. The associations among components of the models and the objects of the systems structurally and semantically are captured using architectural view.

REFERENCES

Ahn, S. W., & Yoo, C. (2012, April). WiP abstract: Virtual network platform for large scale CPS testbed. In *Proceedings of the 2012 IEEE/ ACM Third International Conference on Cyber-Physical Systems* (p. 214). IEEE Computer Society. doi:10.1109/ICCPS.2012.37

Bhave, A., Krogh, B., Garlan, D., & Schmerl, B. (2010). Multi-domain modeling of cyber-physical systems using architectural views. *AVICPS, 2010*, 43.

Derler, P., Lee, E. A., & Sangiovanni-Vincentelli, A. L. (2011). *Addressing modeling challenges in cyber-physical systems (No. UCB/EECS-2011-17)*. California Univ Berkeley Dept of Electrical Engineering and Computer Science.

Khan, R. A. M., & Karl, H. (2011). Multihop performance of cooperative preamble sampling MAC (CPS-MAC) in wireless sensor networks. In Ad-hoc, mobile, and wireless networks (pp. 145-149). Springer Berlin Heidelberg.

Marculescu, R., & Bogdan, P. (2011). *Cyber physical systems: Workload modeling and design optimization*. Academic Press.

Platzer, A. (2010). *Integrative challenges of cyber-physical systems verification*. Academic Press.

Rajhans, A., & Krogh, B. H. (2012, April). Heterogeneous verification of cyber-physical systems using behavior relations. In *Proceedings of the 15th ACM International Conference on Hybrid Systems: Computation and Control* (pp. 35-44). ACM. doi:10.1145/2185632.2185641

Saeedloei, N., & Gupta, G. (2011). A logic-based modeling and verification of CPS. *ACM SIGBED Review*, *8*(2), 31–34. doi:10.1145/2000367.2000374

ADDITIONAL READING

Arya, V., Hazra, J., Kodeswaran, P., Seetharam, D., Banerjee, N., & Kalyanaraman, S. (2011, January). Cps-net: In-network aggregation for synchrophasor applications. In Communication Systems and Networks (COMSNETS), 2011 Third International Conference on (pp. 1-8). IEEE.

Bhave, A., Krogh, B. H., Garlan, D., & Schmerl, B. (2011, April). View consistency in architectures for cyber-physical systems. In Cyber-Physical Systems (ICCPS), 2011 IEEE/ACM International Conference on (pp. 151-160). IEEE. doi:10.1109/ICCPS.2011.17

Li, H., Lai, L., & Poor, H. V. (2012). Multicast routing for decentralized control of cyber physical systems with an application in smart grid. Selected Areas in Communications. *IEEE Journal on*, *30*(6), 1097–1107.

KEY TERMS AND DEFINITIONS

C&C: Component and Connector perspective model represent computational and physical elements as connectors and annotations.

CCN: Cloud Condensation Nuclei evaluate industrial pollution on climate changes and measured using CCN spectrometer.

CLP: Constraint Logic Programming.

FSP: Finite State Process is modeled using process algebra.

GPS: Global Positioning System unit are the elements of the sensor suite in the vehicle.

GSC: Ground Station Controller generate reference routes for quadrotor.

LP: Logic Programming measure the continuous or real time quantities.

PMUs: Phasor Measurement Units are new sensors used to measure the electricity grids.

STARMAC: Stanford Testbed of Autonomous Rotorcraft for Multi Agent Control.

Chapter 10
Heterogeneous Networking Issues

ABSTRACT

To make a network survivable it must be heterogeneous. The functionality of this network is defined by a set of protocols and its operations. In heterogeneous networks, if a protocol is weakened by any attack, it will not affect the entire network. Applying this heterogeneity concept, a new survivability paradigm is described in this chapter. This network architecture improves the network's heterogeneity without losing its interoperability. Several issues discovered in security and survivability applications can be converted into scheduling problems. To overcome this, a new model is described to support design and analysis with security and survivability concerns. A five-step model is introduced to transmute applications into model abstraction and representations with solutions resulting from scheduling algorithms. A reverse transformation converts the solutions back to the application domain.

INTRODUCTION

Several computers are connected with one another to communicate with each other to form a computer network. The reason for this assembling or to form as a network is to share the resources among the interconnected computers. Various hardware and software technologies are utilized to build computer networks. Various kinds of hardware components like optical fiber, Ethernet or just utilizing wireless connections can also be used to form a network. The regular and generally utilized hardware component to build any network is the Ethernet. The network is formed with the help of Ethernet by linking discrete computer components with one another through wiring. Bridges, switches, hubs and routers are some of the different components to be utilized for the Ethernet networks. At the same time, various kinds of cables like coaxial cable, twisted pair wire and fiber optics also are used in the formation of Ethernet network.

Unlike wired networks, physical connection or wiring is not required in the formation of wireless networks. Signals of infrared and radio are utilized for communication process in the wireless technology. According to the literature of wireless technologies, many variations exist. For instance, Bluetooth, cellular systems, satellites, wireless LANs, terrestrial microwaves, etc.

DOI: 10.4018/978-1-4666-7312-0.ch010

Even though initially, wireless technologies are not well established when compared to Ethernet, later they are well developed and made simple to work with. Yet the focal points and economy connected with the physical systems can't be disregarded completely. The topology of the network is the structure of the network formed by either wireless connections or physical connections among the nodes in the network. The requirements of the network determine the topology of the network. Hence, there will be various kinds of topologies.

Various kinds of computer networks include Local Area Network (LAN), Personal Area Network (PAN), Campus Area Network (CAN), Wide Area Network (WAN), Metropolitan Area Network (MAN), and Storage Area Network (SAN). To establish a network in small areas like a single building or individual labs in the colleges, Local Area Network (LAN) is best suitable. High data rate at Giga bits is offered by LANs in a small range. Personal Area Networks (PAN) is intended for personal uses and the corresponding range of communication is approximately 20 to 30 feet. CAN is a network which is larger when compared to LAN. When the computer systems in various locations need to be connected, then CAN is useful. For instance, the systems in administrative office, library, labs and other offices of the university can be connected to form CAN. Wide Area Networks (WAN) is formed from the compound connections among numerous LANs. It can be termed as interconnection of networks. For instance: Internet. Now-a-days, Internet is being used in almost every place like houses, commercial buildings, colleges, etc. The central point of LAN and WAN can be considered and termed as Metropolitan Area Network (MAN). The LAN and WAN are interconnected to form a MAN. The coverage range of MAN is approximately 5 to 50 km. The applications of MAN are military, online reservation systems, banks, etc. (freewimaxinfo.com)

The different network connections are shown in Figure 1. Connections among the devices may be wired or wireless. There are many advantages of computer networks. Some of them are specified below.

- File and thus data sharing,
- Huge data can be stored,
- Resources as well as data can be shared,
- Cost effective, and
- Easy to build.

In the initial stages of introduction of networks, it is expensive to establish a network because more wires are being utilized. But later it became easier and inexpensive and thus reducing the communication complications which virtually reduces the distances between different places in the physical world (freewimaxinfo.com).

Various Types of Network Problems

The network problems are mostly related to the connectivity among the nodes in the network. These problems effect could range from a single node to a network. The network problems might be associated with the concerns of the systems in the network (http://computer-network.wifi-lifestyle.com/page/261).

Network Cable Failure

The network connectivity problems in wired LAN are due to the network cable failures. These failures may range from low level to moderate level. The LAN failure may be due to cable between client computers and the closest LAN switch. This in turn allows a computer to have no access to the network resources. To resolve this issue either new cable has to be replaced or identify the port that causes cable failure and plug it in other port. Another reason for cable failure is that it blocks the

Figure 1. Various network connections

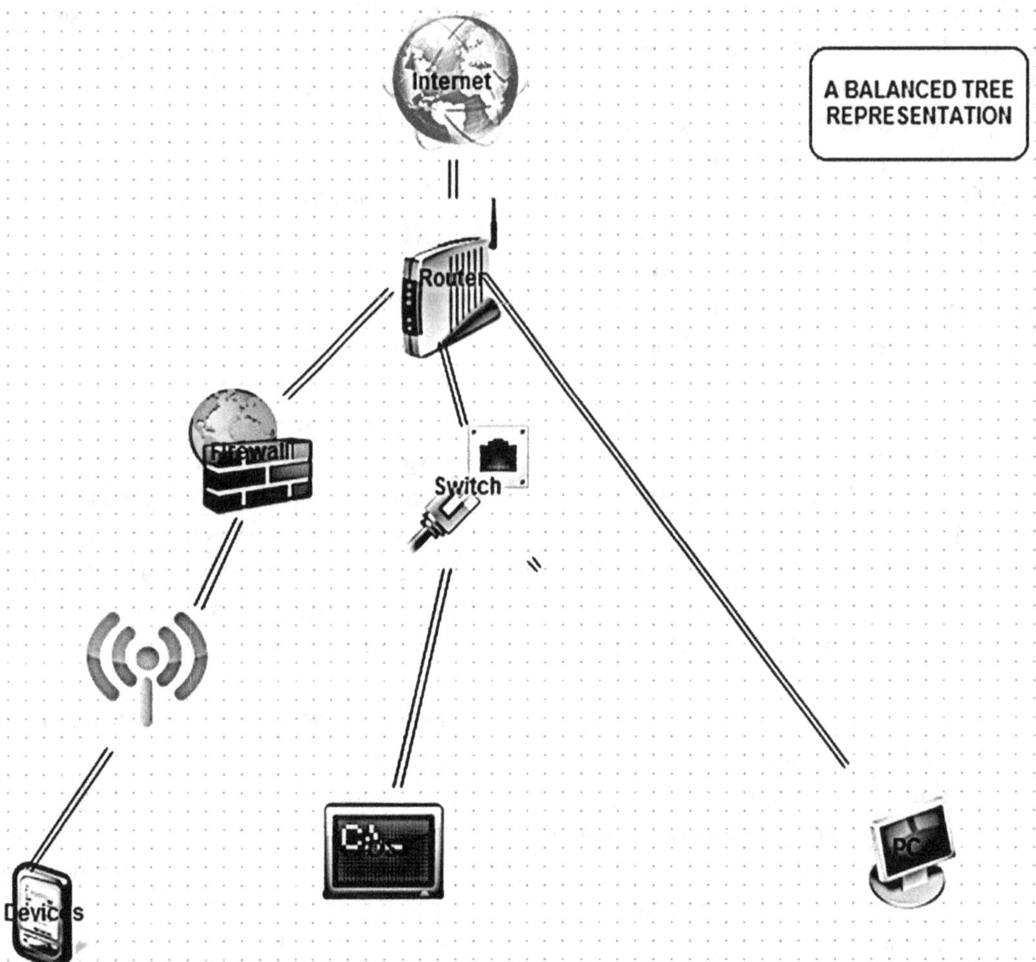

uplink cable in a building (block) which results in network interruption. In LANs cable is essential for connections where as in complex switch networks the Spanning Tree Protocol (STP) is used for connecting LAN switches and identifying loop hole in the bridging of connections.

Network Devices Failure

It is another reason for network failure i.e. due to NIC failure or single witch failure, there will be network interruption in a client device. The computers only are affected because of the network problems which are based on the failure of Network Interface Card (NIC). This is not a major affect as the network card backup can be utilized as an alternate. A question arises when network connectivity problems occurs it is due to due to switch failure or system design. Basically the system design is based on its load balance and great accessibility needs which would be separately evaluated. These factors are depending on using repetitive links, router and switch duplication and multi-homing critical hosts. Guaranteeing the high availability is the main objective of a redundant environment. Redundancy may take an advantage of offering no single point of failure. There are three types of network redundancies which are given below:

- **Switch Redundancy:** Let us assume that switch A and switch B are redundant to each other. So, if the link of any switch (either switch A or switch B) with the rest of the network, then the other switch can be used to maintain the network without any issue. This solution prevents the network system breakdown which occurred due to failure in a particular switch.
- **Router Redundancy:** When there is failure in the routers, this method creates a back up to the WAN connection. The failure in a particular router point is prevented by interrupting the WAN links.
- **Link Redundancy:** It will create a back-up of the link whenever failure occurs in a server connection or in any switches. A collection of switch ports are particularly used as support for connection between switches.

Virus Outbreak

The reason for this kind of network problem is not the connectivity issue. Virus outbreak is a kind of network problem which may degrade the performance of the network by creating an extensive traffic i.e, flooding of huge number of packets. In every entry point, a well organized and protective firewall system as well as anti-virus software is used to avoid the internet risks such as viruses and other malwares (http://computer-network.wifi-lifestyle.com/page/261).

BACKGROUND

Heterogeneous Networks

As described in the above section as data traffic increases there will be raise in the demand for data traffic also. Nowadays Heterogeneous Network has become a noticeable resolution to satisfy this request in comparable to other technologies. Heterogeneous Networks referred as 'HetNets' are an amalgamation of major and minor cells such as Macro, Pico, Femto, relay (El-Arabied, 2012) with various radio technologies such as 3G, Long Term Evolution (LTE), LTE advanced (El-Arabied, 2012). These all function together to offer a good coverage and feasible capacity. The network can be expanded by huge number of Macro cells but it cannot provide proper solution. Because more macro cells means more Capital Expenditure (CAPEX) (El-Arabied, 2012) and demand will not be met. In addition more problems occur related to interferences and frequency reuse issues.

Base Stations

The terms such as Macro, Pico, Femto and relay are used as base stations which have been described below.

Macro Cells

The cell in an outdoor base station which is easily accessible by the community is referred as Macro cell. In this cell range it's the main base station with the transmission power up to 43 milliWatt decibels (dBm) (El-Arabied, 2012). With the help of backhaul connection available in the infrastructure, macro cells are linked to each other. In the rural areas or in the areas with no infrastructure microwave links will be used as a better connection in spite of best communication available such as fiber medium.

Pico Cells

Pico Cells are smaller in all ways compared to Macro Cells. It has a transmission power from 30dBm to 23dBm (El-Arabied, 2012). It coverage area is limited and it is also an outdoor base station which can easily accessible by the community. To improve the capacity in the urban regions, Pico cells are integrated with the Macro layer. The backhauling idea is applied in this also as it is in the Macro layer.

Femto Cells

Femto cells are tiny compared to other types of cell mentioned above. Femto cells are home base station (indoor units) that provides restricted access. It has very low transmission power less than 23dBm (El-Arabied, 2012). Though it has less power transmission, it enhances the data traffic. Since the distance between the User Equipment (UE) and the element inside the building (same) is small, the UE can link with high speed rate over this small range. This type of connection improves the UE's battery life and reduces operator's total cost, backhauling and also reduces the cost of the base station. Though it has some advantages over small range still it has few disadvantages such as restricted access to the base station, handoff, reuse of frequency and interference (El-Arabied, 2012). However there are people who provide way out for the above said problems.

Relays

A relay is a signal which in fact accepts, demodulates, and converts the data to the received signal. And also apply any error correction method to retransmit it as an original signal.

AN ARCHITECTURAL FRAMEWORK FOR HETEROGENEOUS NETWORKING

Handover is one of the most abilities of heterogeneous networking. This is essential because as a mobile node moves randomly then the networks associated with it also be changing. Another main issue in heterogeneous networking is Quality of Service (QoS). In many wireless networks, the QoS of every connection is affected due to vertical handover as QoS vary from one network connection to other wireless network connection. QoS also out looked by other components of the network from the higher layer of protocol stack. As a result of this the system performance carried out by the network and transport operations capabilities are affected. As per the QoS amendments, the system also must react to the changes occur in the channels. Now a query raises that how these QoS amendments are managed and how far it is going to affect the applications of the system used in it. As a solution a system has to be organized to use and utilize changes occur in wireless networks. Additionally new features such as personalization, personal area networks and location-based services (Mapp et al., 2006) can be added to improve the system.

To overcome the above issues a new framework is required to summarize the main challenges of heterogeneous networking and also for the mobile devices in it. The main purpose of framework is to locate the unfamiliar regions of wireless network for better connection. The methodology used in the framework is same as the OSI model. The layers of this model are used to mention each layer's functionality, permitting modular methodology for the expansion of systems and the components exchange to apply various implementations. The researchers have planned to implement a prototype testbed to deal with the proposed architecture.

OSI Model

The simple transmission of information from one node to the other node in the network is the main objective of OSI model. However, in heterogeneous networking there are several new processes which have to be aided by the networks associated to it and one of the functions is vertical handover (Cavalcanti, Agrawal, Cordeiro, Xie, & Kumar, 2005). In vertical handover there will be often smooth communication between the mobile host and the network, whereas this type of communication is not possible in the OSI model. Because vertical handover performs the operation of modifying the network parameters such as permitting resource reservation to enable the quality of service in the available network, which cannot be effectively done in the context of OSI.

The research study has shown that the OSI model function properly, when the network features at the boundary region has the similar characteristics of core network. In the previous network systems, to do so the wired networks such as token ring systems were used to transmit few megabits per second between the boundaries of the associated network. On the other hand right from the previous decade to the current the core network and the end systems have considered its own way of communications. When comparison is made amid the end systems and core network (Mapp et al., 2006), the later take a lead in communication. Because the core network utilizes innovations like MPLS, single mode fiber optics whereas peripheral systems use various wireless technologies that have various characteristics with respect to latency, available bandwidth and error distribution resources. Considering all these remarks researchers have decided to implement a framework to exhibit the concept of future heterogeneous network. The new framework which has the architecture layering is described below.

The Architecture Layering: A Conceptual Framework

From the previous discussion it is true that, for the existing wireless networks the OSI model cannot be considered as a better notional framework. A solution to this is that OSI model framework can be modified instead of considering as it is for future wireless networks. The enhancement in the framework determines the order of operations rather than giving details of interfaces used in it. The arrangement of the priority is the most important concern, because it has been shown that there are several difficulties occur due to the order of operations, for example the process of vertical handover lies over the transport layer.

The proposed architecture model with the conceptual framework with the seven layers like the OSI model is shown in Figure 2. But it uses a new level of processes for an effective implementation. In this model, vertical handover is specified below the policy management by getting input from it and policy management layer is located below the network transport layer. In the same way, QoS is specified its private precise layer to isolate it from both the network transport and application layers. This distinguishes with current methods where QoS happen to be an attachment rather than be a portion of the network stack (Mapp et al., 2006).

It has been noticed that the layering paradigm does not limit the developers with the inflexible components. A framework is considered as an excellent model compared to the complete design requirement. Hence, this model overview the proper ordering of operations rather than reducing the capable cross layer techniques. As discussed earlier policy management and vertical handover operations are combined as an individual element. Similarly, higher layers may lookout the functionalities not only from its lower layers (as per hierarchy) but also from the bottom layers (Mapp et al., 2006). This same concept can be used for the QoS layer with the help of network abstraction layer.

Hence, there is a need for transparent conceptual division which should be highlighted. In turn this will generate challenging options for performing vertical integration and trans-layer interfacing. Following are the description of various conceptual layers using a bottom-up approach (Mapp et al., 2006).

Hardware Platform Layer

This layer uses the hardware components and technologies that are essential to maintain

Figure 2. The architectural model

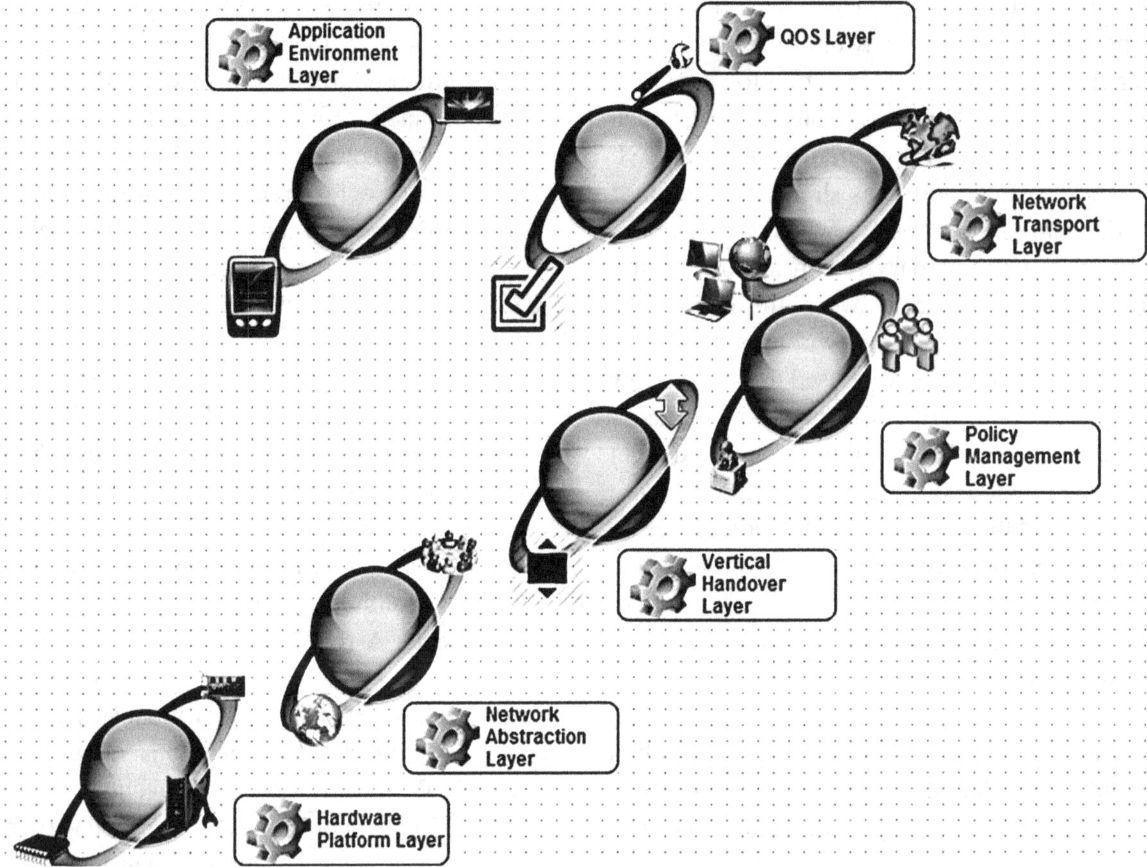

wireless networks. This layer describes several characteristics, various modulation techniques and MAC algorithms for obtaining and maintaining the channels. Due to its incompatibility this layer comprised of vertical sub-layers (Mapp et al., 2006) for determining a network such as 3G, WLAN, WiMax, etc.

Network Abstraction Layer

The Network Abstraction Layer uses common interface to maintain dissimilar networking technologies. Various wireless device drivers are designed to link onto this layer. The network abstraction layer manages and takes care of the network on the mobile node. In recent times, the IEEE arranged the 802.21 working group to look into ways to regulating the interface to various wireless MACs (Mapp et al., 2006).

Vertical Handover Layer

Vertical handover is a main module of heterogeneous networking. It has two different methods such as network-controlled and client-based handover. In network-controlled approach the network uses certain methods to decide when and how the handover will occur. These methods manage all required network information including its relative position on the mobile in various networks. And also it manages network's signal strengths, its direction and speed at the mobile node's location (Glenford,2006). But this approach is not considered as a scalable one, as it will not maintain the information about the networks associated to it. Mainly this approach relies mostly on the operator's network information which has been distributed in its communication environment.

The client-based handover is the second approach in which handover is managed by the mobile device. Following are the advantages of this approach.

- It decides when the handover should occur as it occupies the greater location and maintains the mobile node's network interface information up-to-date.
- While performing vertical handover, the mobile node should be conscious about the status of TCP connections and other higher level issues.
- A cost effective strong core systems can be created by eliminating handover functions from the core network.

Policy Management Layer

Whenever a handover occurs, a policy management system is desired to assess all the situations based certain factors. The factors could be modification in the signal strength and coverage, the network status and the status of transport connections linked with the mobile host. Policy management is categorized as reactive and proactive. The network abstraction layer delivers the notification about the presence or absence of hetnet devices location on which the reactive policy depends. Some of the reactive policy management systems are POLIMAND and PROTON (Mapp et al., 2006).

Proactive policies are used to obtain and utilize the information such as signal strength and coverage of the network before the mobile node reaches its location. A main parameter required from proactive policies is the Time Before Vertical Handover (TBVH) (Mapp et al., 2006). Once the TBVH is known, the higher layers of protocol stack utilize the channels at the most before it becomes busy.

There are two categories of proactive policies: proactive-knowledge-based policy mechanism and proactive-modeling approach. In proactive-knowledge-based approach utilizes the mobile node's location and obtain the each network's coverage and signal strengths in which the hetnet device happened to present in that region of the network. These systems need a technique for finding and monitoring the location. Additionally this approach confirms the type of networks in which data is available and reachable. This mechanism provides the data in a specified format that can be managed by host nodes with restricted resources. And data is transmitted in a low bandwidth networks without any effect. The proactive-modeling method uses mathematical model to define the geometric design based TBVH. In most of the simulations and real networks this approach is widely used in spite of its less accuracy. Though this approach is flexible but proactive knowledge approach is more accurate. To design an effective architecture based on the specified condition both the policies need to be combined. Now the question raises which policy to be chosen. If it is based on accuracy then proactive-knowledge approach is to be applied. When there is no data coverage then the system has to use reactive policy mechanism.

Network Transport Layer

This layer emphasizes the operations allocated to OSI model network and transport layers. Therefore this layer concentrates on peripheral network problems such as addressing, routing and transport concerns.

The networks of type either core or peripheral uses TCP/IP which have been supported by End-to-End opinions. When the internet was considered these opinions have been used during the architectural negotiations. Currently the Internet is growing rapidly in a core network with mobile networks as main stream. These two networks are separated by means of characteristics such as latency, throughput and inaccuracy outlines.

It is an assumption that for heterogeneous networking TCP/IP has to be evaluated whenever it is used in the peripheral networks, though IP can be used in it or not. A statement is that in the existing IP structure each device is assigned with a unique IP address that can be used universally all over the network. But this address is provoked by the accomplishment of Network Address Translation (NAT) methods. In NAT there is a provision for private IP address used in the peripheral network whereas to transfer the information between various machines in the internet only limited global IP addresses are used (Mapp et al., 2006). The NAT software uses private IP address to offer information exchange between the local machine and the global IP connection. All datagrams packets can be examined and filtered at a particular point in a network, as all datagram packets have to pass through the server performing the NAT. Additionally it improves the security by making the local machines invisible in the internet so as to reduce the possible development of security flaws and DoS attacks in particular systems.

The achievement of NAT is to provide unique IP address to all machines in the network globally. NAT creates a situation that in a core network IP addresses can be used only by the data to be transmitted. But in the peripheral networks the local addressing can be represented in a different way so that the data transmission can be done between the local gateways of the networks. Suppose this approach is applied then inadequate IPv4 addresses will be there. Though researchers utilize the IPv6 address, still it requires a huge universal space for connection which is to be inspected again in the real world. It is a fact that TCP is not a correct choice for wireless networks since it infers that the packet loss is due to congestion which is not true. Moreover it reduces the data rate and apply slow start methodology in wired systems. In wireless systems the packet loss is due to interference, channel fading, vertical handover, etc. And many of these transients are impermanent and detached to network jamming. Many attempts have been made to enhance the TCP protocol engine but failed to succeed in that by making it more approachable to network outages provisionally.

The Case for Network Plurality and Application Conformity

The peripheral networks with various networking structures come with many open issues to be solved. But there are several naming and addressing schemes that can be used for packet transmission in various networks. To solve the issues discussed in previous researches, a new framework is expected to be developed. This framework provides a way for connecting various network applications that are performed in different networks. As TCP/IP is considered not only as a protocol in core network but also considered as an interface in peripheral networks and it is not necessary that TCP/IP should be modified to be used in any application. In other words TCP protocol engine creates an overlay over all the networking protocols used in the network. Actually the applications assume that the protocol used is TCP where as it is using other network protocol in it and to support network plurality it has to maintain conformity of application. The application conformity is based on the transport requirements of application to select a particular protocol which is needed (Mapp et al., 2006).

Quality of Service Layer

As many networks uses hetnet device then it has to experience various requirements of quality of service and QoS layer is required to maintain this inconsistency. There are two approaches of QoS such as upward QoS and downward QoS.

- **Downward QoS:** Whenever vertical handovers occur in heterogeneous networks, this QoS establishes a set of methodologies to manage the various qualities of service. This QoS is mainly needed for legacy applications. In order to accomplish this in various accessible channels, a new approach is required to join the connections in a network.
- **Upward QoS:** In future as the hetnet device adjust its location then the applications will be able to respond to the changes occur in QoS. These changes are offered through the QoS layer. In upward QoS, the changes occur in applications are informed by an event-based QoS signaling mechanism. Once the QoS layer delivers event notifications, in response to this the applications start accessing certain routines in it. This concept is same like the X windows system in which events are notified to the X-server to identify the routines to execute it. In the networking community, the TRIGTRAN and PILC projects demonstrate the above said paradigm by lower layers to supply suggestions to higher layers (Mapp et al., 2006).

QoS-Aware Middleware

This is a functional component in the distributed situations to support upward QoS in the design of a QoS-aware middleware platform. This platform has to consider a recognized environment such as CORBA to provide backing for upward QoS which is compatible to the architecture. This in turn permits the distributed applications to operate flawlessly in the heterogeneous mobile networks (Mapp et al., 2006).

The Application Environments Layer: A Toolkit Approach

Many application situations put an effort to summarize various architectural layers. These systems are very huge that it cannot go along with other systems and also providing connection between devices and applications has become an issue. A unconventional way to n alternative approach is to implement a Toolkit philosophy. In this approach certain application is aided with toolkit components to develop application environments. Consequently this would create compatibility which would also summarize the low layers functionality of the architecture.

NETWORK MODEL

The idea behind survivability through heterogeneity is identify the various instances of network elements which provide the same functionality that are exposed to dissimilar security attacks. Therefore the network architecture which has a group of heterogeneous network elements provides similar functional ability to all. Compared to homogeneous networks these functional abilities provide more opportunities for the existing security attacks. Consider the following two examples (Zhang, Vin, Alvisi, Lee, & Dao, 2000) which depict the survivability of heterogeneous networking framework.

- In network architecture a router has an important role. In homogeneous networks the routers are more vulnerable to security attacks, whereas in heterogeneous networking each router is provided with various paths between source and destination nodes to manage the attacks.
- The transport protocols provide end-to-end network services to transmit the data packets consistently in an appropriate time. The survivability of above mentioned network services solely depends on transport protocol capabilities to handle the attacks. In addition to TCP for data transmission, a web service can use User Datagram Protocol (UDP) or Simple Reliable Datagram Protocol (SRDP) that can endure TCP

SYN-flood attack. This attack is an emergence of various denial-of-service attacks on web servers (Zhang et al., 2000).

The above instances use the networking framework that relies on the several vulnerabilities to security attacks. These attacks are various types of network components at every stage of well-designed ability. As the heterogeneous networking framework survivability increases, the network elements vulnerability to attacks also increases its diversity.

Diversity Space

Theoretically the efficient abilities of network architecture and the network elements heterogeneity are represented through diversity space diagram (Zhang et al., 2000). This diagram categorizes the functional resources such as network and transport protocols, routing protocols and router operating systems of a network into a multi-dimensional space. Every network element that represents a operational ability is represented as a point between the communication medium and the operating systems in the dimension.

Figure 3 as in (Zhang et al., 2000) illustrates an example of such diversity space. The protocols like UDP, Real-time Transport Protocol (RTP) and TCP are considered to be the variations of the transport protocols, while as satellite, wireless and fiber-optic networks are considered to be the variations in the case of the communication medium.

Figure 3. The diversity space for heterogeneous networking

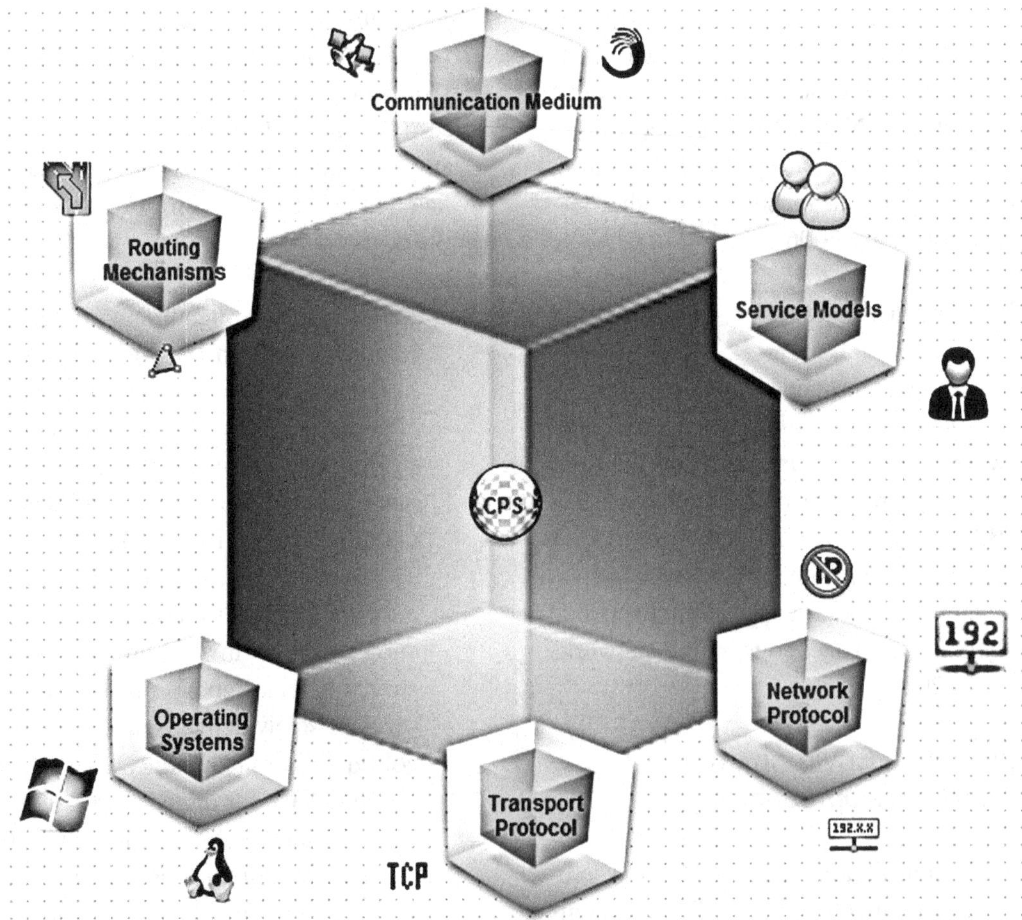

The distance between two components of network in any aspect reveals the range in their liability to attacks. As the distance between the two components of network extends, the vulnerability to attacks are partially covered. For instance, based on the design and implementation of Linux and Windows operating systems, the distance between these operating system dimensions is higher. But in the communication dimension, the distance between IPv4 and IPv6 is quite less because IPv6 is carried out from IPv4 (Zhang et al., 2000).

Liability Model and Survivability Degree

For a specified illustration a question raises that for each dimension, how many network elements are considered for supporting survivable network framework design. The answer to this question is to design a liability model for each component of network by presenting the innovative idea of survivability degree (Zhang et al., 2000). It is a metric used for denoting the various network elements diversity in the vulnerability to attacks. This in turn helps to identify a set of attacks that are vulnerable to particular network element.

This can be explained through by considering A as set of attacks and S as set of network elements. The structure of a survivable network should comprise at least the group S of network elements. At every level of functional ability assuming that at least one network element in S is not exposed to each of the attacks in the set A (Zhang et al., 2000). Practically the set S may include various network elements that are exposed to each of the attacks in set A. A survivability measure is required to observe the level of redundancy in set S so that each network element in S is less exposed to future attacks. As the survivability measure is greater instinctively the diversity in the set also becomes higher. The vulnerabilities of all the elements in the network are identified to devise the attacks on each of it. This is effective when the network has more diversity.

The approach for creating the set S which is survivable is focused by the below assumption. The survivability of the components of Set S in the network to the set of attacks in A is a rational pointer of the grade to which set S will sustain unidentified attacks (Zhang et al., 2000). There are numerous ways to describe assessable survivability degree for a specified set of components in the network that disseminate the similar functional ability. One of the measures is the growing diversity distance among all pairs of network components in the set. The set can tolerate the numerous dissimilar attacks is another measure. To recognize the set of network components at every level of operational ability, it is desired to build a heterogeneous network framework for developing and applying significant network elements. The main challenge is to generate an efficient step for installing network components with affordable budget and controllable complication. An effective installation of these network components will produce a network that will be enormously very strong to a wide diversity of well-known and unidentified security attacks.

SURVIVABLE OVERLAY NETWORKS AND SERVICES

These are serviceable end-to-end services that include layered operation of functional capabilities. This can be accomplished through configuration of network elements. In the heterogeneous networking structure, every functional capability is instantiated by utilizing a set S of heterogeneous network components. Basically in each layer there are various network elements that perform well-designed capability to obtain several types of an end-to- end network service. For instance Figure 4 (Zhang et al., 2000) illustrates a configuration of numerous network components to build WWW and broadcast services. It is noticed that Reliable Layered Multicast (RLM) (Zhang et al., 2000) is used as transport protocol to initiate the broadcast

Figure 4. Interchangeable elements at each layer

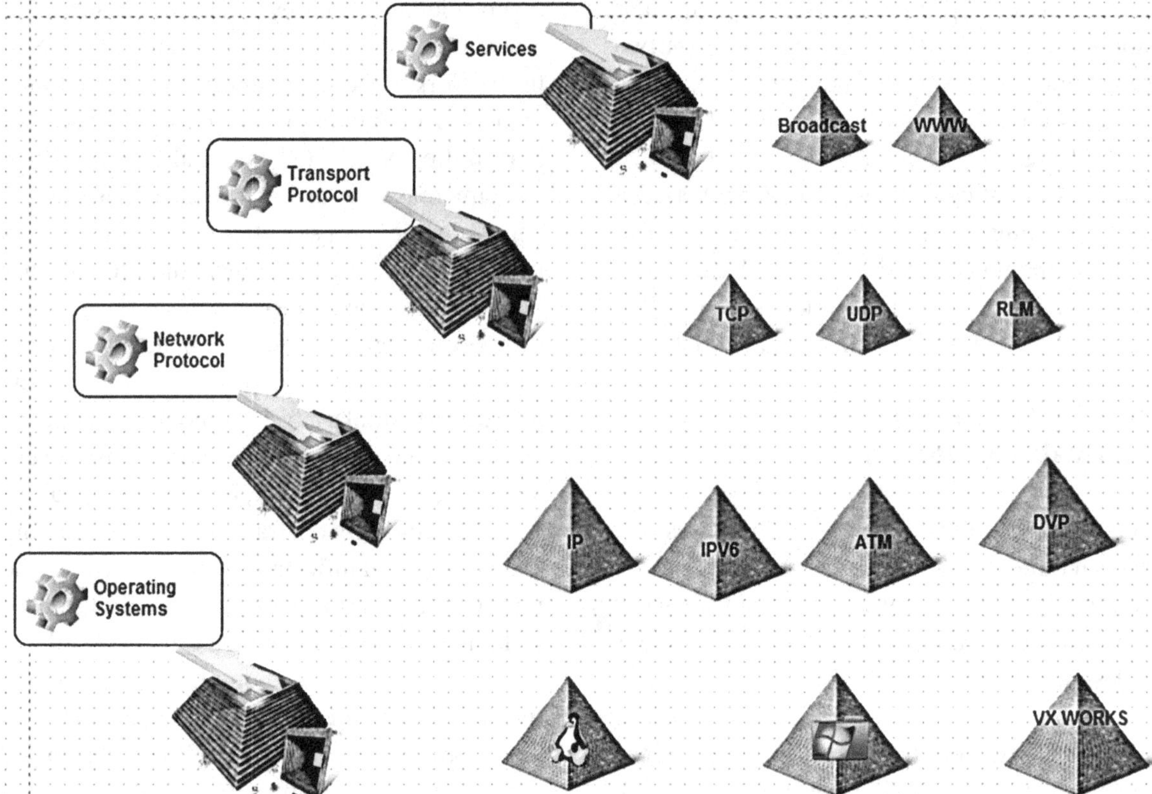

service in place of using UDP as its transport protocol. In this structure some of the network services are maintained by RLM whereas rest of the services are maintained by UDP or during usual operation it can develop any one of the above mentioned two instantiations. To detect the attack it switches to the other instantiation.

Practically it enforces several challenges due to the functionality of network layer. The network elements in this layer have the same functionality from the viewpoint of an application. As an illustration consider the two transport protocols TCP and UDP in which TCP delivers a consistent transport mechanism for congestion control whereas UDP provides nothing. Though these two transport protocols TCP and UDP belongs to same network layer, it is difficult to change between them in an application. This concern can be governed by the subsequent four mechanisms (Zhang et al., 2000):

- **Patching Lost Functionality:** This methodology is used to maintain the loss that occurs when there is a change between network protocol stack of one network element to another. For example when there is a change in the transport protocol level between TCP and UDP, then the session layer fulfill the functionality of reliable communication and congestion control. Though this approach is beneficial for the associated application, it has its own limitation which is exposed to the similar attack of the network component which is to be replaced.

- **Tolerable Operation Region:** The main purpose of this approach is to provide clarity moderately in an application. This is to represent operation of suitable area in the heterogeneous diversity space. If a network service is reconstructed in applications out of range then intimation is given it through an upcall interface (Zhang et al., 2000). In response to this call the application can offer corresponding handlers to change accordingly. Suppose the network functions in the range of application then there will be clarity about the reconstruction of network services build through the different parts of network elements. To facilitate such translucent reconstruction, every network component necessarily be allocated with a definite interface. Additionally, to provide similar functional ability the heterogeneous networking framework should disseminate agreed mechanisms to transform and handover among network elements.
- **Overlay Networks:** The heterogeneous networking structure help logical overlay networks with numerous physical recognitions with the help of above mentioned two approaches. There are various strategy options for executing overlay networks. In a particular circumstance, initially the framework uses any of the physical recognitions and whenever it detects an attack it change to another realization. In a complicated situation the framework may concurrently provide various physical realizations of the logical overlay network. Every physical realization holds the information about the overall overlay network traffic. Traffic can be spread over the several levels of granularity such as from the packet flow level to a set of data flows. As a result of this the design selection has an impact on the Quality of Service (QoS) assurances supported by network's ability. Therefore to assure end-to-end service, a network has to allocate resources throughout the way and also to initialize and preserve state facts at each network element. Subsequently, each packet transformation between various physical realizations affects the QoS requirements.
- **Multiplexing:** It is a process in which each layers element requires to communicate with heterogeneous elements of other layer. For instance, a transport protocol TCP or RLM provides a way for WWW server to serve its clients at a time. This involves multiplexing methods to distribute one service into various methods to be assisted by heterogeneous choices. In another illustration, a mission critical network is covered by various heterogeneous networks that offer same connectivity. The overlay procedure ensures that whenever attack is encountered it will often modify its association with fundamental changes.

Survivability Application

Many of the researches focused more on providing security to networked systems from malicious attacks. But still there are certain security issues that are to be solved. This is because of network systems situated in critical infrastructures. According to President's Commission on Critical Infrastructure Protection (PCCIP) (Krings & Azadmanesh, 2005) in 1997 particular infrastructures are selected whose inability have a deteriorating impression on protection or financial safety. Some of the recognized important organizations are telecommunications, electrical power, gas and oil storage, transportation and water supply. The common factor in the above mentioned critical infrastructures is that their fundamental devices are restricted by communication networks and that their original physical infrastructure is represented by graphs. Moreover there are acceptable problems that are linked with these critical infrastructures have appropriate solutions in areas which uses graphs as universal representation such as graph theory or scheduling theory.

Computer network security and survivability are the key research areas used in the field of cyber attack to focus on protection. Security is frequently observed as issue with respect to secrecy, reliability, accessibility, dependability and accuracy. Compared to security, survivability is expressed as the ability to tolerate the attacks, recognition of attacks and recovery from attacks with accepted changes. Though survivability is represented with respect to above factors it has concern about recovery whereas security is associated with resistance and recognition. In the fault-tolerance field recovery factor accept many notions by considering diverse fault models. These models are more often affected by systems network arrangement and communication protocols used in it.

The network computer systems lack in security due to the absence of theoretical base and mathematical models. The methodologies used for security and survivability are dynamic. Hence it demands for consistent security test procedures such as intrusion detection in systems that cannot be confirmed in the absence of these procedures. To initiate with a proper foundation comparisons are given more importance than comparative results obtained.

To improve the inflexibility of cyber critical problems, security and survivability issues are converted to other regulations. To find solutions to complex problems, it require certain changes in the specified issues that can be used in mathematics and engineering broadly. To do so well recognized instances are used along with exponentiation or Laplace transformation. Converting the actual problem into several other problems is a common approach in which the details of solutions found or cost-effective solutions also exist. Once a new explanation is found, a reverse modification is considered to retrieve the area of original problem.

Model Overview

The essential viewpoint of the transformation model is depicted in Figure 5. The following section gives an explanation about the model and represented by a mobile agent along with a distributed agreement application. The model overview is considered for network of computers having crucial infrastructure like electric power grid combined with data communication network which manages its resources.

The above process is described through certain examples for assumed graph and scheduling difficulties.

Suppose the liability of a data communication infrastructure is to be examined, then the communication network may be denoted by a directed graph. This digraph has weights assigned to particular Quality of Service (QoS) parameter such as maximal data rate. The purpose is to consider a required data rate in spite of connection failure in the system. Such situation may occur when a communication infrastructure is to be examined with reverence to its malicious acts flexibility intended to interrupt communication associations (Krings & Azadmanesh, 2005).

Processors and Tasks

In the process of development, devices are viewed in the customary way such as computers and machines whereas in the security and survivability regions resources are explained in a usual way. There are several characteristics that are linked with dissimilar resources. Processors may be of types such as identical, uniform, unrelated, and dedicated which are described below (Krings & Azadmanesh, 2005).

Figure 5. Model overview

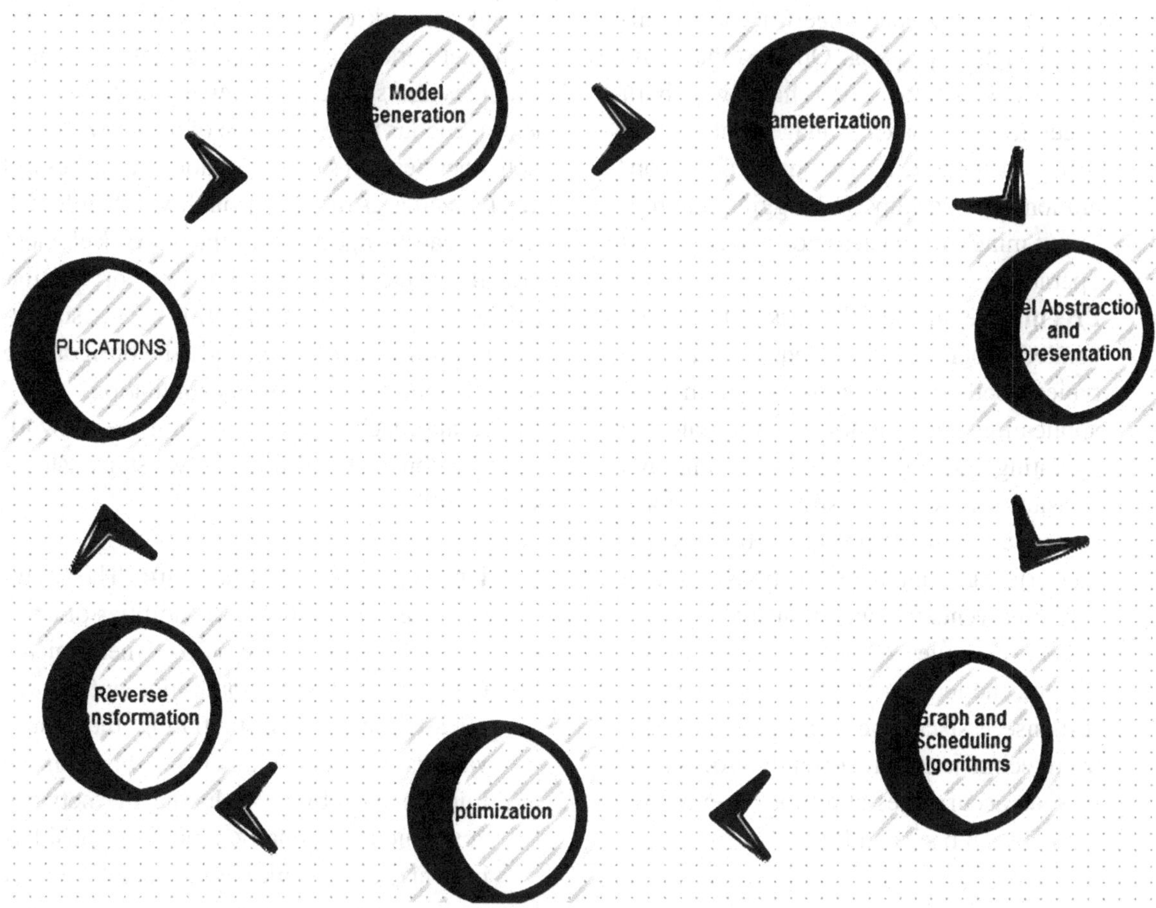

- **Identical:** The processers are of identical situations like homogeneous computers and input/output devices, software licenses, personnel with similar ability level.
- **Uniform:** The processors having various speed like computers and input/output devices with diversity, various bandwidth of network devices, workforce at various skill levels within the similar field, various sniffing abilities of network sniffers and various abilities of vulnerability analyzers.
- **Unrelated:** These are the processors whose speed based on the task carried out. According to classical scheduling theory the individual processor speeds are stable compare to processor speeds which is referred as uniformity. The processors are said to be unrelated if its speed is based on task carried out like network systems with Distributed Denial of Service (DDoS).
- **Dedicated:** These types of processors are used for performing particular jobs. Instance of these types are special purpose computers or computers with various fields of specialization such as UNIX and NT system administrators.

Responsibilities may be of following types such as non-preemptive or preemptive (Krings & Azadmanesh, 2005).

- **Non-Preemptive:** It is a process which cannot be suspended once it has been initiated such as printing. On the other hand security strategies often have well-built necessities for patch management, redundancy management, and maintenance operations like backups and logging that represent minuscule such as non-traceable and operations.
- **Preemptive:** In this the task can be suspended whenever it is required. It is a typical method in many of the commercial applications and the device with real-time operating systems. In spite of conventional translations, security strategies perform some action in response to the various concerns and malicious actions. In that way it prevents the operations of a system. Whenever issues or attacks occur in the system, the technicians from the technical response assistance centers execute many need technicians to recurrently process numerous occurrences at a time by exchanging between back and forth.

NETWORK RECONSTITUTION THROUGH HETEROGENEOUS REPLICATION

One of the fault-tolerance measures of distributed systems is replication. Whenever failure occurs in the system component then the replicated component take a lead in performing it so that the functionality of system can complete its task. According to the discussions done in the previous studies, the network flexibility against unintended failures is enhanced by computer network simulated measures such as support of routes or servers. But these measures won't develop its survivability besides expected attacks.

The heterogeneous networking method supports a new type of replication compared to heterogeneous components. The replication of critical network elements exists in a heterogeneous networking is connectivity infrastructure, resources and services (Zhang et al., 2000). The heterogeneous representation of the network element operates in a same way though a successful attack decreases its functionality. Therefore a network can change to dissimilar network element with the same functionally to support similar end-to-end service to applications. This survivability approach can be referred to reconfigure the network using heterogeneous simulation.

The approach of reestablishing the network has to be done in the following two steps (Zhang et al., 2000).

- **Heterogeneous Replication:** The main purpose is to replicate the abilities of critical network. With the help of mechanisms that transfer these capabilities not by duplicating but by instantiating those into various network elements. This can be implemented by reproducing the network components manually. And also considering various network elements motivated at each component or by considering more than one network element that occurs at the similar physical component. To expand the mechanisms for heterogeneous replication, it is required to construct the off-line tools for interchanging and transmitting network elements in it.
- **Dynamic Reconfiguration:** This is to reconstruct the network with the combination of network elements. When there is a change in the functional ability by any network element, then the whole system change to a replicate of the similar functional capability robustly.

Additionally, self-motivated reconfiguration can be used as a preemptive measure. Due to the frequent change of active elements, the network utilizes its ability for an adversary to recognize flaws and point in time to prepare for a intended attack.

The network reconfiguration techniques (Zhang et al., 2000) are also created based on the following factors:

- A set of strategies that identify the critical elements to be replicated in a network, type of heterogeneous components on which replication to be applied and during standard process and attack how to coordinate between replicas.
- There are certain procedures that act as a mediator between the heterogeneous networking and intrusion detection algorithms. This in turn helps to detect any attack using intrusion detection module so that it can generate dynamic reconfiguration events.

One important issue which is to be concentrated is to identify the type of heterogeneous replications and what we should replicate. This issue is addressed using the threat model with the intrusion detection module in the following section.

Intrusion Detection

One of the optimization measures of new survivable network paradigm is an intrusion detection component. The main objective of this component is to identify the risks in network services and to give attacks data so that the system can perform suitable recovery actions. The network uses threat models to mention the fundamental services and their level of allowable performance degradation or loss. The Intrusion Detection System (IDS) (Zhang et al., 2000) uses the threat models to decide what to observe and what creates threats. Once the IDS identify the threats, then it describes the negotiated services and attack methods which are utilized to decide the heterogeneous repetitions to be activated.

In a survivable network the mission must be satisfied in the existence of attacks at an appropriate time. A threat is a circumstance of attack that intends to compromise or destruct the fundamental components or services. Nonessential services under attack are not considered as threats and also not perform any network recovery actions. This is because when the network is under intended attacks there will be restricted resources and specified time of response.

For a particular task a threat model consider network component or service as critical which is not supposed to be and has adequate quality requirement for every component or service. To facilitate the identification of on-going risks to the network and its mission, the survivability mechanisms with strategies connect with the threat models. Therefore, the way the heterogeneous copies that can be used to regain and reconstruct the work can be managed. For an instance, in a WWW server the threat model contain fundamental service to offer evidence based on demand and include lowest quality constraint to examine at least certain amount of simultaneous demands with the maximum number of seconds per delay. This model determines that if the service is not up to the level of performance constraint then it is treated as risk and appropriate recovery action have to be taken to improve the service (Zhang et al., 2000).

The concept of threat taxonomy is used to group similar threats from the large number of specified threats. The taxonomy provides a way for identifying threats as well as allows similar type of recognition and recovery methods that can be applied on same set of threats. In this way it can decreases the complexity of a system. For an instance the following three dimensions are used to classify the threats such as the effect - which also referred as goal such as denial-of-service, the target - the essential service to be targeted and the technique - how to handle the risk. As an assumption consider Denial-of-Service (DoS) which can be achieved by two methods such as server breakdown or utilization of resource. Two risks are said to be in the same category if they have similar values in all three above mentioned dimensions (Zhang et al., 2000).

In this architecture according to attack scenario study the intrusion detection module can list the identified long-term risks and the forecasted imminent risks. With the help of attacks information such as the effects, targets and techniques suitable recovery events are executed. Meticulously the technique dimension decides how to apply heterogeneous replications for the affected services or what type of heterogeneous replication can be applied. Consider an example in which a DoS attack is carried out through windows fault which caused the server breakdown. Then this fault can rectified through the activation of Linux performance. If the DoS attack is carried out by utilizing TCP handshake such as SYN-flood attack, then it activates other transport layer protocol performances. To simplify the solution, the risk procedures should be mapped to dimensions of diversity space. Moreover a heterogeneous replication should be chosen routinely so that it has the longest distance from the specified one to the identified threat (Zhang et al., 2000).

SERVICE MODEL

This section enlightens the control of new survivable network paradigm which is demonstrated utilizing heterogeneous service model. Explained below are some of the benefits of the new views which are implementable.

The present Internet service model is somewhat homogeneous. Many applications are using the architecture of WWW browser or server model. The regularity of WWW model is cost effective where as the WWW client/server model has its own demerits. This is due to Distributed Denial of Service (DDoS) (Zhang et al.,2000) attacks in which contender is through by systemizing huge number of assumed unauthorized presentation of clients or huge number of ineffective requests that reject the services of authorized users. It happens only in the network with proper bandwidth like the Internet core. In the WWW service model the bandwidth requirements are often asymmetric like data flow from servers to clients rather than in the other direction, so that the consequence of broadband connectivity may be unconstructive. In other words the actual bandwidth used between clients and servers could create successful DDoS attacks. Because of these reasons nowadays WWW services are unprotected in front of DDoS attacks.

The unbalanced network infrastructure helps to detain the DDoS attacker. The bandwidth can used in two different ways such as from clients to servers and servers to clients. If bandwidth is accessible in one direction, then it is restricted by reassuring other direction's bandwidth which eliminates the resources that derive the DDoS attacks. This type of bandwidth allocation is suitable for satellite networks. In these networks it holds the bandwidth inconsistency between the two directions such as downlink from server to client and uplink from client to server which is regularly quite huge as 10000 times. For instance in satellite networks the downlink range will be 100Mbps whereas the uplink range is either 128Kbps or 512Kbps. Thus, DDoS is not suitable for unstructured networks like satellite networks.

Moreover if a simple service model is used rather than heterogeneous service model, then the attacks are unserviceable. Consider a broadcast-based information service in which the information is distributed to WWW server, in turn the servers transmit the information to all clients dynamically. In response to this the clients collect all data inactively and then stream out required information. This type of model is suitable for applications where the stream of information unstructured and efficiently operates in satellite networks. Further the broadcast-based information dissemination model is significantly invulnerable to DDoS attacks because it functions on its own rather than user requirements (Zhang et al., 2000).

Hence, the proposed heterogeneous networking paradigm as in (Zhang et al., 2000) is shown in Figure 6 can be applied. The design of this paradigm is to construct a survivable network application based on two dissimilar sets of service models absolutely and also on two dissimilar network structures. The application easily transfers to the next service, whenever a service is drastically weakened by attacks on one or more components included in it.

CONCLUSION

The theory of survivability through heterogeneity has long been an attractive thought. For instance, in a report issued in 1999, CERT had proposed that one conceivable method for retrieval of fundamental services after assault is to utilize repetitive modules with the same interface however diverse execution. A few DARPA Information Survivability ventures, e.g., the Immunix project by OGI, additionally recorded "heterogeneity" (diverse execution from the same details) as one of the primary destinations. Heterogeneity has additionally been abused to attempt to attain tolerance from programming errors through n-versions programming. Nonetheless, to the best of our awareness there still hasn't been any accomplishment regarding real plan and execution case of the "survivability through heterogeneity" standard. Plans of putting this logic at work through heterogeneous networking model are positively exceptional.

Figure 6. Replications over heterogeneous service models

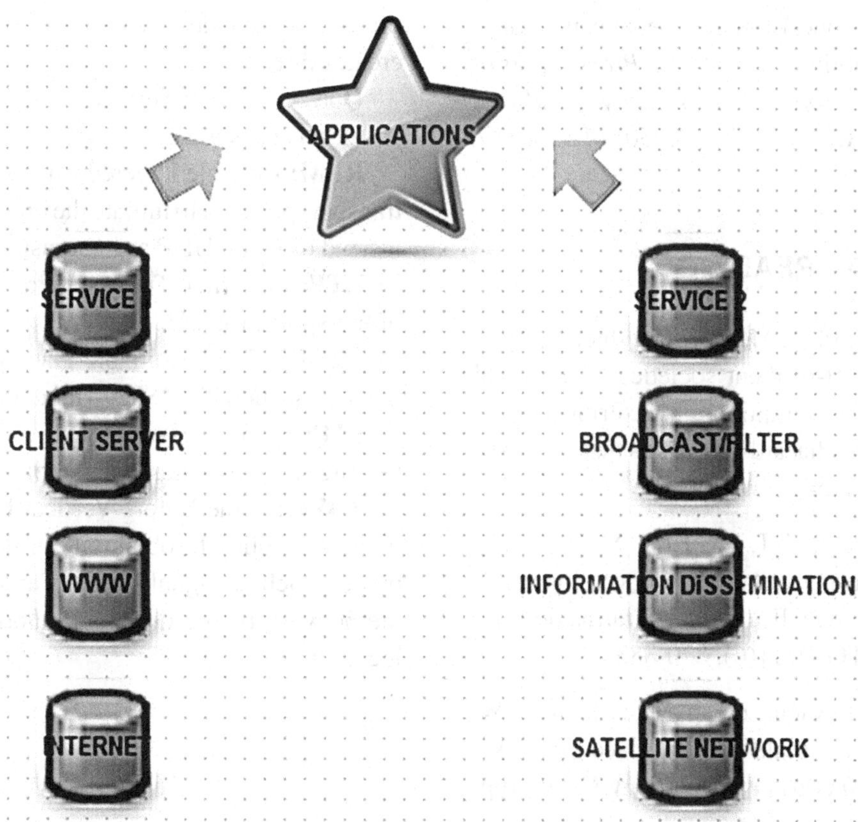

REFERENCES

Cavalcanti, D., Agrawal, D., Cordeiro, C., Xie, B., & Kumar, A. (2005). Issues in integrating cellular networks WLANs and MANETs: A futuristic heterogeneous wireless network. *IEEE Wireless Communications*, *12*(3), 30–41. doi:10.1109/MWC.2005.1452852

El-Arabied, M. (2012). *Heterogeneous networks: An introduction*. Academic Press.

Krings, A. W., & Azadmanesh, A. (2005). A graph based model for survivability applications. *European Journal of Operational Research*, *164*(3), 680–689. doi:10.1016/j.ejor.2003.10.052

Mapp, G. E., Cottingham, D., Shaikh, F., Vidales, P., Patanapongpibul, L., Baliosian, J., & Crowcroft, J. (2006). *An architectural framework for heterogeneous networking*. Academic Press.

Zhang, Y., Vin, H., Alvisi, L., Lee, W., & Dao, S. K. (2001, September). Heterogeneous networking: A new survivability paradigm. In *Proceedings of the 2001 Workshop on New Security Paradigms* (pp. 33-39). ACM. doi:10.1145/508171.508177

ADDITIONAL READING

Birkmann, J. (2006). Measuring vulnerability to promote disaster-resilient societies: Conceptual frameworks and definitions. Measuring vulnerability to natural hazards: Towards disaster resilient societies, 9-54.

Duan, Z., Zhang, Z. L., & Hou, Y. T. (2003). Service overlay networks: SLAs, QoS, and bandwidth provisioning. IEEE/ACM Transactions on Networking (TON), 11(6), 870-883.

Hossain, M. S., Atiquzzaman, M., & Ivancic, W. Survivability and scalability of space networks. In *NASA Earth Science Technology Forum* (pp. 22-24).

Li, N., & Hou, J. C. (2004, March). Topology control in heterogeneous wireless networks: Problems and solutions. In INFOCOM 2004. Twenty-third AnnualJoint Conference of the IEEE Computer and Communications Societies (Vol. 1). IEEE.

Papavassiliou, S., Kato, N., Liu, Y., Xu, C. Z., & Wang, X. (2012). Guest Editors' Introduction: Special Issue on Cyber-Physical Systems (CPS). Parallel and Distributed Systems. *IEEE Transactions on*, *23*(9), 1569–1571.

KEY TERMS AND DEFINITIONS

DDoS: Distributed Denial of Service is an attack that rejects the services of authorized users.

HetNets: Heterogeneous Networks contains huge and small cells such as Macro, Pico, Femto, relay.

IDS: Intrusion Detection System uses the threat models to decide what to observe and what creates threats.

QoS: Quality of Service is to provide end-to-end service assurances.

RLM: Reliable Layered Multicast is used as transport protocol to initiate the broadcast service instead of using UDP as its transport protocol.

RTP: Real-time Transport Protocol is a type of transport protocol.

SRDP: Simple Reliable Datagram Protocol that can sustain TCP SYN-flood attack.

STP: Spanning Tree Protocol is used for connecting LAN switches and identifying loop hole.

TBVH: Time Before Vertical Handover is a proactive policy to obtain and utilize the information such as signal strength and coverage of the network before the mobile node reaches its location.

Chapter 11
Heterogeneous Mobile Computing Issues

ABSTRACT

The fast development of mobile computing has produced a wide variety of technologies that affect systems in the mobile computing realm. Even though mobile computing focuses the importance of interrelated systems, the qualifying of interoperability remains an important constraint. In this chapter, several techniques are explained to manage various heterogeneity characteristics along with the key concepts related to these systems. A general approach is described to manage the heterogeneity. It has been seen that to have a better performance in overlapping networks, it is necessary to switch between the networks due to mobility and congestion. This problem is overcome by overlay networks that identify the existing network and then select the best network and allow transmission from one node to another node in the same network or create a novel network. In this way, this architecture provides a way to transmit packets to the mobile host using the available network.

INTRODUCTION

Both the mobile computing devices and mobile computing systems are affected a lot with the enormous growth in the field of mobile computing which initiated the high range of heterogeneous technologies. The interoperability is the key feature which is highly required to be enabled since the utilization of interconnected systems is concentrated by mobile computing. But the interoperability is difficult to be incorporated in the heterogeneous systems. High level of heterogeneity is supported by mobile computing because of the heterogeneous features of mobile devices, resources, operating system, network capabilities, and applications which includes the persistent access to mobile services and omnipresent communication among mobile hosts.

The two mobile hosts that are able to move around in their respective networks are permitted to utilize the communication link by the communication among mobile devices. The user communicates with the backend systems with the help of mobile device connected to a networks backend system. The respective functions are activated on the backend with respect to this communication process. For example a user's request is serviced with a definite response by the mobile server.

DOI: 10.4018/978-1-4666-7312-0.ch011

The middleware solutions are used to simplify the complexity of heterogeneity. One of the possible solutions is multilevel layer technique. In this multilayer architecture, the topmost layer will be the application layer, the middle layer with the middleware layer and the bottom most layer will be the heterogeneous environment. Thus the heterogeneous environment is accessed evidently with the fundamental heterogeneity hidden.

Multi-modeling means making the communication possible among various Models of Computations (MoCs) by interconnecting them. Different kinds of tools from various vendors are integrated and breakable tool chains are introduced. When various tools are integrated, obviously there will be many challenges to be resolved, but it is important to concentrate on the semantics of interoperation. A better perceptive of semantics of interoperation leads to a better software architectures for interoperation. Figure 1 as in (Schmohl, & Baumgarten, 2008) shows a sample fundamental middleware approach.

BACKGROUND

Basic Approach

An extensive variety of architectural domains are concerned by the heterogeneity problem in mobile environments. Heterogeneity is abstracted (Schmohl, & Baumgarten, 2008) in three different ways as defined below:

- **Hardware Heterogeneity:** The collection of various devices with diverse abilities connected with dissimilar network technologies is referred as hardware heterogeneity.
- **Software Heterogeneity:** The group of various applications and different operating systems is referred as software heterogeneity.
- **Architectural Heterogeneity:** All the architectural features shared by the network interconnections in the environment will be divergent in the case of architectural heterogeneity.

Figure 1. Middleware approach

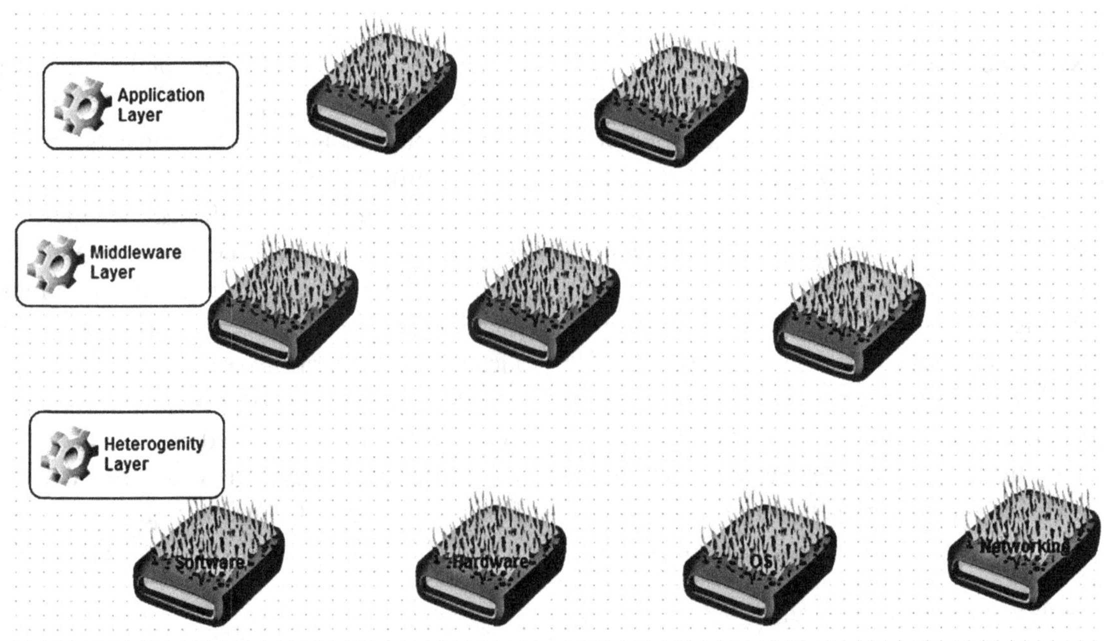

The tribulations that come up from the development of interoperability among various devices and systems can be effectively handled using heterogeneity. The communication models into which interoperability can be categorized are given below (Robert et al,):

- **Direct Communication:** There is a direct collision by heterogeneity in this case as the existing commonly shared principles are used to establish the communication among mobile devices to be taken place directly.
- **Brokered Communication:** The centralized request is used to set up the communication link between devices. The ability to handle a heap of heterogeneous devices by the server is the major challenge in this case.
- **Unidirectional Workflow Activation:** A unidirectional communication is established with the server by the mobile user to activate a particular workflow on the server. The server needs to support the heterogeneous users.
- **Service Provision:** A particular service from a list of services which are provided by the server can be made to be utilized by the mobile device by sending a request to the server and receiving a corresponding response. Previously, the response is sent only after the workflow is completed such that responses delivered after the client request will be used in describing the service. Hence, this application is an extension of the previous case. Even, in this case, the server needs to handle heterogeneous group of devices.

Hardware Heterogeneity

The various physical realization of the core technologies used in mobile devices is referred as hardware heterogeneity. This hardware heterogeneity leads to derive various abilities to various devices. Consequently, the heterogeneous group of devices can be ordered properly because of these different abilities of mobile devices. The following features of hardware heterogeneity are used to categorize the various capabilities of mobile devices.

- **Communication Interfaces:** These permit the device to access the network by connecting the device with its network or surrounding such as GSM, satellite phone networks, 3G networks, Bluetooth, IEEE 802.11, etc.
- **UI Capabilities:** These abilities are used to enable the communication between the device and the user. The input and output interfaces between the device and users such as keypad, microphones, speakers, displays, etc., differ from one device to another. The request from the user and the response from the device both are specific to the device abilities.
- **Performance:** The confines of the mobile device like power supply, the available space, etc., lead to the performance constrained hardware to be equipped in the mobile devices.

The level of limitations varies considerably from device to device even though every mobile device has its own limitations. The ability to compute, store and communicate is considered with respect to the performance.

Software Heterogeneity

The group of software goods on mobile devices is taken into consideration in software heterogeneity. There are four types of software heterogeneity as discussed below:

- **Operating Systems:** Various number and type of operating systems are installed on mobile devices. The heterogeneity regarding the operating systems on mobile devices leads to different architectures and various tasks being handled by the respective OS in parallel. Some applications can make use of some of these OS which provide the required infrastructure like Windows Mobile and Symbian OS.

- **Middleware APIs:** These middleware APIs are used to enhance the operating system. If these APIs are affected by the core functions of the operating system, then they become less efficient than the local APIs of the operation system. Hence these APIs need to be protected from the operating systems core functions like in J2ME.
- **Applications:** The collection of applications that accessible by APIs which are made available by the operating systems and the middleware APIs are described by the abstraction principle.
- **Application Domains:** The application domains such as mobile billing, context awareness, etc., are used to classify the applications. Some common ideology is being shared by various application domains even though they diverge from each other.

Wireless Overlay Networks are the satellite networks, cellular and wireless LAN which superimpose the wide area data networks, building size and the room size. The total ordering determines the "goodness" of these networks; to be precise, the smaller coverage area and the higher bandwidth that can be acquired by the mobile host indicates the level of overlay to be low. A numerous wireless networks emerge with the enormous growth in usage of wireless networks and upcoming trends in wireless technologies. Most of these networks provide almost same coverage area and the required bandwidth over the equivalent overlay level. The dynamic conditions like cost, current traffic load, power consumption of the network usage, etc., are to be considered in order to make the better network evident. The mobility of the mobile node across wireless overlay networks is referred as "Vertical Handoff". The three overlays which are used in the realization of vertical handoff concept are LAN, WaveLAN, Wide Area Wireless networks. The handoff latency can be minimized using mobile IP. Handoffs need to be made conventional in order to attain "Seamlessness". The decision regarding the vertical handoff is implanted in the system and is also simple. The "lowest" level or reachable overlay, i.e., small coverage area is chosen by the mobile host in most of the cases for switching purpose. Regrettably, the system dynamics are not considered by this policy. The acceptance of the new networks becomes complex particularly with similar coverage area and bandwidth if only one fixed single policy is incorporated.

There is a widespread emerge in the area of wireless network technology. Wideband CDMA can provide data rates up to 2 Mbps and is satisfying the third generation wireless communication services requirements. The same user can be provided with the required level of quality and the mixed services of both the packet and circuit switched networks with varying bandwidth at the same time. The combination of GPRS (Generalized Packet Radio Service) and GSM is used to provide the bit rate varying from 9kbps to more than 150kbps. In the circuit switched networks, the charge to the user is made based on the amount of data transferred but not the time for which the connection is established.

Different charge models for various wireless networks are given in Table 1. High network bandwidth is given to the users by information stations in order to make their information tank full such as gas stations. Similarly, global coverage and go-anywhere reliability is to be guaranteed by the satellite networks such as Teledesic and spaceway.

Metricom Ricochet wireless modem, cellular modems, and CDPD are some of the examples for the existing wide area wireless networks but which diverge from each other in many parameters

Table 1. Various network charge models

Wireless Network	Charge Model
Cellular Modems (Circuit Switched Data)	Function of connection time
High speed Circuit Switched Data	Function of time to connect and the rate at which data is transmitted
GPRS, WCDMA (Packet Switched)	Function of transmitted data
Metricom Ricochet	Flat monthly rate
Wireless LANs (IR, WaveLAN)	Free of charge beyond the fixed cost of infrastructure

like bandwidth, power consumption, latency, and mainly their process of charging. Integrating all these networks flawlessly is a challenging task.

When many network access technologies are integrated together, it is assumed to have a universal core network and this is holding a high research interest in recent days. A test bed is being developed with various network access technologies like infrared, GSM, WaveLAN, CDMA, etc with Internet as a backbone core network at U.C. Berkeley as Iceberg project.

It is essential that handoffs are allowed only based on some guidelines. To use the network efficiently, the decisions regarding the handoff need to reflect on the dynamic factors also. For instance, the load across the networks can be balanced based on the information on current network conditions, the specifications of the user currently like moving speed can use only the networks that support mobility and hence do not consider the other networks. The knowledge about the topology of the network and the pattern of the user activities help in making the handoff decisions. The handoff latency must be minimized such that the communication can be carried out with interruption which indicates that the handoff is attained seamlessly. The opinion of the user with less user interaction is required in automating the switching process of the user from one network to the other network. The guidelines for specifying the policy regarding the handoff need to be provided by user involvement. When this involvement of the user is minimized, it is said to be automated. If the specified policy is not simple and spontaneous, then the network will be configured by the users which violate the aim of attaining the handoff seamlessly.

Architectural Heterogeneity

The discrepancies in any phase of the design of the architecture of mobile computing systems are addressed by the architectural heterogeneity (Robert et al,). Some of them are given below:

- **Network Topology:** There are differences between the static and dynamic settings of the network to a large extent. When a static architecture is considered, it differs among various networks. This need to be considered important only when the mobile devices move between such various networks. The mobility of a device across a single network is also considered in the case of dynamically changing network topologies. These give rise to the availability and the handover techniques as challenges.
- **Services:** The mobile devices use the heterogeneous services from the existing wide range of divergent services. The service protocols which specify the access and the delivery of the result are considered.

The components of the heterogeneity aware middleware which are identified from the discussion regarding the approaches to face the challenges of heterogeneity are:

- **Device Database:** A device database is used to store related to the device specifically about the capabilities and semantics of the devices.
- **Device Detector:** The devices which are communicating with the middleware are identified using device detector. The identification attribute is compared with the respective entry in the device database during the identification process.
- **Intermediary Storage:** The information which is represented independent of the device is stored in the intermediate space.
- **Translation Adapters:** The information is translated from the device specific to device independent and vice versa using translation adapters. Conceptually, there exists an adapter which shares common capabilities of each device group.
- **Common Interfaces:** The heterogeneous communication partners' access among themselves using a set of interfaces offered by the middleware. The access to the heterogeneous technology is made transparent using these common interfaces.

The same domain with various abilities is defined as heterogeneity. The capabilities of the heterogeneous devices are captured and organize them into appropriate representations which serve as a foundation to find the solution to the device heterogeneity as the first step of attaining interoperability among heterogeneous devices.

Two sample techniques which are suitable for implementing the representations that adapt to device heterogeneity (Robert et al,) are given below:

- **Device Capability Data Bases (DCDB):** The capabilities of the devices are stored in device capability databases. The system which communicates with the devices utilizes this database in order to select the appropriate device to communicate. The system uses this database to analyze the device request and deliver the result accordingly. Relational databases or XML are the general forms of device capability databases such as open source project WURFL.
- **Ontology:** Ontology's are made use of storing data in a more complicated way. The data can be represented as an interrelated set of concepts and characteristics of heterogeneous devices are described using the Ontology. The ontology concentrates on various device characteristics. The ontology is a complicated enhancement of DCDBs but both the DCDB and ontology serve for the similar purposes. Both the DCDB and ontology are referred as device databases because both are storing the information about devices.

Key Themes

The way the heterogeneity concepts to be addressed are dependent on the application, i.e., each application's heterogeneity challenges need to be handled in a different manner. There are four communication principles into which the realization approaches of heterogeneity which handles middleware and are grouped into general client server and peer-to-peer communication paradigms (Schmohl,& Baumgarten, 2008).

Client-Server Model Communication

The communication between the client (mobile device) and a server in the backend is referred as client server model communication. Either a client or server is chosen to employ the heterogeneity aware middleware or sometimes it is employed on both client and server depending on the application. The communication models which are grouped under this communication paradigm are (Schmohl,& Baumgarten, 2008):

- **Unidirectional Workflow Activation:** The clients activate the workflows on the server using the set of common interfaces offered by the server. The communication is in one direction only. Alteration to the individual client protocols is elementary and is restricted to the perceptive of the clients' invocation.
- **Service Provision:** The server and the client can communicate bidirectional way. The device detection is made possible by the server's ability to react to the client's request. When the client sends a request to the server, it is processed by the application at the backend and the temporary results are stored in the intermediary format in the middleware. At this point, the middleware alters the intermediate results according to the requirements of the client as there is knowledge about the device specifications and the results are delivered to the device which sends a request. Therefore, the clients' requests are realized and the particular responses of device can be altered using the concept of individual adaptation.

The middleware which have consciousness about the heterogeneity are employed on the server only according to the client server communication model. But there may be a need to employ the middleware parts on the clients also. To resolve this issue, the middleware is decomposed from the client and hence increases the varieties of applications as the need to employ the middleware components on the devices is eliminated.

Peer-to-Peer Model

This model concentrates on the communication between inter-devices and no strong centralized control exists in this case.

- **Direct Communication:** In pure peer-to-peer networks, there is will be no component controlling in a centralized fashion. Heterogeneous peers are made interoperable with the employment of middleware in them. As this a direct communication and bidirectional in nature, the devices or partners which involve in the communication need to have an agreement based on the protocols which need to be followed in common by both the communicating partners. In addition to the existing fundamental requirements of the hardware, the middleware provides the communication protocols to the devices. The utilization of the same middleware on every client eliminates the need for individual adaptation and the hence the intermediate representations. The hardware limitations regarding the computation, storage and communication exists on every mobile device. The middleware is aware and has the strong concentration on the general interfaces and the hardware limitations of the mobile devices.
- **Brokered Communication:** In heterogeneous peer-to-peer networks, the centralized control is made possible in the case of inter-device communication by the intermediary devices referred as brokers. The communication between heterogeneous partners is conferred by the middle which is resident on the server. Therefore, device detection, individual adaptation and general interfaces play an important role in the brokered communication.

An entity is used to make the communication among the heterogeneous devices or systems possible by creating a room for it between the two communicating devices. This concept is metaphorically related to the general concept as bridges as bridges or entity between two communicating devices are used to connect probably two dissimilar domains. Various applications or examples can be conceived as this is a very fundamental concept. There are two types of bridges known as hardware and software bridges. The various applications are classified into these two types' bridges as discussed below.

Hardware Bridges

The communication between two different heterogeneous devices is made possible by the hardware device and this is dedicated completely only to this communication. In this scenario, the dedicated hardware device is referred as a hardware bridge. The supported heterogeneous domains are provided with the interfaces by the bridging devices. For instance in the case of heterogeneous sensors, the laptop can behave as a bridging device. The different interfaces like USB, serial port, etc., are used to connect different sensors to the laptop which is acting as a bridging device. The wireless 802.11 is used as a system backend to which the refined sensory data in an appropriate format is sent by the laptop after completing the capturing process of getting the data from sensors. Accordingly, the laptop which is a bridging device transmits the data to the destination from the source.

Software Bridges

The diverse systems on the software level communicate with each other with the help of software bridges as similar to the hardware bridges help in communication among various hardware systems. Software bridging helps in dealing with the abstraction layer in many levels. The intrinsic data types of the systems and the protocols to be translated are to be dealt in the transport level bridging. The new devices are detected and the required services from the existing heterogeneous services are provided to them in the service level bridging. The semantics such as roles and compatibility of various devices are handled and interpreted in the device level bridging.

The adaptation mechanism can be made possible at all the bridging levels as they are exemplified by heterogeneous communication. The adaptation mechanism requires some information in order to adapt the communication according to the particular device which requires some kind of potential databases. All the bridging systems need to deal with the translation of protocols, semantics of services and devices, and data types individually. The complexity of the translation process can be minimized by representing the information in the intermediary format on every bridging level instead of employing the translation technique for every pair of systems. The heterogeneity features related to the hardware and software of the mobile devices are discussed till now. The mobile agents need to be deployed in order to deal with the heterogeneity related to the architecture.

Any kind of heterogeneous problems can be dealt by the autonomous programs that are employed on the backend systems but not on the mobile devices. Let us assume that there are mobile devices which can access a group of heterogeneous services. The service requests from these devices can be handled by employing the mobile agents to execute the workflow as given below: The request for the service from the mobile device is accepted by the mobile agent using a standardized interface. Then, the inquiry is done about a particular service by the mobile agent, obtain the detailed regarding the service, adaption to the group of heterogeneous services is carried out. After adaptation, the service is delivered to the requesting device. The heterogeneity of the services is masked from the mobile devices as the adaptation process of heterogeneous services is being carried out by the mobile agent.

OVERLAY NETWORKING

The best performance of the networks can be attained by overlapping with one another. But in such cases, there is a need of mechanism to change the networks easily and transparently due to mobility and congestion. Hence, the best available network is chosen by the architecture to forward the packets to a mobile host.

The tasks of the overlay networking subsystem are:

- Find all the available networks,
- Select the best network out of available networks, and
- A cell of the same network or the best network is chosen for switching transparently when required. (management of transparent handoff).

The mobile host can be in any cell of a particular network, but at the same time it indicates that it belongs to the networks above the network in which actually it is. For instance a mobile host actually is present in the in-building network but it can be considered that it is present in the campus area network, metropolitan area, the regional networks, etc. horizontal handoff takes place when a mobile host moves from one cell to another. When a mobile host changes its location from one network to another network like one metropolitan area to another metropolitan area, then it is referred as vertical handoffs. According to the overlay networking concept, both the horizontal and vertical handoffs are supported. Hence both the heterogeneous networks and the transparent handoffs are maintained by the overlay networking. The heterogeneous networks are said to be supported by overlay networking as the definition of overlay networks itself is the heterogeneous networks overlapping each other. The transparent handoff is said to be supported by overlay networking as it is able to identify the existing networks.

Some of the principles (Brewer et al., 1997) of overlay networking:

- **Highly Available:** The availability of connectivity can be attained and enhanced as the redundancy is introduced by utilizing multiple networks.
- **Localized Services:** The localized services are made available with the provision of information about the location of the client to the infrastructure using multiple networks. It can be made a note that the details about the clients location is provided only by the available networks.
- **Performance:** The capability of overlay networks to choose the best network of all available networks helps in enhancing the performance.
- **Dynamic Adaptation:** Overlay networking performs the dynamic adaptation with the knowledge of the current network of the client. Hence, the user can be provided with more appropriate content in a specific format.

Generally, there are two types of base stations. They are black box base stations (Brewer et al., 1997) and Daedalus-aware base stations (Brewer et al., 1997). The black box base stations are not controllable. Daedalus-aware base stations can be controlled, or modified to the required level to execute the protocols. This division is significant as there is a need of utilization of existing network where the control is not required. There are proprietary protocols to detect the networks and perform horizontal handoff in the black-box base stations.

The tasks to be performed by the black box base stations:

- Offer routing to client.
- Local wireless network management.

The handoff can be controlled with the help of Daedalus-aware base stations. The tasks to be performed by the Daedalus-aware base stations are:

- Client is provided with a signal.
- Network need to be optimized in opposition to wireless losses.
- Location information is provided.
- Clients in its respective cell are served with bootstrap name.

The non-mobile or official location of the client is the home agent. The Daedalus-aware base station delivers the packets to the client at their current location and at the same time keeps track of the actual location of the client.

Home agent helps in eliminating the "triangle routing" and optimizing the route.

The important tasks to be performed by the home agent are:

- The current position and IP address of the client are to be determined.
- Packets are forwarded to the client at their current location.
- Optimized routes are established.

The tasks specified above indicate that the mobility is not dealt by the server and the proxy. There is a possibility of adding some of the responsibilities of the proxy to the server. The dynamic adaptation is performed by the proxy to alter the content of the server according to the requirements or format of the client. The proxy enables the indirect communication between the servers and the clients. The server cannot notice the changes or troubles in the network as they are masked by the proxy and at the same time, the client is provided with the optimized content. A single proxy can be used to many clients to a server.

Some of the tasks of proxy are:

- Servers are provided an optimized access,
- Client connection management,
- Server name and the services are to be provided,
- Data formats are to be optimized,
- Network connectivity is to be observed,
- End-to-end security for simple clients is to be allowed, and
- Location of the clients is to be determined.

Each base station covering a region is allied with local services. For instance users connected to their respective base station can access the services like web server with local information or a local printer.

The client request is to be sent to the server which might happen via proxy, i.e, the request from the client is received by the proxy, processes it and finally forwards to the server. When the response is returned by the server, it is received by the proxy. As the proxy do not know the current location of the client, the response sent by the server is forwarded to the home agent which always keeps track of the location of the client. Hence, the home agent delivers the response to the client through the suitable network.

As the home agent need to keep track of the current location of the clients, updating the home agent is mostly required in the case handoffs. Handoff might take place because of the disconnection of the network to which it is connected actually or a better network availability. There is a possibility of explicit forced handoff request by the users.

The periodic signals are propagated by the clients to determine the base station in order to detect the network in Daedalus-aware base stations. When the base station receives the signal sent by the client, it indicates its presence and the quality of the signals from the base stations of the multiple network connections determines the network to take handoff.

Heterogeneous group of networks face many challenges related to the bandwidth, performance, error rates, latency, etc., to offer the access anytime anywhere in the wireless wide-area. The effect of these parameters can be diminished with the extension of TCP. The performance of the connections can be enhanced by replacing a single lengthy connection many short connections referred as "session".

The principle of performance is supported by the transport performance subsystem. Some other principles are listed below:

- **Highly Available:** The network can be made highly available by enhancing the error handling mechanism.
- **Multimedia:** The performance of multimedia data can be enhanced by permitting the application to use delivery classes to specify its necessities. For example the missing packets can be avoided to be retransmitted if the packets are of video or audio as the interpretation of data will not vary much without the missing data.
- **Dynamic Adaptation:** The efficiency of the transfer can be improved by adapting the content according to the actual bandwidth by observing the connection between the proxy and the client.

The scalable proxy is the main important module of the architecture. The users' device, preferences and the network connectivity are used by the proxy to employ dynamic adaptation of data to be sent to the users. The disconnections or the limitations of the client are masked by the proxy as an intermediary between client and the server and provides the data in time irrespective of the restrictions of the network. The performance of the network is further improved with the deployment of caching. The proxy obtain the data from the cache if available in cache otherwise from the server or internet when a request is sent by the client. The verification and validation process will be carried out by the proxy to restrict the access to the specific resources like email or any logon information to any website.

The objectives of the dynamic adaptation and heterogeneous clients can be attained by using the proxy. In general, the standard servers cannot handle all the heterogeneous clients. Hence, the adaptation process is carried out by the proxy in order to transform the data as per the clients' request. The scalability property of the proxy allows to extending the number of users that it can support. The highly cost effective architecture can be designed using a proxy by integrating the assets taken as a whole of the dynamic users.

Proxy supports the image, postscript, video, etc., cases of multimedia through translations; service name is used in the case of localized services, global authentication by helping the needy clients to authenticate, transparent access by making the servers free from the issues related to the mobility and connectivity. The access to the network is improved by administrating and detecting the local resources.

It is possible to automate the detection of local resources like maps or printers as similar as the selection of the best available network is automated. The access to the resources can be limited to specific users, an authentication process is required. The Kerberos can be used in the design and employment of an authentication process which can be used by low cost mobile devices also. The contradictory objectives of the global authentication with low-cost mobile devices which cannot employ the Kerberos locally are determined. Similarly, another conflict is that the global authentication do not has faith in the local infrastructure with their identification.

The global authentication and the localized service are the two main principles of the network services subsystem. The local clients are served only with the registered local services. Either local or remote Kerberos resource can be accessed by the user after completing the authentication process. The discrepancies are permitted to have an effect on the available services to maintain heterogeneous networks and heterogeneous clients.

By permitting a variety of local servers, the multimedia can be supported. The available services are involuntarily detected by local proxies to facilitate the transparent access and assist the clients to discover the other important services such as SMTP and DNS.

Vertical Handoff

The mobility among various heterogeneous wireless networks is known as vertical handoff (Chen, Liu, & Huang, 2004). In general, the position of the handoff system is above the present routing system. Multicast based handoff system is exhibits low latency handoffs, improves the Mobile IP design and can be altered to sustain with several wireless network interfaces.

Multicast Based Handoff System

The base stations are wired connected to the mobile hosts. In this case, the base station behaves similar to the foreign agents in Mobile IP (Stemm, & Katz, 1998). The abstraction of the packets from the source is delivered to the foreign agents by the home agent who functions similarly in Mobile IP. The mobile host chooses the small set of base stations and it listens only to the address of these base stations only in order to identify the multicasting of abstracted packets sent by the home agent. The home base station behaves as the forwarding base station for the mobile host. The abstracted packets sent by the home agent are de-capsulated by the forwarding base station before sending it to the mobile host. The other base stations besides the forwarding base stations behave as buffering base stations which is used to buffer packets from the home agent. When the handoff process is initialized by the mobile host, the present base station will change its behavior to the buffering mode and the new home base station changes from the buffering mode to the forwarding mode. The home agent behaves as base station where the infrastructure of base stations is not manual control. In general the forwarding agent functions at the gateway between various networks but it can be installed at the home agent also in the case of wireless networks. The mobile host home or local address is related to the multicast care-of address (address of the multicast group of base stations) using a translation table in the network layer of the home agent. The mode of the base station as forwarding base station or buffering base station is also included in the translation table. The entries of the translation table are compared with every incoming packet and the respective action (to forward or to buffer) specified in the table is performed if match occurs. Every base station has two user level agents known as beacon agent and de-capsulation agent. The beacon packets are transmitted by the beacon agent. The kernel level translation table is adapted and the control messages from the mobile host are received by the de-capsulation agent. The mobile host local address is appended in all outgoing packets by the translation table at the mobile host.

The mobile receives packets via multiple network interfaces. As there are multiple network interfaces, there is a chance of receiving duplicate packets. The network interface specific table is maintained in order to enroll the number of packets sent via each network interface to the mobile host and eliminates the duplicate packets. The changes in the table are notified if the callback is registered with the networking stack during the user level process. The user level process notifies if a single interface forwards the packets more than the threshold number of packets.

A mobile host has two user level agents as handoff controller and user control panel. The overlay network is determined using beacons and connection is established using base station by the handoff controller. The network and the base station can be chosen by the user using the user control panel.

These are applicable only when the handoff is expected soon but not in all the cases where the applications demand low handoff latency. The situations (Stemm, & Katz, 1998) where the handoff is likely to happen soon are:

- **User Input:** This input suggests the mobile host to be more forceful regarding the handoff process. The mobile host can be switched to multicast mobile IP mode while the user is about to change the campus area network. The mobile host can be brought out from this state when the user is not on move.
- **Signal Strength Received:** The received signal strength might not indicate the occurrence of handoff accurately but it might indicate the accurate distance between the mobile host and the base station. In general, the mobile host is assumed to be moving towards the base station when the received signal strength is high and away from the base station when the received signal strength is low. The mobile host is assumed to have vertical handoff when the best signal strength that the mobile host hears is low.
- **Geographic Hints:** In the new overlay network, the cells which behave as gateways are determined with the help of traces. The transitions between networks in the overlay network where the user can possibly connected to more than one network are similar to the task of the building topography. From some locations of the particular cells in the building only, there is a possibility for vertical handoff to occur. For example entry and exit from the building can be only from some locations. The information indicating that a particular cell is at the borders of the network and a chance of occurring vertical handoff is more from these cells by the base stations of respective cells.
- **Handoff Frequency:** The frequency of handoffs is observed and when it is increased, the enhancements are utilized.

The following improvements (Stemm, & Katz, 1998) can be attained at the expense of power or bandwidth:

- **Fast Beaconing:** The multicast group of base stations from which the mobile host can listen is requested to send more than one beacon packets per second, i.e., with higher frequency. The handoff can be taken place faster as the beacon packets are received rapidly. Hence the handoff latency is minimized.
- **Packet Double Casting:** The multicast group of base stations to which the mobile host is able to listen can be pushed into the forwarding mode by the mobile host which indicates the possibility of receiving multiple packets by mobile host from various base stations. If it is assumed that there are only two base stations in the multicast group, then they are the current base station and the next level overlay network base station. The IP ids are maintained in the cache and the IP id of the received packet is compared to the entries in the cache. If match occurs, it indicates the received packet is a duplicate packet and hence it is filtered out. This process is taken place in the network layer at the mobile host. This process of eliminating duplicate packets is helpful in minimizing the congestion at the transport layer. The number of packets received from both the base stations is maintained at the network layer of the mobile host and are compared with each other. The base station which sent more number of packets is

treated as the nearby, can be selected for the handoff to be taken and the base station from which there are no packets or less number of packets is said to be unreachable. The packets in the cache maintained at the network level are forwarded to the next higher levels. When the mobile host does not receive packets, then handoff is activated using beacons. This process can be takes place at different places in different applications. For instance at the network layer in the case of IS-95 CDMA cellular phone standard, at the physical layer in the case of ARDIS wide area data system, etc.

- **Header Double Casting:** In the packet double casting approach, the handoff is indicated by the duplicate or more number of packets through a particular interface. Hence, this advantage can be considered and the full packets can be sent only after the handoff process is completed. i.e., in this approach, the packets are buffered by the base station which are destined for the mobile host and forwards the IP header of the buffered packet to the mobile host. The received packet headers by the mobile host are maintained at the network layer. When the mobile host receives the number of packet headers more than the threshold value, then the handoff to the new base station is taken by the mobile host. After the handoff process, the new base station forwards the full packets as similar as in the fundamental system. The advantage of this approach is that the short packets are sent on the upper overlay before handoff which helps in reducing the congestion.

Advantages of the double casting approaches (packet double casting and the header double casting) when compared to the beaconing systems:

- In general, the mobile host utilizes less number of resources and uses additional resources when it is able to receive data actively.
- The handoff process is activated without duplicate packets.
- Reduces the congestion.

All the mobile devices in the wireless cell are affected with the beacons sent by the base station. The effectiveness of the bandwidth utilization will be dramatically reduced with the increase in the frequency of the beacons. Also, the increase in the number of beacons, it will compete with the number of application level data packets to acquire network resources and hence there is a chance of network congestion.

The disadvantage of double casting approaches is that the network load maintained by both the overlays (before and after handoff) must be equal. The same beacon packets can be used by multiple users in a cell to trigger the handoff is the advantage of the beaconing systems.

Handoff Mechanism

The switching process from one network to the other in the heterogeneous wireless networks is referred as vertical handoff (Chen et al.,2004). To trigger the vertical handoff, the wireless networks that can be reached are discovered initially. The mobile host determines whether to trigger the handoff or not after determining the listenable wireless networks. The time at which the handoff process to be triggered by the mobile host based on the candidate resources and the application in use.

Many suitable and favorable mobile services are provided by the wireless networks. Various wireless technologies are introduced for various intensions such as technology like HIPERLAN/2 is introduced in the case of local area networks while GSM and UMTS are introduced in the case of wide area networks. The parameters such as bandwidth, coverage area, frequency band, latency of data transmission, etc., are used to vary these technologies. Generally, larger bandwidth is provided in the case of smaller service area and low bandwidth is provided in the case of larger service area. It is significant that the established connection of the mobile host is sustained while it is moving through different wireless networks and at the same time, flawless integration of these technologies is decisive.

There are three key constraints to be considered for the perfect integration of various dissimilar wireless technologies:

- Automatic process of triggering vertical handoff without the interference of the user.
- The automatic selection of the best available network among the many interfaces by the mobile host.
- During the handoff process and when the mobile host is moving between 2 different service providers, the redirection of data flow is to be switched to the new wireless network effortlessly.

RELIABLE DATA TRANSMISSION

Error free transmission is required in any digital communication system. There is a chance of incorrect data being received by the receiver or destination in the transmission system. Hence, making the data to be received by the receiver correctly is a major challenge in designing the transmission systems of digital communication and storage systems and which can be achieved by using the error control coding technique. The message should be received by the receiver error free if it is transmitted and the stored message should be able to be retrieved correctly without any error in the case of storage system by many applications. Whenever the error detection and correction mechanisms are essential to maintain the reliability, then techniques like Forward Error Correction (FEC) can be utilized. In forward error correction mechanism, the limited errors in the transport or storage system can be detected and corrected without the requirement of retransmissions. The forward error correction mechanism based on the convolution codes is powerful in performing the error correction, efficient and flexible channel utilization. The systems with either high or low data rate can employ the FEC mechanism which is based on the convolution codes implemented using VLSI technique effortlessly and inexpensively.

The data formatting mechanisms and the buffer management systems are integrated with the forward error correction mechanism in some of the new systems. Additional message is added to the original message which helps in detecting and correcting the errors if any on the receiver side, this is basic idea in the channel coding process. This type of coding mechanism enables the receiver to detect and correct the errors which might have been introduced because of the noise without appealing for the retransmission to efficiently use the limited range of the bandwidth.

The mathematical notion of information transmission is introduced by C.E. Shannon in 1948. According to this concept, digital information can be transmitted after encoding using a noisy channel with a random and low error probability and the decoding process being carried out at the receiver side. The rate of transmission is to be maintained less than the capacity of the channel in order to attain this goal.

In general, the classification of the fading effects in mobile communications is made as small scale fading and large scale fading. The reduction in the average signal power and the loss of the path because of the mobility over large areas is referred as large scale fading. In general, large scale fading is caused because of the receiver being hidden by high territories like hills, tall buildings, forests, etc. When the transmitter and the receiver are separated spatially, signal strength and the phase will undergo vivid modifications. This is referred as small scale fading which also is known as Rayleigh fading as the envelope of the received signal is depicted by a Rayleigh. There will be no line of sight signal and more number of reflective paths is constituted in the received signal. A leading non-fading signal component leads to the line-of-sight propagation path. A fully distributive sensing and an inexpensive computing solution is provided by wireless sensor networks for the environments where conservative networks are not viable. In sensor networks, the problem of transmitting the data reliably is versatile. The weak paths should not be artificially strengthened during the determination and selection of the route using the Automatic Repeat Request mechanism in order to offer prominence on energy conservation in the wireless sensor networks. The well-engineered recovery enhances the path maintenance at the MAC layer or the transport layer or at both. Since most of sensor network applications are resistant to irregular packet loss, the standard delivery should depend on common small event descriptions in order to make the recovery to be inexpensive. Detection and correction of loss are the necessities in some other applications. The guaranteed delivery, segregation and assembling pieces of data are the features of the reliable data transmission system. The limitations of the sensor networks are different from the traditional wired networks. Since, the nodes of the sensor networks cannot be recharged whenever required, it wastage of energy reduces the lifetime of the nodes. Hence, the energy constraints play a vital role in sensor networks. The in-network processing in wireless sensor networks is made possible and attractive with low bandwidths and energy constraints. Optimization of the shared network is concentrated on the throughput instead of fairness as the nodes in the sensor network work together to attain a common mission instead of representing independent users. The interoperability with existing standards is less necessitate as the sensor networks are frequently organized as a single unit with economical hardware. All the reasons lead to the enhancement or improvement of the traditional communication protocols in the sensor networks. As it is already indicated that the reliability for data transmission system can be implemented at different layers, it can also be noted that MAC layer and transport layer reliability is crucial. The transport layer can be provided with the hop by hop error recovery and the route can be discovered and maintained only with the reliability of MAC layer. Hence, the reliability plays a vital role in MAC layer.

Reliable Multi-Segment Transport (RMST) (Stann,& Heidemann,2003) is modification to the transport layer which can guarantee delivery even during the very high error rates through multiple hops. The diffusion routing becomes an advantage of RMST with the addition of negligible control traffic.

The hop-to-hop recovery of frames is referred as link layer Automatic Repeat Request (ARQ). The methods which offer reliability in the MAC layer using IEEE 802.11 are RTS/CTS control packets, Acknowledgements (ACK) and selection of slot randomly. The RTS/CTS mechanism assures that a single transmitter will acquire the channel access and reduces the collisions and improves the reliability. In the acknowledgment (ACK) process, the receiver sends back the ACK control packet as acknowledgement after receiving the data packet to the transmitter indicating the successful transmission. This mechanism is also referred as "Stop-and-wait" ARQ mechanism (Stann,& Heidemann, 2003), where the transmitter retransmits the packet for which it did not receive the acknowledgement after waiting for a certain period of time. The RTS/CTS or ACK mechanisms are not implemented in the case of multicasting or broadcasting transmission of packets. The medium is sensed; choose the idle slot for transmission to reduce the probability of broadcast collision.

Three modes of ARQ (Stann,& Heidemann, 2003) in MAC layer:

No ARQ

MAC address is broadcasted. At the routing layer, address screening is used to achieve unicast. The reliability in this mode is delayed to the transport or application layer.

Advantages of No ARQ:

- The overhead of RTS/CTS or ACK control packets is eliminated as these mechanisms are not employed in the MAC layer in this mode.
- High quality paths are selected by the routing protocols for data transmission.
- The poor paths chosen by the reliable mechanism are by mistake realized as strong by the higher layers.

ARQ Always

Stop-and-wait protocol is used to transmit using single node address. The assumed reliability can be strengthened with retransmissions using the RTS/CTS or ACK mechanisms. The acknowledgement must be sent as unicast by all the multiple neighbors to which the node communicated.

Advantages:

- The reliable paths determined during the route discovery process are used to transmit the packets irrespective of the temporary intrusion in the wireless domain.

Selective ARQ

This method is a combination of previous two methods No ARQ and the ARQ always. ARQ, a stop-and-wait mechanism is employed in the case of unicast or single receiver or neighbor. When there is a requirement of broadcast or more neighbors, No ARQ method is employed. The advantages of both ARQ and No ARQ are integrated in this method. ARQ mechanism is used to transmit the data and control packets on traditional paths to improve reliability. No ARQ mechanism is used to broadcast the packets to all the neighbors during the route discovery process. Hence, the route discovery process does not increase the overhead in order to improve reliability and at the same time, risk is not being taken in transmitting the packets without using ARQ mechanism.

In wireless communication, transmitting the data larger than the network MTU is a challenging task, more particularly in directed distribution. There is a limit to which extent an entity can be decomposed in order to provide guaranteed delivery even though there is a capacity of fragmentation and reassembly for IEEE 802.11. The data packet cannot be reassembled and made useful when a single fragment is missed among a large binary object.

The main reason for loss of packets is assumed to be congestion by the traditional transport layer protocol like TCP. Hence the concentration of such transport layer protocols is on congesting control. The interference and low power are the main reasons of packet loss in the sensor networks. The tradeoff between hop-by-hop and end-to-end functionality is very important in the design of transport layer. The receiver or the in-network nodes can start the repair requests on a predetermined path.

There are two variations in transport layer schemes (Stemm, & Katz, 1998). They are:

- **End-to-End Selective Request NACK:** Only the sink enables the repairing process. The missing data is retransmitted using the reverse unbreakable path which is used to send the request for repairing the particular missing fragments by the sink to the source.

- **Hop-by-Hop Selective Request NACK and Repair from Cache:** The fragments of a large data are cached by the caching nodes on the unbreakable or reliable path from the source to the receiver. When there is a request for repair from the receiver in the transmission, a response is sent by the caching node if the lost fragment is in the local cache of caching node when the caching node receives this repair request. If caching node does not find the requested fragment, then NACK is forwarded towards the source.

It is possible to provide the reliability even at the application layer. Reliability is a parameter which plays a vital role at every layer of the network. Waiting for the subsequent sensor reading is quite straightforward reliability scheme in the case of sensor networks where the periodic data is automatically generated. Conversely, this simple and straightforward approach is not applicable to entities which are large. The probability of receiving a whole entity over several hops is very less still at the reasonable per-packet loss rates. The large information element which is divided at the source is sent as per the request of the receiver. The request of the receiver is removed when all the fragments of a large data entity are received by the receiver. All the fragments of a large data entity are transmitted at regular and pre-calculated periods of time by the source until the receiver deletes the request. Whether the additional cost induced by the transport system is worth to provide sufficient advantages in terms of utilization of energy or not is determined using this "transport less" standard.

CONCLUSION

The high level of heterogeneity is one of the characteristics of the mobile computing. One of the few standards that are followed by the software developers, device manufacturers, and network providers to exemplify the mobile computing by a high level of heterogeneity is middleware solutions. In mobile environments, the extensive variety of architectural domains is the main consideration to be taken into account while dealing with the heterogeneity. The interoperability among various devices and systems need to be attained while addressing the heterogeneity. The variation in the technology of physical implementation of the mobile devices is referred as hardware heterogeneity. The devices that exhibit different capabilities are the resultant of the hardware heterogeneity.

There is an extensive emerge in the technologies of wide area wireless network. The requirements of the third generation wireless communications are satisfied by CDMA which is capable of providing 2Mbps data rate. The combination of packet and circuit switched services with unpredictable bandwidth can be activated at the same time to the same user with the particular levels of quality. Metricom Richochet wireless modem, cellular modems and CDPD are some of the examples of wide area wireless networks. The interoperability can be attained among the heterogeneous devices by organizing them into appropriate representations after observing all the capabilities of various heterogeneous devices. Application specific instantiation is required to address the heterogeneity concepts.

The communication between the client and the server is referred as client server model communication. The middleware which has the knowledge about heterogeneity is employed only on the server. Another type of communication is possible by inserting an additional entity between a pair or more heterogeneous systems. The additional device or entity inserted in between 2 devices or systems is referred as bridge between two systems or proxy. The differences in the protocols and the data types of the two systems connected are adapted with each other using proxy, referred as transport level bridging. Similarly, service level bridging is used to identify new devices and suitable services are delivered to these devices. The semantics of different devices are translated in the device level bridging. There are limitations to the protocols like IEEE 802.11 in decomposing the entity into smaller units even though it has the properties of fragmentation and reassembly in order to provide guaranteed delivery. If all fragments of the data entity transmitted are not properly received by the receiver, i.e, if any single fragment is missing, then the data becomes worthless. The main reason for the loss of packets is assumed to be congestion by the traditional transport layer protocol like TCP. In sensor networks, the concentration on energy conservation should not lead to the assumption of the poor paths to be strong enough.

REFERENCES

Brewer, E. A., Katz, R. H., Chawathe, Y., Gribble, S. D., Hodes, T., & Nguyen, G. et al. (1998). A network architecture for heterogeneous mobile computing. *IEEE Personal Communications*, *5*(5), 8–24. doi:10.1109/98.729719

Chen, W. T., Liu, J. C., & Huang, H. K. (2004, July). An adaptive scheme for vertical handoff in wireless overlay networks. In *Proceedings of Parallel and Distributed Systems*, (pp. 541-548). IEEE.

Schmohl, R., & Baumgarten, U. (2008, July). A generalized context-aware architecture in heterogeneous mobile computing environments. In *Proceedings of Wireless and Mobile Communications*, (pp. 118-124). IEEE. doi:10.1109/ICWMC.2008.59

Stann, F., & Heidemann, J. (2003, May). RMST: Reliable data transport in sensor networks. In *Proceedings of Sensor Network Protocols and Applications*, (pp. 102-112). IEEE.

ADDITIONAL READING

Bartlett, K. A., Scantlebury, R. A., & Wilkinson, P. T. (1969). A note on reliable full-duplex transmission over half-duplex links. *Communications of the ACM*, *12*(5), 260–261. doi:10.1145/362946.362970

Stemm, M., & Katz, R. H. (1998). Vertical handoffs in wireless overlay networks. *Mobile Networks and Applications*, *3*(4), 335–350. doi:10.1023/A:1019197320544

Wang, H. J., Katz, R. H., & Giese, J. (1999, February). Policy-enabled handoffs across heterogeneous wireless networks. In Mobile Computing Systems and Applications, 1999. Proceedings. WMCSA'99. Second IEEE Workshop on (pp. 51-60). IEEE. doi:10.1109/MCSA.1999.749277

KEY TERMS AND DEFINITIONS

Brokered Communication: The centralized request to set up a communication link between devices.

Daedalus-Aware: A base station to control hand.

DCDB: Device Capability Data Bases to select an appropriate device to communicate.

Device Database: To store the capabilities and semantics of the devices.

Device Detector: To communicate with the middleware.

Middleware APIs: APIs are used to enhance the operating system.

Multi-Modeling: Making the communication possible among various models of computations by interconnecting them.

Vertical Handoff: The mobility of the mobile node across wireless overlay networks.

Wireless Overlay Networks: The satellite networks, cellular, and wireless LAN.

Chapter 12
Scalable Architecture for Heterogeneous Environment

ABSTRACT

Along with the heterogeneous devices, Web-based content increases the necessity for computational services. However, recent trends make it difficult to execute such computations at the terminal side, whereas service providers often allow computations during different load operations. Many computational services are using conventional distributed systems, which provide successful packet transmission in IP networks. In this chapter, proxy architecture and its related tasks are discussed. Some of the necessary requirements, such as incremental scalability, 24x7 availability, and cost-effectiveness, are recognized for scalable network services. To administrate a large cluster and to construct a cluster-based scalable network services, a layered architecture is recommended. This architecture captures the scalable network service requirements and utilizes service-programming models to perform Transformation, Aggregation, Caching, and Customization (TACC) of Internet substance. For better performance, the architecture with the TACC programming model uses data semantics to create novel network services.

INTRODUCTION

Different types of environments like multiple radio access technologies, architectures, base stations with altering transmission power are involved in the heterogeneous mobile network environment. The swift growth of mobile computing with mixed range of technologies affects both the devices and the systems in the mobile computing domain.

The systems that employ various types of computational units like General Purpose Processor (GPP), special purpose processor, co-processor or custom acceleration logic are known as heterogeneous computing systems. Digital Signal Processor (DSP) or Graphics Processing Unit (GPU) can be used as special purpose processor and Application Specific Integrated Circuit (ASIC) or Field Programmable Gate Array (FPGA) can be used as custom acceleration logic (Pandey, & Glesner, 2006).

In general, various processors with diverse Instruction Set Architectures (ISAs) are constituted in heterogeneous computing platform. The requirement of high performance and spontane-

DOI: 10.4018/978-1-4666-7312-0.ch012

ous systems that can communicate with other environments had increased the demand of heterogeneous computing systems. The performance of most of the computer applications is increased without making any modifications in the structure or traditional hardware and was possible with enormous advancement in the technology and frequency scaling. Specialized resources which make the computing system to be heterogeneous are launched in addition to the primary method to gain an extra performance. There is a possibility for the designer to select different processing elements based on the tasks that a system need to perform in the case of heterogeneous computing systems. These heterogeneous systems are also referred as parallel computing systems or multi-core systems or hybrid computing because they incorporate independent computing resources and asymmetric computational units. As the area of the chip increases and the technology of fabrication are enhanced, it is possible to integrate more number of discrete components on chip, hence increases the level of heterogeneity in the modern computing systems. For instance presently, the logic for interfacing the devices with the processor (SATA, PCI, Ethernet, RFID, Radios, UARTs, and memory controllers), programmable functional units and hardware accelerators (GPUs, cryptography co-processors, programmable network processors, A/V encoders/decoders, etc.) are built-in in most of the new processors.

Many new challenges are imposed by the heterogeneous computing systems when compared to the homogeneous systems. The problems related to the homogeneous parallel processing systems are also included heterogeneous systems because it includes multiple processing components. At the same time, non-uniformity is introduced in the development of the system, practices of programming and the complete system capability.

Areas of heterogeneity (Chawathe, Fink, McCanne, & Brewer, 1998) can include:

- **ISA or Instruction Set Architecture:** Two-fold incompatibility arises because of the different instruction set architectures for different computing elements.
- **ABI or Application Binary Interface:** Memory is interpreted in various ways by different computing elements. The interpretation may be based on the convention, memory layout, architecture and the compiler being used.
- **API or Application Programming Interface:** All the computing elements may not be uniformly obtaining a chance for the library and OS services.
- **Low-level Implementation of Language Features:** In heterogeneous environments, additional translation or abstraction is required in the case of function pointers, which are used to implement the language features like functions and threads.
- **Memory Interface and Hierarchy:** Cache structures, cache coherency protocols might be different for different computing elements. Similarly, the memory access might be uniform or non-uniform and the arbitrary data length that a processor can read at a time might be byte, word or burst access.
- **Interconnect:** Besides basic memory/bus interfaces, different computing elements might have different types of interfaces like dedicated network interfaces, direct memory access (DMA), mailboxes, FIFOs, scratchpad memories, etc.

Various computing elements in the heterogeneous computing environment require different types of compilers. Hence, the development process of heterogeneous systems is complicated when compared to the development process of homogeneous systems. In order to satisfy the aim of heterogeneous systems, an organized way of interfacing different compilers and linkers is required. The heterogeneity can be hidden with the help of interpretive techniques but the cost of interpretation requires just-in-time compilation mechanisms to be utilized. But these mechanisms are not suitable for the embedded systems or real time scenarios which are more complex runtime systems.

As the device manufactures, network providers or software developers do not obey the common standards for exchange of information in the mobile computing environment. Hence, it is considered as a high level of heterogeneity. Heterogeneous characteristics of mobile devices, operating system, network capabilities and resources are replicated by this aspect. Recently, the technological trends like wireless networking and multimedia are emerging hastily. When the infrastructure is less or the inconvenient or expensive to use, then the flexible means of communication is provided by the mobile networks (Sun,Gao,Belding-Royer, & Kempf, 2004). There is a chance of having many heterogeneous nodes in the mobile networks.

The type of clients and embedded wireless devices such as PDAs and mobile VoIP clients increased the heterogeneity (Sun, Belding-Royer, Gao, & Kempf, 2007). In classrooms or in a multi-hop mesh, fixed wireless routers behave as a network backbone. Users can communicate among them through PDAs, laptops or any other wireless devices by moving freely within the network. The enhancement in employment and a balanced nature of multi-hop mesh networks made them more established. The varying network load, battery and processing power are hold by the devices within these networks as heterogeneous facilities. Heterogeneous networks are quickly emerging and turning out to be the most important component of the wireless Internet.

There are many variations in the appearance and the characteristics (size, disk, computational power, memory, battery life) of different kinds of mobile devices. The performance of communication and the communication protocol design are affected by these differences or heterogeneity. This heterogeneity determines the capability of one device to be more powerful than the other; some can act as servers while some other can behave as only clients. The design and architecture of the network infrastructure in heterogeneous and potentially overlapping networks need to be in such a fashion that the clients can be provided with optimized network access.

Architectural Requirements for Heterogeneous Networks

The features that the architecture of the heterogeneous networks which handle specific requirements are given below:

- **Heterogeneous Wireless Networks:** The wireless networks with restricted and global coverage need to be included in the architecture.
- **Seamless Mobility:** The flawless mobility or roaming facilities need to be supported by the architecture in order to eliminate the disruptions during the communication in inter-system or intra-system roaming.
- **Scalability:** The fault tolerance and the scalability in terms of users need to be supported by the architecture which integrates various wireless systems of both the present and the future service providers.
- **Automated Localized Service:** The architecture must be in such a fashion that the local network services can be detected and connected to the users automatically without the users having the knowledge about the services in their current location.
- **Economical:** The architecture need to ensure economical and rapid deployment, by using the existing infrastructures instead of going for the new ones.
- **Availability, 24x7 Coverage:** The users should be able to access the network any time any day.

- **Automatic Network Setup:** The network must be automatically detected without the knowledge of the users about the networks in the range and this setup need to be supported by the infrastructure.
- **Functionality and Performance:** The quick and reliable access to data and sharing of data need to be ensured by the architecture.
- **International Authentication:** The globally available security infrastructure such as Kerberos or public key cryptography is used by the architecture to authenticate the users.
- **Heterogeneous Clients Support:** Specifications are different in different devices. The architecture must be able to contain any type of devices like smart-phones.
- **Multimedia Support:** A large variety of data like graphics, audio, video, text, etc., need to be supported by the architecture.
- **Speed and Precision:** Any type of data needs to be transferable error free without any delay must be made possible by the architecture.

The architecture of the heterogeneous mobile networks is defined using these specifications. The principle elements given below which may be individually or jointly work in order to satisfy these specifications:

- Overlay networks,
- Scalable proxy architecture,
- Data transport performance, and
- Network services and authentication.

Overlay Networks

The wireless networks which have some area in common, i.e, whose coverage areas are overlapped are referred as wireless overlay networks. Lower bandwidth and larger coverage area is offered at the higher levels and the vice versa as the higher bandwidth and the smaller coverage area at the lower levels in the hierarchy.

A group of nodes are placed in particular locations in an existing network framework as shown in the Figure 1 as in (Brewer et al.,1997) is referred as overlay network structure. While the user is in mobility, the best available network will be chosen to switch from the existing after determining new networks by a mobile device in overlay networks. This optimizes the fast handoff procedure and gives quick and transparent access to the best accessible system.

A group of different wireless networks must exist among which the mobile terminal need to switch in order to achieve overlay networking as in (Brewer et al.,1997) is shown in the Figure 2. In order to switch among the different wireless networks, the mobile terminal need to have multiple network interfaces.

Wireless overlay, the next generation wireless network is used to give more user satisfaction by allowing the mobile terminal to switch among different networks and choose the best network at any moment.

Scalable Proxy Architecture

Proxy means alternative. In the areas of computing like www, mobile computing, etc., the concept of proxy is initiated and is being widely used. The wireless networks face many challenges like frequent disconnections and limited resources which may be overcome by the use of proxy. The mobile devices on heterogeneous platforms will lead to new concerted applications because of the synergy between networking and mobility. One of such applications is "System on Mobile Devices" SYD. The integration of middleware and client-ware technologies is SYD. The development

Figure 1. Overlay networking

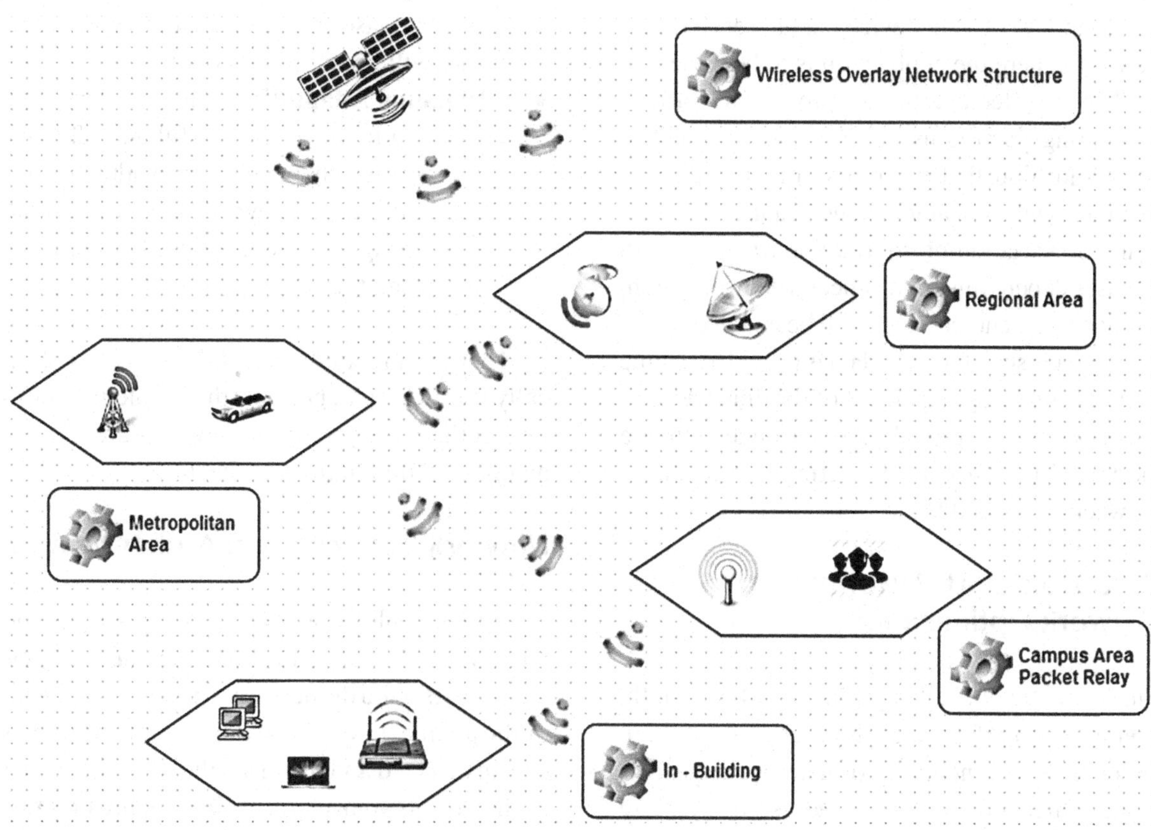

Figure 2. Basic architecture of network level

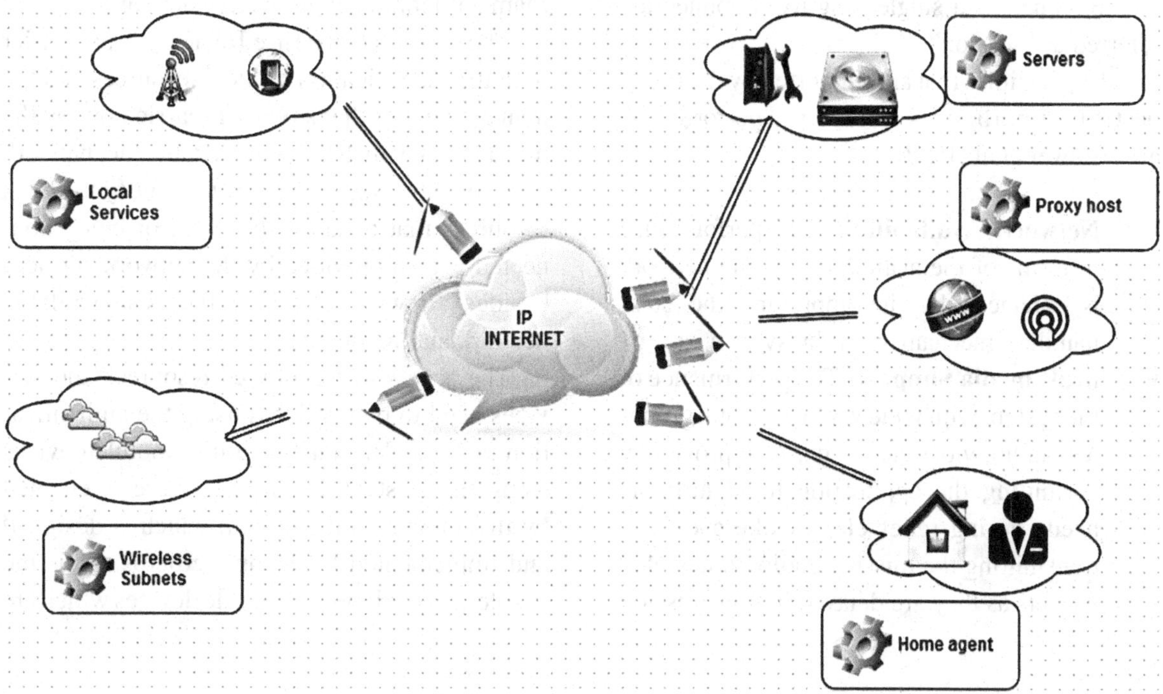

of the application is independent of the detailed environment of the device, data, services, or network where the application is to be executed.

The architecture of the proxies in various computing paradigms needs to be designed in such a fashion that the proxy tolerates disconnections and is scalable. The features like the dynamic variation of information transmitted to the user depending on the client's device, system connectivity, choices, etc., will be enabled by the proxy if it is scalable. The data is provided in time without any delay regardless of the drawbacks of the network using proxies. The disconnections are hidden by the proxy while acting as a mediator between client and the server.

Data Transport Performance: Network Optimization

There are many challenges like low bandwidth, asymmetric performance, high error rates, high latency, etc., in the group of heterogeneous networks which provide wireless access to anywhere anytime. All these issues are resolved using the extended TCP. The performance of the connections is enhanced when several short connections are combined as a single long lived connection referred as "session".

The principles that are supported by the transport subsystem besides the theory of performance are (Brewer et al.,1997):

- **Network Availability:** The performance in terms of the availability of the network is enhanced by the improving the error handling mechanism of the system.
- **Multimedia Support:** The performance of the system with wide variety of data, graphics, audio, video, text, etc., is improved by permitting the application to identify its needs during relief classes like avoid re-transmitting the missing audio, video, etc., packets as they are delayed in transmission and cannot be placed at the original position and also image or picture without this data will be in a good condition.
- **Dynamic Adaptation:** The transfer of the data can be made successful and effective by adjusting the actual bandwidth according to the content which is possible with monitoring the connection between the proxy and the client.

There is a requirement of the parts of practically useful system because the problems identified in the wide variety of networks are not just an optimization in this architecture

Network Services and Authentication

The use of application specific proxy servers and the advances in the routing and the transport network layers build the network services component of the architecture. The local available resources can be detected and the make the resources adapt to the "on-the-move" reconfiguration using this component. The specified ability of the component is crucial in order to enable the interaction with the environment to be flawless while the clients roam autonomously in overlay networks.

The network can be used efficiently and easier with the identification of local resources and the management of the network is carried out by the mechanism which is provided by the network services. The systematic way to identify the local resources that enhance the value of being connected is also provided by the network services besides allowing choosing the best available network automatically.

The access to the limited resources and services need to be restricted using the authentication process. The verification of mobile devices using the trustworthy infrastructure is enabled by the authentication system which is designed and implemented based on Kerberos. Thus the problem of the low-cost mobile devices which are not able to run Kerberos in the vicinity and are exhausted to belief the local infrastructure with their identification and the conflicting goals of global authentication are resolved.

The two important principles of the network services subsystem are the localized service and global authentication. The services to local clients are provided after the services are registered locally. The users are permitted to access either local or remote Kerberos resource by the authentication process. By permitting the available services to be flexible and affected to the variations, the heterogeneous networks and heterogeneous clients are supported. For example the user can obtain the details of the other users in the cell using the service which is based on the network in use.

Few important techniques need to be utilized in order to obtain this architecture (Brewer et al., 1997):

- The signals of the standard mobility can be improved using the service discovery protocol by providing the additional information related to location, copying features and broadcasts.
- The integration of an interface definition language and the semantics of a model based user interface based on the interface specifications. The scripts of the function which can relate the exported object interfaces to the client device control interfaces are located in the infrastructure. The object communications are created which helps in remapping the destination of the object to dynamic locations of the server.

BACKGROUND

Proxy Architecture

In today's networks, the common place where the proxies are used where many different types of network services are required (Endler,Rubinsztejn,da Rocha,& do, 2005). Proxy is normally located in between the server and its clients. The network bandwidth can be efficiently used; access latency can be reduced, network and device heterogeneity are utilized to perform the copy operation using proxies. Throughput and differences of latency between the wired and wireless paths, movement of the host from one place to another, and restricted number of resources of the Mobile Hosts (MH) are the three foremost problems of the mobile computing and wireless communications which are handled using the proxies in an efficient manner (Endler et al., 2005). In general, proxies are used in infrastructure based mobile networks as the functions of proxies are normally used in processing and memory. But at the same time, it can also be used to realize precise services in mobile ad hoc networks i.e, which are infrastructure less based.

Bridging the differences between the networks and the devices is the main aim of proxies. The new joint applications are created with the mobile devices on heterogeneous platforms because of the synergy between networking and mobility. The protection of the clients from the drawback consequences of the networks which operate slowly and providing significant data appropriately to the clients which it needs by adapting the Internet content are the two key responsibilities of proxy. The maintenance of the information that has utmost semantic value and the layout to be modified in order to optimize the presentation on the target device are two goals of a proxy. Many architectural advantages can be imposed if the representation is updated and modification is done at the proxy.

Networks with varying characteristics are allowed to be used by the wide variety of mobile clients to interoperate evidently with legacy servers. The revision of the clients takes place at the proxy which gives the impact to the server that the clients are powerful and strongly connected. The adaptation can be done both at the server and the proxy. But adaptation at the proxy gives a chance to the server to concentrate on providing the content and the individual content can be presented by the proxy.

The following benefits attained by segregating the task of the proxy and the server are:

- Maintenance improvement,
- Paying back of proxy resources,
- Cost effective in providing the orthogonal content, and
- Providing QoS which decouples the administration and billing.

It is better to use proxy based architecture instead of using end-to-end approach in order to serve the mobile clients. The advantages are given below (Endler et al., 2005):

- The proxy transforms which are dependent on mobile and wireless devices permitting mobile access the legacy services directly.
- The overhead of the servers can be reduced by distributing the tasks which are required to transform the protocol and content to any node where they are required.
- The quality of the wireless link can be more responsibly and perfectly monitored, disconnections of MH can be detected, and better choice of modification can be selected by placing the proxies at a node or close to a node with wireless interface.
- Any communication layer transformations can be employed, modified or personalized based on the precise abilities of the wireless links.

Some examples of services or application in mobile and wireless computing are web access, multimedia streaming, databases, etc. The problems related to these kinds of applications are solved using proxy-based middleware. There are different terms like gateway, intermediary or agent which can be used interchangeably instead of proxy.

Generally, the proxy is defined as an entity that seizes communication or carries out some service in aid of some mobile client (Endler et al., 2005). The proxy needs to be implemented on a well-connected network of service workstations and so the design needs to be carried out appropriately.

The following are to be delivered in order to achieve the goal of the proxy architecture:

- **Scalability:** The proxy must be able to serve any number of users. To facilitate this, proxy architecture should the ability of integration various wireless systems with present and future service providers. The per-user performance is maintained constant with the addition of nodes in the network of service workstations when there is an increase in the number of users.
- **Functionality and Performance:** The access to the data must be without any delay and reliable. Any individual user should be served with minimized latency. When a proxy is used, the overhead must not be visible yet during the high speed connection.
- **Availability, 24x7 Coverage:** The access to the network must be available anytime any day. The services to the user need to be continuously provided. So, the flaw in any individual component must be evidently shrouded by the architecture. This is discussed as a requirement of the architecture specification also.
- **Mass Customization:** For each proxy user, an everlasting preference report is kept. The proxy's behaviour is updated automatically using the user's preference report when there is request from the corresponding user.

In order to make the system scalable, available or both, there is a need of duplicating the components of the proxy. But, the substitute transcoder supervisor and client tendency database, else every component of the proxy are duplicated.

Classifying Proxy-Based Approaches

The differences between the network and devices need to be overpass and eliminate, application specific revisions are to be achieved by the proxies. Hence, the functions of the proxies (Endler et al., 2005) are developed based on the following points:

- The various features like throughput, latency, reliability, probability of disconnection, etc., of the wired and wireless networks that need to be overpass.
- Specific features like display size, user input/output method, processing capacity size, RAM size, restricted supply of energy, etc., of the mobile host.
- The applications nature and precise prerequisites like quick reaction time, low system latency, dependable correspondence, versatility or detachment transparency, cache coherence, etc.

Broad range of modification and management functions which may be probably allocated to proxies could be designed based on the above features.

The problems related to the communication protocol, communication of data and programming, particular device customizations, handoff and mobility management, security and certification, failure recovery, etc., may be handled by the proxies. All proxy based approaches are compared using two orthogonal forms of categories instead of developing massive variety of proxy centred architectures. Proxy based architecture's general features are considered as first dimension and the proxy's functions are determined in the second dimension.

Architecture-Based Classification

The proxy based approaches are categorized by highlighting the common features of the software architecture. This categorization is completely independent of the specific task assigned to the proxy.

The features such as level, placement, single/multi-protocol, communication and extensibility described below are used to categorize the proxy based approaches.

Level: Revision or alteration / customization are handled by the proxies generally at three software levels (Endler et al., 2005):

- **Communication-Level:** The problems related to the communication protocols are handled by the proxies at this level. Making the movement of device and the utilization of the wireless links visible to the higher software layers is the key objective. The optimizations or modifications of the wired or wireless protocols, buffering, handoff management, etc., are the variations which takes place at this level. For instance TCP proposals of various flavours in the case of wireless networks and wireless CORBA.
- **Middleware-Level:** The tasks are performed in a generalized mode only instead of customizing them to a particular type of application or a particular communication protocol by the proxy. Examples of general tasks are modification of the content, management of cached data consistently, detecting the services or resources, security and certification, etc.
- **Application-Level:** At this level, proxies perform the application specific tasks. i.e the functions of a particular application are executed by the proxy based architectures. Some of the example tasks that are application specific are web browsing, access to

the database, peer to peer data sharing, etc. When the operation of caching is to be compared in the case of web and database applications, the web application need to deal with the heterogeneous objects with fast response time whereas the database application need to deal with the homogeneous data with cache consistency maintenance.

Placement and Distribution

In proxy based architectures, proxy can be placed in different places or positions. Four different cases (Endler et al., 2005) are defined below:

- **Server–Side:** The proxy performing only at a fixed node of the network.
- **Client–Side:** The proxy performing only at the mobile node of the network such as CODA.
- **Interceptor Model:** A pair of proxies is used in this case. one proxy is implemented at the fixed node and the other at the mobile node.
- **Migratory Proxy:** In this case, the proxy will be able to move between the fixed node and the mobile node.

In general, proxy is located at the server side or an interceptor model is used in most of the systems. There are no restrictions in the case of devices to incorporate server side proxies, but the client side proxy can be used only in the devices which have more computing resources. When there is a need to transfer the computing tasks between the mobile node and the network, migratory proxy is used assuming that a particular mobile node is moving throughout the network.

The distribution of the proxy specific adaptation and the management functionality can be centralized or decentralized (Endler et al., 2005). In the case of centralized distribution, each proxy need to perform the complete functionality whereas in the case of decentralized distribution, a set of proxies share the complete functionality and performs only a part of the whole functionality.

- **Single-/Multi-Protocol:** The number of communication protocols that proxy architecture supports is used to classify them into two groups: A proxy architecture which supports only single protocol and a proxy architecture which supports multiple protocols. Protocols like TCP or HTTP are used in the case of single protocol based proxy architectures and try to bridge the gap between the wired-wireless by modifying these protocols. In multiple protocol based proxy architectures, many protocols like UDP, SMTP, SMS, WSP, etc., are used to support the wired-wireless translation. The data will be delivered to the user irrespective of the wireless network with which the user is connected by dynamically toggling between these multiple protocols such as iMobileEE, TACC, eRACE, etc.
- **Communication:** The proxy can communicate with the server, client or other proxies either in synchronously or asynchronously. In the synchronous mode of communication, the client sends an explicit adaptation request to the proxy and then the particular task is performed by the proxy and responds back to a particular client. In an asynchronous mode of communication, the proxy plays the role of the user and notifications are sent to the client asynchronously. In this mode, the proxy performs the functions like search, collection, information aggregation as it plays the role of the user. WAP, WBI, MoCA's proxy framework are some of the examples where both the synchronous and asynchronous modes of communications are supported.

- In order to perform the functions like session management, handoff management, check pointing, multicasting, etc., the communication is carried out among proxies either directly or indirectly. In the direct mode of communication, the proxy will have the knowledge about the other proxy with which the communication need to be carried out, through its client node. In the indirect mode of communication, the proxies will not have the knowledge of other proxy with which the communication is being carried out. A server behaves as a router in order to exchange the messages between the pair of proxies.
- **Programmability/Extensibility:** The chance to adapt and personalize the functions is referred as extensibility. The proxy architectures are classified based on extensibility also. In general, the behaviour of the proxy is predefined and it depends on the current state of the environment it is executing. Some of the architectures are designed in such a fashion that the proxy can adapt the existing framework to the requirements of the particular application at the development time such as MoCA's proxy framework. Some of the other architectures are designed such that a new module or new functionality can be tailored to the existing framework.

Common Proxy Tasks

The proxy based architecture can be classified based on the major task or the function that the proxy performs. There are many tasks that a proxy can perform, but only few which are the most common tasks that can be assigned to a proxy are given below (Endler et al., 2005).

Protocol Translation and Optimization (Endler et al., 2005)

In general, most of the conventional communication protocols which are designed for wired networks are not suitable for wireless networks because they are highly error prone, expensive, and have low throughput, high latency, mutual interference, irregular connectivity, etc. Hence, the proxy's role in this case is to transform and optimize these protocols of wired network to wireless networks.

Besides the above mentioned task, proxies can optimize the multimedia transmission and presentation using various communication optimization techniques.

Content Adaptation (Endler et al., 2005)

Adaptation to content is irrespective of the protocol and the transmission and the presentation at the mobile device are optimized by transforming the payload whereas the protocol translation is protocol dependent adaptation/optimization. The requirements of the application like quality of the wireless link, features of the device as computational power, output capabilities, supported protocols, etc., determines a particular type adaptation that can be used. Examples of content adaptation comprise various techniques like data distillation or enhancement, aggregation, intelligent filtering and transcoding.

Distillation and Refinement (Endler et al., 2005)

Filtering the data to preserve the semantic data by removing the duplicate or superfluous data using the process referred as distillation. It is a highly lossy, real time compression technique which can be applicable for a particular type of data only. It is also referred as data compression which might be focused around coding guidelines. For instance, JPEG is a lossy compression scheme and is based on coding where the required quality of the image determines the rate of compression, i.e, varied compression rate. In GIF type of images, the compression rate is fixed and the level of reduction in the colour palette for display determines the compression rate. Example of distillation which is not based on coding is the scaling down of images in all direction thereby sinking its binary representation.

Fading the colours or reducing the numbers of shades in the colour palette is another type of compression technique which is based on the colour. Even though the image do not have the similar colours when compared to the original image, it is useful to the user since there will no change in the image except the colours. Similarly, the image can be zoomed in when the user requires observing some part of the original data with high precision and vice-versa.

A part of the image or data or document can be selected in the original quality using a process called refinement. When the binary size of data is to be reduced, the processes of distillation and refinement are applied orthogonally.

Summarization (Endler et al., 2005)

Using the process of summarization which is also a lossy compression technique, particular required parts of the original image can be chosen for presentation with less information loss. Video and text are the most familiar data types used by the mobile and wireless devices. As today, there is a need to display large contents like web data on small screens, text summarization techniques are evolved. The motionless or moving pictures with or without audio are defined as a video summary. The brief information of the image content is provided to the user by maintaining the important information of the original image. The compressed video or video summary might be the combination of individual segments which are not in a series in the original image without a break in the presentation but still holding the essence of the longer video file or original video file.

When the connection is low throughput and need to send a video, then video summarization is helpful because it is less in size when compared to the original video. Hence, the summarized video can be sent to the users in a shorter time and comprehensively.

Intelligent Filtering (Endler et al., 2005)

Based on the conditions of the network or the target device, filters are used to transform or drop the data or data delivery is delayed. This process is known as intelligent filtering.

Transcoding

The format and the representation of content are altered using the process described as transcoding. In order to make variety of devices access the data, the data might need to be filtered, altered, converted or reformatted. Video formats are converted using the transcoding process such as VHS – to – Quicktime – MPEG. In order to enable the mobile devices to handle the HTML and graphics files, transcoding process need to be carried out in order to transform HTML to WML. Transcoding is used when original format of the content cannot be used in presentation because of the limitations of terminal characteristics.

Caching and Consistency Management (Endler et al., 2005)

The caching of data at the mobile host is the general function performed by the proxies. The traffic reduction, limiting the latency, efficient usage of wireless bandwidth, saving the mobile devices battery power, dealing with client disconnections are some of most important and general objectives of caching. The data is cached at a node on the edge of the network using server side proxy in order to minimize the traffic and latency. Client side proxy is used to achieve the rest of the objectives by caching the data on the mobile host.

The cache consistency approaches are applicable to distributed file systems, data-sharing applications as similar to the networks.

Session Management (Endler et al., 2005)

The features that the session management is able to perform are given below:

- Representation, summarization, and adaptation of the session state.
- Session state transfer and installation at new device.
- Control the online sessions.

Session is a series of logical actions that are performed by a user. The service or session both has the same notion similar to the session state. In some applications refer it as service and some other applications refer it as session. The disconnections of the links and the movement of the user are not dealt in the session management of mobile and wireless computing environment instead it is used only to maintain the session state of the applications.

There are middleware level proxy architectures which are capable of working only with voice and web data, users will be able to share the data among them and the session states can be transferred seamlessly between various states.

Handover Management (Endler et al., 2005): One of the provisions that are offered by wireless networks to the user is mobility and the data from various places can be accessed by the users. In order to provide these facilities to the users by the wireless or mobile networks, there is a need of mobility management and handover management. When there is disconnection of a mobile device / user with the network it is being connected and connects to other network, handoff is said to be taken place. The handoff need to be done without any delay otherwise the communication will be discontinued or data will be lost. During the handoff process, the handoff management need to identify the network to which the mobile device can be connected base on the location of the mobile device and transfer the connection or the session state from the old network to the new network. Hence, there is a need to make the handoff process to be transparent to the applications by the handover management.

Discovery and Auto-Configuration (Endler et al., 2005)

The service discovery mechanisms are strongly required for dynamic mobile computing environments when compared to the traditional distributed environments. Because the nodes in mobile computing environment are mobile in nature, there is a need to manage the changes in the service availability and the most suitable service need to be chosen for each client based on its present position.

The complexity of control mechanisms can be minimized, dynamic nature of the networks and heterogeneity can be concealed by the proxy based architectures. The overhead of choosing the best service by the client can be eliminated by accessing a service via proxy instead of accessing the services by the client directly. Proxy based approaches are used to discover the services by distributed systems like Jini.

Security and Privacy (Endler et al., 2005)

A proxy-based approach can be utilized by services for secure mobile communications. The authentication or certification process in the mobile environment can be decentralized using proxies. The computed functions at the device need to be maintained as uncomplicated as possible because more computational effort is required to employ a public key security model by the application. Proxy hides the details of the requester and provides a natural and efficient secrecy for the mobile application when it is acting as a mediator between the clients and the servers. In such cases, the mobile clients are represented by the proxies and are liable to handle privacy, authorization, user authentication, or data encryption. The right to use the shared resources like file, printer, etc., is controlled by the proxies employing the public key security model in the proxy based security architecture. There are two protocols devised separately in order to guarantee the security and privacy. One protocol is devised for secure communication between a device and a proxy and another is designed for secure communication between a pair of proxies.

The use of proxy based architectures is evolved in the field of mobile computing. But still, the flexibility, scalability, and adaptation to the precise needs of the present and future mobile network and applications are the challenges of proxy based architectures in the area of mobile computing.

The increase in the number of applications of mobile network leads to the increase in the complexity and customization of the services and the proxies need to be involved in more number of specialized functions. Even though each application will have its own explicit requirements for the functions or services that are provided by the proxy, there will be some functions, structures or architectures which can be reused in many applications during the implementation of proxies for a specific application. The application and the middleware level proxy based architectures require simple, flexible and extensible tools and framework in order to develop and customize the architectures quickly.

The proxy based architectures need to be extended such that they can be configured dynamically, adaption of the functions of proxy to the clients dynamic demand, server load, or the mobile network conditions at that instant. Preferably, it is suggested that the collection of standard modules for content adaptation, protocol translation, cache management, etc. to be maintained such that they can be incorporated in the existing proxy framework based on the precise requirements and the network conditions.

CLUSTER-BASED PROXIES

The cluster architecture consists of small modules. When the complete architecture is implemented as modules or blocks, it will be cost effective and the performance can be increased. The cutting edge technology is used in the case of memory, data storage and other components of the blocks. The development, installation and maintenance of the independent nodes is easy and simple when compared to the large centralized server.

The scalable network services should be able to perform the tasks given below (Pancholi, 2002):

- Incremental scalability,
- Providing overflow growth,
- 24 x 7 availability, and
- Cost effective.

When a high speed system area network is used to integrate the clusters of product terminals, the challenges of Internet server workloads can be successfully handled assuming that the partial failures are managed using the existing software infrastructure and a large cluster need not managed or reinvented for each new service. The cluster based scalable network services where the above requirements like incremental scalability, availability etc., are abstracted for reuse are built on a general layered architecture. The model that is used to perform Transformation, Aggregation, Caching and Customization (TACC) (Pancholi, 2002) on Internet content is service programming model. Basically Available, Soft state and Eventual consistency are referred as BASE semantics

(Fox, Gribble, Chawathe, Brewer, & Gauthier, 1997) and Atomicity, Consistency, Isolation, Durability are referred as ACID semantics (Fox et al., 1997). BASE semantics are weaker than the ACID semantics and are used in the development and the operation of the architecture and TACC programming model in order to make it simple and less complex. Hence, the consistency is relying on the availability and robustness on soft state while managing failures.

The scalability, availability and cost effectiveness are three basic challenges still make the setup of network services to be complicated.

The elemental properties of the clusters of workstations are used to meet the following requirements:

- The service is enabled to be carried the leading edge of the cost/performance curve with the use of product PCs as the unit of dimension.
- The temporary failures are hidden using the intrinsic duplication.
- Relating the network service workloads to the network of workstations.

Nevertheless, the cluster software initialization and management are still complicated. A layered framework can be used to handle this complexity. The revision and aggregation services are combined into a particular service like a search engine or hastened web browsing on the top layer. In the middle layer, caching, conversion among MIME types, integrating the data from various sources, customizing the service for each user individually of a large number is made possible. Finally, the scalability, sustainability of more offered load, availability, system screening, and load balancing are provided in the lower layer. Hence, any new services use this layered framework as a skeleton in order to handle to scalability, availability, etc., and concentrated on the development of the service content.

When the data is modified by the network service, most of it is able to tolerate the BASE semantics which are weaker the ACID semantics BASE semantics are introduced with the combined trade-off between consistency and availability, and replacing robustness with the soft state.

Advantages of Clusters

The three fundamental benefits that the clusters exhibit in the field of Internet service employment are (Fox et al., 1997):

- Scalability,
- Availability, and
- Cost/performance and maintenance.

Scalability

Clusters are most appropriate for the workloads of Internet service as they are highly parallel.

When there are large clusters for these types of workloads, there is chance of power dwarf in the largest machines. The plan for the required capacity in the case of Internet service is mostly impossible because it depends on more unknown variables. Hence, the ability to increase the number of clusters over time is the benefit in the field of Internet service deployment.

Capacity planning is substituted by the incremental scalability with moderately fluid reactionary scaling. Thus, the clusters stops the previously used "forklift upgrade" method of scaling where the current or old machine including the related investments should be washed away and substitute with a larger one.

High Availability

The nodes independency causes the usual duplication in clusters. The components like bus, disks, power supply, etc., exist individually for every node. Hence, temporary failures are to be masked using the software. A subset of nodes is disabled for the short term in order to carry out a natural extension. Network services highly require these kinds of abilities.

Commodity Building Blocks

Using commodity building blocks is an advantage of clustering instead of using a big sized and single blocked machine. Since the cutting edge can be tracked by the memory, node, and disks lead to the advantage in terms of cost/ performance. The stability and robustness can be guaranteed by selecting the reliable high volume previous generation products whenever there is a change in the building block.

In addition, if a product can be obtained from one of many vendors, it is easy to obtain, install and maintain but it there is only one vendor, and then it is difficult to get maintenance when required. It is always better to build a product with heterogeneous blocks.

Challenges of Cluster Computing

Clusters have disadvantages in some areas when compared to SMP's. Some of the challenges (Fox et al., 1997) which affect the architecture are described below:

- **Administration:** When there are more nodes in a system, management which is referred as administration is a tedious task. A tool which integrates supervision and reporting tasks with the data visualization support is effective to reduce the complexity of cluster administration and make it simple.
- **Component vs. System Replication:** A complete service cannot be supported by a single product PC in a cluster but it can support more than one component of service. Hence, incremental scaling is provided by the commodity PCs with component level duplication instead of whole system duplication assuming that the modules of the software are divided into loosely coupled modules. An architecture where each component is defined a particular function and possibility of interchanging the functions among components of similar type will be able to handle this challenge. For instance a cache process carries out whatever the disk type is available and a component which performs data compression can consider any available CPU cycles.
- **Partial Failures:** The difference between the clusters and SMPs is the handling partial failures using the component level replication, i.e., failures of subsets of the system need to be adapted and be able to survive. Partial failures will never occur in the case of SMPs and traditional workstations, because the complete machine is either in working condition or down.
- **Shared State:** When the requirement of shared state in cluster is reduced or evaded, the performance can be enhanced and the complexity can be minimized.

The partial failure and the shared state will concentrate to share the required semantics by network services.

BASE Semantics

The data semantics required by each service determines how the design space needed to be partitioned for network services. ACID (Fox et al., 1997) properties provide the strong semantics in the traditional transactional database model but the cost and complexity are high. Availability is not assured using the ACID properties. It is better to make the ACID services to be unavailable instead of unwinding the constraints of ACID properties. For applications like Internet commerce transactions, maintenance of user profile information, and billing users for customizing the services, the most appropriate and preferable semantics are ACID semantics.

The availability is more required for the user of Internet services when compared to consistency or durability of data:

- **Basically Available:** Old data can be preserved until the complete data reaches to point of consistency after a short time.
- **Soft State:** Soft state is a state to which the data can be restored at the cost of additional calculations. It is used to enhance the performance.
- **Eventual Consistency:** Answers which are delivered rapidly and are based on the old data or partial soft state will be not accurate but only are approximate answers. But these answers are preferable and more valuable when compared to the precise answers which delay in delivery.

The integration of the above techniques lead to the data semantics referred as BASE (Fox et al., 1997). All the semantics which do not obey ACID semantics strictly are classified as BASE semantics. The partial failure in clusters can be handled by the users using BASE semantics with low complexity and less cost. The complication in implementing the service might be minimized using the BASE. Sometimes the consistency is traded for simplicity and some other times, it is traded for availability. The performance can be enhanced using BASE semantics.

For instance the communication or disk activity is evaded or delayed by the users till a suitable time in order to attain durability and consistency using BASE semantics. In general, every service can be classified as either ACID or BASE. In any case different parts of administrations obliged diverse information semantics at different times like Yahoo maintains database according to BASE semantics but maintains user personalized profiles according to ACID semantics. The online Internet content is altered using the transformation proxy which is accommodated between the clients and the servers. The data before transformation can be obtained back using rollback process as the transformed data is BASE data. If the data is related to the billing process, then the data need to be maintained as an ACID data.

Cluster-Based Scalable Service Architecture

Both the cluster computing issues and the network services issues are dealt in the cluster based scalable service architecture using the advantages of clusters. The Scalable Network Service (SNS) (Fox et al, 1997) are abstracted to detach the network services content with its implementation. High availability, fault tolerance, and scalability are the SNS requirements with thin boundaries in the reusable layer. The programming model can be related perfectly with cluster based scalable service architecture and various present services can be related to it directly.

Advantages of Clustered Architecture

A cluster-based architecture is mainly extensively established for proxy-based services. Development of proxy applications can be efficiently carried out by considering the advantages of the clustered architectures.

Scalability, availability, and commodity blocks are the three main advantages of the clustered architectures when compared to single large servers.

GENERALIZED PROXIES

Presently, there will be countless clients and servers connected to each other via Internet. There are many parameters like screen size, resolution, processing power, etc., in which they vary. As the new smart applications are introduced, there is continuous growth in these devices. As the number of clients increase, the task of server becomes difficult to provide the precise information required by the clients. Generally, the server and the client communicate directly with each other. The server sends the requested data by the client when a HTTP request is sent by the client to the server. It is expected or assumed that the data received by the client is similar to the data sent by the server without any change. At the same time, the server does not consider the type of client to which it is sending the data or the data will not be modified according to the requirements of the client. Suppose that a proxy is placed in between the server and the client making the communication to be indirect and via proxy. In this scenario, the server and the client will have no knowledge about the proxy. The client request is channelled and extracted it according to the projected work by the proxy in the network. For an instance the requested page is searched by caching proxy in the cache before it is forwarded. If the target server is exhausted, then the request is sent to the mirror site if the proxy is a load balancing proxy. In both cases of caching proxy or load balancing proxy, the client will receive the requested information without being forwarding the request to the target server. The alteration in the proxy based services need to be carried out depending on the variation in the network, hardware and software.

Proxy-Based Services

In client based adaptation approach, the functionality of the clients is minimized to the lowest level to adapt to the frequently changing environment. In the server based approach, the required functionality is updated in the server to make adaptable.

The proxy based services exhibit advantages over the client based approach and server based approach as are some are specified below:

Presently, the infrastructure is increasing rapidly in the Internet. The current servers and the clients must be abandoned to facilitate the heterogeneous clients and servers. Proxy based approach is successful in making the Internet be scalable and able to be advanced. In this approach, proxy is placed in between the client and the server; hence client and the server do not require any changes. One of the requirements for proxy based architecture is easy extension.

New characteristics and actions can be added to the client using the proxy based approach. The simple clients are sufficient to support the huge applications when proxy is used to transfer the complex subsystems. The services can be installed incrementally, simple way and in a cost-effective way using proxy based approach when compared to a traditional large scale network.

Scalability, adaptation, fault tolerance, and cost effectiveness are some of the important features to be considered during the design of proxy based services.

TACC Model

Proxy based services can be implemented based on TACC (Transformation, Aggregation, Caching, Customization) programming model (Fox et al., 1997).

Transforming or changing the data content from one form to the other is referred as transformation such as encryption, decryption, encoding, decoding, format conversion, filtering, etc.

Integrating the data which is collected from various sources according to the user's requirements is referred as aggregation.

Caching means storing the frequently, and recently accessed data locally. In proxy based systems, only the data after transformation is stored in cache. The cache is also used to store original content of Internet, cumulative information, and temporary results.

The key service or heart of the proxy based services is the personalization or customization. User preferences are used to parameterize the services and attain customization. User preferences are maintained as a database and the output is given depending on the user preferences.

Features of TACC

The various tasks need to be performed by the TACC architecture is assigned to different building blocks or workers which are connected using a set of API's. Every building block will be an expert in performing a particular task. As the workers of the application are connected to each other, they communicate with each other. The output of one building block might be given to another building block or a particular building block can call a function or service provided by another building block. The final model is common or universal and uncomplicated to utilize in developing the proxy based application.

In TACC architecture, the client sends the user profile information along with the input to be processed by the workers. This is an important characteristic in TACC architecture because of which reusability of workers is made possible. For example the same building block can be used to perform two different tasks like image compression to reduce the image resolution and size reduction by minimizing the colour level provided with the required set of parameters.

The building blocks of TACC architecture can be classified as passive building blocks and active building blocks. The building blocks which receive the information from other blocks of the architecture or system, perform the computations according to the predefined task and the output is delivered back is referred as passive building block. These blocks do not communicate with the outside world. The building blocks which receive the input information or request for the task from the outside world and communicate with the outside world are referred as active blocks. Once the request is received by active blocks, it either performs the task as per the request or it forwards the request to the other blocks in the architecture which it can perform the requested task.

Regarding the HTTP request from the client in a web based service, the active workers will receive this request and direct it to the internal passive workers/building blocks to complete the computations related to the request of the client. The response or output of the request is sent to the active worker by the passive worker which in turn is forwarded to the requested client. The passive workers only work at the backend and are involved in performing the actual computation whereas active workers depend on the passive workers to complete the requests.

The design complexity of the architecture can be minimized with some of the characteristics of the workers. The workers which perform the similar tasks are classified or grouped into the same class. The workers of the same class are treated as similar workers and so can be used interchangeably. A simple serial interface is used to assign the tasks to the workers. The worker which received the task from the interface forwards the task to the consuming worker with the additional information like class of the worker and the input data.

The tasks are assumed to be single and tiny as atomic and able to be restart. This atomicity and restart-able of the tasks can be attained if the workers are made as stateless. Hence, if a task is performed multiple times or a fault occurs in the worker while performing the task do not impact the consistency of the system.

TACC programming model can be used to develop different types of services at the TACC and service layers. Some services can be implemented by modifying the existing scalable network services with precise low-level performance requirements.

CONCLUSION

Various radio access technologies and base stations with varying transmission power are the different components in the heterogeneous mobile network environment. The proxies are used to conquer the three main challenges – the differences between the wired and wireless links in terms of throughput and latency, mobility of the nodes, inadequate number of resources of mobile nodes in the field of mobile computing and wireless communications. The new applications can be developed using mobile devices on heterogeneous platforms with the collaboration between networking and mobility. The proxy is used to provide efficient delivery to the clients by eliminating the effect of slow networks and integrate the content from various locations to deliver significant presentation to clients.

A unit which interrupts the communication or which is used to perform actions in place of a mobile client is referred as a proxy. A network of product workstations which is well-connected without any frequent disconnections is used by a proxy to perform its actions. Scalability, availability, functionality, and mass customization are the important features to be exhibited by the proxy.

The cluster architecture is divided into small building blocks which improves the performance of the system and is cost effective. The advantage of the architecture as small blocks arise from the fact that installing, organising and maintenance of small individual blocks are easy when compared to the large centralized server. Scalability, cost effectiveness and availability are the three basic challenges which make the deployment of the network services still stay complicated. These requirements can be attained using the basic properties of the clusters of workstations.

Incremental scalability, cost, availability, maintenance and performance advantages of product PCs become as the advantages of clusters when compared to single larger machines like SMPs in the field of Internet service deployment.

Maintenance, partial failures exhibited by clusters, dividing the software into loosely coupled parts, and less amount of state sharing among clusters are the key challenges of cluster based proxies.

REFERENCES

Brewer, E. A., Katz, R. H., Chawathe, Y., Gribble, S. D., Hodes, T., & Nguyen, G. et al. (1998). A network architecture for heterogeneous mobile computing. *IEEE Personal Communications*, *5*(5), 8–24. doi:10.1109/98.729719

Chawathe, Y., Fink, S. A., McCanne, S., & Brewer, E. A. (1998, September). A proxy architecture for reliable multicast in heterogeneous environments. In *Proceedings of the Sixth ACM International Conference on Multimedia* (pp. 151-159). ACM. doi:10.1145/290747.290767

Endler, M., Rubinsztejn, H. K. S., da Rocha, R. C. A., & do Sacramento Rodrigues, V. J. (2005). *Proxy-based adaptation for mobile computing* (Vol. 736). PUC.

Fox, A., Gribble, S. D., Chawathe, Y., Brewer, E. A., & Gauthier, P. (1997). Cluster-based scalable network services. ACM.

Pancholi, G. (2002). *Proxy-based services in distributed systems*. Academic Press.

Pandey, S., & Glesner, M. (2006, July). Statistical on-chip communication bus synthesis and voltage scaling under timing yield constraint. In *Proceedings of the 43rd Annual Design Automation Conference* (pp. 663-668). ACM. doi:10.1145/1146909.1147078

Sun, Y., Belding-Royer, E. M., Gao, X., & Kempf, J. (2007). Real-time traffic support in heterogeneous mobile networks. *Wireless Networks*, *13*(4), 431–445. doi:10.1007/s11276-006-9198-y

Sun, Y., Gao, X., Belding-Royer, E. M., & Kempf, J. (2004, October). Model-based resource prediction for multi-hop wireless networks. In *Proceedings of Mobile Ad-Hoc and Sensor Systems*, (pp. 114-123). IEEE.

Welling, G., Ott, M., & Mathur, S. (2001). A cluster-based active router architecture. *IEEE Micro*, *21*(1), 16–25. doi:10.1109/40.903058

ADDITIONAL READING

Aron, M., Sanders, D., Druschel, P., & Zwaenepoel, W. (2000). Scalable content-aware request distribution in cluster-based network servers. In Proceedings of the 2000 Annual USENIX technical Conference (No. LABOS-CONF-2005-025).

Flachs, B., Goldrian, G., Hofstee, P., & Vogt, J. S. (2009). Bringing Heterogeneous Multiprocessors Into the Mainstream. In *Proceedings of 2009 Symposium on Application Accelerators in High-Performance Computing (SAAHPC'09).*

Guo, J., & Bhuyan, L. N. (2006). Load balancing in a cluster-based web server for multimedia applications. Parallel and Distributed Systems. *IEEE Transactions on*, *17*(11), 1321–1334.

Stemm, M., & Katz, R. H. (1998). Vertical handoffs in wireless overlay networks. *Mobile Networks and Applications*, *3*(4), 335–350. doi:10.1023/A:1019197320544

KEY TERMS AND DEFINITIONS

ACID Semantics: Atomicity, Consistency, Isolation, Durability.

ASIC: Application Specific Integrated Circuit which also referred as Field Programmable Gate Array used as custom acceleration logic.

BASE Semantics: Basically Available, Soft state and Eventual consistency are also referred as data semantics.

DSP: Digital Signal Processor is a graphical processing unit used as special purpose processor.

Heterogeneous Computing Systems: General Purpose Processor, special purpose processor, co-processor or custom acceleration logic.

ISAs: Instruction Set Architectures in processors are constituted in heterogeneous computing platform.

Migratory Proxy: The proxy will be able to move between the fixed node and the mobile node.

TACC: Transformation, Aggregation, Caching, and Customization is a service programming model.

Wireless Overlay Networks: Networks whose coverage areas are overlapped.

Chapter 13
Network Services

ABSTRACT

A novel framework formed from a collection of independent agents that interact with each other is determined to provide a network service. Agents in this structure have the capability to perform independent activities such as duplication, migration, etc. A new method is developed in this chapter by means of genetic algorithms to change the behavior of agents over peers and also to improve the network service performance in a distributed and well planned way. Architecture with a remote control device, Personal Universal Controller (PUC), is described. The PUC provides two-way communication with the applications for copying specification for its functionality and constructing an interface for monitoring that electrical device. The requirements of every application hold the information about its dependency information and availability of appliance conditions. The network protocols, such as Service Discovery Protocols, are explained with their types and functionality.

INTRODUCTION

The evolutionary framework (Nakano & Suda, 2004) is a network service which creates a group of agents which are independent from each other. These agents communicate with each other and have the ability to perform the autonomous actions like reproduction, migration and death. The genetic algorithms (Nakano, & Suda,2004) are used to change the actions being performed by the agents over generations in this evolutionary framework. The network service performance in terms of response time, bandwidth utilization, resource usage, etc., can be enhanced using this mechanism in a decentralized and self-controlled approach.

BACKGROUND

Adaptive Network Services

Recently, the fields like optimization, clustering, communication networks, robotics, etc., utilize the concept of swarm intelligence immensely. Swarm intelligence is intelligence which is observed in

DOI: 10.4018/978-1-4666-7312-0.ch013

the group of simple insects like ants, birds etc. According to this, the information about the environment is only partially used instead the operation is carried out the individuals based on their capability of sensing their environment. The objective can be satisfied only by the intellectual behavior of the group of folks but the individuals will not be able to achieve the goal. The group of individuals offers the network services like adaptation and scalability.

The services of distributed system which comprise contented distribution networks, content service networks, distributed record offering system, etc., and need a bulk of network components to be duplicated, migrate, and remove in a decentralized procedure (Nakano, & Suda, 2004).

In this framework, the group of agents offers only one network service. Even though, every agent individually employs the same network service, they exhibit various behaviors. The behavior of the agent depends on the set of genes which are induced into it and the agent from which it is developed through reproduction process in genetic algorithms. There exists a central control in generational genetic algorithms which selects and evaluates the individual agents whereas in the evolutionary framework, the neighbor agents are involved in the evaluation and selection in a decentralized and autonomous mode. The behavior of the agents is advanced over generations and adapt to different network environments in evolutionary framework.

Evolutionary Framework for Developing Network Applications

The control in the network environment is distributed and the network service is controlled individually by each agent. Here, only the local agents can communicate with each other. Local agents are the agents that belong to the same network platform or the platforms which are adjacent to each other.

The three network components used in the modeling of the network are agents, users and platforms are shown in the Figure 1 as in (Nakano, & Suda, 2004). The energy is the common resource which exchanged among these components. The users get the network service from the agents and give energy to the agents. The platform where the agents reside is referred as the hosting platform. The hosting platform offer computing resources like CPU power, memory and network bandwidth to agents in order to exchange the energy. The actions like reproduction, migration and deletion are performed by the agents using this energy. The efficiency with which the service is offered by the agent using the computing resources and with which the action is performed can be measured by the level of energy. The independent systems connected to each other are referred as platforms. Agents reside on these platforms and the computing resources like CPU, memory, bandwidth, etc., are provided by the platforms. The agents perform the actions like reproduction, migration and deletion using the energy provided by the users on the hosting platform. The agents with no energy are ejected by the platforms. In this way, the energy efficient agents are supported and are selected by the platforms. The exchange of energy efficiently can be observed in Figure 1.

Agents and Their Performance

The actions performed by the agents are determined by their internal states like energy intake, age, the activeness and the agent's performance is in direct proportionate to a network service like response time. The environmental conditions like request rate, request rate change, population, resource cost, behavior cost of the hosting platform and the adjacent platforms can be sensed by the agents with their ability.

The definitions of the environmental conditions (Nakano, & Suda,2004) are given below:

Figure 1. Exchange of energy

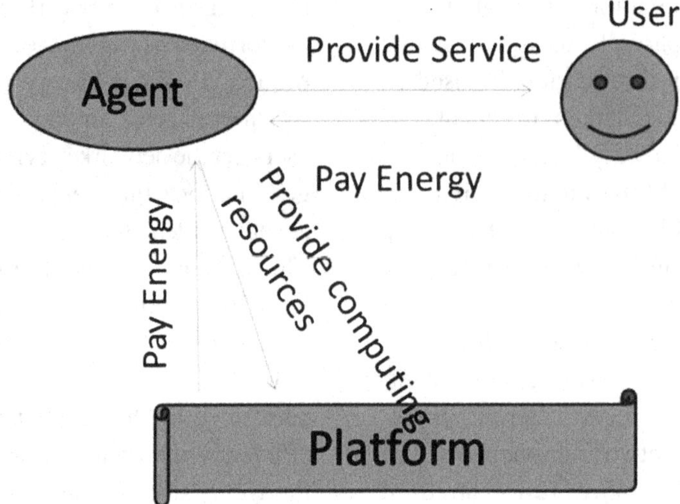

- **Request Rate:** The rate at which the user send request to the hosting platform.
- **Request Rate Change:** The amount of increment or decrement in the request rate.
- **Residents:** The number of agents on the platform.
- **Price of the Resource:** The resource cost on the platform. Ex: Energy resource.
- **Cost of Behavior:** The energy cost to execute an action on the platform.

The action to be performed by the agent depends on the environmental state or their interior condition. When the request rate is high which indicates there is a more service demand, then there is a need to perform the reproduction action. To provide the service in the surrounding areas of the users, the migration action is to be performed. When the service being provided by an agent is expired, then the agent needs to perform the death action.

The selection of the action to be performed by the agent as in (Nakano, & Suda,2004) is shown in Figure 2. A set of associated weights W_i are multiplied with the input value (V_i) which is based on the internal states and the environmental conditions. The behavior whose weighted sum (Σ ($V_i \times W_i$)) exceeds the threshold value (θ) is selected to be performed by the agent. If the condition has been satisfied by more than one behavior, then the behavior with highest weighted sum is selected. If the action to be performed is migration, the agents need to select the platform to which it needs to migrate from the hosting platform.

Methods for Evolutionary Adaptation

The behavior of the agents is managed by a block of genes and the variation in these genes lead to different behavioral agents. The genetic operations like mutation and crossover generates the diverse behavioral characteristics. The performance of the service can be improved by the reproduction action. During this process, the agent chooses a reproduction partner such that the performance of minimum one of the administrations like reaction time, transmission capacity utilization, resource usage, etc., is improved. The network service is made adapt to the network environment by repetitive generations which retains the favorable and valuable features and detains the features that are not useful. Some of the evolutionary mechanisms (Nakano, & Suda, 2004) are given below:

Figure 2. Process to invocate the behavior

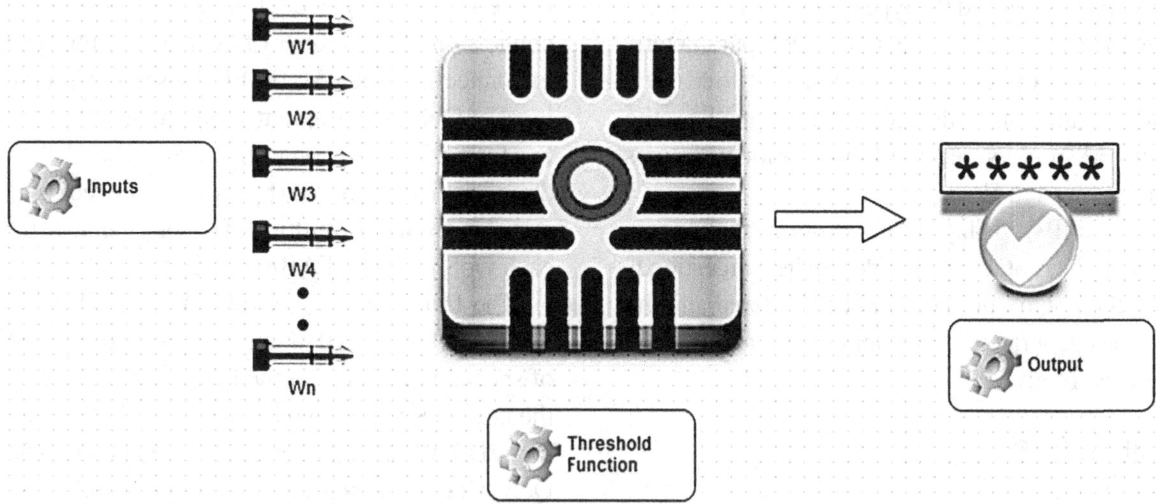

- **Representation:** A vector of real values which correspond to the weights is used to represent an agent.
- **Natural Selection:** It is a process of eliminating the agents whose energy vanishes. The elimination process will be carried out by a platform. Natural selection ensures that the efficient behavioral agents are favored and inefficient behavioral agents are eliminated.
- **Partner Selection:** Waiting time, hop count, and energy efficiency are the numerous robustness values which are used to choose an associate by an agent during the reproduction process. The fitness assignment strategy is followed by an agent to select an associate agent from the host platform or a neighboring platform.

The difference between the time at which the request for the service is arrived at the platform and the time at which the service is provided by an agent is referred as waiting time. The number of platforms that a request needs to migrate from the user to an agent is referred as hop count. The portion of energy consumed from the acquired energy is referred as energy efficiency.

The agents on the platform might be free or might be servicing the request. So, when a service request is arrived at a platform, it will be processed if any agent on the platform is free otherwise, the request is placed in the queue indicating all the agents present on the platform are active in executing other service requests. With the intention to reduce the number of service requests that are being queued, the number of agents needs to be increase which is possible by the reproduction action. In this way, this fitness value can be improved (Nakano, & Suda, 2004).

There are four types of services in Adaptive Networking architecture (FABRIC, 2013):

- Quality of Service (QoS),
- Traffic management,
- Fabric dynamic profiling, and
- Resource recovery.

Quality of Service

TCP/IP communication networks initiated the concept of Quality of Service. It is introduced in order to improve the performance of the network by identifying the frames to be dropped by the routers during the congestion. The selection of frames to be discarded by the router depends on the application and the type of traffic. The frames are prioritized according to the QoS parameters. So, during the congestion, firstly the lower priority frames are allowed to be dropped by the network routers and the higher priority frames are allowed to flow.

TCP/IP QoS play a role only during the congestion in the router's queue. When the congestion is not there, QoS priority is not considered and the frames generated by the application are allowed to flow freely.

Fabric QoS

The information in the header of frame and the proprietor configuration of zoning services are used to determine the QoS priority by a fabric access port in the Brocade Fibre Channel Environment. For instance the host designer and the storage objectives for which the association is needed are identified by the fabric zone. After identification, they are logically associated and allow the data to flow from the initiator to the target(s). A special zone with QoS priority prefix in its name is created by the Storage Area Network (SAN) (FABRIC, 2013) administrator in order to employ QoS for a data flow. When the data flow through this QoS priority prefixed zone, the initiator and the target(s) realize the data is prioritized. The QoS priority can be associated to the frame payload which is described as virtual fabric, the Logical SAN (LSAN) (FABRIC, 2013)besides specifying the QoS at the zone level.

The three QoS priorities in the fabric can be associated with the multiple virtual channels. There will be input queues for each virtual channel of their own. All the switches in the fabric follow the same QoS queuing algorithm. The frames in the input buffers are serviced based on the weights according to the QoS queuing algorithm. The QoS priority determines the weight of each frame. The queue with high QoS priority allows more number of frames to flow when compared to the queue with low QoS priority. The service in the low priority is continued even during the congestion. The number of switches or the type of connections like ISL or IFL does not affect the level of QoS to be implemented on the data flow in a fabric. The ISL congestion caused by a "slow drain" device is removed by the resource recovery services by using multiple virtual channels for each QoS priority (FABRIC, 2013).

The frames Source ID/Destination ID (SID/DID) (FABRIC, 2013) are compared to the list of special QoS zones at the fabric access port by the fabric QoS. If it finds a match it indicates that the SID/DID are in that particular QoS zone. The QoS priority is assigned to the flow depending on the QoS "name tag" in the zone name. If the high QoS priority is assigned, then the frame in queued whose virtual channels have high priority traffic by the fabric access port. The same queuing algorithm is used to schedule the frames to be forwarded from the virtual channels by each switch. Hence, it indicates that there is no priority in forwarding the frames across random sized fabric.

Application QoS (Future)

The interface to the fabric can be used to request the required QoS priority by the host. The fabric QoS service interface receives a QoS priority request for the data flow using the Brocade's Intelligent Server Adapter (FABRIC, 2013).

If the request can be satisfied by the fabric with sufficient resources, the virtual channel which is to be used for forwarding the frame is determined and the details about this virtual channel and the acceptance are returned. The QoS request cannot be made when each frame is sent but instead it can be done only per data flow. Now, the host adapter has the knowledge of the adapter queue with particular QoS priority into which this frame need to be put.

The QoS priority is not assigned by the fabric access port but this port is configured such that the frame is accepted from the virtual channel and forward to the suitable output port using the same virtual channel through which it is received.

The host accepts the lower priority QoS when the fabric does not have sufficient physical resources to satisfy the host requested QoS service level. The priority requested by the host interface will be memorized in the case of adaptive network management applications and the assigned priority is upgraded whenever it is possible, i.e., the availability of the physical resources. When the priority is upgraded then the data flow is moved from the virtual channels with existing priority level to the virtual channels with the priority to which it is upgraded.

Traffic Management Services

The network bandwidth allocation and control, reduction in latency along the data path, congestion minimization at the ports of network, segregation of traffic, limiting access rate, etc., are the services (FABRIC, 2013) provided by the traffic management.

Understanding Ingress Rate Limiting

Let us assume a freeway with an entrance ramp for the vehicles to enter and there exists traffic light on the ramp. The vehicles can enter the ramp only when signaled to go. So, the access to the freeway is controlled which reduces the congestion. The congestion can be prevented or avoided by controlling the rate at which the frames enter into a fabric using the services provided by the traffic management services. The priorities are assigned to the application such that the workloads of the applications which are having less priority are controlled during the congestion. The service to the lower level priority workloads will be continued when the physical resources are about to exhaust in the shared network data paths. But this process will be carried out at a lower rate in order to avoid congestion. When the congestion reduces at physical data paths, the network allows the workloads of the lower priority applications as similar as the green light is left on continuously throughout the night at freeway entrance ramp assuming that the traffic during nights to be less. Hence the cars can enter the freeway without waiting. The ingress rate limiting is similar to the traffic light before the freeway entrance ramp. The number of frames to be received by the port can be controlled by setting the ingress rate limiting on.

Traffic Isolation

Traffic isolation is another service provided by the traffic management. The Fabric Shortest Path First (FSPF) (FABRIC, 2013) routing need not be modified in order to allocate the user defined data flows to specific ISLs. The continuous and high bandwidth traffic created by the workload of the application requires the dedicated network resources which are ensured by the traffic isolation like array to array duplication application providing synchronous or asynchronous block duplication which uses the physical or virtual tape devices utilize this service. The physical connections used for traffic isolation are not used by any other application workloads. So, the high bandwidth workloads do not impact the performance.

Congestion Management (Future)

The third service provided by the traffic management is congestion management which provides fine-grained management by applying the service at the virtual channel level. The congestion control and congestion avoidance are the two forms of congestion management. The profound system intelligence about the utilization of resource at each port along the data path is used in order to offer these progressed administrations (FABRIC, 2013).

Congestion Control

The load from the network is discarded during the congestion in order to get rid of the congestion. Hence the congestion control is reactive. Ingress rate limiting is performed manually in the adaptive networking (FABRIC, 2013).

The process of ingress rate limiting by virtual channels with QoS to reduce congestion as in (FABRIC, 2013) is shown in Figure 3.

Congestion Avoidance

The utilization of the physical resources is observed and is compared with the threshold value or high water mark in order to prevent the congestion. Hence, congestion avoidance is proactive.

Exceptional congestion avoidance mechanisms are turned on along the data path when consumption of the resources goes beyond the high water mark (FABRIC, 2013). The profound knowledge about the network is required to observe the usage of the resources like queues, bandwidth, etc., at all ports in the fabric and avoid the congestion. The special queuing and rate limiting algorithms are used to lessen the usage of resources or to make the resources to be shared in the anticipation of reducing the resource utilization below the high water mark in the case of congestion avoidance. The modification in the resource allocation and application specific ingress rate limiting are allowed by favoring the workloads of high priority application at the cost of lesser precedence ones in order to prevent congestion.

Fabric Dynamic Profiling

The summary of the usage of baseline resources across the entire fabric is provided by the service of adaptive networking. The points at which congestion might take place are determined and the physical resource utilization is observed and

Figure 3. Virtual channels with QoS using ingress rate port to reduce congestion control

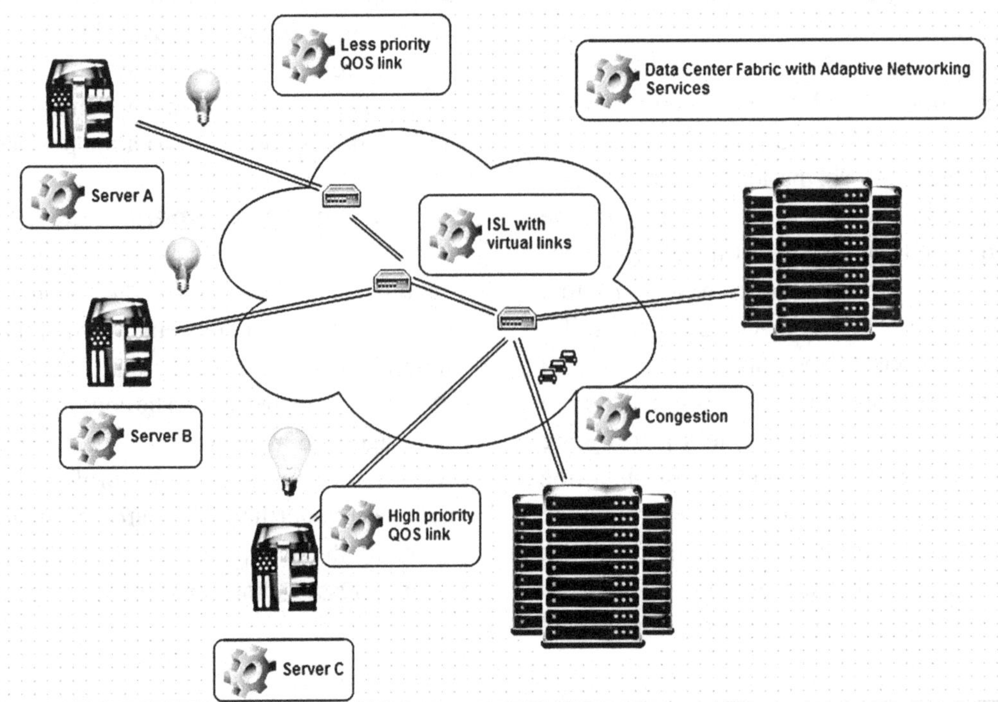

reports the statistics. To make fabric management simpler, these reports are used to support the capacity planning and end-to-end fault isolation tools (FABRIC, 2013). The "Top Talker" profile is a sample of fabric dynamic profile.

Resource Recovery Services (Future)

The availability of the resources at the destination port is represented by a flow control mechanism, Buffer-to-Buffer (BB) (FABRIC, 2013) credit. The traffic flow over the data paths which are shared is prohibited by subjecting the fabrics to conditions in which BB credit resources are fatigued. Damaged or missing frames and "slow-drain" devices are the two conditions which lead to congestion. BB credit recovery is used to overcome the problem due to the damaged or missing frames and the dynamic virtual channel mapping of data flows is used to overcome the problem caused by "slow-drain" devices.

Dynamic Virtual Channel Mapping of Data Flows

As soon as a slow-drain device on an imparted data path avoids other information streams from utilizing that path it is appropriate for using another resource recovery service. This situation may take place on ISL associations when a storage target is not able to process accepted frames rapidly, because of shortage of inner resources like internal queue flow, storage array cache misses. This results in deficiency of BB credit for sending E_Port of the ISL (FABRIC Data Center Fabric, 2013). All the data flows without available BB credit using that ISL are halted. BB credit fatigue propagates regressive to the ingress ports for all information flows that utilized the congested ISLs, when data path navigates through multiple switches over multiple ISLs (FABRIC, 2013).

If the slow-drain condition is detected before the BB credit is exhausted, then the data flow is allowed to be moved to a different virtual channel with its own BB credit pool as long as the condition holds. The original virtual channel can be used to continue the remaining data flows which share that ISL without seizing them. The physical resource in an end device can be prevented from exhaustion by dynamic virtual channel mapping. When the resource is not exhausted then there is no chance of disturbing the workloads of the application which do not depend on that resource.

VC1,VC2 -> Virtual Channels

The medium level QoS priority is assigned to both the server A and server B as shown in the Figure 4 (FABRIC, 2013). It is shown that the BB credits on the ISL ports of one of the arrays is about to exhaust as it is behaving as a slow drain. The slow-drain flow is allowed to move from virtual channel 1(VC1) to virtual channel 2 (VC2) between server B and its array port by activating the dynamic virtual channel flow mapping. BB credits are allocated individually to each virtual channel. The BB credits of virtual channel 1 will be recovered immediately but the slow-drain flow is isolated by the virtual channel 2 in order to prevent the congestion because of the ISL traffic.

Adaptive Networking Services Management (FABRIC, 2013)

The simplification of fabric management is the main aim of adaptive networking services. The detailed information about the usage of fabric wide resource need to be made available by the fabric intelligence in order to create the highly dynamic application workloads as the data center is used to implement the virtual servers and virtual storage. Across all virtual devices, there is a need that the resource utilization needs to be associated with the workloads of the application. Therefore, the simple configuration and the adaptive networking service management are provided with the extension of the device management and fabric management software (Brocade Fabric Manger and Brocade

Figure 4. Slow drain devices for which dynamic virtual channel flow mapping is applied

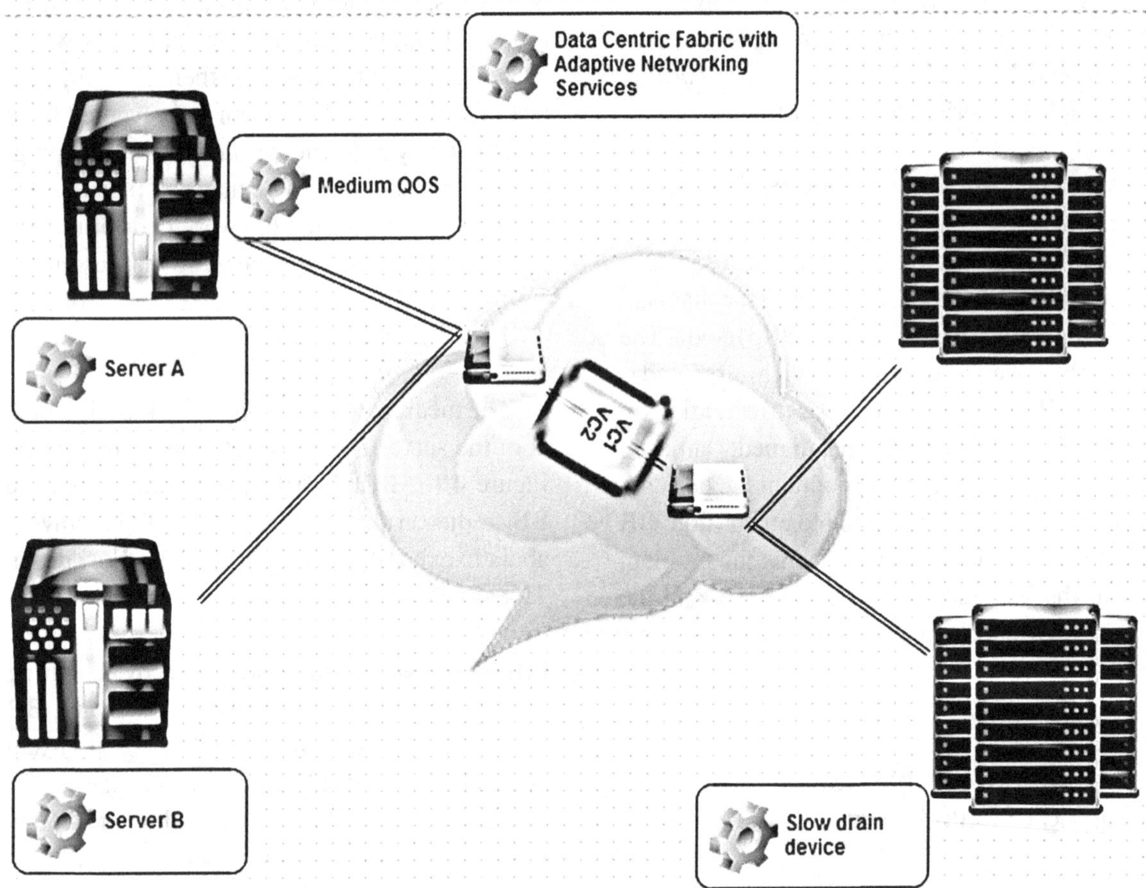

EFCM) (FABRIC, 2013). The workload provisioning, capacity planning, and end-to-end fault isolation management tools are integrated by the management layer as application QoS is accessible in adaptive networking. The IBM Tivoli, HP Open View, EMC ECC, Microsoft Management Console, etc., are the fault isolation management tools available in higher level management applications.

SERVICE DISCOVERY

The services offered by the components on a computer system are automatically detected using the network protocols called Service Discovery Protocols (SDP) (Kreger, 2001). The services of one agent can be made to use by another agent without the requirement of interference of the user continuously. This is made possible only when there is common language used on service discovery.

The hardware networking devices and services of the computers on a network are detected automatically and instantly using a service discovery networking protocol. The manual configuration of the network hardware is a difficult task for most of the novice users and this difficulty can be made easy with the help of working service discovery. All the modern operating systems are incorporated with the service discovery techniques which are used to connect computers to form a network and make the job of the user to be simple which might not need more technical knowledge.

The service discovery protocols will be active as soon as the computer is switched on. The services and hardware offered by the network can be made used by all the computers which are connected in the form a network. The verification process whether the process is being carried out or not is made simpler from the view point of the user as it just to verify the network connection lights on the computer and popup messages of network connection by the operating system. This method seems to be simple in the view point of the end user but the actual work being performed by the operating system is tedious in order to perform different tasks like scanning the network for available connection methods, other computers on the network, available files and services located through the network and provide the required information instantly to the user.

The internet is used in the form of web pages by the end users because of the services of the service discovery techniques. It is impossible for a user to connect all the web pages visited by them manually. This process can be made automatic and make the job of the user to be simpler and efficient when browsing the internet only using the service discovery protocols.

Dynamic host configuration protocol (DHCP) is used to connect the computers to internet through service discovery protocols. The advanced model used on Internet is DHCP. The IP address of the computer is obtained by DHCP before connecting and establishes the network connection without the interference of the user. The required information like IP address is obtained when a message is sent to the network server as soon as the computer is on.

The below mentioned are service discovery protocols:

- Bluetooth Service Discovery Protocol (SDP).
- DNS Service Discovery (DNS-SD), part of Apple's Bonjour technology.
- Dynamic Host Configuration Protocol (DHCP).
- Internet Storage Name Service (ISNS).
- Jini for Java objects.
- Service Location Protocol (SLP).
- Session Announcement Protocol (SAP) used to discover RTP sessions.
- Simple Service Discovery Protocol (SSDP) as used in Universal Plug and Play (UPnP).
- Universal Description Discovery and Integration (UDDI) for web services.
- Web Proxy Auto discovery Protocol (WPAD).
- WS-Discovery (Web Services Dynamic Discovery).
- XMPP Service Discovery (XEP-0030).
- XRDS (eXtensible Resource Descriptor Sequence) used by XRI, OpenID, OAuth, etc.

As the caching service might need to search by the web service, there might be services which need to search for another service in the case of SOA/distributed systems. The DNS helps in solving this problem of searching a service by the other, but it will have less impact in the case of services that are more dynamic.

The following are performed by the mechanism which is provided by service discovery system as shown in the Figure 5 as in (Gottschalk,Graham, Kreger, & Snell,2002):

- Services to register their availability,
- Locating a single instance of a particular service, and
- Notifying when the instances of a service change.

Figure 5. Service discovery protocol

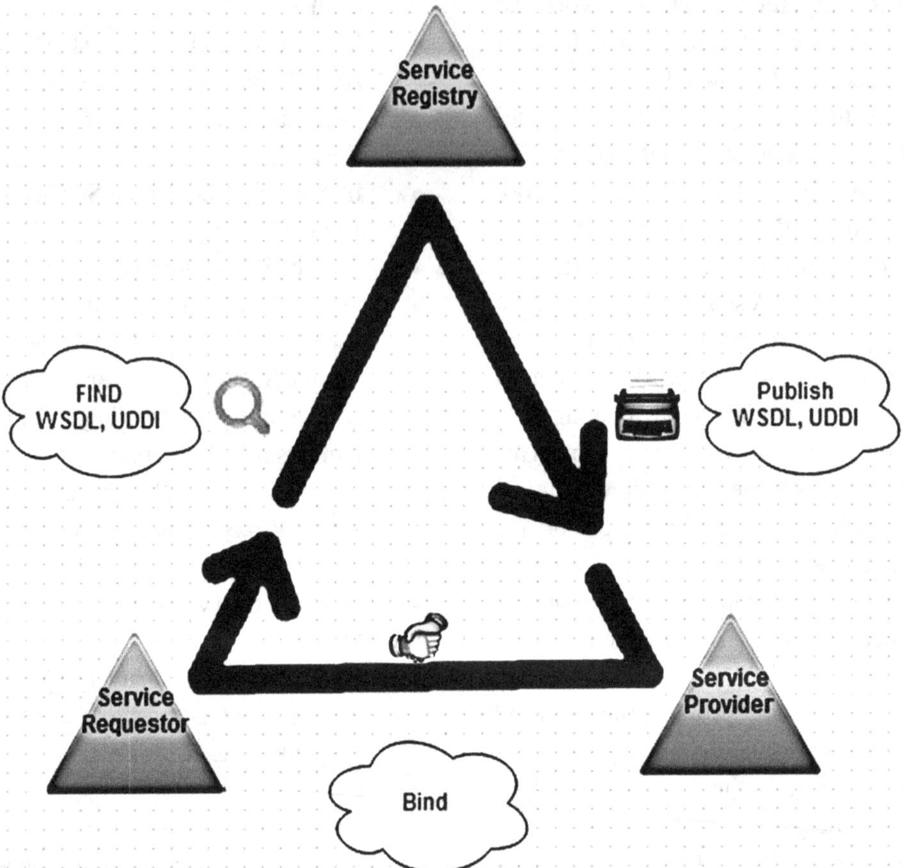

The user configured network like domestic security, lighting control system, etc., uses the service discovery whenever there is an entry of a new node in the network. The integrated process need to be initialized by the user when a new node/device join the network in order to integrate this newly entered node/device into the network. Firstly, it searches for the devices with which it can communicate such as devices with TCP load controllers will be searched by the switch in compliance with TCP profile so that it can send the information related its state. The process which associates both the devices like switch and the device with TCP load controllers is referred as the binding process.

Service Discovery Protocols for Infra-Structure Less Networks

The most awaiting technology is which makes the communication irrespective of the time, place, and device. The wireless networks which do not have infra structure and is self-organized make this type of communication to be possible as the nodes in the wireless networks can directly communicate with each other and can transfer the data among them. The concentration of the researches till the past decade is on the low level technology. But presently, it is emerging that how to make the exchange of data and the services of one mobile user by the other. So, there is a need to develop and discover the higher level services.

A wireless network where nodes are mobile in nature and infrastructure less is referred as mobile ad hoc network (MANET). The areas where the wired networks cannot be established, search and rescue operations after the disasters need to be carried out, MANET is highly applicable. MANET like self-organizing networks utilizes the service discovery which facilitates the devices to identify the services of the network automatically by the service discovery functions and broadcast their own functions to the network. The natural disaster situations are needs to be dealt with the service discovery system and this type of situations needs to be handled properly without any faults is the important requirement of the service discovery system. In MANETs, the requests are distributed by the clients using diffusion mechanisms; another common approach to service discovery is another limitation. As the service provider's location is not known on before, this technique is commonly used. When the diffusion mechanism is used by the protocol, the specified service is made available by the different providers. The discovery success rate is improved, guaranteed and the number of acknowledgements is reduced with the combination of fault tolerant service discovery mechanism and service selection mechanism in some protocols.

Fault-Tolerant Service Discovery Mechanism Viz. Location Aware Discovery Service (LADS)

The delivery of service discovery packets in the aggressive environment like MANET is guaranteed by making LADS function over MANET which utilizes redundancy.

In Location Aware Service Selection (LASS), intermediate nodes uses data fusion scheme to merge the responds sent by different providers which reduces the number of transmissions and in turn improve the performance of the network. LASS is an automatic, distributed and location aware data fusion service selection mechanism (Kniess et, al 2011).

The characteristics identified for a successful result are:

- The requested geographic location where the service need to be provided.
- The maximum response time, or the maximum time within which the service provider reach to the specified geographic location.
- The Service provider's speed.
- The number of providers that must be requested.

The above specified features are considered by the LASS data fusion scheme to reply summative in the network.

Two types of failures that are considered by LADS mechanism are components and messages. The failures related to the physical devices such as electromagnetic interference are referred as component failures. The failures because of congestion, signal fading, and unintentional disconnections are referred as message failures.

Application Scenario

MANET is used in assisting the target scenarios like emergency search/rescue missions. The area affected with natural disaster like an earthquake where there is power cut, no service of telephone and the struggle facing by the relief workers through wrecked streets. In such scenarios, the specialized rescue team with wireless devices connected like an ad hoc network, sensor network will be highly helpful in rescuing the survivors.

The resources provided by some of the mobile elements of the rescue team in the above discussed scenario might be an ambulance, a robot which is helpful in reaching the places like contamination risk, highly fired, etc., where the man is not able to go or any other person helping in medication. Some of the nodes in the scenario behave as providers and some behave as requestors. Provider nodes provide the service and the requestor nodes requests for the service.

All the devices in the network are synchronized in time and are equipped with GPS. Hence, it is known that the nodes have the knowledge about their geographic position. A node analyzes and identifies the type of service needed and then the request message is sent to the network for a particular type of service/resource.

The characteristics of ad hoc networks are limited power for processing and communication, distributed management, infrastructure less and dynamic network topology. Because of these characteristics, the nodes/devices in these types of networks must have the ability to identify the services dynamically and share them effectively.

The Secure Pervasive Discovery protocol is a service discovery protocol with security features and is a fully distributed in nature (Elwahsh, Hashem, & Amin, 2011). The services offered by a device can be identified by the other devices even without a centralized control. It provides the trusted services location, protects the private information, safe communications, or access control as it depends on the chaos trust model.

The network based service discovery technology in wireless and mobile networks is emerged because of the high increase of mobile devices and the popularity of wireless technology (Helal, Desai,Verma,& Lee, 2003). The complexities of the ad hoc environment are not supported by the existing service discovery protocols and delivery mechanisms. The concentration is made on devices instead of software services which lead them not to be suited for m-commerce oriented scenarios. The protocol which is designed especially for networks like ad hoc, peer-to-peer and targeted towards m-commerce oriented software services is a Konark protocol (Helal et al., 2003) The two important features of Konark are service discovery and advertisement and service description and delivery. The services are stored in a tree structure in Konark. The registration and advertisement of services on mobile devices and the services on other devices in the environment are discovered based on the tree where the services are stored. The service description is XML based approach. The services are described in a language which is easily understood by human and the software using a description template which is included in the Konark. Service delivery which is based on SOAP is handled by a micro HTTP server installed on each device. Presently research is being carried out in order to introduce a Personal Java based virtual machine based protocol of Konark.

The computing network devices like tiny sensors, highly dynamic and powerful devices are integrated with the people and their ambient environment by the techniques of pervasive computing.

The features like discovery, configuration and communication are exhibited by the devices and services among them. Presently, these features are implemented manually. Sometimes some special skills are required in the case of configuration, which actually are not required to realize the required tasks.

The design of service discovery protocols is carried out in such a fashion that the administrative overhead can be reduced and the usability can be increased. The probable communications and the states among devices and programs at design time need not be predicted and be coded by the beginner system designers because the service discovery protocols make their task easier by adding a layer of indirection.

Pervasive Environment Challenges

The environment of pervasive computing is more vibrant and diverse when compared to the enterprise environment. The network which is confined by firewalls and controlled by system administrators is only suitable for the enterprise network services to be functioned. In pervasive computing environments, the ambient services cannot be easily defined by the network scope and the system administrator task to manage the services is also so simple. In office environment, the discovery of pervasive service may aim at the service of any domain like enterprise computing.

Since 1970's, one of the milestone in a line of work is a pervasive computing. Distributed systems and mobile computing are the two major steps in the evolution before pervasive computing (T. Murgan et., al, 2004). The technical problems identified and realized before are also involved in the pervasive computing. Some of the techniques or algorithms which exist already will be applicable to pervasive computing also but some new techniques need to be introduced for some of the demands of pervasive computing.

Distributed Systems

When the concept of personal computers and local area networks are combined, it leads to the field of distributed systems. The conceptual framework and the algorithms introduced during the period of 1970's – 1990's, are the foundation of different type of computer networks like wired or wireless with mobile or static devices.

Mobile Computing

Since 1990s, the research towards the distributed system with the mobile clients has emerged because of the physical appearance and the properties of the laptops and wireless LANs. The mobile computing which evolved holds many fundamental principles of distributed systems but however, there is a requirement of introducing some specialized techniques because of the four major constraints of mobile computing called unpredictable and dynamic network topology, lowered trust and the robustness of mobile elements, and the weight, size and energy/battery limitations of mobile devices. The concept of pervasive computing is an extension of mobile computing and four such additional problems as in (Satyanarayanan, 2001) are shown in Figure 6.

The concepts of mobile computing and distributed systems which are incorporated in the pervasive computing are shown in Figure 6. It can be observed from the figure that there is multiplicative increase in the complexity of the previous problems. The robustness and maturity properties lead to the increase in complexity to design and develop pervasive computing system when compared to a simple distributed system. The relationships illustrated in the Figure 6 are logical but not temporal.

In future, there is lot of scope of research in the field of pervasive computing. The more discussion and analysis of the previous designs help in solving the problems related to pervasive computing. More research needs to be carried out in various areas like human computer interaction, software agents, expert systems, and artificial intelligence. The ability of the above mentioned areas and different kinds of computer systems will lead to novel developments.

REMOTE-CONTROL INTERFACE

The interfaces to complex applications can be enhanced using a remote control device called the Personal Universal Controller (PUC) (Nichols et al., 2002). The everyday appliance is employed in two-way communication using PUC. Firstly, the

Figure 6. Taxonomy of computer systems research problems in pervasive computing

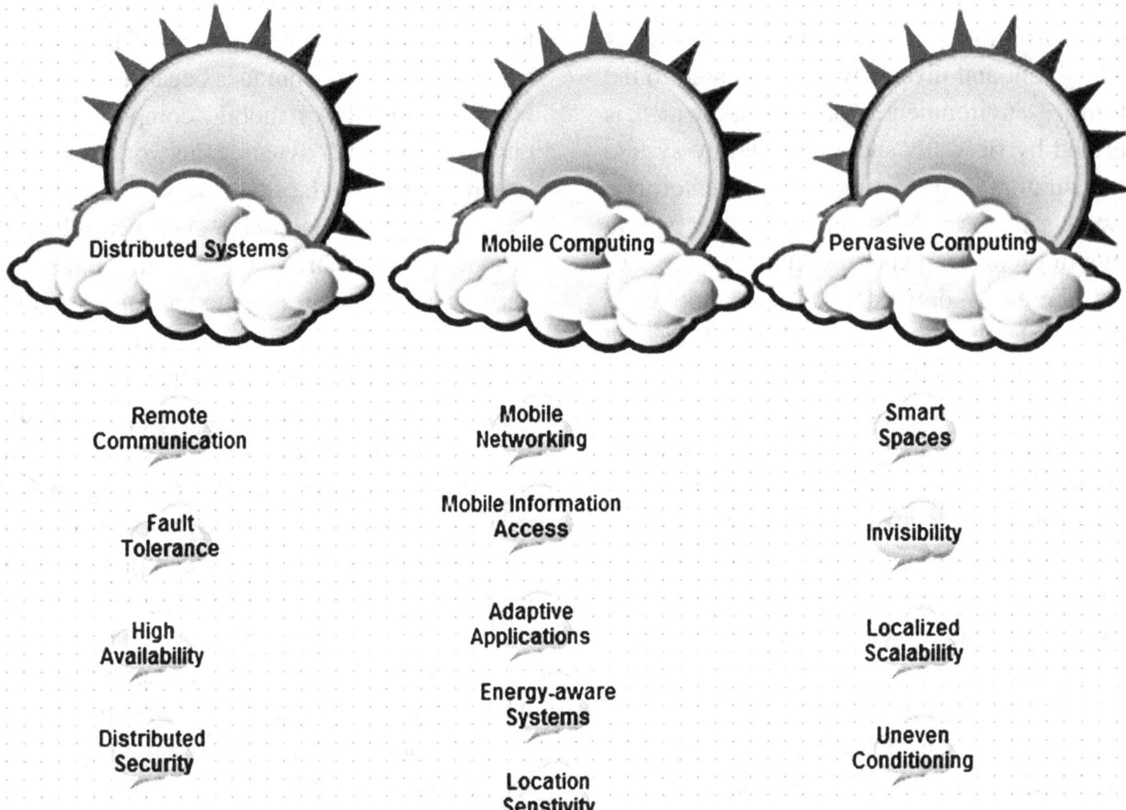

specification of the functions of the appliance is downloaded and then an interface is developed automatically to control the appliance. The high level description of all the functions, the information related to their connections in a hierarchical manner, and the applicable function to a particular state of the appliance will be included in the specification of the corresponding appliance. The quality of the interfaces developed automatically will be satisfactory because the designers create specifications based on the dependency information.

Presently, most of our home appliances like televisions, stereo equipments, AC's, light switches, etc., are composed with numerous complex procedures and can be operated with the remote. When there is an increase in the features in the appliances, the complexity in the design increases and the user interface will be more difficult to operate.

Now-a-days, it has become more common to use mobile phones, pagers, Personal Digital Assistants (PDAs), laptop by the people while moving from one place to the other. These kinds of devices which are in the short range can be connected to each other enabling the communication to be possible among them using the short distance radio technology like 802.11b, RF-Lite, and Bluetooth.

Research is being carried out in order to enhance the interfaces to home and office appliances with the help of Personal Universal Controller (PUC) and handheld devices. PUC is a self-programming approach which varies from the regular remote control approach such as BPL Pronto. As the user communicates with the interface, similarly the PUC communicates with the appliances to exchange messages. The appliance is able to revise the interface and the feedback is provided to the user because of the two-way communication.

PUC has the capability to supply an interface to perform all the operations of each device whereas the Pronto do not have the similar capability. PUC can be used to choose one among the multiple functions or modalities like choosing one among a record of songs on MP3 player and communication interface using a graphical interface. The details related to the information which can be used to develop the high quality user interface will be included in the explanation of the device's functions but the details regarding the appearance of the interface will not be included. So, the interface developer has the freedom of choosing the interface outlook. The dependency information which is represented in the form of a tree is useful to disable the components which are not in use by the interface and create better layouts by the interface developers. The main objective of the dependency information is to improve the layout. The information required to know how to structure an interface can be obtained by interface generators using dependency information. For example the different panels are used to lay sets of functions which are never accessed at the same time.

The structure of the resultant interfaces need not be similar to the group tree which is developed by the designers using the dependency information. So, it is easy to construct the group tree using the dependency information. The approximate structure of the appliance is estimated by the designer from the group tree and the dependencies are helpful is obtaining the remaining information by the interface generator. The information stored in the group tree related to the structure of the appliances by the designer, is more than that is required for the interfaces to be developed. Ex: constructing tree with smaller group which increases the depth of the tree.

The generators develop the interfaces which can be used to control the actual appliances by the PUC system. The proprietary communication protocols are translated to the PUC protocol on most of the appliances using software referred as appliance adaptors.

Universal interactor is similar to PUC which is used to control many devices. Universal Information Appliance (UIA) which can be illustrated on PDA uses MoDAL (Nichols et al.,2002) which is based on the XML to access the information by creating the user interface panel. The MoDAL processor is used to deal only simple layouts and the text strings only is the input type. The highly device independent method which is used for the design of user interface is provided by UIML which is based on XML language. The difference between the UIML and the PUC is the strong coupling with the interface. The type of component to be utilized in an interface and the code to implement as soon as events happen are defined by the interface generator but not described in the specifications in the case of PUC.

Architecture

There are four sections in the PUC architecture as shown in Figure 8 as in (Nichols et al., 2002)

1. Appliance adapters,
2. A specification language,
3. A communication protocol, and
4. Interface generators.

The design benefits (Nichols et al., 2002) include:

- Involuntary production of interfaces.
- Scalability is permitted with the model which connects peer to peer.

Figure 7. An architectural diagram of the PUC system showing one connection (multiple connections are allowed at both ends)

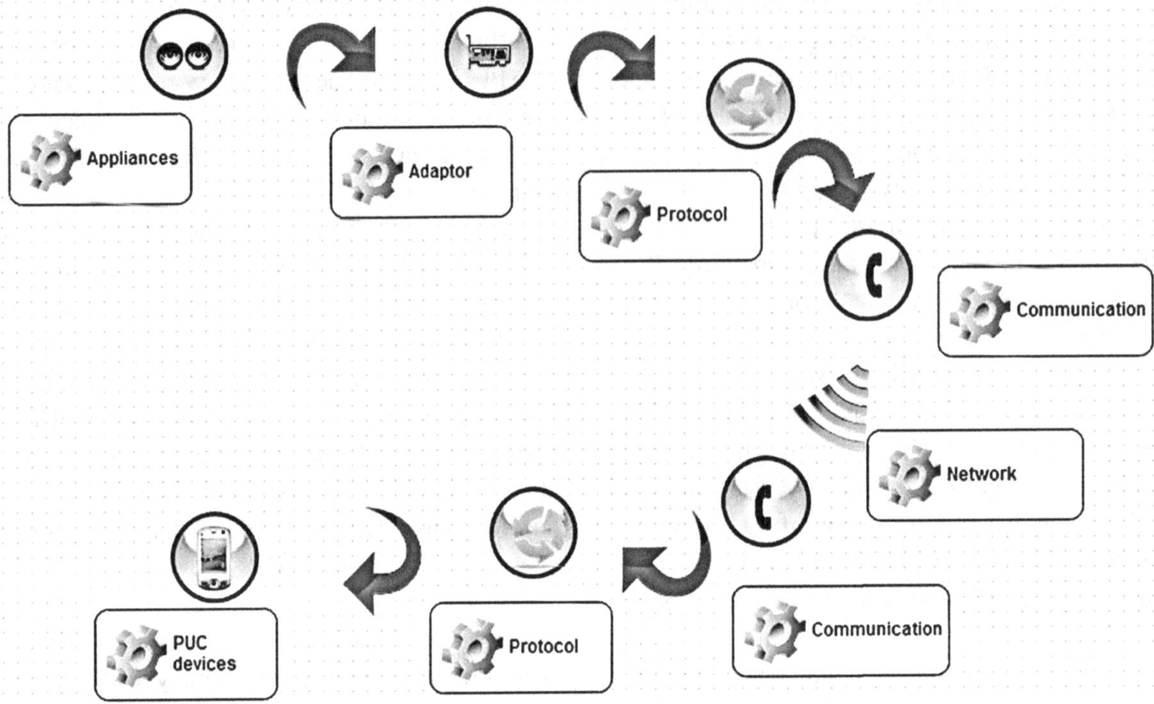

- The easy communication is made possible as the PUCs are independent of the appliances at the transport layer.
- The isolation of exclusive machine control conventions from the PUC structure is possible.

Appliance adapters are used to translate the proprietary appliance protocols to the PUC protocols. A wide range of devices generate the automatic interfaces using the PUC architecture in a wide range of modalities. Automatic interface generation is possible using the two-way communication protocol and a specification language. The functions of the appliances are described to an interface generator using a two-way communication protocol and a specification language. Examples of interfaces are graphical interface on a handheld device, speech interface on a mobile phone, etc (Nichols et al., 2002). These interfaces which are used to control the appliances are separated from its appliances by the specification language. PUCs and the appliances communicate with each other using a network which is the major component of the architecture shown in the Figure 7. The architecture of PUC is highly scalable when compared to the I Crafter and UIA because the appliances have the ability to connect it to PUC. The requests are broadcasted occasionally by PUC to determine the appliances as similar to the discovery segment of the Bluetooth.

Few assumptions in the fundamental transport mechanism make the communication to be simpler. As IEEE 802.11b, wireless Ethernet protocol is designed to function with an ample range of transport layers and less number of messages, it is not possible for every controller device to communicate.

Communication Protocol

The appliances and PUCs exchange the information between them in a bidirectional mode and asynchronously using the communication protocol. Six messages are defined by the protocol. Two out of six are sent by the appliances and four out of six are sent by the PUC. The four different type of messages from the PUC are specification request, every state value, state change information and the invocation of a command. The two different messages that can be sent by the appliances are specification of a particular state and the current value of a particular state. The state's current value message is sent by the appliance for the request message regarding the state value sent by PUC. The protocol is network independent, realized on TCP/IP and based on XML.

SECURITY ISSUES

The security plays a vital role in the field of computers or Internet. The five most important security issues considered are:

1. Reliability.
2. The risks are necessary to be indulgent.
3. Relationship between corporation and security issues.
4. The place of the data initializes the role of legal factors.
5. Best practices for the corporations.
    a. The corporations need to maintain the customer information secure.

A Survey of Survivability in Mobile Ad-Hoc Networks

Research towards ad hoc network security is enhanced. But it is not still possible to eliminate all attacks or interferences on the predictable lines of protection.

There is an increase in the applicability and use of mobile ad hoc networks and ubiquitous computing as there is emerging trend using wireless portable devices like laptops, PDAs, wireless telephones, wireless sensors or any other wireless devices (Lima, dos Santos,& Pujolle, 2009). Presently, use of mobile networking is widely increased in the specialized and household activities because of the Internet services and the transferability. In MANET, the nodes communicate among themselves without the support of any infrastructure or any central control. The nodes in MANET have the ability to transfer the data in multiple hops.

The mobility and the wireless communication properties of the nodes in MANET pose restrictions on network management, control and security.

Extensive research has been carried out and still continuing in the area of security and privacy. Many techniques have been developed and introduced in order to protect the required information, avoid network attacks as intrusion using firewalls, etc. Recently, single and closed jurisdictional control is implemented for the computing environments of before generation. The complexity of implementing security and privacy in the environments like ad hoc, dynamic and where more number of systems involve in the communication and information sharing is increasing day by day. The characterizing and analysis of security and privacy are not well operational with the traditional models and techniques in the case of the Internet based applications because of the higher social complexity.

The desired security can be achieved by making a detailed design of the system which makes the users, administrators easily understand by illustrating the different kinds of threats and vulnerabilities that may occur and the measures that need to be taken in order to handle these threats and vulnerabilities. The usual requirement process itself includes the process of analysis such that the process of providing security and privacy are considered from the initial stage only. The analysis process of security requirements can be carried out in top down approach or bottom up approach. The tradeoff between the security and the rest of the requirements in the system design like cost, performance, etc., can be obtained by the evaluation techniques which are based on qualitative goal. The desired properties can be verified as the details are provided by the requirements models if the techniques of model checking are applicable at any stage of the requirement process.

The necessity to secure the information from the inadvertent failure and fraud, intentional unapproved efforts to get to or modify the information, against excessive interruptions in obtaining or utilizing the information, or against intrusion to the point of denial of service leads to the analysis for the requirements of security. The cost of implementing this security is becoming overhead to small companies and globally, it is going beyond billions of dollars yearly.

The dynamic nature of the requirements leads to the development of new protocols, algorithms and technologies. On the other hand, new technologies are rising in unauthorized utilization or accidental or deliberate misuse which affect the stable products and environments. Hence, in order to overcome all these circumstances, the existing solutions need to be used and at the same time new solutions need to be developed to handle the security in a right mode.

The connection to a server or schema, access to database, modification of database, applica-

Figure 8. Realms needing protection in an Internet world

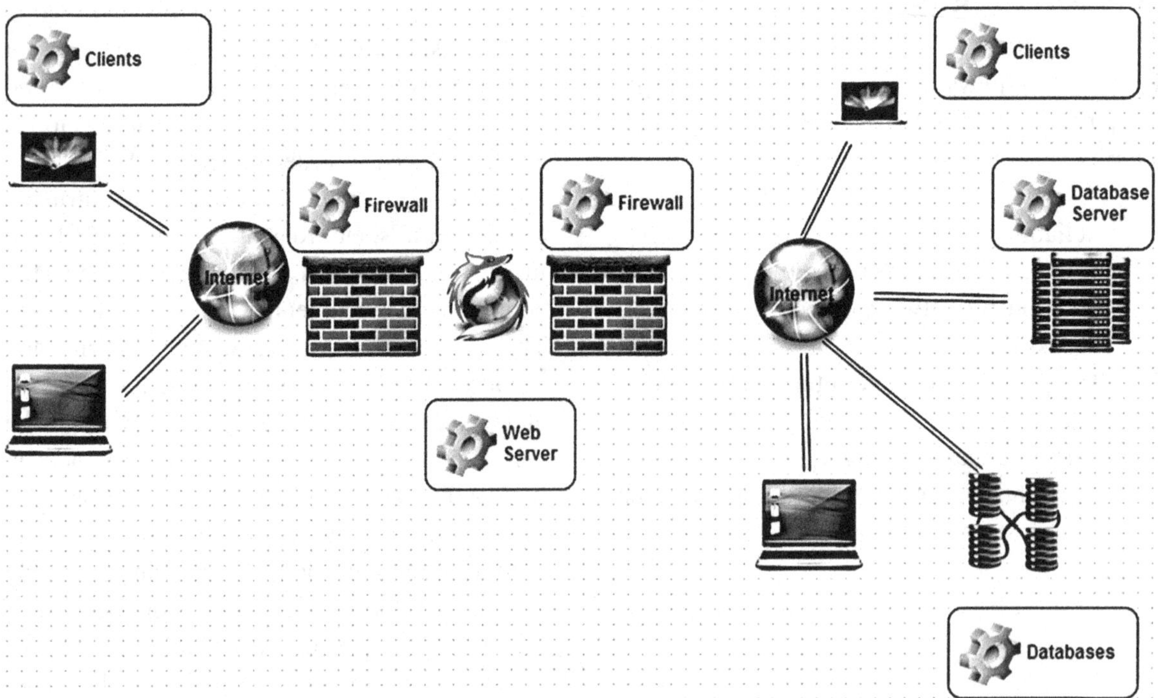

tion usage, etc., is some of the functions of the database environments. The security officers, administrators and the application programmers are in charge to handle and secure this data against unintentional or intentional misuse. As there is a possibility of accessing the databases via Internet from anywhere in the world, the rights of internal database users need to be managed, guarded and the electronic commerce secrecy need to be guaranteed. The risk level towards the valuable and sensitive data, access to users is increased with the introduction of Internet. The complex computing environment that must be protected by the security plans is shown in Figure 8.

CONCLUSION

Previously, the static stovepipes of dedicated servers are used as data centers. Now, there is an emerging change in this regard where the virtual environments are used as data centers. The virtual environment is where the applications are executed on virtual servers which share the computing resources and virtual storage pools are used to store the data. There is a persistent growth in different types of data as the transformation is being taken place and the infrastructure management needs to be simplified by increasing the usage of physical server and storage resources.

The reduction in power, cooling, floor space, etc., is the convincing benefits of the increased device utilization in the virtual environments. But to make this real, it is expensive and is becoming inadequate. The better connectivity to high capacity arrays improves the utilization of high end storage.

Virtual servers and the virtual storage are the two most important technologies required for transformation but at the same time they bring in the intricacy to the information center. The information from one virtual machine can be transferred to another virtual machine as the workloads of the machines change over time when the data center is a virtual environment. The unexpected congestion in the network which deals with server to storage traffic, server to server clusters and storage to storage replication might occur and unanticipated bottlenecks might be created because of the dynamic movement of application workloads and data. It is difficult to provide configuration management, capacity planning, security and fault isolation in virtual environment (FABRIC, 2013).

REFERENCES

Elwahsh, H., Hashem, M., & Amin, M. (2011). Secure service discovery protocols for ad hoc networks. In Advances in computer science and information technology (pp. 147-157). Springer Berlin Heidelberg. doi:10.1007/978-3-642-17857-3_15

Fabric, D. C. (2013). *Adaptive networking—Advanced data center fabric technology*. Retrieved from http://www.dell.com/downloads/global/products/pvaul/en/dcf_adaptive_networking.pdf

Gottschalk, K., Graham, S., Kreger, H., & Snell, J. (2002). Introduction to web services architecture. *IBM Systems Journal*, *41*(2), 170–177. doi:10.1147/sj.412.0170

Helal, S., Desai, N., Verma, V., & Lee, C. (2003, March). Konark-A service discovery and delivery protocol for ad-hoc networks. In Proceedings of Wireless Communications and Networking, (Vol. 3, pp. 2107-2113). IEEE. doi:10.1109/WCNC.2003.1200712

Kniess, J., Loques, O., & Albuquerque, C. V. (2011, March). A fault-tolerant service discovery protocol for emergency search and rescue missions. In *Proceedings of Test Workshop* (LATW), (pp. 1-6). IEEE. doi:10.1109/LATW.2011.5985903

Kreger, H. (2001). Web services conceptual architecture (WSCA 1.0). *IBM Software Group, 5*, 6–7.

Lima, M., dos Santos, A. L., & Pujolle, G. (2009). A survey of survivability in mobile ad hoc networks. *IEEE Communications Surveys and Tutorials, 11*(1), 66–77. doi:10.1109/SURV.2009.090106

Nakano, T., & Suda, T. (2004, January). Adaptive and evolvable network services. In Proceedings of Genetic and Evolutionary Computation–GECCO 2004 (pp. 151–162). Springer Berlin Heidelberg. doi:10.1007/978-3-540-24854-5_14

Nichols, J., Myers, B. A., Higgins, M., Hughes, J., Harris, T. K., Rosenfeld, R., & Pignol, M. (2002, October). Generating remote control interfaces for complex appliances. In *Proceedings of the 15th Annual ACM Symposium on User Interface Software and Technology* (pp. 161-170). ACM. doi:10.1145/571985.572008

Satyanarayanan, M. (2001). Pervasive computing: Vision and challenges. *IEEE Personal Communications, 8*(4), 10–17. doi:10.1109/98.943998

ADDITIONAL READING

Djenouri, D., Khelladi, L., & Badache, N. (2005). A survey of security issues in mobile ad hoc networks. *IEEE Communications Surveys, 7*(4), 2-28.

Lakshmanan, K., De Niz, D., Rajkumar, R. R., & Moreno, G. (2012). Overload provisioning in mixed-criticality cyber-physical systems. *ACM Transactions on Embedded Computing Systems, 11*(4), 83. doi:10.1145/2362336.2362350

Wang, C., Carzaniga, A., Evans, D., & Wolf, A. L. (2002, January). Security issues and requirements for internet-scale publish-subscribe systems. In System Sciences, 2002. HICSS. Proceedings of the 35th Annual Hawaii International Conference on (pp. 3940-3947). IEEE.

KEY TERMS AND DEFINITIONS

BB: Buffer-to-Buffer; a flow control mechanism to provide resources at the destination port.

DHCP: Dynamic Host Configuration Protocol connects the computers to internet through service discovery protocols.

FSPF: Fabric Shortest Path First is to allocate the user defined data flows to specific ISLs.

PDA: Personal Digital Assistant a communication device.

PUC: A remote control device called the Personal Universal Controller.

SAN: Storage Area Network used as administrator to employ QoS for a data flow.

SDP: Service Discovery Protocol is a network protocol that detects the devices and services offered by the devices on a computer network.

UIA: Universal Information Appliance which can be demonstrated on PDA to access information.

Chapter 14
Cyber Physical Control Systems

ABSTRACT

The focus of algorithmic design is to solve composite problems. Intelligent systems use intellectual concepts like evolutionary computation, artificial neural networks, fuzzy systems, and swarm intelligence to process natural intelligence models. Artificial intelligence is used as a part of intelligent systems to perform logic- and case-based reasoning. Systems like mechanical and electrical support systems are operated by utilizing Supervisory Control and Data Acquisition (SCADA) systems. These systems cannot accomplish their purpose, provided the control system deals with the reliability of it. In CPSs, dimensions of physical processes are taken by sensors and are processed in cyber subsystems to drive the actuators that affect the physical processors. CPSs are closed-loop systems. The adaptation and the prediction are the properties to be followed by the control strategies that are implemented in cyber subsystems. This chapter explores cyber physical control systems.

INTRODUCTION

Cyber Physical Systems is described to be an integration of computation and physical processes. The physical processes are observed and controlled by the embedded computers and networks. The computing process is affected by the feedback sent by the physical processes and vice versa. It has been realized that the financial and societal possibility of such kind of systems is larger than what is expected it to be. So, to develop the technology, huge amount of speculations are made throughout the world wide. The embedded systems, computers and devices which are embedded with software such as cars, toys, medical devices and scientific instruments whose main focus is not computation are the foundation to develop the new technology. The software and network which presents the abstraction and modelling, design and analysis techniques are integrated with the dynamics of the physical processes by the Cyber Physical Systems as shown in the Figure 1 (Sundar & Lee, 2012).

The CPS is categorized as engineering discipline whose main focus is the technology and has the very good basics and foundation in mathematical abstractions. The adjoin abstractions which are progressed over decades for modelling physical processes like differential equations, stochastic processes, etc., the abstractions that are developed over centuries in the field of computer science like algorithms and programs is one of the critical challenges in technology. A "procedural

DOI: 10.4018/978-1-4666-7312-0.ch014

Figure 1. CPS applications

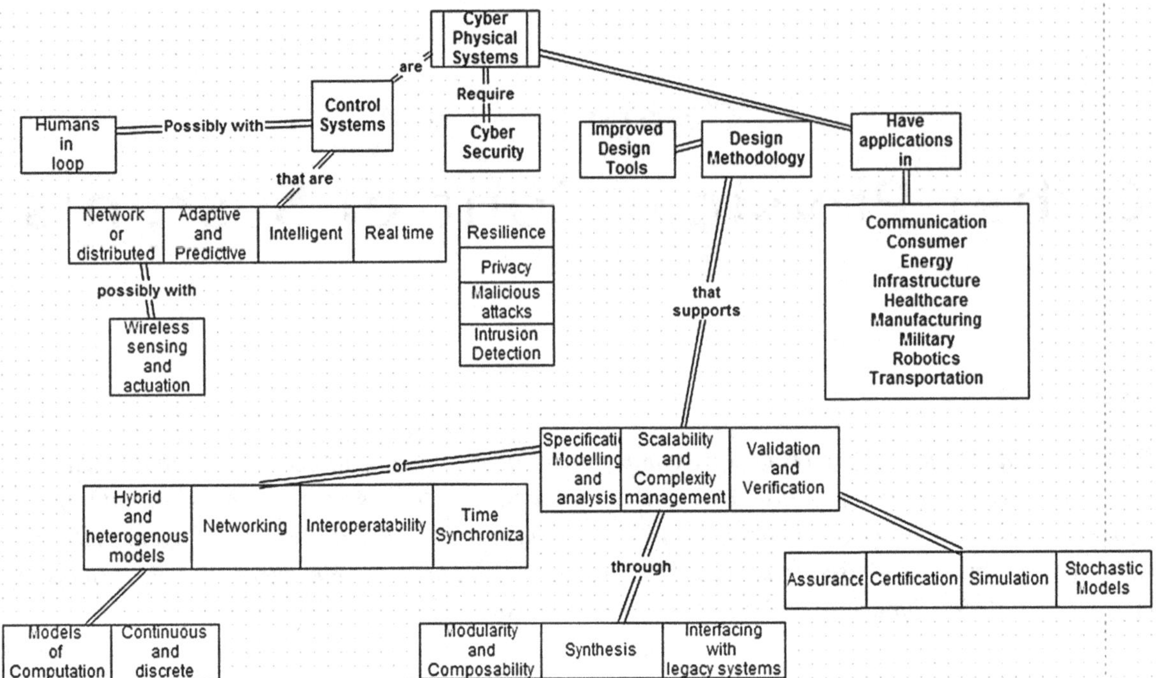

epistemology" is provided by the abstractions of the algorithms and programs [Abelson and Sussman]. The physical process abstractions focus mainly on the development of the system state over time whereas the computer science abstractions focus on the data transforming processes or computation processes.

The core physical properties like passage of time which require the progress of the physical world to be included in the discussion area are abstracted away by computer science as rooted in the Turing-Church view of computability (Zhang, 2012).

The progress of powerful methods and tools in the field of science and engineering has been evolved by the systems and control researchers. Some of these methods and tools include the time and frequency domain methods, state space analysis, identification of system, filtering, prediction, optimization, robust control, stochastic control, etc (Baheti & Gill, 2011). Simultaneously, the key advancements has been brought by the researchers in computer science field in the areas like new programming languages, real-time computing techniques, methods involved in visualization, compiler designs, embedded systems, architectures, systems software, approaches to guarantee the consistency of the system innovatively, security of the cyber world, fault tolerance. The formal and potential representation and the tools which are used for authentication purpose are also introduced by the computer science researchers (Baheti & Gill, 2011). The integration of the knowledge and engineering principles across these two disciplines is the main aspiration of Cyber Physical Systems in order to introduce novel CPS science and supporting technology

To detach the details of the hardware/software implementation from the details regarding the control system design, many industrial systems are developed in the customs of industry. Modelling uncertainty and random disturbances are addressed by the ad hoc tuning methods following the design and verification of control system by extensive simulation. Making the system effective and efficient while various subsystems are being integrated is neither a cost effective nor a time-efficient. For example, in automotive industry, different vendors manufacture the system components using their own software and hardware on which the complete vehicle control system is dependent. The Original Equipment Manufacturers (OEMs) deliver the individual components to a supply chain. To retain the low costs of the individual components which need to be integrated with different kinds of vehicles by the Original Equipment Manufacturers (OEMs) (Baheti & Gill, 2011) is a real challenge.

The most critical challenge of next generation vehicle control systems is the amplification in the complication of the components and the sophisticated technology requirement in the case of sensors and actuators, wireless communication and multi-core processors. The systems that integrate the individually developed system components required by both the supplier and the integrator need to be reliable and cost-effective.

In particular, theory and tools are needed for developing cost-effective methods (Baheti & Gill, 2011) to:

1. Design, analyze, and verify the components at various levels of abstraction. The system and software architecture levels are also included. The constraints from other levels are also need to be considered.
2. Investigate and realize the communication between the vehicle control systems and the other subsystems like engine, transmission, steering, wheel, brake, suspension, etc.
3. Guarantee the security, stability, and the performance while reducing the cost of the vehicle to the consumer. In automobile industry, the major differentiating factors for a practical business are the new functionality and the cost of vehicle control systems.

BACKGROUND

Intelligent Systems

The human brain is an extraordinary system. The brain in the human body indicates the body and the mind to carry out different kinds of simple or complex tasks like identifying the people, identifying the taste of the food we eat, perform mathematical calculations (Rudas & Fodor, 2008), to decide which action to be performed based on the knowledge gained. Today, computers can perform the very complicated tasks also very easily and faster when compared to the human but they are deficient in recognizing the reasons or to learn as the human brain.

To reduce the gap between the humans and computers by enabling the computers to be able to act intellectually by equipping with the machines is the main focus of the Artificial Intelligence (AI). It can be observed that it is difficult to implement the artificial human brain in the near future. But at the same time, it can be observed that the complex computations are being carried out which are assumed to be difficult to be performed by the computer in the present stage. This leads to the growth of the intelligent systems which have the ability to resolve some real time problems where the human intervention is expected. Some of the intelligent systems are mobile devices which have the facility to translate the foreign languages and make it easy to understand, system which can play any game like chess, beach volleyball etc., like a grand master, and machines which are used to identify the tumours or any fractures by automatically analyzing the medical images like Computer Axial Tomography scans (Rudas & Fodor, 2008).

The main aim of the intelligent systems is to identify a standard procedural approach to crack the important and moderately complex problems. The consistent results are obtained over time. The capability to realize and revenue from experience is depicted as intelligence. The capability to gain and preserve the awareness, mental ability, and the capability to react rapidly and effectively to a new condition, so on is also because of the intelligence (Rudas & Fodor, 2008).

The classification of the intelligent systems can be done based on flexibility, learning, memory, chronological dynamics, analysis, and the ability to control indecisive and inaccurate information from the computation as a point of view.

Intelligent systems are built based on the artificial intelligence. There are two main directions in the artificial intelligence known as Humanistic Artificial Intelligence (HAI) (Rudas & Fodor, 2008) and Rationalistic Artificial Intelligence (RAI) (Rudas & Fodor, 2008). The formal is used to study about the machines which have the capability of thinking and act like humans and the later is used to realize the machines which are built based on the intelligent human behaviour perspective.

Human require certain level of intelligence in order to perform some typical functions. In order to make the operation of these functions to be simpler, machines are developed by the art referred as Humanistic Artificial Intelligence. This is the research being carried out to enable the computers to perform certain things which are better performed by the human.

The explanation and the imitation of the intelligent behaviour in terms of computational processes is a research in the field called Rationalistic Artificial Intelligence.

The system that imitates some aspects of the natural intelligence is defined as an intelligent system. Some of these aspects that intelligence system imitates are learning, robustness across problem domains, flexibility, efficiency improvement, compressing the information like data to knowledge, extrapolated reasoning etc (Imre et al, 2008).

Computational Intelligence

The design of human engineered systems which demonstrate the intelligent behaviour or features is made feasible with the growth in the area of digital computers (Rudas & Fodor, 2008). The symbolic representations and manipulations are the restrictions intended by the AI research community on intelligent systems. The structure of the problem is analyzed and certain reasoning procedures are applied within that structure by an artificial intelligence to build an intelligent system. An unordered source discovers and evolves the structure in the bottom-up approach. Intelligent systems also know about the non-symbolic and bottom-up approaches. The perspective and the expectation about the behaviour of the systems by the conventional approaches which is carried out based on the analytical approaches are verified to be insufficient still at the early phases of launching a suitable mathematical model. The high definiteness and the high rigid properties of the computational environment utilized in such an analytical approach may cause difficulty to survive with the intricacy of the real world industrial systems (Imre et al, 2008). A high level of ambiguity, tolerate impression, and the expense while trying to increase the precision need to be experienced in order to deal with such systems.

Computational Intelligence (Rudas & Fodor, 2008) integrates fuzzy logic, neural networks and evolutionary computation making it as a hybrid system.

Definition of computational intelligence by Bezdek: If the system functions only with the numerical data then it is referred as computationally intelligent. The knowledge in the artificial sense is not used as it is having the component which identifies the patterns.

In addition, it begins to exhibit the following (Rudas & Fodor,2008):

1. Computational fault tolerance.
2. Error rates that approximate human performance.

A computational intelligence system whose additional significance arrives from integrating the knowledge in a non-numerical way is an artificially intelligent system

In modern terminology, the evolutionary computing means the genetic algorithms and the evolutionary programming. The methodology involving computing is said to be Computational intelligence. The capability to discover and/or handle new conditions from which the system is supposed to acquire one or more attributes of reason like generalization, discovery, association and abstraction (Rudas & Fodor, 2008). Computational intelligence and variation are identical. Computational intelligence does not depend precisely on human knowledge. One of the major characteristics of intelligent systems is adaptability.

It can be concluded that the computational intelligence is a part of artificial intelligence only when the analysis of the system complexity is completed on all the three levels.

One of the major attributes of the intelligence is adaptation. It can be examined that the new problems are not being personalized by the traditional symbolic artificial intelligence systems in new ways. Artificial is highlighted when compared to the intelligence in the AI systems. Thus it is incidental that the CI systems are intelligent where as AI systems are artificial but not intelligent (Rudas & Fodor, 2008).

Soft Computing

The computation intelligence which depends on soft computing mechanisms is isolated from artificial intelligence which depends on a hard computing mechanism to introduce a new approach called machine intelligence (Rudas & Fodor, 2008). The analysis and the design of the physical processes and systems is the main focus of the hard computing. The precision and the formality are its characteristics.

Artificial Intelligence vs. Computational Intelligence

Soft computing is familiar in the direction of the analysis and design of intelligent systems. Artificial intelligence is based on the fuzzy logic, probabilistic reasoning, artificial neural networks etc. Although ambiguity and uncertainty are the objectionable properties in hard computing, they are used to make the most of an adequate result at economical, tractability, high Machine Intelligence Quotient (MIQ) (Rudas & Fodor, 2008). The soft computing is considered as a base of real machine intelligence instead of the hard computing as shown in Figure 2 (Rudas & Fodor, 2008). Utilization of acceptance for ambiguity, uncertainty and unfair fact to realize tractability, robustness, inexpensive result and enhanced affinity with reality is the steering theory of soft computing.

The ambiguity and estimated reasoning are the two main concerns of Fuzzy logic (FL), learning and curve fitting are the concerns of Neural Networks (NN) where as searching and optimization are the concerns of Evolutionary Computation (EC). The constituents of soft computing constituents oppose each other instead of being cooperative (Rudas & Fodor, 2008).

The fact that the combined use of fuzzy logic, neural networks and evolutionary computation is more effective when they are used individually is elevated from the years of experience. For example: there are numerous assorted applications varying from chemical process control to consumer goods which already has become well known as the applications of the combination of the fuzzy logic and neural nets (Rudas & Fodor, 2008).

Figure 2. Comparison of hard computing and soft computing

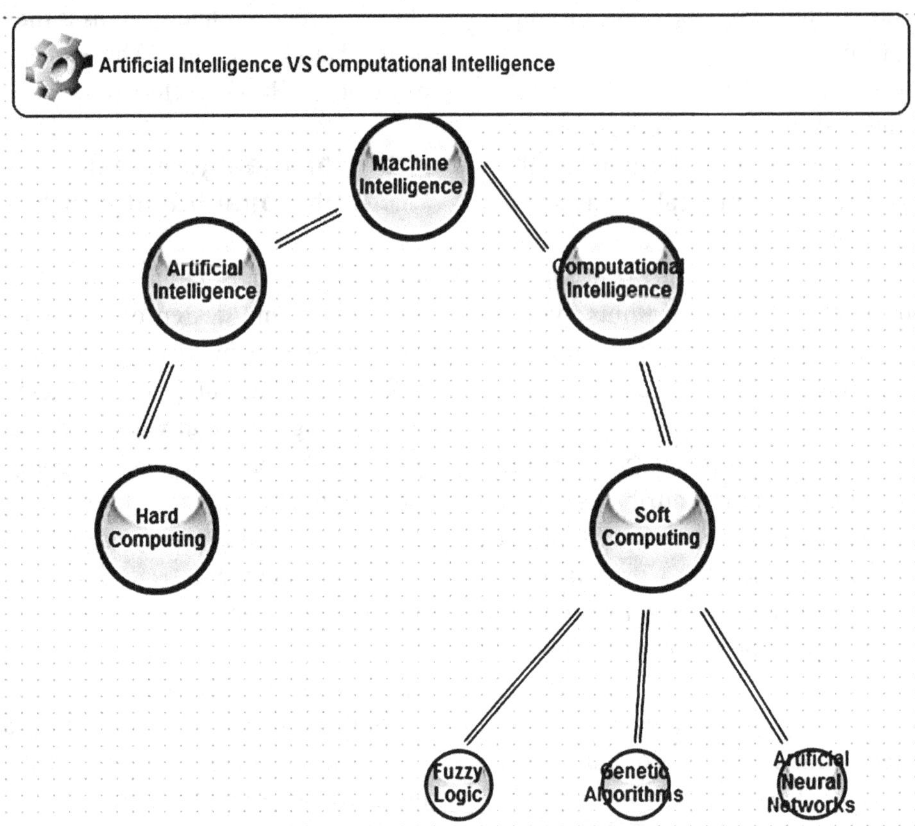

Intelligent Control

Adaptation and learning are the significant features of human intelligence. Planning under high ambiguity and copying huge quantity of information are emulated by intelligent control methods. Recently, everything which is not described as conventional control is included in the intelligent control. However, there will be shifting boundaries like "intelligent control" at present to "control" in the future. From years of experience it can be observed that the human intelligence and intelligent behaviour are not having full pledged definitions. This leads to the fact of difficulty in defining the term "Intelligent Control" (Antsaklis, 1994). Currently, the old discussion among engineers, computer scientists, psychologists, and educators about the definition of "Intelligence" is still going on.

Intelligent Control Systems

There are number of ways and dimensions along which the intelligent systems can be characterized. The control systems concentrate on some of the attributes of intelligent systems.

Intelligent systems are characterized as (Antsaklis,1994):

- The capability of behaving in a suitable manner under the ambiguous conditions such that the success probability is increased. The accomplishment of system's ultimate goal from the behaviour of the sub-goals indicates the successful behaviour.
- The functions of living things and finally human mental power are emulated to make the man-made intelligent system to behave appropriately.

There are many levels of dimensions of intelligence that can be calculated based on which the intelligent system can be categorized. The capability to sense the environment, the ability to decide and manage the action is the low level requirements of the intelligence. At the same time, the ability to identify the objects and events, real time knowledge representation and future plan are the high level requirements of intelligence.

The ability to observe and realize are made possible by the advanced forms of intelligence. Intelligence chooses intelligently to behave effectively under various circumstances to withstand and perform well in a complex and aggressive environment. The development in the computational power and knowledge gain to sense, conclude and operate in a intricate and dynamic world lead to the growth and evolution of intelligence.

Intelligent Control and Its Usage

Intelligent control has evolved to be an interdisciplinary area. The features like decision making, image recognition, adaptation to the uncertain media, self organization, planning, etc., are out of scale of conventional control theory but are linked with the intelligent control (Meystel & Messina, 2000). Albus (1995) provided the intelligent control definition which is very famous and comprehensive: "Intelligence will be defined as an ability of a system to act appropriately in an uncertain environment, where appropriate action is that which increases the probability of success, and success is the achievement of behavioural sub-goals that support the system's ultimate goal."

The controller which is used to formulate the behaviour of an intelligent system is described as intelligent controller by Pang.

The features provided by the various properties of this controller are:

- The ability to decide the action to be taken and the point/time at which it need to be performed.
- The ability to bring the desirable and feasible actions together.
- The details of the control heuristics resolution can be altered.
- The control heuristics obtained must be the most appropriate and should adapt to dynamic changes.
- The ability to integrate various control heuristics.

Characteristics of Intelligent Systems

Intelligent systems have many fundamental properties at different levels. The level of the intelligence is measured based on these fundamental properties which are also referred as intelligent system characteristics (Rudas & Fodor, 2008).

Three fundamental characteristics of intelligent control systems are discussed below:

- **Adaptation and Learning:** Intelligent system must be able to adapt to dynamic conditions. Generally, learning is not an essential feature for adaptation but it becomes essential for the systems to enable to adapt to various unforeseen conditions. So, the ability to learn becomes as one of the important properties of intelligent systems.
- **Autonomy and Intelligence:** Establishing and accomplishing objectives independently is one of the significant properties of intelligent control systems. The system is said to highly autonomous if the system is able to behave successfully in unpredictable situations for the period more than which it is intended to work without any external interference. Autonomy is having different levels. An adaptive control system is said to highly autonomic when compared to the control system with fixed controllers because of the property of adaptive control system being able to adapt with greater ambiguity. Intelligence in the system is not

essential in low level autonomy where as it is essential at higher levels of autonomy.

- **Structures and Hierarchies:** Intelligent systems require an appropriate functional architecture for performing the analysis, evaluating control strategies and to manage the complex issues. This architecture should be able to reduce the complexity by providing a technique to build different levels of generalization such as granularity and resolution. A method or procedure with entropy which emphasizes such efficient computational architectures analysis the intelligent machines. The complexity can be handled by behaving as main vehicles in such construction. The term hierarchy need not always imply as hierarchical hardware but it can also be referred as functional hierarchies, or hierarchies of range and resolution along spatial or temporal dimensions. Hardwired constructions also might be a part of these. The ability to learn is essential in order to adapt to dynamic situations so that these architectures will be able to cope with unexpected and important changes.

The learning is essential as they need to be highly adaptable to unexpected important changes and must be highly independent in order to deal with changes. Significant complexity need to handle by these systems which lead to hierarchical architectures.

Characteristics of Intelligent Control

Intelligent control systems depend on soft computing methods, such as genetic algorithms, neural networks and fuzzy logic. An additional point of view is to examine intelligent control systems concerning their features. Whether the control system is intelligent or not, its heart is the control laws. The goal of the control system is to reduce the variation from a pre-determined path and/or ultimate status. It is suggested that the control laws are passive to the control system from the analysis of control laws. In the current hypothesis of automatic control, it is difficult to assume the control laws to be a larger fraction of the control strategy taken as a whole system. The mission of the control laws is that a certain variable of interest is kept within some limits around a reference path. The control laws mission is achieved by making some external intelligence is functioning away from the limits of the intelligence of particular control law. These assignments and their origin are incorporated into the function of the controller by the intelligent controllers (Meystel & Messina, 2000). This is a fundamental difference.

Fuzzy Logic

The tool of fuzzification is used to transform the input data set from the high decree realm to low decree realm in fuzzy logic controllers. The search for adjacency among data units, focus and grouping is performed by Fuzzification and hence it is implied that a role of generalization procedure is played by Fuzzification (Meystel & Messina, 2000). Non-statistical ambiguity in information and data is referred as fuzziness. Fuzzy is used to describe and is used to deal with many concepts in reality. In classical logic, the logic like an aspect is either an element or not a element of a set is known as crisp logic. This indicates that the membership degree of each element in the set is either 1 or 0. In a fuzzy set, the membership grades of the elements in the set are reflected by the values of fuzzy membership. The fuzzy logic is the logic of estimated analysis which is the basis for the membership function, the fundamental initiative in fuzzy set theory (Rudas & Fodor, 2008). The conventional logic is the general form of it. The properties like ambiguity, approximation, etc., are modelled by fuzzy sets. There are some problems which would not have the solution using crisp logic but fuzzy logic solves such problems.

There are many applications of fuzzy logic in the areas of engineering like robotics and control, architecture and environmental engineering. The applications of fuzzy logic in the non-engineering field are medicine, management, decision analysis, and computer science (Rudas & Fodor, 2008). The applications where fuzzy logic plays a role would be increasing from day-to-day. Fuzzy control and fuzzy expert systems (Antsaklis, 1994) are the two major application areas.

Neural Networks

A computation tool for abstracting the surrounding area, spatial or temporal is said to be neural networks. The information is moved from the higher to lower levels of resolution by a natural tool which is referred as neural networks. Hence, neural networks are referred as multi-resolution systems. A decision related to the abstractions and the rules to be applied at the lower resolution are made by controllers which are based on expert systems. They are also operated in a multi-level, multi-resolution framework (Meystel & Messina, 2000). An analysis hypothesis of the structure of the brain is roughly modelled as an artificial neural network. Numerous comparatively uncomplicated individual processing components are utilized in modelling highly interconnected and parallel computational structure. The noisy and variable information are dealt with its ability.

The neural networks can be applied in following five areas (Rudas & Fodor, 2008):

- Classification,
- Content addressable memory or associative memory,
- Clustering or compression,
- Generation of sequences or patterns, and
- Control systems.

Hybrid Logic Control Systems

There can be multi-levels in the hybrid logic control systems. The lower resolution levels are logical controllers and analytical controllers are higher resolution levels. At the minimum, there will be dual-level architecture of control systems with different resolutions (Meystel & Messina, 2000). Intelligent systems are built by integrating two or more individual technologies like fuzzy logic, neural networks, genetic algorithms, etc., using hybrid systems. The various aspects of human intelligence are represented using the individual technologies in order to improve the performance (Rudas & Fodor, 2008). Anyways, there will be constraints and limitations for every individual technology. The systems abilities and the performance can be improved by integrating two or more of them making as a hybrid system. This leads to better understanding of human condition.

Behaviour-Based Controllers

A superposition concept of the multiple controllers activities, each offering a distinct kind of behaviour working simultaneously are utilized by behaviour-based controllers. In general, some kind of a hierarchical structure lies beneath implementation (Meystel & Messina, 2000). The behaviour controller to be invoked at a particular instant of time is selected by a low resolution level. Sub goals are generated by each of the individual behaviour generation controller for themselves. There are several underlying characteristics that define the systems of intelligent control. Since the issue of control is a part of the intelligent systems, there is a lot of scope in expansion. The definitions of intelligence are extracted by observing the abilities of the overall system and estimating the user's expectations. The fundamentals of prescribed hypothesis of intelligent systems and the performance metrics of such systems are developed using the parameters of system capabilities and the constituent modules (Meystel & Messina, 2000).

ADAPTIVE AND PREDICTIVE METHODS

In Cyber Physical Systems, measurements of physical processes are taken by sensors and are processed in cyber subsystems to drive the actuators that affect the physical processors. So, it is said that the cyber physical systems are closed-loop systems. The adaptation and the prediction (Meystel & Messina, 2000) are the properties to be obeyed by the control strategies which are implemented in the cyber subsystems.

Adaptive Control

The ability to adaptation during operation, the multi-dimensional complexity of multi-functionality, heterogeneous distributed architecture, efficient usage of resources are the important properties of the cyber physical systems (Phan & Lee,2011). For example, the configuration of an unmanned aircraft avionics system must be able to face the situations like collisions or aircraft system failures and continue the safe operation and the accidents need to be avoided by controlling the speed according to the current road condition.

The type of control applicable to process the changing dynamics in normal operating conditions subjected to stochastic disturbances is called as adaptive control (Phan & Lee, 2011).

Reasons for using adaptive control are:

- Variations in process dynamics,
- Variations in the character of disturbances, and
- Engineering efficiency.

Normally, it is not simple to control a process with changing dynamics. Currently, adaptive control and robust control are the two possible solutions existing for that situation. The type of control which controls the process in closed-loop is referred as adaptive control. The information about the system characteristics is obtained during the operation of the system. The specific involvement in the control loop is made in order to fulfil the control goal by obtaining the latest information during the operation of the systems. There are various interventions and can be categorized as signal adaptation, parameter adaptation, and structure adaptation.

Adaptive control is used when the process is being executing, there is a chance of the process undergoing some kind of unexpected changes and the changes are being taken place in process parameters during the operation (Landau et. al, 2011).

When the process parameters are indefinite or adjust with time, the desired level performance is acquired or sustained using adaptive control by defining a set of techniques for adjusting the real time in controllers automatically. When there is a lack of knowledge about the present values of the process parameters, high performance control systems are designed using these techniques. The tuning of control systems is made automatic using these techniques. The expansion of these techniques is taken place only after the extensive research which started in 1950s and the introduction of microprocessors.

Basic Principles

Figure 3 (Landau et. al, 2011) depicts that the performance of the control systems is reduced because of the vague and immense deviations of the process parameters, which are termed as parameter disturbances.

The classifications of the disturbances that are acting on the control systems are:

- Disturbances acting on the controlled variables.
- Parameter disturbances acting on the performance of the control system.

Figure 3. Adaptive control systems

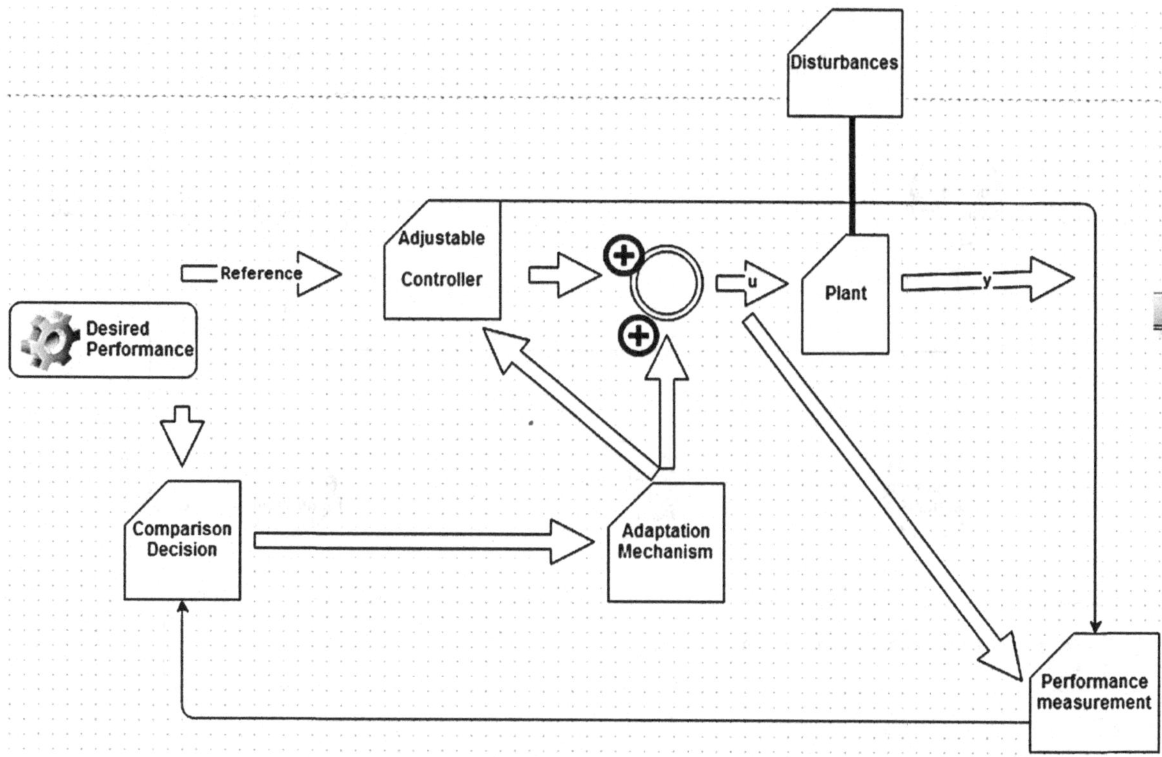

The effect due to the former disturbances is eliminated and the desired values of the performance are brought to a certain index using the feedback in the conventional control systems. The required performance of a control in the existence of parameter disturbances can be acquired and maintained in the similar manner.

The index of performance (IP) is measured only after defining it for the performance of a control system, ex: damping factor. The adaptation mechanism is fed with the difference between the measured IP and the desired IP. When IP behaves as a controller variable, an adaptive control system can be described as a feedback system. To observe the performance of the basic feedback control system, an additional feedback loop called an adaptive control loop is used as shown in the Figure 3.

Basic Techniques of Adaptive Control

Open-Loop Adaptive Control

Simple open-loop systems such as gain scheduling techniques as shown in the Figure 4 as in (Landau et. al, 2011) are also developed along with the development of the closed-loop adaptive control systems. The gain scheduling technique makes an assumption that there exists a tight association between the variables of the environment that are assessable and the process model parameters. The controller parameters are modified in order to minimize or eradicate the consequence of deviations in the parameter using this relation. It is observed that the gain scheduling scheme can change the performance of the system. So, there is

Figure 4. Gain scheduling

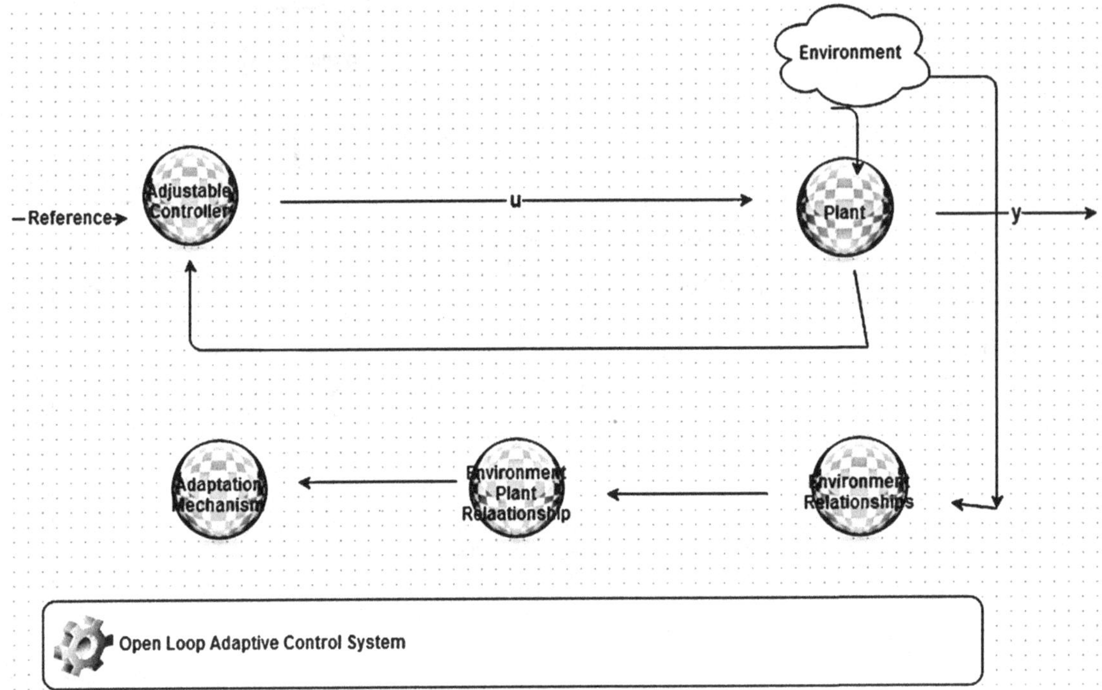

a chance that this scheme might not be successful because of the changes in the tight bond between the environment measurement and the process parameters (Landau et. al, 2011).

Direct Adaptive Control

The desired behaviour of the closed-loop system (Landau et. al, 2011) determines the features of a dynamic system which are identified by the required outcome of the feedback control system in many cases. For example: A given function determines the input-output behaviour which is specified by a tracking objective. The design of the controller is made such that the features of the required dynamic system are realized by the closed-loop control system using the given plant model.

Indirect Adaptive Control (Self Tuning Control)

The linear control scheme (Landau et. al, 2011) is extended and is referred as indirect adaptive control scheme or self-tuning control scheme. Designing a suitable controller by estimating the model of the plant using the available input and output data is the basic idea of this scheme. The adjustable predictor for the plant output is only by estimating the parameter online. Recursive estimation algorithm is used to fine-tune the adjustable predictor parameters by utilizing the error between the output of the plant and the predicted output (predicted error). Making the estimated error asymptotically to zero in a deterministic environment is the main objective. A accurate input-output report of the plant for a specified input series is used to obtain an estimated model asymptotically using this scheme called as adaptive predictor.

Direct and Indirect Adaptive Control

The adaptation mechanism directly adapts the controller parameters. The controller parameters are calculated using the adjustable predictor parameters which are adapted by the adaptation mechanism 1. The adjustable predictor is parameterized appropriately to estimate the controller parameters by the parameter adaptation, yielding a direct adaptive control scheme. Since the indirect adaptive control schemes approximate the controller parameters directly, they are in fact Direct Adaptive Control (DAC) (Landau et. al, 2011) schemes. The simpler implementation and the elimination of the numerical problems related with the parameters of the computing controller by the approximation of the plant parameters make the direct adaptive control a very attractive approach. Unfortunately, the plant models are the only applications to which it is limited.

Basic Design of Adaptive Controllers

It is possible to extend the ideas and the organization in a deterministic environment to the functions in a stochastic environment in a straightforward manner. The model for the stochastic disturbance needs to be considered along with the model of a plant while a control system is being designed in a stochastic environment.

Irrespective of the type of linear controller used, the plant output is an Auto Regressive Moving Average (ARMA) (Landau et.al, 2011) process when the disturbance is modelled as ARMA. Hence, ARMA model with the required statistical properties, average value and variance is used to specify the control performance. The design of the controller needs to be done such that the resultant imitates the required ARMA model.

An adaptive control systems design steps (Landau et.al, 2011) are as given below:

- Outline of the linear controller accepting that the parameters of the plant model and disturbance model are known.
- The adaptive control loop organization is to be defined.
- Algorithm design which adapts the parameters.

The know disturbances are inputs, outputs and the states and are utilized to evaluate a definite performance index (IP) by an adaptive control system. The control system is given a set of performance indices. The performance index of the control system is maintained to be close to the set of the given indices, i.e., within the set of acceptable ones, an auxiliary control is generated by modifying the adjustable controller parameters from the similarity of the calculated performance index with the set of given indices (Landau et.al, 2011).

Model Predictive Control

Since 1980s, in process industries like chemical plants and oil refineries, a sophisticated method of process control called Model Predictive Control (MPC). Dynamic models of the process and the linear empirical models obtained by system identification are the models on which model predictive controllers depend. Model Predictive Control (MPC) is also known as Dynamical Matrix Control (DMC), Generalized Predictive Control (GPC) and Receding Horizon Control (RHC).

The control algorithms are based on:

- At each step, an optimization problem is solved numerically.
- Constrained optimization – typically QP or LP.
- Diminishing horizon control.

Currently, MPC is the technology of choice and is being used in most of the existing multivariable control applications (Gorinevsky, 2005).

Predictive Control Approach

Computer systems that host information technology stringent performance or quality of service are very important requirements that must be satisfied when operated in the highly dynamic environments (Gorinevsky, 2005). Ex: military command and control, commerce and banking, transportation, etc. It is required to observe many performance related parameters and also sometimes it is required to optimize in order to make it to react quickly to the operating conditions which vary with time to attain QoS goals in computing systems. It is difficult to tune the important operating parameters manually when these increase in size and complexity. Hence, highly autonomic or self managing, guidance only from high level administrators, tune the important operating parameters adaptively to maintain the specified QoS are the properties that need to be obeyed by the future systems. While designing self managing computing systems using predictive control approach, it needs to emphasize that actions are selected using a control policy by optimizing the system behaviour as anticipated by the system model for the precise QoS conditions over a limited prediction horizon (Abdelwahed, Bai, & Kandasamy, 2009) Optimization problem clearly represents both the control objectives and the operating constraints and at every instant of time they are solved.

Applications (Abdelwahed et al., 2009) of this control method:

- Issues of Performance management vary from simple linear dynamics to more complex.
- Systems with long delay or dead times.
- Systems that exhibits non-linear and event driven behaviour.

The changes caused by resource failures and/ or changes in time-varying system parameters are accommodated to the behavioural model itself.

The behaviour of the complex dynamic systems is to be represented by the models used in MPC. Generic PID controllers are often used to control simple systems adequately and so, there is no need of more complex MPC control algorithm. Large time delays and higher order dynamics are the common characteristics that are critical for PID controllers (Ahmadzade, Shahgholian, Tehrani, & Mahdavian, 2011).

The variations in the independent variables cause changes in the dependent variables of the modelled system which will be predicted by MPC models. The set points of regulatory PID controllers or the final control elements are adjusted by the controller very frequently in a chemical process. Examples of PID controllers are pressure, flow, temperature, etc. Examples of final control elements are valves, dampers, etc. Disturbances are the independent variables in which the modification is not possible to be made by the controller. The other measurements in the processes are dependent variables which are represented in the form of control objectives or process constraints. The future changes in the dependent variables are calculated using the existing measurements of the plant, present dynamic state of the process, the MPC models, the targets and limits of the process variable by the model predictive control. During the process of enforcing the constraints on both independent and dependent variables (Sebaa, Moulahoum, Houassine, & Kabache, 2012), the dependent variables can be maintained to be close to the target by computing these changes. The initial changes observed by MPC in every independent variable are implemented and the process of implementing the subsequent changes is repeated whenever required. The real processes are considered to be almost linear over a small operating range while many of them are not linear. The differences between the model and the process generate the prediction errors which are balanced by using the linear MPC approaches with the feedback mechanism in most of the applications. The response of the dependent variables is predicted by integrating the changes of various independent variables as one using the principle of superposition in linear algebra when there are linear models in the model predictive controllers. Hence, the control problem is simplified to the fast and robust calculations such as a series of direct matrix algebra (Sebaa et al., 2012).

Theory behind Model Predictive Control

MPC is based on the optimization techniques like iteration and finite horizon of a plant model. The sampling of the present state of the plant is done at time t. Numerical minimization algorithm is used to apply the cost minimizing control strategy for a short period of time, t+Δt. The cost minimizing strategy is discovered through the solution of Euler-Lagrange equations by exploring the state trajectory that originate from the present using the exclusive online calculations during the period of time, t+Δt. The implementation is carried out only on the first step of the control strategy at the initial stage. The process is repeated after sampling the state of the plant and a new control and new predicted state path are obtained from the new present state (Sebaa et al., 2012). MPC is also referred as diminishing horizon control as the prediction horizon is being shifted forwards always. The better results are attained even though this is not an optimal approach. An extensive research is being carried out in order to enhance the MPC method, to discover the methods which find the solution of Euler-Lagrange type equations in a faster way and to realize the global stability properties of MPC's local optimization.

Principles of MPC

Model Predictive Control (MPC) is a multivariable control algorithm that uses (Sebaa et al., 2012):

- An internal dynamic model of the process,
- A history of past control moves, and
- An optimization cost function J over the receding prediction horizon is used to estimate the optimum control moves.

The cost function of the optimization without violating the low/high limit constraints is given as:

$$J = \sum_{i=1}^{N} w_{xi}(r_i - x_i)^2 + \sum_{i=1}^{N} w_{u_i} \Delta u_i^2$$

with:

- x_i controlled variable (e.g. measured temperature),
- r_i reference variable (e.g. required temperature),
- u_i manipulated variable (e.g. control valve),
- w_{xi} weighting coefficient reflecting the relative importance of, and
- w_{ui} weighting coefficient penalizing relative big changes in.

Nonlinear MPC

The variation of model predictive control (MPC) (Nikolaou, 2001) is a Nonlinear Model Predictive Control (NMPC). In NMPC, the models used during the process of prediction are nonlinear system models. NMPC also desire the solution of the optimal control problems on a limited prediction horizon to be iterative as similar to the case in linear MPC. As the optimal control problems in nonlinear MPC are not considered to be convex as in the case of linear MPC, the stability theory and the numerical solution of NMPC need to face many challenges. Direct single shooting, direct multiple shooting methods and direct collocation are the direct optimal control methods which use the Newton-type optimization schemes. One of these schemes behaves as a foundation for the numerical solution of the NMPC optimal control problems. The fact that consecutive optimal control problems are similar is utilized by NMPC algorithms to make a correct guess and efficiently initialize the Newton-type solution procedure from the optimal solution which is calculated in the previous step. Significant amount of computation time also is saved in this process of initialization. In general, the path following algorithms or "real time iterations" converge the optimization problem iteratively. But the property of subsequent problems similarity is also utilized by the path following algorithms or "real time iterations" that considers only single iteration in order to obtain the solution for the current NMPC problem with the proper initialization before proceeding to the next problem.

Since the first IDCOM and DMC applications of MPC technology, it has been evolved significantly in twenty two years. Till today, there are nearly more than 2200 applications like solid foundation in refining and petrochemicals, food processing, etc.

Even though the controllers still maintain an IDCOM or DMC like behaviours in most of the cases, significant new potentiality is introduced in MPC technology. Multiple objective functions and graded constraints are used in the development of SMC-IDCOM and HIECON algorithms which are IDCOM like controllers. Similarly, evaluation of control and economic trade-offs using weighting factors is carried out by DMC, RMPCT and OPC algorithms which are DMC like controllers using single dynamic objective function. IDCOM behaviour is inherited by the PFC controller. The variation is that the nonlinear and unstable processes can be accommodated and the input function is parameterized using the basic functions.

Emerging MPC applications (Gorinevsky, 2005):

- Nonlinear MPC:
  - Just need a computable model (simulation).
  - NLP optimization.
- Hybrid MPC:
  - Discrete and parametric variables.
  - Combination of dynamics and discrete mode change.
  - Mixed-integer optimization (MILP, MIQP).
- Engine control.
- Large scale operation control problems:
  - Operations management (control of supply chain).
  - Campaign control.

The report on significant applications in progress by all the vendors makes the future MPC technology to be bright. The features like various objective functions, boundless prediction horizon, nonlinear process models, better use of model uncertainty estimates, and to handle ill-conditioning in a better way might be included in next generation MPC technology.

CONTROL SYSTEM ARCHITECTURES

The clear vision is obtained during the early stages in the expansion of the computer control systems that some overall efficient organization is required. Assigning a device driver to the machines in order to overview the operation of the machines is failed. Few of these devices attain high attention where as others attain less attention.

The device to be operated is identified and their activities are synchronized by executing some type of program in an ordinary system. It is evident that the control machines which are controlled by a computer need to be managed by a supervisor. Supervisor must ensure that it concentrates on every machine adequately and when required in order to keep the system up to date and run smoothly. Nevertheless, any device must be able to handle or send any type of signal from/to it. The input from the devices is more difficult to handle when compared to the output to the devices. Signals may persist for long time or last only for a moment and handled as interrupts when they vanish which is sent by various devices. Polling need to considered when devices do not send any signals in order to determine the status of the devices.

Types of Control System Architectures

Generally, the range of the architecture of control systems vary from effortless local control to highly redundant distributed control (TM5-601, 2006). The sensors, controller and the controlled equipment will be in a close proximity in the architecture of the local control system. Each controller's range is restricted to a specific system or subsystem. Single controller or group of controllers which are accommodated in a common control room are used to connect all the sensors, actuators and other equipment in a system which is defined by a centralized control. The best features of the local control and the centralized control are combined and are offered by architecture of the distributed control system. In distributed control system, each system or group of systems are provided with a controller, but a digital communication circuit is used to connect them to one or more operator stations to form a network in a central location (TM5-601, 2006).

Control system architectures are classified into three different types as discussed below:

Standalone System

The self-sufficient and self-contained are the two properties of a standalone control system. Its constituents depend on the type of the controller used. The individual unit operations, packaged systems, small processes, skid-mounted systems, etc., are the applications where mostly the standalone systems are used (Merritt, 2005). A standalone system performs its job without the direct control of the higher level system. The standalone system operated on its own when the communications become worse due to unavoidable conditions otherwise it is connected to the other control element in a plant.

Distributed Control System (DCS)

The range of DCS varies from the conventional distributed process control systems to the modern process automation system (PAS). All the elements of DCS are connected by a network like field bus or Ethernet. Some of the elements of DCS are multiple direct control elements, HMI workstations, SCADA systems, control processors, logic processors, I/O processors, servers, process historians, and high level software packages. As various devices operate various tasks, a DCS is said to be truly "distributed". Major applications of the DCF are the controlling the large processes and integrating high level software packages like asset management (Merritt, 2005).

Server-Based System

The elements of a conventional standalone or distributed control system are accommodated in the plant (like on-chip in the case of processor). Some of the non-critical elements of the control system are placed outside the plant in the case of the server based system (like off-chip in the case of processor). While all I/O, critical controls, shutdown systems, and other real-time functions are kept in the plant, all the advanced DCS-type supervisory control, SCADA (supervisory control and data acquisition), asset management, ERP, loop tuning and related functions can be operated from afar by the remote servers. These types of remote servers can be placed at any location in the world. Secure or non-secure communications like microwave, satellite, virtual private networks, the web, dial-up modems or cell phones can be used to connect with these remote servers. Server based system supports both the standalone system and DCS systems (Merritt, 2005).

SCADA (Supervisory Control and Data Acquisition) systems are relevant to the services that are sufficiently large where a central control system is required (TM5-601, 2006).

Local Control

The architecture of the local control systems (TM5-601, 2006) accommodates the sensors, controller, and the controlled equipment narrowly. The specific system or the subsystem is a scope of each controller. The initialization or termination of the automatic sequences which are controlled locally, modification of the control set points is done based on the inputs accepted from a supervisory controller. But the local controller determines the control action by itself. Operator interfaces and the displays that are required are also local. Trouble shooting with the system is the main advantage of these systems. But the intricacy is that supervising the systems or react to the unforeseen events of the system. Packaged control panels which are furnished with chillers and skid-mounted pump packages are the examples of local control.

Centralized Control

The single controller or group of controllers are used to connect all sensors, actuators and other equipment in a common area in the centralized control systems (TM5-601, 2006). This improves the knowledge about the operation of the system and makes the action to be taken during the unforeseen conditions faster. Earlier, power plants, digital controls and other facilities using single loop controllers use this type of system architecture. But it is expensive in case of routing and wiring all the control system to a central location. Hence, it has been replaced with the distributed control system. If centralized control systems are used in small C4ISR facilities, then fully redundant processors are needed. Centralized control systems accommodate the redundancy. The faults like electricity, physical and environmental threats must not be affecting the signals to or from the equipment of all the redundant processors. In order to ensure this, the wiring needs to be isolated from one to the other processor.

Distributed Control

The advantages of both local control and centralized control are presented by the distributed control system (TM5-601, 2006) architecture. In a distributed control system, each local system has its own controller and the central operator station to control all these local controllers. Local controller controls the action of each system or subsystem. The status of all the systems, each controller's input and output data is possible to be viewed by the central operator station. At the same time, it can interfere in the process of local controllers whenever it is required. The system elements which work together and exhibit the structural and behavioural ability which cannot be produced with a single system or a system working alone are integrated using control systems architecture. The fundamental construction of networks, command and control systems, spacecraft and computer hardware and software together is termed as "architecture".

Real-Time Control Methods

The reference model (Albus & Rippey, 1994) which is appropriate for a lot of software concentrated, real time control problem fields is a real time control system. A reference model is the one which is like a skeleton of the human body. It can be used to develop any system by adapting the reference model with some changes to obtain some important relationships among the entities and supporting standards or specifications development. A reference model is based on a small number of unifying concepts and may be used as a basis for education and explaining standards to a non-specialist. Real-time control system is open and scalable.

The system complexity is organized using a hierarchical control model which is based on a set of well-founded engineering principles in RCS. A generic node model is shared among all the control nodes at all levels. The process of designing, engineering, integrating and testing the control systems is done by an ample methodology which is provided by RCS. The systems tasks are made into granular, finite subsets by iterative procedure of partition in order to make control of the system easier and the system to be efficient by architects. Real-time control system concentrates on intelligent control that adjusts to vague and amorphous operating environments.

Sensing, perception, knowledge, costs, learning, planning, and execution are some of the important considerations made by RCS.

RCS applies to many problem domains including:

- Manufacturing example:
  - Vehicle Systems.
- Wider RCS applications examples:
  - Space.
  - Underwater.
  - U.S.P.S.
  - Underground coal mining.

RCS METHODOLOGY OBJECTIVES

The objectives in developing RCS are outlined below (Quintero & Barbera, 1992):

- To improve human understanding of the design result.
- To manage software complexity.
- To provide robust, verifiable, efficient, coordinated, real-time performance.
- To provide extensibility, portability, and software reuse.

RCS Methodology Approach

Developing an RCS methodology involves (Quintero & Barbera, 1992):

- Organization of complete set of integration rules.
- Identifying information models and real-time software execution models which explicitly highlight critical components of the RCS problem domain.
- Selecting software engineering implementation techniques which are compatible with the integration rules, the models and the RCS methodology objectives.

The architecture models are divided into software and hardware (Quintero & Barbera, 1992). The information models and the execution models are included in the software architecture model. The people, machines, sensors, actuators, computing hardware, and a communications network are included in the hardware architecture model.

The critical design components include the following:

- Real-time task behaviour and software execution models.
- Interfaces and communications methods between software modules, hardware resources and human operators.

- Information models and knowledge base management.
- Allocation of resources.
- Rules for decomposing the design spatially and temporally.

RCS Methodology

The traditional software engineering methodologies like functional decomposition, structured design, etc., and the promising methods that highlight the RCS task decomposition approach are used to depict the RCS methodology.

This RCS Methodology is based on the following empirically established method tenets (Quintero & Barbera, 1993):

- Use task oriented decomposition (driven by scenarios)
- Use hierarchical organization and assign responsibility and authority
- Organize the control hierarchy around tasks top-down and equipment bottom-up
- Partition by an order of magnitude between levels (spatial and temporal resolution) and roughly ten decisions or less per plan
- Use seven + or - two subordinates per supervisor and only one supervisor at a time.
- SP/WM/BG functions are distributed throughout RCS and assumed to exist in each node
- Allow human I/F at any node
- Controller modules are finite state machines communicating through Global Memory
- Design for concurrent processing: Measure execution time performance; allocate sufficient computing resources
- Use synchronous control at the lowest levels transitioning to asynchronous control at the highest levels

Real time control system (RCS) is evolved based on intelligent agent architecture and designed to enable the intelligent behaviour up to human levels of performance. Thirty years before, the theoretical model of the cerebellum is the inspiration for RCS. The coordination and the control of motions in the fine motor are introduced from the stimulation of the brain. It was initially intended for sensory-interactive goal-directed control of laboratory manipulators. Over three decades, it has developed into real-time control architecture for intelligent machine tools, factory automation systems, and intelligent autonomous vehicles (Albus & Barbera, 2004). There are many domains like manufacturing and vehicle systems where the RCS is applicable. A wide variety of applications like loading and unloading the parts and tools in machines, controlling the workstations function, controlling tele-robots in the space station, various undersea vehicles which are independent, land vehicles which are not controlled by a man, coal mining automation systems, postal service, and submarine operational automation systems are designed, developed, and realized using the RCS architecture (Albus & Rippey, 1994).

CONCLUSION

A new generation of engineered systems that integrates the computation, networking and physical processes are referred as Cyber Physical Systems. The computing and the communication cores interact with the physical environment in order to observe, coordinate, control and integration, which are the operations of cyber physical systems. Humans can interact with CPS through many new modalities because of the integrated capabilities of computational and physical processes.

Time and frequency domain methods, state space analysis, system identification, filtering, prediction, optimization, robust control, and stochastic control are some of the powerful science and engineering methods and tools (Baheti & Gill, 2011). Researches in the field of systems and control are involved over the years in initializing the development of these kinds of methods and tools.

In recent times, there has been an enormous scientific and industrial interest in Cyber Physical Systems. Hence, there is an improvement in the design and operation of these systems in terms of theory, tool development and practise. The main aim of intelligent systems is provide the solution for vital and fairly complex problems to achieve reliable results over time using a standardized methodological approach. The flexibility, learning, adaptability, memory, temporal dynamics, reasoning, and the ability to manage uncertain and imprecise information are categories of the intelligence of the system in terms of computation (Krishnakumar, 2003).

The important basic requirement for building the intelligent systems is the Artificial Intelligence. The systems in the field of intelligent control are defined using their underlying characteristics. Only a fraction of the complete intelligence in a system is controlled. So, there is chance of intelligent systems to be extended. In the broader scope, the capabilities of the overall system can be looked at as estimate in opposition to the user's expectations, so as to haul out descriptions of intelligence. The formal theory of intelligent systems and the study of metrics for such systems are inspired from the measures of both the overall system's capabilities and the parameters of the constituent modules (Meystel & Messina, 2000).

A few descriptions of intelligent control would restrict it to those systems that depend on soft computing techniques, such as fuzzy logic, neural networks and genetic algorithms. Another point of view is to study intelligent control systems concerning their characteristics. The heart of a control system is the control laws, whether the control system is intelligent or not. An analysis of control laws suggests that they are passive to the control system's goal of minimizing the variation from a pre-determined path and/or the finishing position. It is additional characteristic in the current hypothesis of automatic control to consider control laws to be portion of a broader control strategy for the whole system (Meystel & Messina, 2000).

The ambiguity and estimated reasoning are the two main concerns of Fuzzy logic (FL), learning and curve fitting are the concerns of Neural Networks (NN) where as searching and optimization are the concerns of Evolutionary Computation (EC). The constituents of soft computing constituents oppose each other instead of being cooperative (Rudas & Fodor, 2008).

REFERENCES

Abdelwahed, S., Bai, J., Su, R., & Kandasamy, N. (2009). On the application of predictive control techniques for adaptive performance management of computing systems. *IEEE Transactions on* Network and Service Management, *6*(4), 212–225.

Ahmadzade, B., Shahgholian, G., Tehrani, F. M., & Mahdavian, M. (2011, August). Model predictive control to improve power system oscillations of SMIB with fuzzy logic controller. In *Proceedings of Electrical Machines and Systems* (ICEMS), (pp. 1-5). IEEE. doi:10.1109/ICEMS.2011.6073337

Albus, J. S. (1995, March). RCS: A reference model architecture for intelligent systems. In *Proceedings of AAAI Spring Symposium on Lessons Learned for Implemented Software Architectures for Physical Agents* (pp. 1-6). AAAI.

Albus, J. S., & Barbera, A. J. (2005). RCS: A cognitive architecture for intelligent multi-agent systems. *Annual Reviews in Control*, *29*(1), 87–99. doi:10.1016/j.arcontrol.2004.12.003

Albus, J. S., & Rippey, W. G. (1994, September). RCS: A reference model architecture for intelligent control. In *Proceedings of From Perception to Action Conference*, (pp. 218-229). IEEE. doi:10.1109/2.144396

Antsaklis, P. J. (1999). Intelligent control. In Wiley encyclopedia of electrical and electronics engineering. Wiley.

Baheti, R., & Gill, H. (2011). Cyber-physical systems. In *The impact of control technology*, (pp. 161-166). Academic Press.

Gorinevsky, D. (2005). A lecture on model predictive control. *IndaBook*. Retrieved from www.indabook.org/d/Model-Predictive-Control.pdf

Krishnakumar, K. (2003). *Intelligent systems for aerospace engineering-an overview*. National Aeronautics And Space Administration Moffett Field Ca Ames Research Center.

Merritt, R. (2005). *Control system architectures: Remote control*. Retrieved from http://www.controlglobal.com/articles/2005/417/

Meystel, A., & Messina, E. (2000). The challenge of intelligent systems. In *Proceedings of Intelligent Control*, (pp. 211-216). IEEE.

Nikolaou, M. (2001). Model predictive controllers: A critical synthesis of theory and industrial needs. *Advances in Chemical Engineering*, *26*, 131–204. doi:10.1016/S0065-2377(01)26003-7

Phan, L. T., & Lee, I. (2011, August). Towards a compositional multi-modal framework for adaptive cyber-physical systems. In *Proceedings of Embedded and Real-Time Computing Systems and Applications* (RTCSA), (vol. 2, pp. 67-73). IEEE. doi:10.1109/RTCSA.2011.82

Quintero, R., & Barbera, A. J. (1992). *A real-time control system methodology for developing intelligent control systems*. Academic Press.

Quintero, R., & Barbera, A. J. (1993, August). A software template approach to building complex large-scale intelligent control systems. In *Proceedings of Intelligent Control*, (pp. 58-63). IEEE. doi:10.1109/ISIC.1993.397723

Rudas, I. J., & Fodor, J. (2008). Intelligent systems. *International Journal of Computers, Communications & Control*, *3*(3).

Sebaa, K., Moulahoum, S., Houassine, H., & Kabache, N. (2012, May). Model predictive control to improve the power system stability. In *Proceedings of Optimization of Electrical and Electronic Equipment* (OPTIM), (pp. 208-212). IEEE. doi:10.1109/OPTIM.2012.6231972

Sundar, S. S., & Lee, E. A. (Eds.). (2012). *Proceedings of the NIST CPS Workshop*. Chicago: NIST.

TM5-601, Department of the Army. (2006). Supervisory control and data acquisition (SCADA) systems for command, control, communications, computer, intelligence, surveillance and reconnaissance (C4ISR). *Facilities*, *21*. Retrieved from http://wbdg.org/ccb/ARMYCOE/COETM/tm_5_601.pdf

Zhang, L. (2012). Aspect-oriented formal techniques of cyber physical systems. *Journal of Software*, *7*(4), 823–834. doi:10.4304/jsw.7.4.823-834

ADDITIONAL READING

Cao, X., Cheng, P., Chen, J., & Sun, Y. (2013). An online optimization approach for control and communication codesign in networked cyber-physical systems. *IEEE Transactions on* Industrial Informatics, *9*(1), 439–450.

Engelbrecht, A. P. (2007). *Computational intelligence: An introduction*. John Wiley & Sons. doi:10.1002/9780470512517

García, M. R., Vilas, C., Santos, L. O., & Alonso, A. A. (2012). A robust multi-model predictive controller for distributed parameter systems. *Journal of Process Control*, *22*(1), 60–71. doi:10.1016/j.jprocont.2011.10.008

Hill, J., Szewczyk, R., Woo, A., Hollar, S., Culler, D., & Pister, K. (2000, November). System architecture directions for networked sensors. *Operating Systems Review*, *34*(5), 93–104. doi:10.1145/384264.379006

KEY TERMS AND DEFINITIONS

Adaptive Control: A control method used by a controller which must adapt to a controlled system with parameters which vary.

AI: Artificial Intelligence is a technology that studies and develops intelligent machines and software.

Fuzzy Logic: It deals with reasoning that is approximate rather than fixed and exact.

Intelligent Control System: A system with a class of control techniques that use various AI computing approaches.

Intelligent System: A system decides which action to be performed based on the knowledge gained.

Neural Networks: Compute values from inputs by feeding information through the network.

OEM: Original Equipment Manufacture is a company whose products are used as components in another company's product.

Soft Computing: A process which is characterized by the use of inexact solutions to computationally hard tasks.

Chapter 15
Cyber Physical Systems Management

ABSTRACT

Most of the systems are unsuccessful during integration due to insignificant consequences occurring in them. This is due to lack of system scalability that fails to provide an improved workload of the system. This chapter describes the parameters to be measured while evaluating the scalability of the structure. The parameters to be measured are described in a scalability review that represents the problems in it. The primary requirement of CPSs is system reliability because an unreliable system yields service interruption and financial cost. A CPS cannot be set up in critical applications in which system reliability and predictability are inefficient. To provide safety critical systems, a high volume of data is dealt, containing operator-in-loop and operating online constantly. The combined characteristics of physical and computational components allow CPSs to use hybrid dynamical models to integrate discrete and continuous state variables that use computational tools to resolve composite problems.

INTRODUCTION

In modern times, the recent and emerging trends enabled the researches to view the complex engineering systems in a different direction. Previously the focus is only on the computational system elements but now it has been extended to the system level and also the interaction of the system with the environment in which it functions. Cyber Physical System is evolved from this new visualization which integrates both the computational and the physical processes and makes the representation of the system to be more practical. As it is becoming more realistic, the analysis, design, testing, monitoring and maintenance become more challenging. The operational flexibility and the efficient resource management are possible only by making such systems as self-managing systems. The more complex and the non-stop functioning in the flexible environment can be carried out only just by increasing the complexity of the CPS. Ultimately, this leads CPS to design with autonomic computing and self-management technology which also turn out to be an attractive area for researchers. Some of the Cyber Physical Systems and autonomic management include

DOI: 10.4018/978-1-4666-7312-0.ch015

Hybrid modelling and fusion of models, Formal modelling methods, Requirements analysis, architecture and implementation and so on.

Restful Management for Cyber Physical Systems

The integration of the physical world and the cyber world is the main focus of the Cyber Physical Systems and should be able to provide continuously reliable services (Zhang,Cai & Zhu, 2012). On the other hand, the physical have its own complexity, ambiguities and many numbers of mobile devices, different kinds of controlled and heterogeneous devices are coming into sight.

Various services and different levels of services like single user to multinational companies, user should be able access any service irrespective of their devices, technology and location are to be provided to different users by Cyber Physical Systems. The users will have a choice of choosing the service providers to obtain the services which are simple, customized and independent. These various constraints impose enormous challenges in managing the CPS. Presently, there is a wide usage of the applications which are based on web. The connectivity in CPS can be attained by using a latent approach as Web-of-Things (WoT) approach. The collection of web services is determined, compiled or created and implemented with the help of WoT approach.

The vision of WoT can be achieved in two steps. In the first step, various kinds of physical things are integrated with Web. In the second step, the concept of devices is converted into interoperable and reusable web services and the services are made more intellectual by organizing different kinds of web services.

At present, there are two ways to integrate a variety of devices to the web known as direct integration and indirect integration. In direct integration, devices which are IP enabled and are also embedded with web server are integrated with web (Zeng, Guo, & Cheng, 2011). Indirect integration is used in the case where devices with very less number of resources and embedded with the web server or in the case where all the devices need not required to be integrated with web with the consideration of cost, energy and security. The World Wide Web Consortium (W3C) introduces two paradigms of web services to abstract the devices. They are RESTComplaint web services and arbitrary web services. In RESTComplaint web services, the design style followed is "REpresentational State Transfer" (REST) (Zhang et al., 2012), where a set of stateless operations which are homogenous are used in controlling the web resources.

The properties like interoperability and simplicity in managing CPS are achieved by implementing it based on the idea on WoT. There are two types of entities in this context referred as manager and agent. The manager is an entity which manages and the agent is an entity which is being managed. The integration of these two entities is carried out by RESTful (Zhang et al., 2012) management of CPS. The existing management information is used in the process of integrating administration elements to the web and the generalization of the incorporated administration substances to Restful web services.

The requirements of the distributed CPS are satisfied by a five layer framework whose design is based on the Representational State Transfer design style. The aim of this framework is enabling the cyber world to monitor, investigate, realize and manage the physical world. It permits the cyber world to carry out the tasks where the time factor plays a major role using the data obtained. The architecture of the CPS becomes as a foundation of this five layer framework which highlights the significance of the context-aware information-centric CPS protocol stack (Zhang et al., 2012).

RESTful web services are said to be both service-oriented and resource-oriented. According to the concept of REST, each resource is identified with a name and a depiction. Hyperlinks are used to connect various resources with each other. A client receives the resource depiction in the form of image or symbol when there is a request from the corresponding resource.

The design of the RESTful web services consists of two steps. In first step, the data set based on which the service will function is identified. In the second step, the identified data set are used to determine the resources. For each resource, the design principles of REST have four steps as given below (Zhang et al., 2012):

- **The First Action:** The resource is to be named with a URI.
- **The Second Action:** The part of the standardized interface is identified which is assumed to be exposed by the resource.
- **The Third Action:** Devise the depiction(s) of the resource.
- **The Fourth Action:** Determine the ordinary course of actions by examining how the service performs and what happens throughout a thriving implementation.

The overhead of the management entities in CPS can be handled by added intricate and intelligent management services using various other technologies.

BACKGROUND

Scalability

In general, the property of the CPS integrating the physical process to the computational process makes it to be heterogeneous. CPS is heterogeneous even in the case of integrating the physical and the cyber domains. As the physical domain may integrate the mechanical motion control, chemical processes, biological processes, human operators etc., it might be termed as multi-physics. The networking technologies, programming languages, software component models, concurrency mechanisms etc., may be integrated in the case of the cyber domain.

In CPS, the methodologies and the tools followed for the design process should be able to sustain different levels of designs from small scale designs to large scale designs, smooth the process of analysis and make the understanding of the complex system to be simpler.

Some of the challenges are listed below:

- Systems engineering;
- Software engineering processes;
- Software engineering technologies (refactoring tools, program analysis, etc.);
- Design tools;
- Co-simulation technologies;
- Model exchange.

The software systems which interact and communicate with the dynamic and unpredictable physical environment in the open contexts need to be discovered, designed and implemented to be error free, efficient and flexible. But this is a very big challenging problem. An alternative of a single software segment can be expressed, examined and realized by many of the existing techniques. Techniques like model checking, mathematical analyses and countless derivative tools throw light on many local invariants (e.g., well-formed output, minimum throughput, maximum response time, etc.) (Bestavros, Bradley, Kfoury, & Matta, 2005).

There is a fairly good handle which shows the way the single software components view in case of different invariant properties and the way to express and test them. The description, testing and realization of the global invariants in open, extensible software systems are not yet a solid grasp. Similarly, bridging the gap between the local and the global invariants is a challenging task. The acceptable range of behaviours and the emergent properties (Bestavros et al., 2005) like timeliness, stability, convergence, freedom from deadlocks, fairness etc are described by the global invariants during the interaction of the system with the components or agents .

There is a chance of the systems to become faulty during the initial stages of the system use or when in the stage of integration. Similarly, the level is also is an important factor to be considered as the negligible effects will have less impact while the systems are operated under fewer loads but will have considerable impact while the systems are operated under heavy loads. This inability of the system to work for various loads referred as scalability has been there since many years.

Defining Scalability

The ability of the system (hardware or software) to handle various workloads without the variation in the system resources by repeatedly applying a cost effective strategy to extend the system's capacity is defined as scalability (Weinstock & Goodenough, 2006). When the system is designed to work on heavy loads, it must be able to work on fewer loads also and vice versa.

Some of the examples of scalability failures are listed below:

- Available address space is exceeded.
- Memory is overloaded.
- Available network bandwidth is exceeded.
- An internal table is filled.

The addition of new resources to the system may become as overhead instead of solving the scalability problem. For instance increase in the number of processes may be overhead instead of enabling the system to meet the additional demand.

When there is a requirement of more number of resources than that are available or than that the system can accommodate, then the scalability problems may rise. The scalability problem is serious in the human operated systems or autonomic computing systems.

A More Complex Concept: Scalability by Extension (Weinstock & Goodenough, 2006)

According to the definition of scalability, one-time increase in capacity is a strategy that is applied and the number of times that strategy can be applied. For example increase in the number of processors to support heavy workloads on the system is a strategy. How many processors can be added without reducing the efficiency? The increment in the number of processors makes the coordination among the added processors to be tedious. The addition of processors for more number of times will not benefit in increasing the system capacity as it is not cost-effective.

The Interdependency of Resources and Scalability (Weinstock & Goodenough, 2006)

Scalability is not pertained only to a single resource. When a complex system is utilizing a number of different resources and a limitation of any one of the resources may lead to the system to experience the scalability problem. In such cases, identification of the resources that can be increased in capacity is to be carried out carefully. The trade off with the attributes of the system is required during the development of the scalable system. The higher levels of operation can be accomplished at the expense of the price, performance, usability or any other important attribute.

Performance vs. Scalability

The increase in the demand or the complexity of the system beyond the threshold level in non-scalable systems degrades the performance of the system. The overall system performance can be improved by sacrificing the negligible level of performance at the lower levels which increases the performance at higher levels. So, the design of the system will be carried out in such a way that it supports during the higher levels of usage or complexity which might be introduces later at the expense of negligible level of some performance at the initial stages. The designer must be cautious about the level of the performance need to be relinquished and this trade off is used to support the definition of scalability.

Cost vs. Scalability

The system with more scaling capability is more expensive when compared to the system with less scaling capability. So, the customer who can invest less need to choose less scalable design and which can be upgraded later without efforts but the cost of modifying will be extreme and sometimes which may be unfeasible. On the other hand, if the customer can invest more and choose the more scalable design, the cost for the design process would go waste if the expected level of demand never occurs. The scalable requirements in the RFP and an approach in estimating the cost for different scenarios would help in taking a decision of level scalable to be incorporated in the system design.

Operability vs. Scalability

It is difficult to manage the integrated or distributed systems as they grow larger and larger. Autonomic computing and man operated systems is the emergent significance of this phenomenon. The human control of the system is the tradeoff between operability and the scalability. The small amount of human control needs to be sacrificed in order to achieve the required levels of scalability. When the system requires higher levels of scalability, there is a chance of system becoming unmanageable, i.e., which cannot be managed by the human.

Functionality (Usability) vs. Scalability

There is a possibility for the system to be more scalable when it is providing less service. The system offering different levels of functionality may be designed to be less scalable. The system can be designed to be scalable at the expense of other attributes of the system.

How Capacity Can Be Improved

Once the design of the system is completed, it need to be tested the workload that the system can handle and the extent to which it can withstand the increment in the work load determines the level of the scalability. To improve the scalability of the system, there are two ways. One way is without adding additional resources and the other way is adding more resources. Examples in the first case, i.e., without adding the additional resources are enhancing an algorithm, altering a data structure, or the decreasing the quantity of work that the system need to perform by reducing the functionalities that the system can provide (Weinstock & Goodenough, 2006). Example in the second case is the addition of processors during heavy loads.

There may be different number of strategies to make the system more scalable. The strategy which increases the system capacity is more or less dependent on the cost of the system. So, the strategy which is cost-effective needs to be applied in order to increase the system capacity during heavy workload to make the system more scalable. The increase in the system capacity in order to make the system more scalable must be cost-effective. For instance a big company can effort to invest for 32-bit event-ID as the server on which the system runs might have more disk space but a small company which have limited funds cannot effort to buy a disk with larger capacity (Weinstock & Goodenough, 2006).

A Scalability Audit

Various factors need to be considered during the assessment of the system in terms of scalability. The designer need to be careful while applying the determined strategy to increase the system capacity and observe that whether the significant factors to be considered are addressed properly or not. Cost effectiveness is the important parameter to be concentrated in order to make the system to be able to increase its capacity. This process is referred as scalability audit.

A scalability audit (Weinstock & Goodenough, 2006) is performed on the system to verify whether the architectural design of the system can be effectively improved to support heavy workloads over its predictable life-time or strong enough to withstand an unexpected and considerable increase in workload. The damage to the system might be severe or terrible when there is an increase in the workload if the system fails to handle the situation.

The scalability audit is found to be useful when conducted in two situations:

1. The significant increase of the load needs to be supported by the system over its existence.
2. The system is sensitive in some cases and the failure may cause serious damage to the system. In this case, the system needs to be evaluated how probable the system is likely to fail under unforeseen load conditions.

Before the system is implemented or the redesign being taken place, the scalability audit needs to be performed in either situation.

There are four subparts into which the audit questions are categorized and which are not completely exclusive from each other:

1. The strategy for identifying and relieving the potential resource bottlenecks.
2. How the incorrect assumptions about the scaling strategy are revealed.
3. The strengths and weaknesses of the general scaling strategies.
4. Assurance methods for supervising the confidence in the scalability strategy.

Resource Bottlenecks

The identification and justification of the bottlenecks is one of the important issues in case of the scalability issues. The scalability of the system is improved by tuning the performance which aims at efficient use of the existing resources. The system can support more load than it is intended to when the algorithm is modified. For example if the algorithm with time complexity, O (n log n) is replaced with an algorithm whose time complexity is $O(n^2)$ then the system satisfies the load more than that it can support.

The tuning becomes tedious when it is not identified where the focus is needed. The point of focus is determined when the actual workload and actual measurements are known from the implementation by effectively using a tuning approach. However, the focus point is not the after-the-fact tuning analysis. The type of questions that need to be investigated to determine the probable resource bottlenecks when the scalability audit is performed before implementing the system.

- **Administrative Bottlenecks:** How do the administrative workload effects with an increase in the system workload? Is the growth of the administrative staff is directly proportional to the growth of the workload? Is any analysis has been carried out with respect to the workload which is associated to the system administration?
- **Limitations of the Capacity:** What are the considerations related to the limitations of the capacity? For example, consider the capacity of the system to be 64000 data entries. If the capacity limit is exceeded more than 64000 data entries, then what is the

level of the impact on the system and to which level the architecture of the system need to upgraded?

- **Client Interface:** The quantity of data that must be accessible to a client utilizing one of the interfaces will be taken into account (Weinstock & Goodenough, 2006).

Revealing Scaling Hypothesis

Aspects that are barely noticeable when a system is moderately small turn out to be critical as the system expands. These aspects demonstrate how the development of a system can uncover new issues that are required to be taken into account by a scaling procedure (Weinstock & Goodenough, 2006).

- The details about the system's configuration (software and hardware together) are prone to hold faults as the system gets extend. Except a proper mechanism is utilized, it is progressively hard to reveal these faults. On the off chance that the system for sustaining or overhauling a system holds (hidden) suspicions that the configuration data is right or that configuration distortion is inside boundary points of confinement, there may be considerable issues to experience these inaccurate suppositions as system develops.
- There is a chance of increasing the frequency of failures which occur rarely when the system extends or as there is an overload. This happens as the circumstances beneath they take place turn out to be more recurrent. For instance, an event state may appear just once out of a million transactions. Hence there is a chance of "rare" fault to arise every day on an average with increase in the system's load to the intensity of million transactions daily. As the rate at which faults arise is proportionate to the quantity, the frequency of hardware faults raise as the hardware quantity increases.
- The system design is significant to restrict the effect of failures as the system becomes larger and larger. The failure may humiliate the entire system when it is small but this should not be the case as the system grows. On the other hand, some kind of mechanism need to be incorporated in order to guarantee the user that the considerable amount of work is not lost and hence redoing can be avoided when the system starts to work normally.
- As a system extends, it can get perplexing and hard to comprehend unless suitable methods are set up to decrease the amount of communications that help to system activities.

Scaling Strategies

The scaling strategies are evaluated to determine their limitations using the following methods (Weinstock & Goodenough, 2006):

- The hypotheses about the system utilization which are made in the initial stage need to be changed when a system need to last for long time. The continuation of the usage of the assured prototypes may be assumed by the scaling strategy.
    - How perceptive are these hypotheses to conceivable modifications in utilization designs, and how probable are those progressions?
    - Is there a methodology set up to track utilization designs so that re-assessment of the scaling method could be focused around real information?

 - How do modifications in forms of utilization influence the nature of the limit that needs to be included?
 - What resources are focused by progressions in variety and quantity of utilization? Is the procedure vigorous against a diversity of conceivable changes in utilization designs?
- The scaling technique may rely on upon clients not exploiting information about how the system is realized. (For instance, the significant guess made by applications about where the specific code is accomplished make the load rebalancing to be much simple).
 - What exactly is the degree to which the scaling procedure is perceptive to clients having the capacity to "look behind the curtain" to exploit apparently concealed data?
- The assumptions regarding the viewpoints like capacity of the devices, supporting devices will be altering throughout the life of the system. The modification in utilization designs may be because of the modifications in hardware capabilities. For instance, the capacity of utilization changes because of the changes in the capacity of the disk. Thus, distinctive computational requests on a system may be due to alternate usage. For instance, multimedia applications are possible if the disk size is expanded and the speed is increased (Weinstock & Goodenough, 2006).
 - Has the hardware patterns are used in the evaluation process of scaling strategy?
- The system is to be organized in order to support numerous user environments if the intention of the scaling strategy is to make the system be used by numerous users. If the environment of the systems' software (operating system, database technology and middleware) is to be altered, the system needs to be portable.
- Try to find "infinite" hypotheses in the system (i.e., hypotheses so as to some bound on demand will never be exceeded). Every system has some upper limits on specifications such as file size or number of database fields. When these limits begin to be approached, the system may be stressed and begin to fail more often or totally. Some examples of such assumptions are as follows: a certain type of file can be completely processed in memory; there will never be more than X transactions processed in a certain time period; or no file will ever need to be more than X bytes. Various problems have been experienced by real systems when these (usually unexamined) limits were exceeded.
 - What is the existing limit cut-off? How those limits are identified with usage and utilization development assumptions?
 - If the resources are expected to have expansive capacities, then what are their decentralized asserts? The limit of the capacity is attained very rapidly if everybody expects that the aggregate limit is accessible (Weinstock & Goodenough, 2006).

Mechanisms which Guarantee Scalability

There is no accepted approach to analyze if a system is adaptable. It is normally difficult to create a practical load—substantially less to really add processing ability to check whether the designed scaling technique will work efficiently. Adaptability confirmation addresses the techniques set up to give more significant trust that a designed scaling method will work or, on the off chance that it won't work, to give an early cautioning that issues (Weinstock & Goodenough, 2006) are upcoming.

- Observe the performance of the different resources for varying requests. How is the performance described as curves - O(n), O(n^2), or O(n log n)? How do the performance of the specific scaling technique is effect with the increase in the capacity?
- Strategies to uncover the bottlenecks are to be discovered or the point at which the assumptions of the scaling design are starting to be abused. What are the existing routines for evaluating patterns that are important to design decisions? (Weinstock & Goodenough, 2006)
- Strengths, Weaknesses, Opportunities, Threats (SWOT) (Weinstock & Goodenough, 2006) study is a tool which is used plan strategies utilized in assessing scheme and business enterprises. This technique is projected here almost as an intension to examine scalability. Carry out a SWOT9 investigation on the scalability mechanism:
    - **Strengths:** The sorts of development the methodology is intended to handle.
    - **Weaknesses:** Development that would not be taken care of by the procedure effectively.
    - **Opportunities:** Conceivable changes in workload or innovation that the technique would have the capacity to adventure truly well.
    - **Threats:** Conceivable changes in the workload or innovation that would lay the technique in uncertainty.

The capability or failure of the systems to manage with the problem of scaling is getting to be progressively imperative. The failure of the considerable number of systems might happen during their initial stage of usage or during the process of integration. This is due to the reason that the effect of some of the parameters is minor when the system usage is less and major when the system usage is high. This scalability issues is not new (Weinstock & Goodenough, 2006).

Scalability could be characterized as the capacity to handle expanded workload (without increasing the number of resources of a system). It is the capacity to hold with the expanded workload by using a cost-effective method again and again for enlarging the capacity of the system. If any of the resource of the system is over-stacked or depleted with the increase in the number of requests to the system, then scalability is said to be unsuccessful.

Scalability audit will concentrate on variables to be measured while evaluating whether a system is liable to be versatile. In the event that the capacity to enhance a system's capability inexpensively is a concern in a system's configuration, then the designers ought to inspect any projected system for expanding ability to check whether all important elements have been addressed accurately. This analysis is referred as a scalability audit.

An scalability audit might be used to assess whether the configuration of a system architecture (1) could be effectively increased to deal with a considerably more load than its foreseen life-time or (2) is powerful as much as necessary to hold an unforeseen, considerable raise in workload where breakdown to handle the expanded workload would be grievous or exceptionally serious for the system (Weinstock & Goodenough, 2006).

RELIABILITY

As the Cyber Physical Systems is an integration of computation and physical system, the range of the systems may vary from the system with significant infrastructure like power grid and shipping to the health and biomedical devices. Reliability (Wu, 2011) is one of the important QoS parameter to be considered in CPS. The unreliable systems may cause many severe problems like interruption of service, economic loss or even loss of life in some cases.

Criteria to be followed in order to improve the performance of CPS in terms of reliability:

- Transforming huge quantity of information,
- Utilizing software as a system element, and
- Non-stop online execution.

The reliable CPSs are significant and ubiquitous. One of the solutions to develop the reliable CPS is automated online evaluation approach. The evaluation of the system is automated at more number of stages in parallel with the operation of the system. The feedback is provided to the operator in the loop to facilitate the improvement of the system reliability. Here, the data is analyzed and evaluated. For example the input and output data is analyzed and the data (input or output) which is irregular are identified and marked. Based on this analysis, the result is sent to the operator in the loop which determines the action to be taken to improve the reliability of the system and achieve minimal system downtime (Wu, 2011).

The data analysis is performed by the computational intelligence in automated and proficient way to guarantee the quality of the data and ensure that the system reliability is improved. The technology like machine learning, data mining, statistical and probabilistic analysis facilitates the computational intelligence. In a cyber physical system, the database is used in order to store data like software bug reports, system status logs and error reports, etc (Wu, 2011). The data mining techniques or any other intelligent techniques are used to analyze the data, identify the erroneous data and segregate the useful information to improve the system reliability. In this method, abnormal states of the system can be eliminated. The functioning of the system is made more reliable by sending this analyzed and correct data to the operator who determines the action to be performed.

Another technique is autonomous. This technique self-manages and self-configures automatically. Hence, it is self-tuning. According to this technique, the system adjusts itself to the changes in it and considers the feedback from the operator to make the system stronger and more reliable.

NOVA (Neutral Online Visualization-aided Autonomic) (Wu, 2011) is a system which analyzes the data to improve the reliability in the case of power grid cyber physical system. This technique makes the system to be able to do robust tests which the system is not able to perform before the actual deployment.

Systems Reliability

The operation of the system is tested using the components of the system (Wu, 2011). The various components in different systems have diversified configurations. The reliability of the system need to be analyzed based on specifically defined concepts. Since the probability concept can only be used in order to say that a particular system of existing two similar systems which are functioning under the same conditions and environments, similar system load may be failed. Hence, the concepts of probability theory are used to define and quantify the QoS parameter, the reliability of the system.

In general, the systems with different reliability are used to perform different functions. At the same time, the probability of performing the function successfully under different conditions by the same system might be different at different times. The inability of the system to perform the required function is referred as "failure".

Reliability Measures

As there are various definitions provided by various researchers, here the general definition of reliability if given:

The probability that the system succeeds or the anticipated function is performed under the given conditions is referred as reliability.

Some more definitions of reliability:

The probability that a part of the system functions properly without any failure for its intended duration of time under the specified conditions is also referred as reliability.

One of the QoS parameter to be guaranteed by the manufacturer of products to the consumers is the reliability.

Maintainability

Maintainability means making the system to work perfectly without any faults and the system must able to be repaired by identifying and correcting the fault in order to make the system perform satisfactorily. The fault component is corrected or substituted with a new component makes the system to reset to its initial state and function in a regular way.

The approved procedures are used to maintain the system and the probability with which the system with fault can be repaired to reset it to particular conditions within a predetermined amount of time is referred as maintainability. Similarly, the probability of separating and fixing the fault of the system within a given time is also known as maintainability.

The maintenance of the system needs to be efficient and effective and which need to be guaranteed by the system designers in combination with the system engineers. Analysis of the failed part of the system needs to be carried out in terms of the required time to remove the specific part or replace the part and rebuild the product to restore the operation, the technology required and the tools required in order to maintain the system.

Availability

Reliability is a measure that the system needs to operate successfully for a specified amount of time. In this regard, no failures must be occurred and there must be no requirement for repairs. For instance failures are not encouraged in the case of space missions and aircraft flights as it cause a serious problem. Hence, the reliability needs to be high in these applications. The possibility of the system to be repaired when failure occurs is referred as availability.

System Reliability with Multiple Failure Modes

Multiple types of failures may be caused due to the different features of reliability and optimization of the system. It is believed that the state of the components in the system is independent and is distributed identically. For example relay networks, diode circuits, fluid flow valves, etc., are the systems where the failure may occur in different modes like open or closed modes.

The reliability of the system can be improved without any variation in the reliability of the individual components of the system with the use of redundancy. There is a chance that redundancy may improve or degrade in the reliability of the system in the case of two-failure mode problem. Hence, the reliability of the system is not related to the number of components of the system, i.e., reliability of the system may not be increased by increasing the number of the components of the system.

Reliability Calculations

Some of the components of the system will have the ability to determine the functionality of the system. The components of different systems may have different types of configurations (Pham, 2007):

- **Series System:** All the components of this type of system will be cascaded to each other. So, all the components need to work in order to operate the system successfully. Otherwise, if any of the components is failed, the operation of the system cannot be continued.

- **Parallel System:** Here, all the components work in parallel. Hence, malfunction of one section does not influence the operation of the system and the system fails only if all the components fail.
- **Series-Parallel System:** Here, some of the components which are connected in series are made redundant to be operated in parallel.

Reliability of Series System

Consider a scenario where 'n' components of a system are connected in a series fashion. In open mode, failure of one component leads to the failure of the system whereas in close mode, failure of all components only can lead to the failure of the system (Pham, 2007).

Example:

The three main components of the computer system are memory, CPU and I/O device. It is evident that the computer works properly only if all the components are working without any fail. Let us assume that the probability of the memory functioning properly is 0.98, CPU is 0.96 and the I/O device is 0.97.

The probability that the computer will operate adequately is:

$$Rel = 0.98 \times 0.96 \times 0.97 = 0.912576$$

It can be observed that the reliability of all components is greater than 95% but still the reliability of the computer is less than 95%.

This is a sample example where the system with three components is considered and connected in series fashion. In this example, it can be realized that the system reliability is much less than the reliability of the individual components. But in general the systems like computing and electrical systems will have hundreds and thousands of components. If the components are connected in series, the high reliability of the individual components of the system does not lead to the high reliability of the system; instead it may not be sufficient also.

Reliability of a Parallel System

The redundancy of the equipments will be there in the case of parallel systems. So, the operation of the system can be continued even when any of these cease to perform its task (Pham, 2007).

Example

A system which has five components with parallel connection among them is considered. If the reliability of the five components of the system is 0.98, then the calculation of the reliability of the system is the Figure 2.

The system will continue operating until all the components fail. Hence,

Rel = P(At least one component is functioning).

Taking the complementary approach,

P(at least one component functioning) = 1- P(all components fail).

Figure 1. Probability of system functioning

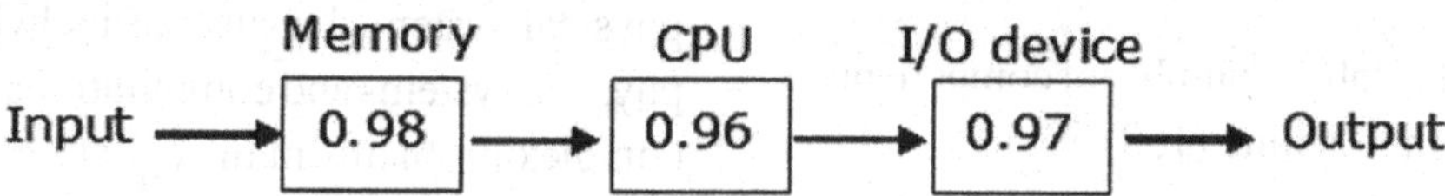

Figure 2. Calculation of system reliability

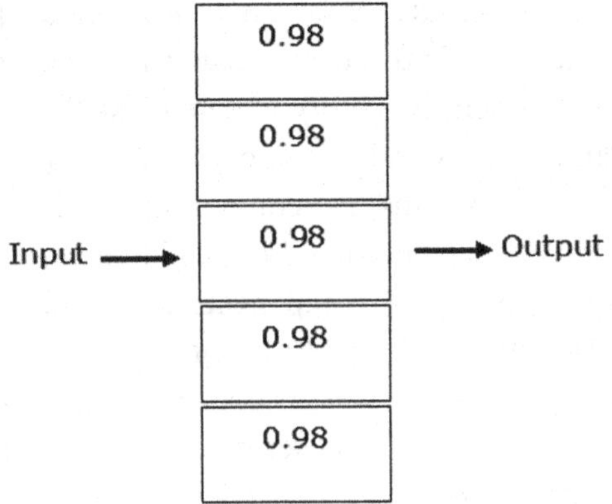

If all the components of the systems fail, then the reliability of the system is

$Rel = 1 - (0.02)^5 = 0.999999997$.

With parallel systems the "law of diminishing returns" operates:

- With first 2 components Rel = 1 – (0.02) * (0.02) = 0.9996
- With first 3 components Rel = 1 – (0.02) * (0.02) * (0.02) = 0.999992
- With first 4 components Rel = 1 – (0.02) * (0.02) * (0.02) * (0.02) = 0.9999999841

Parallel system reliability is proportionate to the quantity of components.

Number of Components

Reliability

k<-1:10

p <- .97

plot (k, 1-(1-p)^k, xlab = "Number of components: ylab = "Reliability")abline (1, 0).

Series-Parallel Systems

Example

Consider a system with 5 kinds of component, with reliabilities:

- Component 1: 0.97,
- Component 2: 0.72,
- Component 3: 0.93,
- Component 4: 0.96,
- Component 5: 0.63.

In this scenario, the component 2 and the component 5 are having low reliability and need to be made redundant.

The System

In R:

$0.97 * (1 - (0.28)^2) * 0.93 * 0.96 * (1- (0.37)^3) = 0.97 * 0.9216 * 0.93 * 0.96 * 0.949347 = 0.7576693155$

The reliability of the individual components of the system and the type of the system determines the reliability of the system.

TOOLS AND TECHNIQUES

Computational Tools for Cyber Physical Systems

The integration and the tight coordination of physical systems with the computational system lead to cyber physical systems. The dynamic hybrid model which includes both continues states and discrete states are used in modelling the cyber physical systems because of its hybrid nature of physical systems and computational systems. The complex problems in the cyber physical systems

Figure 3. Sample scenario for series parallel system

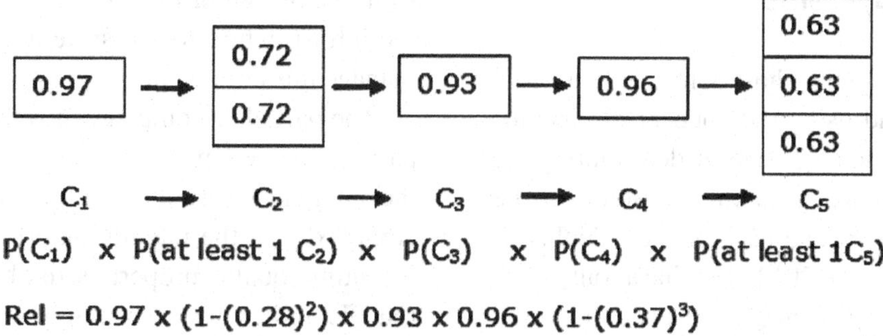

perspective are solved by applying the optimal control algorithms.

Three computational tools that are used to add the abilities of the hybrid dynamic models and optimal control algorithms to the cyber physical system applications are listed below (Gonzalez,2012):

- Optimizes switched hybrid dynamic system under prescribed conditions.
- The route of hybrid dynamic systems is approximated.
- The pseudo spectral approximations are used to compute the optimal control of a nonlinear dynamic system.

The widely used algorithms are extended to new classes of dynamic systems using these tools. The new tools which are computationally efficient in the field of hybrid dynamic systems can be developed by applying mathematical techniques.

The control theory fundamental results are used to address some of the problems of the cyber physical systems.

The cyber physical systems can be controlled and analyzed in two different ways (Gonzalez, 2012):

1. Mathematical model of cyber physical systems can be developed using hybrid dynamic systems.
2. Hybrid dynamic models are solved using the computational developed optimal control algorithms.

Hybrid Dynamical Models

When the states of a dynamical system contain the variables that can hold both the continuous and discrete values, then it is said to be a hybrid system (Gonzalez,2012). In classical systems, differential equations are used to model the dynamics of continuous variables and the finite state machines are used to model the dynamics of discrete variables. Since both the dynamics of continuous and discrete variables need to be modelled in the dynamical system, the theories of both the differential equations and the finite state machines need to be incorporated into a single framework.

This new framework introduces many hypothetical challenges but it can be used to depict the fact which cannot be done by the differential equations. Some of the challenges are the non-unique and non-continuous trajectories produced by the hybrid systems for a given specific conditions and continuous inputs. These challenges which are not able to be solved by the existing tools are the key points in order to introduce new tools whose design is carried out based on the hybrid systems.

Optimal Control of Dynamical Systems

The extreme mappings whose domain is functional spaces are found using the concept of calculus of variations. The challenge of determining the optimal control of a dynamical system can be considered as a special case of the calculus of variations (Gonzalez, 2012). Finding a control law which is used to determine the constraints used to define a certain criteria are satisfied and which is used to minimize the real range of an objective function of a specific dynamical system is the main challenge of the optimal control.

The optimal control algorithms can be used to solve many problems in the context of cyber physical systems. For instance safety and performance of the system can be guaranteed while performing the scheduling in the electric power grid systems using the optimal control algorithms.

However, there exists a gap between the formulation of these problems and the ability to solve them because the existing optimal control algorithms are not completely compatible with the hybrid dynamic systems and the scaling problems also come into existence.

Techniques

The challenges of CPS to provide the required quality are listed below (Ermagan, Krüger, & Menarini, 2006):

- Integration complexity,
- System assurance, and
- Agility demands.

These challenges lead to develop the next generation CPS with a definite rational demand of the related issues. The challenge of system integration is said to be multi-dimensional as CPS integrates the IT and physical components and also integrates the abilities of individual system into a single complex system. An extensive range of skills, techniques and technologies varying from the design of the architecture to providing the infrastructure to the system are required to manage this complexity.

The partial or complete knowledge about the parts of the system is required while developing the integrated systems in order to manage the complexity of the integration effectively. In the meantime, quality properties, like breakdown and risk flexibility are exceedingly cross-cutting in nature (Ermagan et al., 2006). A widespread end-to-end software and systems engineering approach and a model based strategy to software and systems engineering are required in order to overcome the three major limitations of complexity during integration. This will essentially integrate parts of system with the suitable tooling, and comparing middleware infrastructure to release a number of the requests, cross-cutting, high trust quality necessities by relieving them from architectural design (Ermagan et al., 2006).

The three research challenges identified in order to make advancement towards a comprehensive engineering approach are given below:

- Methods, systems, and instruments for prerequisites and configuration space conception for high-confidence systems of systems.
- Methods and devices for fast architecture configuration, investigation, execution and quality certification under incomplete knowledge about interfaces and quality properties of subsystems.
- Techniques and instruments for quick composition, configuration and re-design of systems of systems architectures to address agility requests throughout both design and run-time (Ermagan et al., 2006).

Promising Innovations and Abstractions

During recent years, there is a promising research carried out in the regard of service-oriented approaches. Based on the services exhibited by the subsystems of integrated system, the rapid, flexible composition of subsystems is enabled using the service-oriented approaches. They are used in the extensive advancement in development of business intelligence systems and also in the process of makeover in the area of embedded systems. It has the ability to integrate itself with the cyber physical systems.

The improvement in the Model-Driven Architecture (MDA) (I.H.Krüger et al, 2006) and Model-Driven Design (MDD) (I.H.Krüger et al, 2006) makes the idea of reflective, highly reconfigurable and adaptive systems to be almost real. The extraction of the appropriate models of the subsystems and the extraction of the infrastructure of integration in order to capture the QoS properties and obtain the solution of 3/3 concrete integrated systems of systems.

The partiality and assurance demands of CPS are addressed by the integration of service oriented development techniques and MDA/MDD techniques. The complexity of the CPS can be reduced using the services which are defined by partial interaction patterns. The complete components need not taken into consideration, instead only the specific services which are required are considered for an integration solution. The validation and the verification of the level of assurance of the integrated solution are enabled by capturing the required information about the quality demands by the service interfaces. The subsequent contribution to the MDA/MDD approach during the design and runtime makes the quality demand information to be obtainable. This would probably direct to a multi-dimensional perceptive of systems of systems, such that services emerge as the location for cross-cutting behaviour and quality aspects within an integration solution (Ermagan et al., 2006).

Cyber Physical Systems of Systems

In systems engineering field Systems of Systems (SoS) (Maier, 1998) is a latest concept, which has certain characteristics like self-government of system components with respect to operation and management. Systems of systems enlighten on rising performance and growth processes of systems. According to (Jamshidi, 2009) systems of systems is a combination of dissimilar systems which are connected together to reach its goal for a specified period. The main purpose is to provide services to the whole system; where as a single system cannot provide the function in an effective manner. In systems of systems the components can easily be linked and disconnected so that it can be dynamically reconstituted. This key point is a main characteristic of systems of systems.

Systems of systems follow the concept of partial self-government of various components which is referred as autonomy (Engell, 2014). It does not mean that it is fully automated without any human intervention. In few areas administration and involvement of human is required in the whole system along with its subsystems also. This is to improvise the system in a translucent way to avoid the unexpected results arising from the systems. From an manufacturing point of view, systems of systems is a combination of present and new systems abilities to develop, evaluate and systemize, which is referred as Systems of Systems Engineering (SOSE) (Engell, 2014).

SOSE is derived from dissimilar disciplines to tackle the uncertain composite circumstances (Sousa-Poza, Kovacic, & Keating, 2008). Since Cyber Physical systems are tightly coupled with real time and physical systems, it is sometimes called as embedded systems. Because implanted systems mostly relies on connectivity with the physical world through internet. Now we consider cyber physical systems as huge composite physical systems that communicate with substantial elements of distributed computing. These elements are helpful in supervising; organizing and managing the information conversed with the humans (Engell, 2014). In physical systems the information of elements are associated with the objects and power, whereas administration and organization of system elements are associated with the transmission networks. Some of the examples of such systems are energy plant, automaton, electrical grid, a structure with disseminated HVAC control, etc (Engell, 2014).

When cyber physical systems include some of the characteristics of systems of systems then it is called Cyber Physical Systems of Systems (CPSoS) (Engell, 2014). The characteristics of CPSoS with description points are:

- **Huge, Automated Composite Disseminated Physical Systems:** Basically an integrated system comprised of partly connected objects that perform definite process, offer a service and produce some results. The whole performance of the system relies on the components, though the elements of a system present service separately. In this regard the physical size of the system in not important. And also it is difficult to derive the complexity of the system. Automobile vehicle with various organizers connected with a transmission system is an example of cyber physical system (Engell, 2014). This is possible when all the components of a vehicle functions together, since there is limited self-determination of subsystems.
- **Manageable, Self Administrative, and Organizable:** Most of the time the organization and management of the processes are carried out either in a vital or hierarchical manner in a system. Because the management and the control functions executed on a real-time complexity are dispersed with power as a particular structure to supervise and manage the whole system. Connection among elements and subsystems of control and supervision systems is an important factor of the largely structure (Engell, 2014). Though many scientific systems provide easy access through internet, but it is required to limit the illegal access against safety, which is a key challenge while designing any system. In CPSoS the supervision and control of the whole system is managed not only by practical measures but also by customer satisfaction and cost of devices. As a whole, system is determined as human-technological structure to provide service at a huge level.
- **Biased Self-Government of Subsystems:** According to the meaning of CPSoS, self-determination of subsystems is to offer particular services separately (Engell, 2014). But subsystems show self-interested method in limited supervision, liking and attaining objective. In this regard the controller or user can derive certain conclusions independently. Moreover the assessment structures of the whole system can be different when it comes to subsystems. As these subsystems function independently to obtain its objectives, the technological and cost-effective factors create a bond among them(Engell, 2014).
- **On Various Time Dimensions Reconstitution of Whole System:** Reconstitution of whole system is nothing but connecting or eliminating modules based on various time dimensions, characteristics, functioning method and purpose to modify the system (Engell, 2014). It incorporates the system on entry

and exit of components to observe errors and alterations that occur in requirements and policies. The significant challenge in this is a management of easily attachable components.

- **Capable of Obtaining Expected Behaviour:** Prevailing behaviour is a collection of expected models, variations in huge systems and the way the system is configured (unpredicted) and connected with the subsystems (Engell, 2014). And also varies in its communication strategies. Expected behaviour is different from errors occur in a system. In other words expected behaviour is an error that leads to total collapse of any system resulting in instability like power failure. In practical this should be avoided as it affect the functioning of the system. So expected behaviour should be focused on design and analysis of a system to face the differences, errors and difficulties that affects the subsystems and its adjacent systems. To avoid such situations systems have to be created with vibrant approaches.
- **Development Process of Overall System Constantly:** CPSoS are huge systems that functions for extended period. In these systems the existence of mechanical and chemical devices are for many years (Engell, 2014). Whereas new methods have to be carried out for enhancing the operation of the system, as software and transmission in structure are quickly changing. So huge systems can be reconstructed with fewer modifications rather than a new structure.

The design of cyber physical systems of systems behaviour should be a combination of representation, investigation and replication methods. The approaches and methods have to be derived from computational systems for generating disseminated distinct systems. And apply security methods for authentication and verification to necessitate behaviour at low in this huge complex system.

CONCLUSION

The operational resilience and the efficient resource management are supported only by self-manageable cyber physical systems. The complexity of it and the requirement of performing the more complicated and continuous functioning in a dynamic environment is payable. Hence, the attention is turned towards the technologies that are self-manageable like autonomous computing.

The interoperability and the simplicity are accomplished towards the management of the CPS based on the concept of WoT (Web-of-Things). The management information model is used to integrate the organization units to the web and the generalization of the integrated organization units to restful management service. Recently, it is vital to determine the capability of dealing the issues related to scaling by the systems or systems of systems. The factors that have less impact during the low loads may have severe impact during the high usage of the system which may lead to the failure of the system during their initial stage of use or while the integration is being carried out.

The system might be designed to work under heavy loads or low loads only. The term scalability is the ability to make the system adapt to handle the increased or decreased loads by applying a cost-effective strategy. When the system is exhausted in increasing the resources and still cannot satisfy the requested demands is referred as scalability failure. The system is evaluated to determine whether the system is scalable or not. This process is referred as scalability audit which is performed whenever the system need to be scaled.

Cyber physical systems provide immense opportunities in various fields for research, development and improvement. There are many challenges to be conquered in order to bring the future CPS into existence. One of the challenges in CPS is the network QoS management. In this regard, a feedback scheduling mechanism is one of the solutions to fight with network QoS management. The role of WSAN QoS management is vital in CPS design and implementation.

Since the cyber physical system is an integration of systems, reliability is an essential and important QoS parameter to be satisfied. The systems that are integrated in cyber physical systems vary from the power grid systems to health and biomedical devices. The systems that are not reliable may lead to many drawbacks like additional expense, life loss or disturbance in the service. The next generation CPS which include the rational command of the associated issues can be developed by overcoming the challenges like the integration complexity, system assurance and agility demands. There is a wide scope to develop the tools, skills, techniques and technologies to manage the complexity of CPS.

REFERENCES

Bestavros, A., Bradley, A. D., Kfoury, A. J., & Matta, I. (2005, November). Typed abstraction of complex network compositions. In *Proceedings of Network Protocols*, (pp. 10-pp). IEEE. doi:10.1109/ICNP.2005.44

Engell, S. (2014). *Cyber-physical systems of systems – Definition and core research and development areas* (Working Paper of the Support Action CPSoS). Academic Press.

Ermagan, V., Krüger, I., & Menarini, M. (2006). *High-confidence service engineering for cyber physical systems.* Paper presented at National Workshop on High-Confidence Software Platforms for Cyber-Physical Systems (HCSP-CPS). Blacksburg, VA.

Gonzalez, H. (2012). *Computational tools for cyber-physical systems.* Academic Press.

Jamshidi, M. (Ed.). (2008). *Systems of systems engineering: Principles and applications.* CRC Press. doi:10.1201/9781420065893

Maier, M. W. (1998). Architecting principles for systems-of-systems. *Systems Engineering*, *1*(4), 267–284. doi:10.1002/(SICI)1520-6858(1998)1:4<267::AID-SYS3>3.0.CO;2-D

Pham, H. (2007). *System software reliability.* Springer.

Sousa-Poza, A., Kovacic, S., & Keating, C. (2008). System of systems engineering: An emerging multidiscipline. *International Journal of System of Systems Engineering*, *1*(1), 1–17. doi:10.1504/IJSSE.2008.018129

Weinstock, C. B., & Goodenough, J. B. (2006). *On system scalability (No. CMU/SEI-2006-TN-012).* Carnegie-Mellon University.

Wu, L. L. (2011). *Improving system reliability for cyber-physical systems.* Academic Press.

Zeng, D., Guo, S., & Cheng, Z. (2011). The web of things: A survey. *Journal of Communication*, *6*(6), 424–438.

Zhang, Y., Cai, H., & Zhu, M. (2012, April). RESTful management for cyber-physical systems. In *Proceedings of Object/Component/Service-Oriented Real-Time Distributed Computing Workshops* (ISORCW), (pp. 43-47). IEEE. doi:10.1109/ISORCW.2012.18

ADDITIONAL READING

Mitchell, R., & Chen, I. R. (2013). Effect of intrusion detection and response on reliability of cyber physical systems. *IEEE Transactions on Reliability*, *62*(1), 199–210. doi:10.1109/TR.2013.2240891

Zhang, L. (2011, August). Formal specification for real time cyber physical systems using aspect-oriented approach. In Theoretical Aspects of Software Engineering (TASE), 2011 Fifth International Symposium on (pp. 213-216). IEEE. doi:10.1109/TASE.2011.37

KEY TERMS AND DEFINITIONS

Availability: A system needs to operate successfully for a specified amount of time.

Hybrid Dynamical System: System that contain both analog (continuous) and logical (discrete) components.

Maintainability: Making the system to work perfectly without any faults.

MDA: Model-Driven Architecture is a software design approach for the development of software systems.

Reliability: A system that performs and maintains its functions in routine circumstances.

Scalability: The ability of the system (hardware or software) to handle various workloads without the variation in the system resources.

SWOT: Strengths, Weaknesses, Opportunities, Threats is a strategic planning tool used in evaluating projects and business ventures.

Compilation of References

Abdelwahed, S., Bai, J., Su, R., & Kandasamy, N. (2009). On the application of predictive control techniques for adaptive performance management of computing systems. *IEEE Transactions on* Network and Service Management, *6*(4), 212–225.

Abdelzaher, T. (2006). Towards an architecture for distributed cyber-physical systems. In *Proceedings of the 2006 National Science Foundation Workshop on Cyber-Physical Systems*. Academic Press.

Ahmadi, H., & Abdelzaher, T. (2009, December). An adaptive-reliability cyber-physical transport protocol for spatio-temporal data. In *Proceedings of Real-Time Systems Symposium*, (pp. 238-247). IEEE. doi:10.1109/RTSS.2009.45

Ahmadzade, B., Shahgholian, G., Tehrani, F. M., & Mahdavian, M. (2011, August). Model predictive control to improve power system oscillations of SMIB with fuzzy logic controller. In *Proceedings of Electrical Machines and Systems* (ICEMS), (pp. 1-5). IEEE. doi:10.1109/ICEMS.2011.6073337

Ahn, S. W., & Yoo, C. (2012, April). WiP abstract: Virtual network platform for large scale CPS testbed. In *Proceedings of the 2012 IEEE/ACM Third International Conference on Cyber-Physical Systems* (p. 214). IEEE Computer Society. doi:10.1109/ICCPS.2012.37

Albus, J. S. (1995, March). RCS: A reference model architecture for intelligent systems. In *Proceedings ofAAAI Spring Symposium on Lessons Learned for Implemented Software Architectures for Physical Agents* (pp. 1-6). AAAI.

Albus, J. S., & Barbera, A. J. (2005). RCS: A cognitive architecture for intelligent multi-agent systems. *Annual Reviews in Control*, *29*(1), 87–99. doi:10.1016/j.arcontrol.2004.12.003

Amin, S., Cárdenas, A. A., & Sastry, S. S. (2009). Safe and secure networked control systems under denial-of-service attacks. In Hybrid systems: Computation and control (pp. 31-45). Springer Berlin Heidelberg. doi:10.1007/978-3-642-00602-9_3

Anand, M., Cronin, E., Sherr, M., Blaze, M., Ives, Z., & Lee, I. (2006). Security challenges in next generation cyber physical systems. In *Beyond SCADA: Networked embedded control for cyber physical systems*. Academic Press.

Anastasi, G., Conti, M., & Gregori, E. (2004). IEEE 802.11 ad hoc networks: protocols, performance and open issues. In *Proceedings of Mobile Ad Hoc Networking*, (pp. 69-116). Academic Press.

Antsaklis, P. J. (1999). Intelligent control. In Wiley encyclopedia of electrical and electronics engineering. Wiley.

Anwar, R. W., & Ali, S. (2012). Trust based secure cyber physical systems. In *Proceedings of Workshop on Trustworthy Cyber-Physical Systems*. Academic Press. Retrieved from http://www.cs.ncl.ac.uk/publications/trs/papers/1347.pdf

Baheti, R., & Gill, H. (2011). Cyber-physical systems. In *The impact of control technology*, (pp. 161-166). Academic Press.

Balasubramanian, J., Tambe, S., Dasarathy, B., Gadgil, S., Porter, F., Gokhale, A., & Schmidt, D. C. (2008, April). Netqope: A model-driven network qos provisioning engine for distributed real-time and embedded systems. In *Proceedings of Real-Time and Embedded Technology and Applications Symposium*, (pp. 113-122). IEEE. doi:10.1109/RTAS.2008.32

Balasubramanian, J., Tambe, S., Gokhale, A., Dasarathy, B., Gadgil, S., & Schmidt, D. (2010). *A model-driven QoS provisioning engine for cyber physical systems*. Academic Press.

Bestavros, A., Bradley, A. D., Kfoury, A. J., & Matta, I. (2005, November). Typed abstraction of complex network compositions. In *Proceedings of Network Protocols*, (pp. 10-pp). IEEE. doi:10.1109/ICNP.2005.44

Bhave, A., Krogh, B., Garlan, D., & Schmerl, B. (2010). Multi-domain modeling of cyber-physical systems using architectural views. *AVICPS*, *2010*, 43.

Bogdan, P., & Marculescu, R. (2011, April). Towards a science of cyber-physical systems design. In *Proceedings of Cyber-Physical Systems (ICCPS)*, (pp. 99-108). IEEE. doi:10.1109/ICCPS.2011.14

Brewer, E. A., Katz, R. H., Chawathe, Y., Gribble, S. D., Hodes, T., & Nguyen, G. et al. (1998). A network architecture for heterogeneous mobile computing. *IEEE Personal Communications*, *5*(5), 8–24. doi:10.1109/98.729719

Cardei, M., & Wu, J. (2004). Coverage in wireless sensor networks. In Handbook of sensor networks, (pp. 422-433). Academic Press.

Cardenas, A. A., Amin, S., & Sastry, S. (2008). Secure control: Towards survivable cyber-physical systems. *System*, *1*(a2), a3.

Cárdenas, A. A., Amin, S., & Sastry, S. (2008, July). Research challenges for the security of control systems. HotSec.

Cardenas, A., Amin, S., Sinopoli, B., Giani, A., Perrig, A., & Sastry, S. (2009, July). Challenges for securing cyber physical systems. In *Proceedings ofWorkshop on Future Directions in Cyber-Physical Systems Security*. Academic Press.

Cardenas, A. A., Amin, S., Lin, Z. S., Huang, Y. L., Huang, C. Y., & Sastry, S. (2011, March). Attacks against process control systems: risk assessment, detection, and response. In *Proceedings of the 6th ACM Symposium on Information, Computer and Communications Security* (pp. 355-366). ACM. doi:10.1145/1966913.1966959

Cardoso, J., Derler, P., Eidson, J. C., & Lee, E. A. (2011, Jun). Network latency and packet delay variation in cyber-physical systems. In *Proceedings ofNetwork Science Workshop (NSW)*, (pp. 51-58). IEEE. doi:10.1109/NSW.2011.6004658

Cavalcanti, D., Agrawal, D., Cordeiro, C., Xie, B., & Kumar, A. (2005). Issues in integrating cellular networks WLANs and MANETs: A futuristic heterogeneous wireless network. *IEEE Wireless Communications*, *12*(3), 30–41. doi:10.1109/MWC.2005.1452852

Chaudet, C., Dhoutaut, D., & Lassous, I. G. (2005). Performance issues with IEEE 802.11 in ad hoc networking. *IEEE Communications Magazine*, *43*(7), 110–116. doi:10.1109/MCOM.2005.1470836

Chawathe, Y., Fink, S. A., McCanne, S., & Brewer, E. A. (1998, September). A proxy architecture for reliable multicast in heterogeneous environments. In *Proceedings of the Sixth ACM International Conference on Multimedia* (pp. 151-159). ACM. doi:10.1145/290747.290767

Chen, W. T., Liu, J. C., & Huang, H. K. (2004, July). An adaptive scheme for vertical handoff in wireless overlay networks. In *Proceedings of Parallel and Distributed Systems*, (pp. 541-548). IEEE.

Conklin, W. A. (2009). Security in cyber-physical systems. In *Proceedings of Workshop on Future Directions in Cyber-Physical Systems Security*. Newark, NJ: Academic Press.

Dahleh, M. A., Frazzoli, E., Megretski, A., Mitter, S. K., Ozdaglar, A. E., Parrilo, P. A., & Shah, D. (2006), Information and control: A bridge between the physical and decision layers. In *Proceedings ofNSF Workshop in Cyber-Physical Systems*. NSF.

de Morais Cordeiro, C., Gossain, H., & Agrawal, D. P. (2003). Multicast over wireless mobile ad hoc networks: Present and future directions. *IEEE Network*, *17*(1), 52–59. doi:10.1109/MNET.2003.1174178

Demeester, P., Gryseels, M., Autenrieth, A., Brianza, C., Castagna, L., & Signorelli, G. et al. (1999). Resilience in multilayer networks. *IEEE Communications Magazine*, *37*(8), 70–76. doi:10.1109/35.783128

Derler, P., Lee, E. A., & Sangiovanni-Vincentelli, A. L. (2011). *Addressing modeling challenges in cyber-physical systems (No. UCB/EECS-2011-17)*. California Univ Berkeley Dept of Electrical Engineering and Computer Science.

El-Arabied, M. (2012). *Heterogeneous networks: An introduction*. Academic Press.

Elwahsh, H., Hashem, M., & Amin, M. (2011). Secure service discovery protocols for ad hoc networks. In Advances in computer science and information technology (pp. 147-157). Springer Berlin Heidelberg. doi:10.1007/978-3-642-17857-3_15

Endler, M., Rubinsztejn, H. K. S., da Rocha, R. C. A., & do Sacramento Rodrigues, V. J. (2005). *Proxy-based adaptation for mobile computing* (Vol. 736). PUC.

Engell, S. (2014). *Cyber-physical systems of systems – Definition and core research and development areas* (Working Paper of the Support Action CPSoS). Academic Press.

Ermagan, V., Krüger, I., & Menarini, M. (2006). *High-confidence service engineering for cyberphysical systems*. Paper presented at National Workshop on High-Confidence Software Platforms for Cyber-Physical Systems (HCSP-CPS). Blacksburg, VA.

Fabric, D. C. (2013). *Adaptive networking—Advanced data center fabric technology*. Retrieved from http://www.dell.com/downloads/global/products/pvaul/en/dcf_adaptive_networking.pdf

Fan, G., & Jin, S. (2010). Coverage problem in wireless sensor network: A survey. *Journal of Networks*, *5*(9), 1033–1040. doi:10.4304/jnw.5.9.1033-1040

Farag, M. M., Lerner, L. W., & Patterson, C. D. (2012, Jun). Interacting with hardware Trojans over a network. In *Proceedings of Hardware-Oriented Security and Trust* (HOST), (pp. 69-74). IEEE. doi:10.1109/HST.2012.6224323

Fox, A., Gribble, S. D., Chawathe, Y., Brewer, E. A., & Gauthier, P. (1997). Cluster-based scalable network services. ACM.

Gonzalez, H. (2012). *Computational tools for cyber-physical systems*. Academic Press.

Gorinevsky, D. (2005). A lecture on model predictive control. *IndaBook*. Retrieved from www.indabook.org/d/Model-Predictive-Control.pdf

Gottschalk, K., Graham, S., Kreger, H., & Snell, J. (2002). Introduction to web services architecture. *IBM Systems Journal*, *41*(2), 170–177. doi:10.1147/sj.412.0170

Haque, M. M., & Ahamed, S. I. (2006). Security in pervasive computing: Current status and open issues. *International Journal of Network Security*, *3*(3), 203–214.

Helal, S., Desai, N., Verma, V., & Lee, C. (2003, March). Konark-A service discovery and delivery protocol for ad-hoc networks. In Proceedings of Wireless Communications and Networking, (Vol. 3, pp. 2107-2113). IEEE. doi:10.1109/WCNC.2003.1200712

Jamshidi, M. (Ed.). (2008). *Systems of systems engineering: Principles and applications*. CRC Press. doi:10.1201/9781420065893

Jensen, J. C., Chang, D. H., & Lee, E. A. (2011, July). A model-based design methodology for cyber-physical systems. In *Proceedings of Wireless Communications and Mobile Computing Conference* (IWCM), (pp. 1666-1671). IEEE. doi:10.1109/IWCMC.2011.5982785

Kang, W., & Son, S. H. (2008). The design of an open data service architecture for cyber-physical systems. *ACM SIGBED Review*, *5*(1), 3. doi:10.1145/1366283.1366286

Katz, R. H., Brewer, E. A., Amir, E., Balakrishnan, H., Fox, A., Gribble, S., et al. (1996, February). The bay area research wireless access network (BARWAN). In Proceedings of Compcon'96: Technologies for the Information Superhighway (pp. 15-20). IEEE.

Khan, R. A. M., & Karl, H. (2011). Multihop performance of cooperative preamble sampling MAC (CPS-MA) in wireless sensor networks. In Ad-hoc, mobile, and wireless networks (pp. 145-149). Springer Berlin Heidelberg.

Kisner, R. A., Manges, W. W., MacIntyre, L. P., Nutaro, J. J., Munro, J. K., & Ewing, P. D. et al. (2010). Cybersecurity through real-time distributed control systems: Oak Ridge National Laboratories report. *ORNL. U. S. Atomic Energy Commission*, *TM-2010*(30), 4–5.

Kniess, J., Loques, O., & Albuquerque, C. V. (2011, March). A fault-tolerant service discovery protocol for emergency search and rescue missions. In *Proceedings of Test Workshop* (LATW), (pp. 1-6). IEEE. doi:10.1109/LATW.2011.5985903

Kosut, O., Jia, L., Thomas, R. J., & Tong, L. (2010, August). On malicious data attacks on power system state estimation. In *Proceedings of Universities Power Engineering Conference* (UP), (pp. 1-6). IEEE.

Koubâa, A., & Andersson, B. (2009, July). A vision of cyber-physical internet. In *Proc. of the Workshop of Real-Time Networks* (RTN 2009). RTN.

Kreger, H. (2001). Web services conceptual architecture (WSCA 1.0). *IBM Software Group, 5*, 6–7.

Krings, A. W., & Azadmanesh, A. (2005). A graph based model for survivability applications. *European Journal of Operational Research, 164*(3), 680–689. doi:10.1016/j.ejor.2003.10.052

Krishnakumar, K. (2003). *Intelligent systems for aerospace engineering-an overview*. National Aeronautics And Space Administration Moffett Field Ca Ames Research Center.

Lee, E. A. (2006, October). Cyber-physical systems-are computing foundations adequate. In *Proceedings of NSF Workshop on Cyber-Physical Systems: Research Motivation, Techniques and Roadmap* (vol. 2). NSF.

Lee, K., & Modiano, E. (2009). Cross-Layer Survivability in WDM-Based Networks. In *Proceedings of INFOCOM 2009. IEEE.* doi:10.1109/INFCOM.2009.5062013

Lehman, T., Yang, X., Ghani, N., Gu, F., Guok, C., Monga, I., & Tierney, B. (2011). Multilayer networks: An architecture framework. *IEEE Communications Magazine, 49*(5), 122–130. doi:10.1109/MCOM.2011.5762808

Lima, M., dos Santos, A. L., & Pujolle, G. (2009). A survey of survivability in mobile ad hoc networks. *IEEE Communications Surveys and Tutorials, 11*(1), 66–77. doi:10.1109/SURV.2009.090106

Lin, S., & Stankovic, J. A. (2009). Performance composition for cyber physical systems. In *Proceedings of the Ph. D. Forum of the 30th Real-Time Systems Symposium* (RTSS'09). RTSS.

Lin, S., He, T., & Stankovic, J. A. (2008). CPS-IP: Cyber physical systems interconnection protocol. *ACM SIGBED Review, 5*(1), 22. doi:10.1145/1366283.1366305

Liu, M., Talpade, R. R., Mcauley, A., & Bommaiah, E. (1999). *AMRoute: Adhoc Multicast Routing Protocol* (Technical Report, 1999). Academic Press.

Maier, M. W. (1998). Architecting principles for systems-of-systems. *Systems Engineering, 1*(4), 267–284. doi:10.1002/(SICI)1520-6858(1998)1:4<267::AID-SYS3>3.0.CO;2-D

Mapp, G. E., Cottingham, D., Shaikh, F., Vidales, P., Patanapongpibul, L., Baliosian, J., & Crowcroft, J. (2006). *An architectural framework for heterogeneous networking*. Academic Press.

Marculescu, R., & Bogdan, P. (2011). *Cyber physical systems: Workload modeling and design optimization.* Academic Press.

Meguerdichian, S., Koushanfar, F., Potkonjak, M., & Srivastava, M. (2001, July). Coverage problems in wireless ad-hoc sensor networks. *IEEE Infocom, 3*, 1380–1387.

Merritt, R. (2005). *Control system architectures: Remote control.* Retrieved from http://www.controlglobal.com/articles/2005/417/

Meystel, A., & Messina, E. (2000). The challenge of intelligent systems. In *Proceedings of Intelligent Control*, (pp. 211-216). IEEE.

Miroslav, Š. V. É. D. A., & Radimír, V. R. B. A. (2011). A cyber-physical system design approach. In *Proceedings of the Sixth International Conference on Systems* (ICONS 2011). St. Maarten: International Academy, Research, and Industry Association.

Mo, Y., & Sinopoli, B. (2009, September). Secure control against replay attacks. In *Proceedings of Communication, Control, and Computing*, (pp. 911-918). IEEE. doi:10.1109/ALLERTON.2009.5394956

Nakano, T., & Suda, T. (2004, January). Adaptive and evolvable network services. In Proceedings of Genetic and Evolutionary Computation–GECCO 2004 (pp. 151–162). Springer Berlin Heidelberg. doi:10.1007/978-3-540-24854-5_14

Nichols, J., Myers, B. A., Higgins, M., Hughes, J., Harris, T. K., Rosenfeld, R., & Pignol, M. (2002, October). Generating remote control interfaces for complex appliances. In *Proceedings of the 15th Annual ACM Symposium on User Interface Software and Technology* (pp. 161-170). ACM. doi:10.1145/571985.572008

Nikolaou, M. (2001). Model predictive controllers: A critical synthesis of theory and industrial needs. *Advances in Chemical Engineering*, *26*, 131–204. doi:10.1016/S0065-2377(01)26003-7

Pal, P., Schantz, R., Rohloff, K., & Loyall, J. (2009, July). Cyber-physical systems security-challenges and research ideas. In *Proceedings of Workshop on Future Directions in Cyber-Physical Systems Security*. Academic Press.

Pancholi, G. (2002). *Proxy-based services in distributed systems*. Academic Press.

Pandey, S., & Glesner, M. (2006, July). Statistical on-chip communication bus synthesis and voltage scaling under timing yield constraint. In *Proceedings of the 43rd Annual Design Automation Conference* (pp. 663-668). ACM. doi:10.1145/1146909.1147078

Park, K. J., Zheng, R., & Liu, X. (2012). Cyber-physical systems: Milestones and research challenges. *Computer Communications*, *36*(1), 1–7. doi:10.1016/j.comcom.2012.09.006

Pham, H. (2007). *System software reliability*. Springer.

Phan, L. T., & Lee, I. (2011, August). Towards a compositional multi-modal framework for adaptive cyber-physical systems. In *Proceedings of Embedded and Real-Time Computing Systems and Applications* (RTCS), (vol. 2, pp. 67-73). IEEE. doi:10.1109/RTCSA.2011.82

Platzer, A. (2010). *Integrative challenges of cyber-physical systems verification*. Academic Press.

Quintero, R., & Barbera, A. J. (1992). *A real-time control system methodology for developing intelligent control systems*. Academic Press.

Quintero, R., & Barbera, A. J. (1993, August). A software template approach to building complex large-scale intelligent control systems. In *Proceedings of Intelligent Control*, (pp. 58-63). IEEE. doi:10.1109/ISIC.1993.397723

Rajhans, A., & Krogh, B. H. (2012, April). Heterogeneous verification of cyber-physical systems using behavior relations. In *Proceedings of the 15th ACM International Conference on Hybrid Systems: Computation and Control* (pp. 35-44). ACM. doi:10.1145/2185632.2185641

Rajhans, A., Cheng, S. W., Schmerl, B., Garlan, D., Krogh, B. H., Agbi, C., & Bhave, A. (2009). An architectural approach to the design and analysis of cyber-physical systems. *Electronic Communications of the EASST, 21*.

Rudas, I. J., & Fodor, J. (2008). Intelligent systems. *International Journal of Computers, Communications & Control*, *3*(3).

Saeedloei, N., & Gupta, G. (2011). A logic-based modeling and verification of CPS. *ACM SIGBED Review*, *8*(2), 31–34. doi:10.1145/2000367.2000374

Satyanarayanan, M. (2001). Pervasive computing: Vision and challenges. *IEEE Personal Communications*, *8*(4), 10–17. doi:10.1109/98.943998

Schmohl, R., & Baumgarten, U. (2008, July). A generalized context-aware architecture in heterogeneous mobile computing environments. In *Proceedings of Wireless and Mobile Communications*, (pp. 118-124). IEEE. doi:10.1109/ICWMC.2008.59

Sebaa, K., Moulahoum, S., Houassine, H., & Kabache, N. (2012, May). Model predictive control to improve the power system stability. In *Proceedings of Optimization of Electrical and Electronic Equipment* (OPTIM), (pp. 208-212). IEEE. doi:10.1109/OPTIM.2012.6231972

Shen, J., Xu, F., Lu, X., & Li, H. (2010, October). Heterogeneous multi-layer wireless networking for mobile CPS. In *Proceedings of Ubiquitous Intelligence & Computing and 7th International Conference on Autonomic & Trusted Computing* (UIC/AT), (pp. 223-227). IEEE. doi:10.1109/UIC-ATC.2010.30

Shi, J., Wan, J., Yan, H., & Suo, H. (2011, November). A survey of cyber-physical systems. In *Proceedings of Wireless Communications and Signal Processing (WCSP)*, (pp. 1-6). IEEE.

Slomka, F., Kollmann, S., Moser, S., & Kempf, K. (2011). A multidisciplinary design methodology for cyber-physical systems. *ACESMB*, *2011*, 23.

Sousa-Poza, A., Kovacic, S., & Keating, C. (2008). System of systems engineering: An emerging multidiscipline. *International Journal of System of Systems Engineering*, *1*(1), 1–17. doi:10.1504/IJSSE.2008.018129

Stann, F., & Heidemann, J. (2003, May). RMST: Reliable data transport in sensor networks. In *Proceedings of Sensor Network Protocols and Applications*, (pp. 102-112). IEEE.

Sun, Y., Gao, X., Belding-Royer, E. M., & Kempf, J. (2004, October). Model-based resource prediction for multi-hop wireless networks. In *Proceedings of Mobile Ad-Hoc and Sensor Systems*, (pp. 114-123). IEEE.

Sundar, S. S., & Lee, E. A. (Eds.). (2012). *Proceedings of the NIST CPS Workshop*. Chicago: NIST.

Sun, Y., Belding-Royer, E. M., Gao, X., & Kempf, J. (2007). Real-time traffic support in heterogeneous mobile networks. *Wireless Networks*, *13*(4), 431–445. doi:10.1007/s11276-006-9198-y

TM5-601, Department of the Army. (2006). Supervisory control and data acquisition (SCA) systems for command, control, communications, computer, intelligence, surveillance and reconnaissance (C4ISR). *Facilities*, *21*. Retrieved from http://wbdg.org/ccb/ARMYCOE/COETM/tm_5_601.pdf

Vicaire, P. A., Hoque, E., Xie, Z., & Stankovic, J. A. (2012). Bundle: A group-based programming abstraction for cyber-physical systems. *IEEE Transactions on* Industrial Informatics, *8*(2), 379–392.

Wang, E. K., Ye, Y., Xu, X., Yiu, S. M., Hui, L. C. K., & Chow, K. P. (2010, December). Security issues and challenges for cyber physical system. In *Proceedings of the 2010 IEEE/ACM Int'l Conference on Green Computing and Communications & Int'l Conference on Cyber, Physical and Social Computing* (pp. 733-738). IEEE Computer Society. doi:10.1109/GreenCom-CPSCom.2010.36

Weinstock, C. B., & Goodenough, J. B. (2006). *On system scalability (No. CMU/SEI-2006-TN-012)*. Carnegie-Mellon University.

Wu, L. L. (2011). *Improving system reliability for cyber-physical systems*. Academic Press.

Wu, F. J., Chu, F. I., & Tseng, Y. C. (2011, August). Cyber-physical handshake. *Computer Communication Review*, *41*(4), 472–473. doi:10.1145/2043164.2018527

Wu, F. J., Kao, Y. F., & Tseng, Y. C. (2011). From wireless sensor networks towards cyber physical systems. *Pervasive and Mobile Computing*, *7*(4), 397–413. doi:10.1016/j.pmcj.2011.03.003

Xia, F., Ma, L., Dong, J., & Sun, Y. (2008, July). Network QoS management in cyber-physical systems. In *Proceedings of Embedded Software and Systems Symposia*, (pp. 302-307). IEEE. doi:10.1109/ICESS.Symposia.2008.84

Xia, F. (2008). QoS challenges and opportunities in wireless sensor/actuator networks. *Sensors (Basel, Switzerlan)*, *8*(2), 1099–1110. doi:10.3390/s8021099

Xue, M., Roy, S., Wan, Y., & Das, S. K. (2012). Security and vulnerability of cyber-physical. In *Handbook on securing cyber-physical critical infrastructure* (pp. 5–30). Boston: Elsevier. doi:10.1016/B978-0-12-415815-3.00001-7

Yampolskiy, M., Horvath, P., Koutsoukos, X. D., Xue, Y., & Sztipanovits, J. (2012, August). Systematic analysis of cyber-attacks on CPS-evaluating applicability of DFD-based approach. In *Proceedings of Resilient Control Systems* (ISRCS), (pp. 55-62). IEEE.

Zeng, D., Guo, S., & Cheng, Z. (2011). The web of things: A survey. *Journal of Communication*, *6*(6), 424–438.

Zhang, F., & Shi, Z. (2009, December). Optimal and adaptive battery discharge strategies for cyber-physical systems. In *Proceedings of Decision and Control, 2009 Held Jointly with the 2009 28th Chinese Control Conference* (pp. 6232-6237). IEEE. doi:10.1109/CDC.2009.5400561

Zhang, Y., Cai, H., & Zhu, M. (2012, April). RESTful management for cyber-physical systems. In *Proceedings of Object/Component/Service-Oriented Real-Time Distributed Computing Workshops* (ISORCW), (pp. 43-47). IEEE. doi:10.1109/ISORCW.2012.18

Zhang, L. (2012). Aspect-oriented development method for non-functional characteristics of cyber physical systems based on MDA approach. *Journal of Software*, *7*(3), 608–619. doi:10.4304/jsw.7.3.608-619

Zhang, L. (2012). Aspect-oriented formal techniques of cyber physical systems. *Journal of Software*, *7*(4), 823–834. doi:10.4304/jsw.7.4.823-834

Zhang, Y., Vin, H., Alvisi, L., Lee, W., & Dao, S. K. (2001, September). Heterogeneous networking: A new survivability paradigm. In *Proceedings of the 2001 Workshop on New Security Paradigms* (pp. 33-39). ACM. doi:10.1145/508171.508177

About the Authors

P. Venkata Krishna is a Professor at School of Computing Science and Engineering, VIT University, Vellore, India. He received his BTech in Electronics and Communication Engineering from Sri Venkateswara University, Tirupathi, India, MTech in Computer Science and Engineering from REC, Calicut, India, and he received his PhD from VIT University, Vellore, India. Dr. Krishna has several years of experience working in academia, research, consultancy, academic administration, and project management roles. His current research interests include mobile and wireless systems, QoS, and Cloud computing. He has been the recipient of several academic and research awards, such as the Cognizant Best Faculty Award for the year 2009-2010 and VIT Researcher Award for the year 2009-2010. He has authored over 150 research papers in various reputed journals and conferences. He has delivered several keynote addresses in reputed conferences. He is currently serving as Editor-in-Chief for IJSGGC, Inderscience Publishers.

V. Saritha is with School of Computing Science and Engineering, VIT University, Vellore, India. She received her BTech in Electronics and Communication Engineering from Andhra University, Visakhapatnam, India, MTech in Computer Science and Engineering from VIT University, India, and she received her PhD from VIT University, Vellore, India. Dr. Saritha has several years of experience working in academia and research. Her current research interests include mobile and wireless systems, vehicular networks, etc. She has authored over 50 research papers in various reputed journals and conferences.

H. P. Sultana received the MCA from Madras University, Chennai, India, and MPhil in Computer Applications from Manonmaniam Sundaranar University, Tirulnelveli, India. She is currently with the School of Computing Sciences, VIT University, Vellore, India. She is pursuing her PhD from the School of Computing Sciences and Engineering, VIT University, Vellore, India. Her research interests include mobile and wireless systems and data structures. She has authored a few research papers in various reputed journals and conferences.

Index

M

N

P

R

S

T

U

V

W